VIZ GRAPHIC NOVEL

◆◆◆◆◆◆◆◆◆◆◆◆◆◆

NO NEED FOR TENCHI!™

SAMURAI SPACE OPERA

STORY AND ART BY
HITOSHI OKUDA

CONTENTS

This volume contains NO NEED FOR TENCHI! PART FOUR in its entirety.

STORY AND ART BY
HITOSHI OKUDA

ENGLISH ADAPTATION BY
FRED BURKE

Translation/Shuko Shikata & Mari Morimoto
Touch-Up Art & Lettering/Wayne Truman & Dan Nakrosis
Cover Design/Hidemi Sahara
Editor/Annette Roman

Senior Editor/Trish Ledoux
Managing Editor/Hyoe Narita
Editor-in-Chief/Satoru Fujii
Publisher/Seiji Horibuchi

Printed in Canada

Published by Viz Communications, Inc.
P.O. Box 77010 • San Francisco, CA 94107

10 9 8 7 6 5 4 3 2 1
First printing, December 1998

Vizit us at our World Wide Web site at **www.viz.com** and our Internet magazine, **j-pop.com**, at **www.j-pop.com**!

NO NEED FOR TENCHI! GRAPHIC NOVELS TO DATE
NO NEED FOR TENCHI!
SWORD PLAY
MAGICAL GIRL PRETTY SAMMY
SAMURAI SPACE OPERA

Tales of Tenchi #1

A PIRATE'S TALE

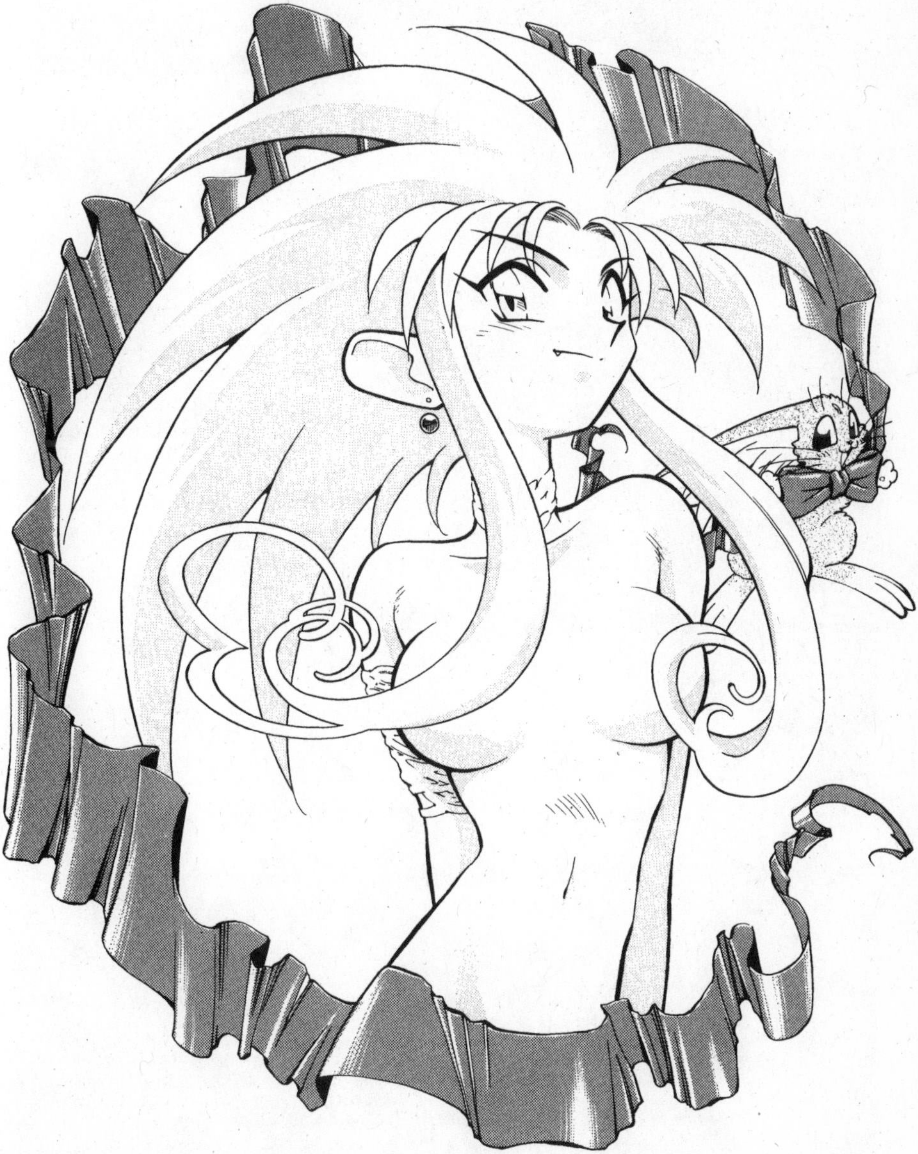

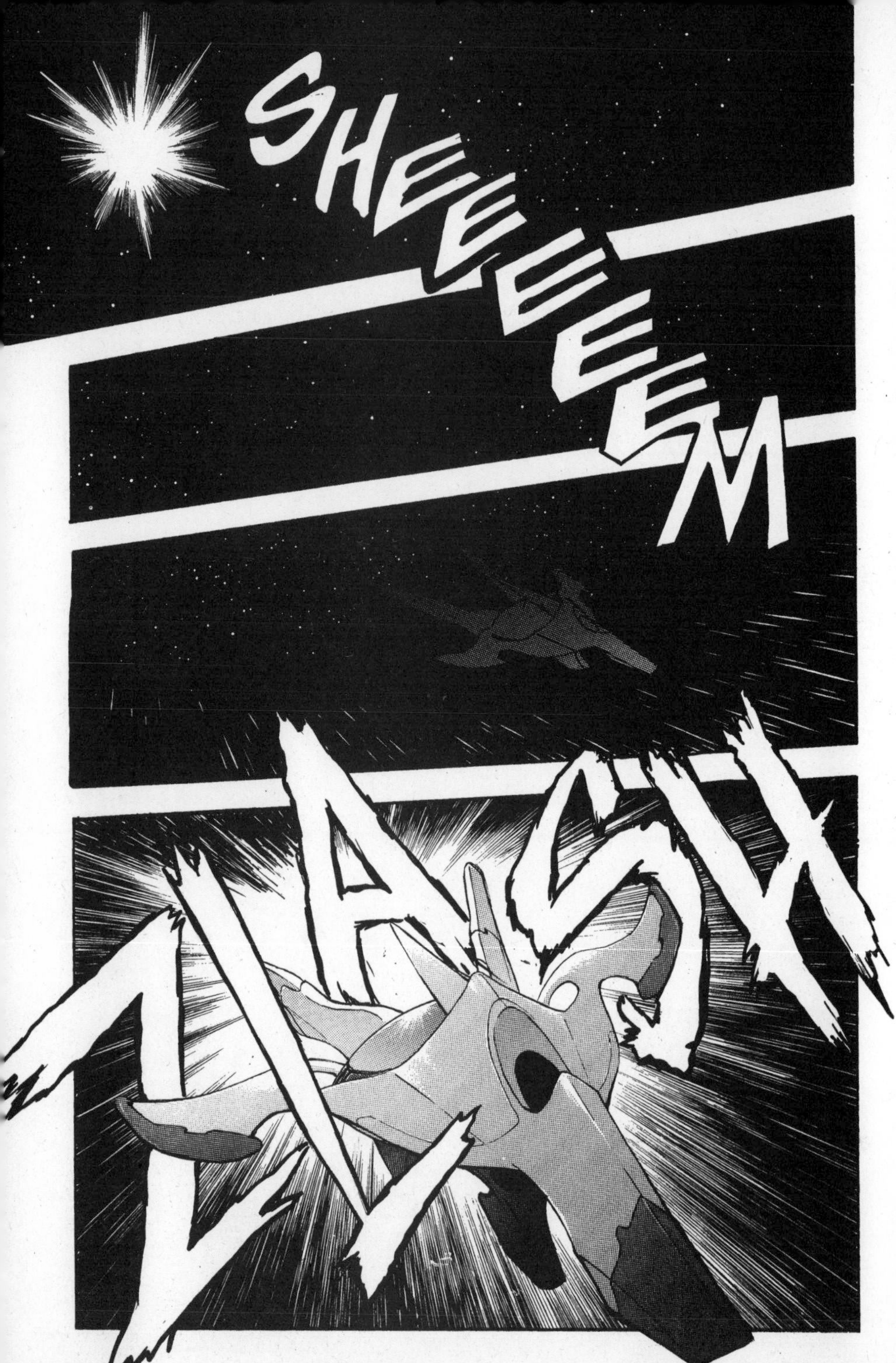
SHEEEEEM

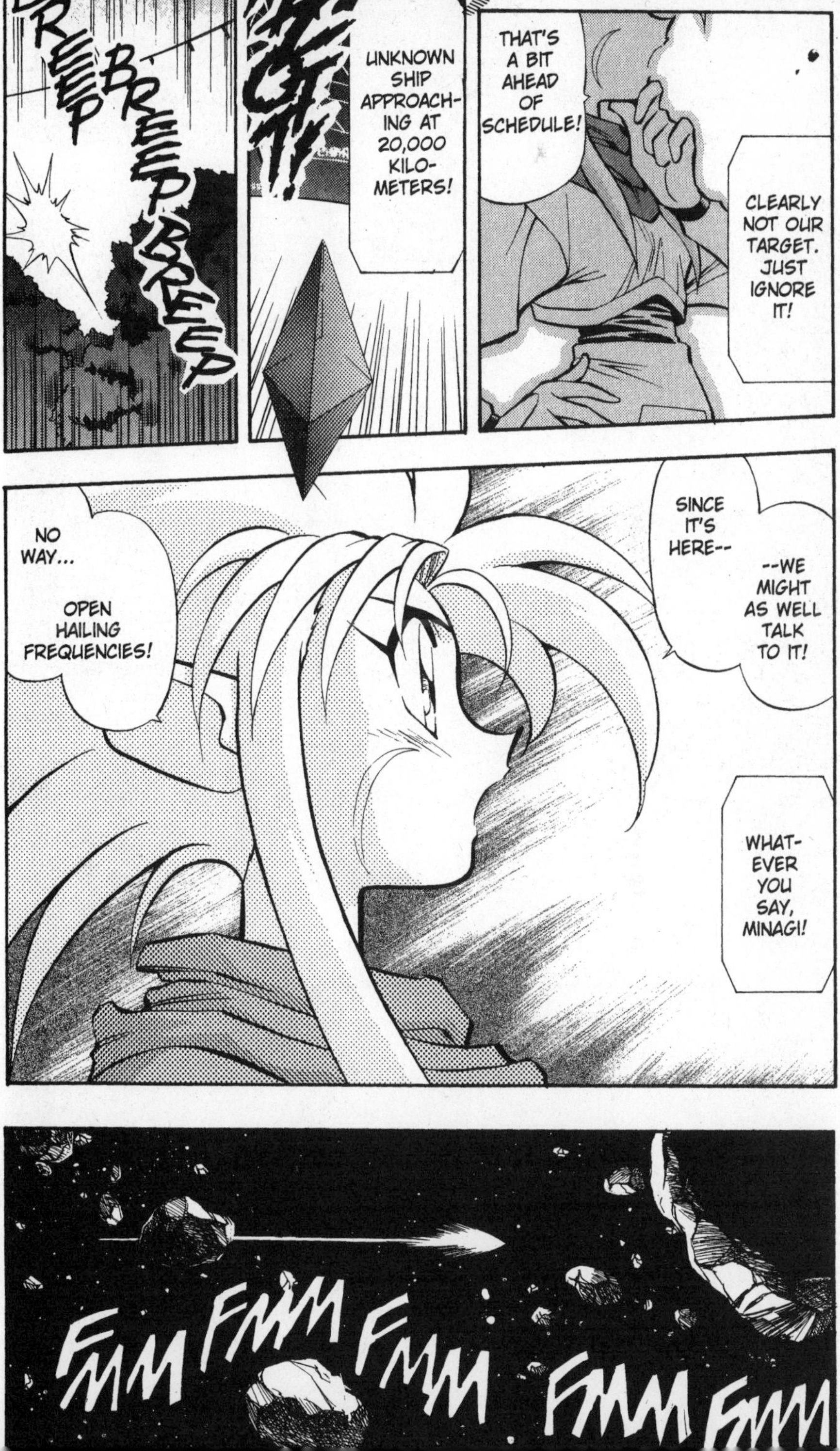
BREEP BREEP BREEP
UNKNOWN SHIP APPROACHING AT 20,000 KILOMETERS!
THAT'S A BIT AHEAD OF SCHEDULE!
CLEARLY NOT OUR TARGET. JUST IGNORE IT!
NO WAY...
OPEN HAILING FREQUENCIES!
SINCE IT'S HERE--
--WE MIGHT AS WELL TALK TO IT!
WHATEVER YOU SAY, MINAGI!
FMM FMM FMM FMM FMM

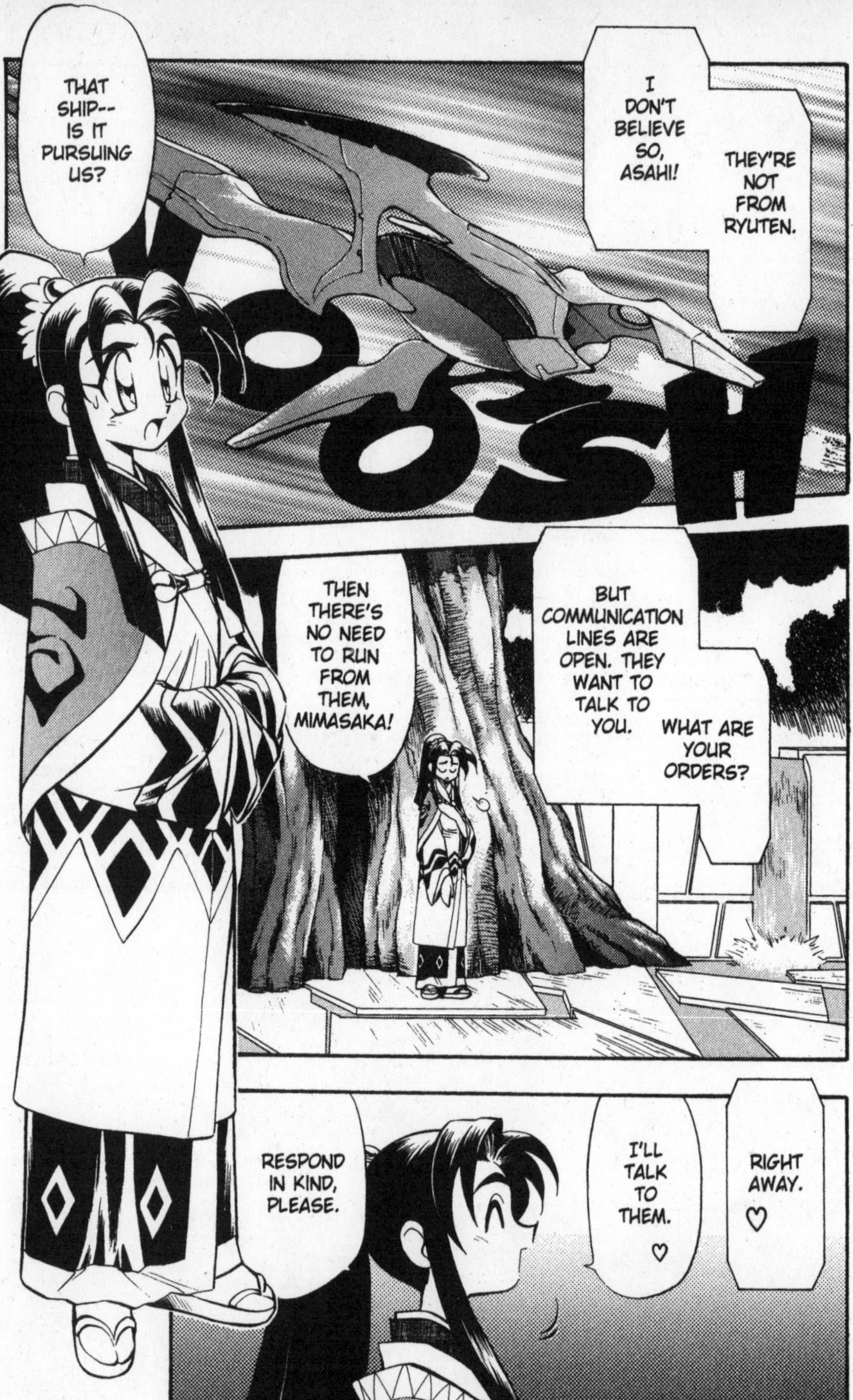
THAT SHIP-- IS IT PURSUING US?
OOSH
I DON'T BELIEVE SO, ASAHI!
THEY'RE NOT FROM RYUTEN.
THEN THERE'S NO NEED TO RUN FROM THEM, MIMASAKA!
BUT COMMUNICATION LINES ARE OPEN. THEY WANT TO TALK TO YOU.
WHAT ARE YOUR ORDERS?
RESPOND IN KIND, PLEASE.
I'LL TALK TO THEM. ♡
RIGHT AWAY. ♡

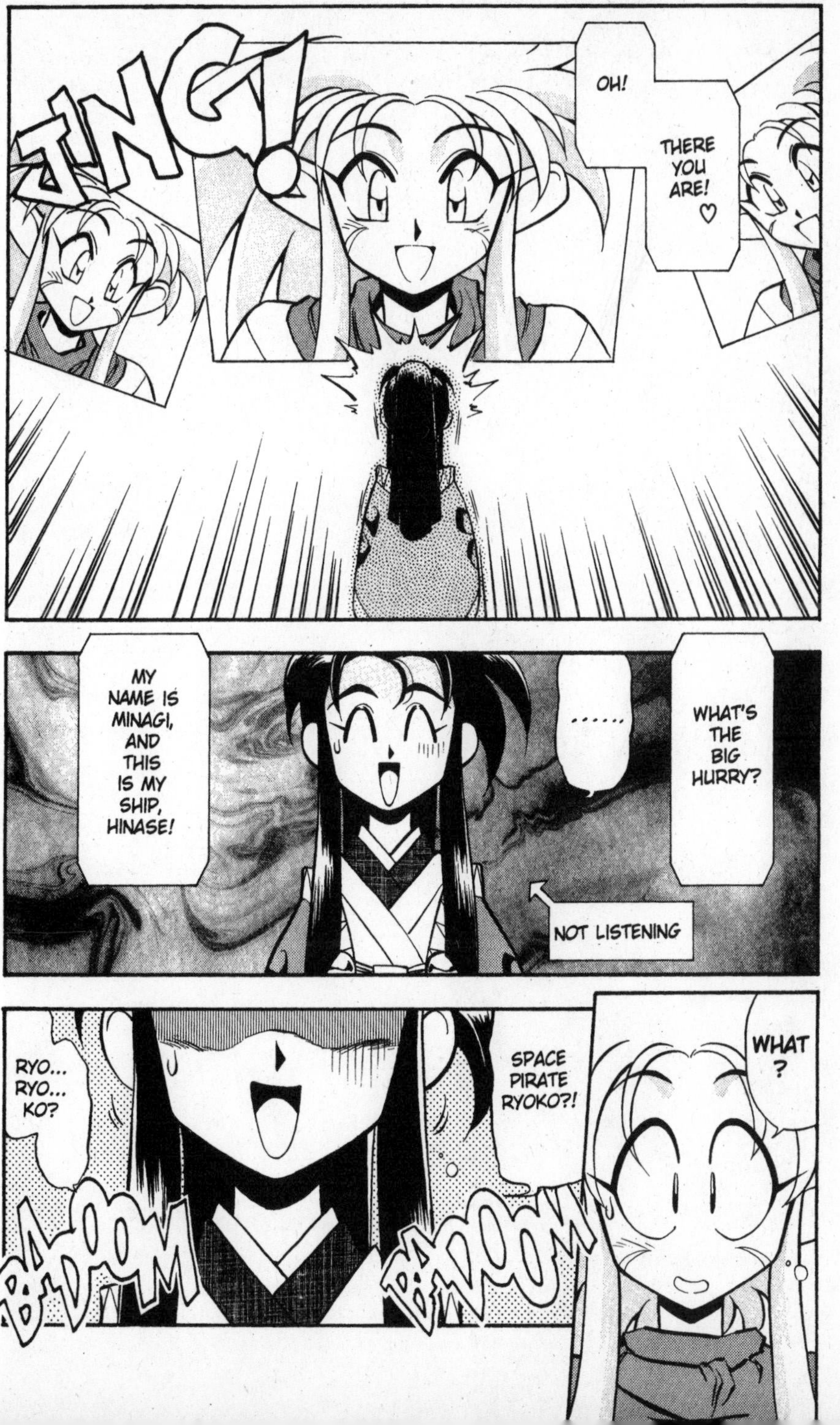
TING!
OH!
THERE YOU ARE! ♡
MY NAME IS MINAGI, AND THIS IS MY SHIP, HINASE!
......
WHAT'S THE BIG HURRY?
NOT LISTENING
RYO... RYO... KO?
BADOOM
SPACE PIRATE RYOKO?!
BADOOM
WHAT?

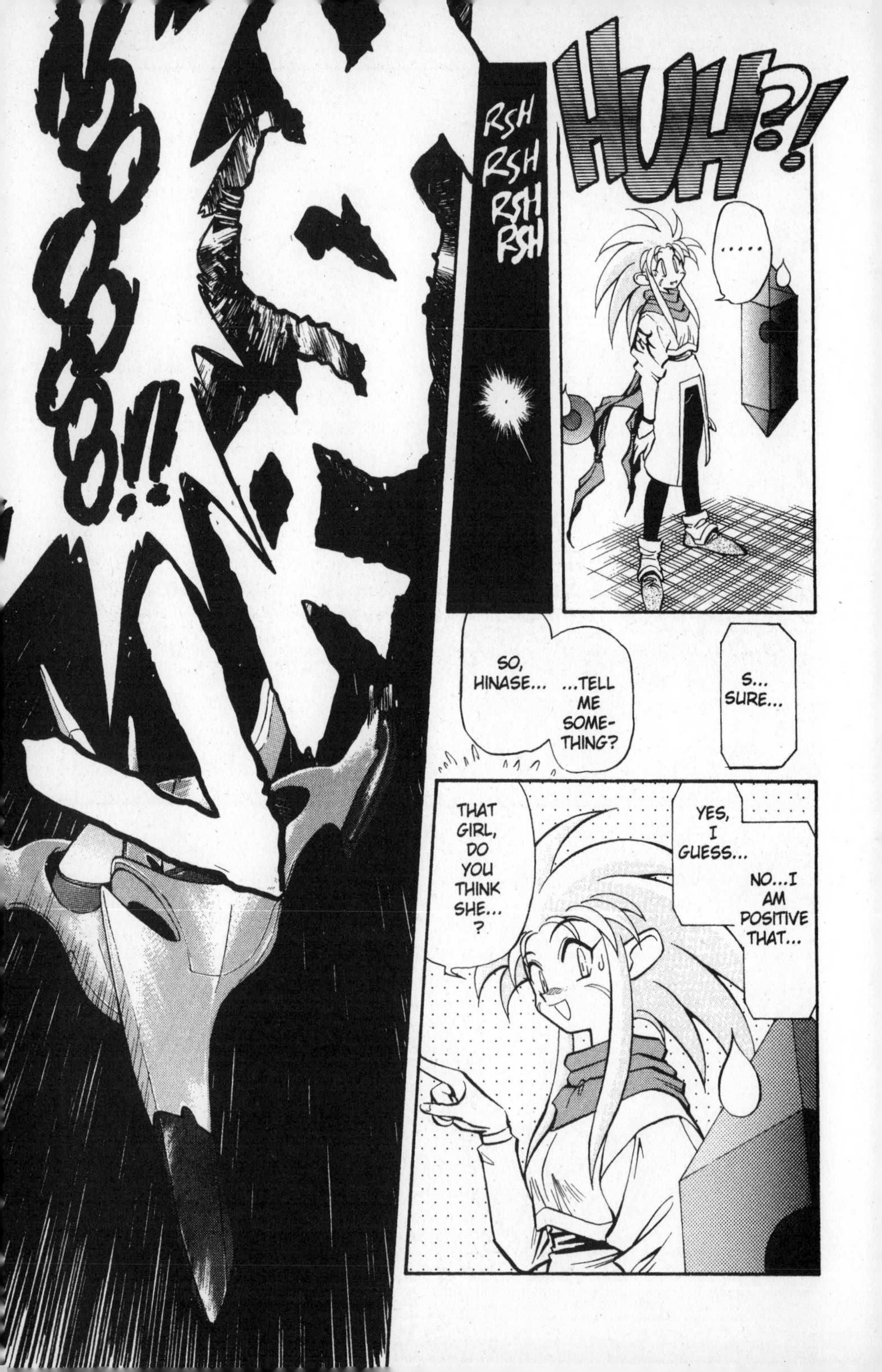
RSH RSH RSH RSH
HUH?!
......
SO, HINASE...
...TELL ME SOMETHING?
S... SURE...
THAT GIRL, DO YOU THINK SHE...?
YES, I GUESS...
NO...I AM POSITIVE THAT...

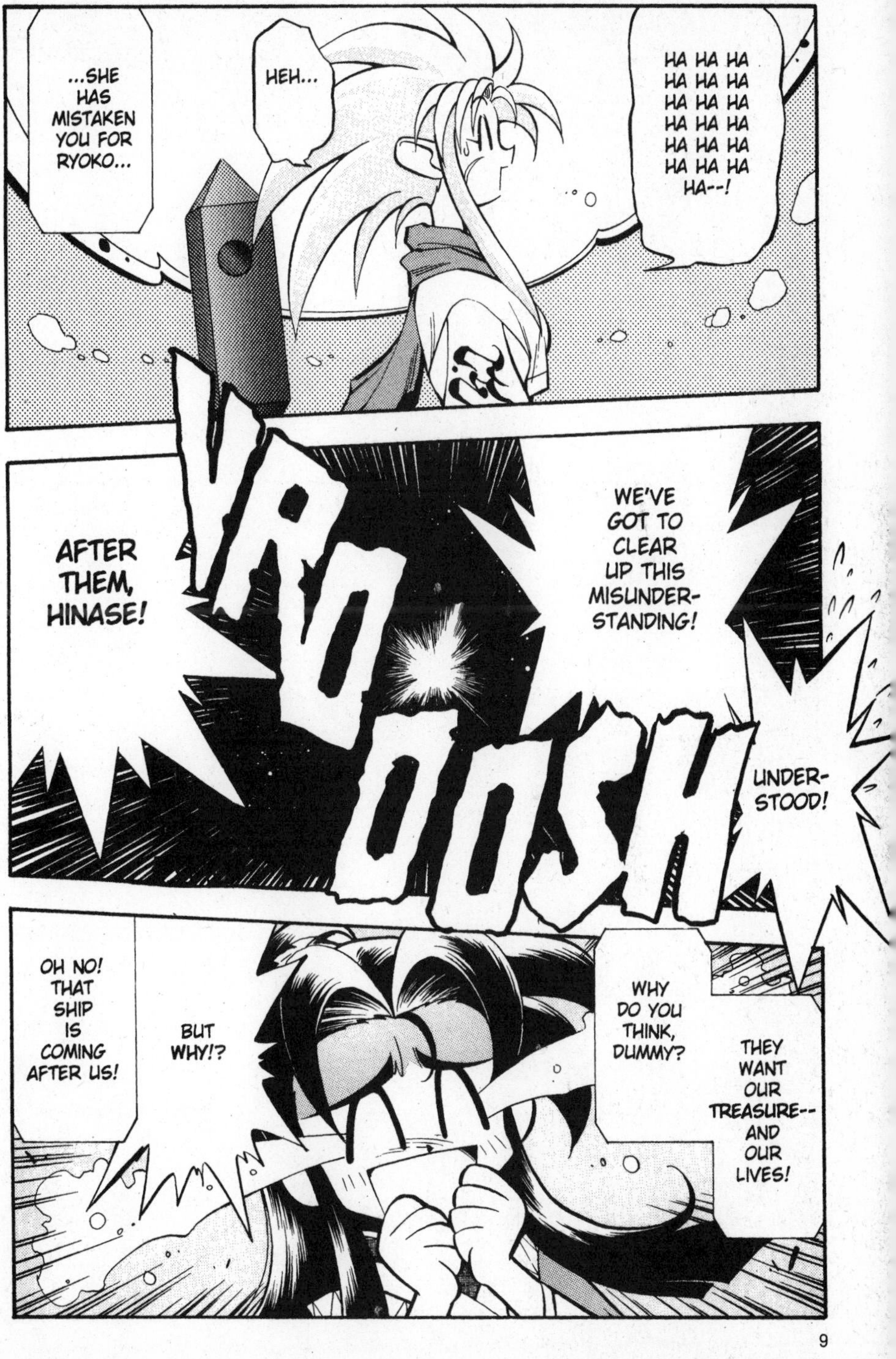
...SHE HAS MISTAKEN YOU FOR RYOKO...
HEH...
HA HA HA HA HA HA HA HA HA HA HA HA HA HA HA HA HA HA HA--!
AFTER THEM, HINASE!
VROOOSH
WE'VE GOT TO CLEAR UP THIS MISUNDER-STANDING!
UNDER-STOOD!
OH NO! THAT SHIP IS COMING AFTER US!
BUT WHY!?
WHY DO YOU THINK, DUMMY?
THEY WANT OUR TREASURE--AND OUR LIVES!

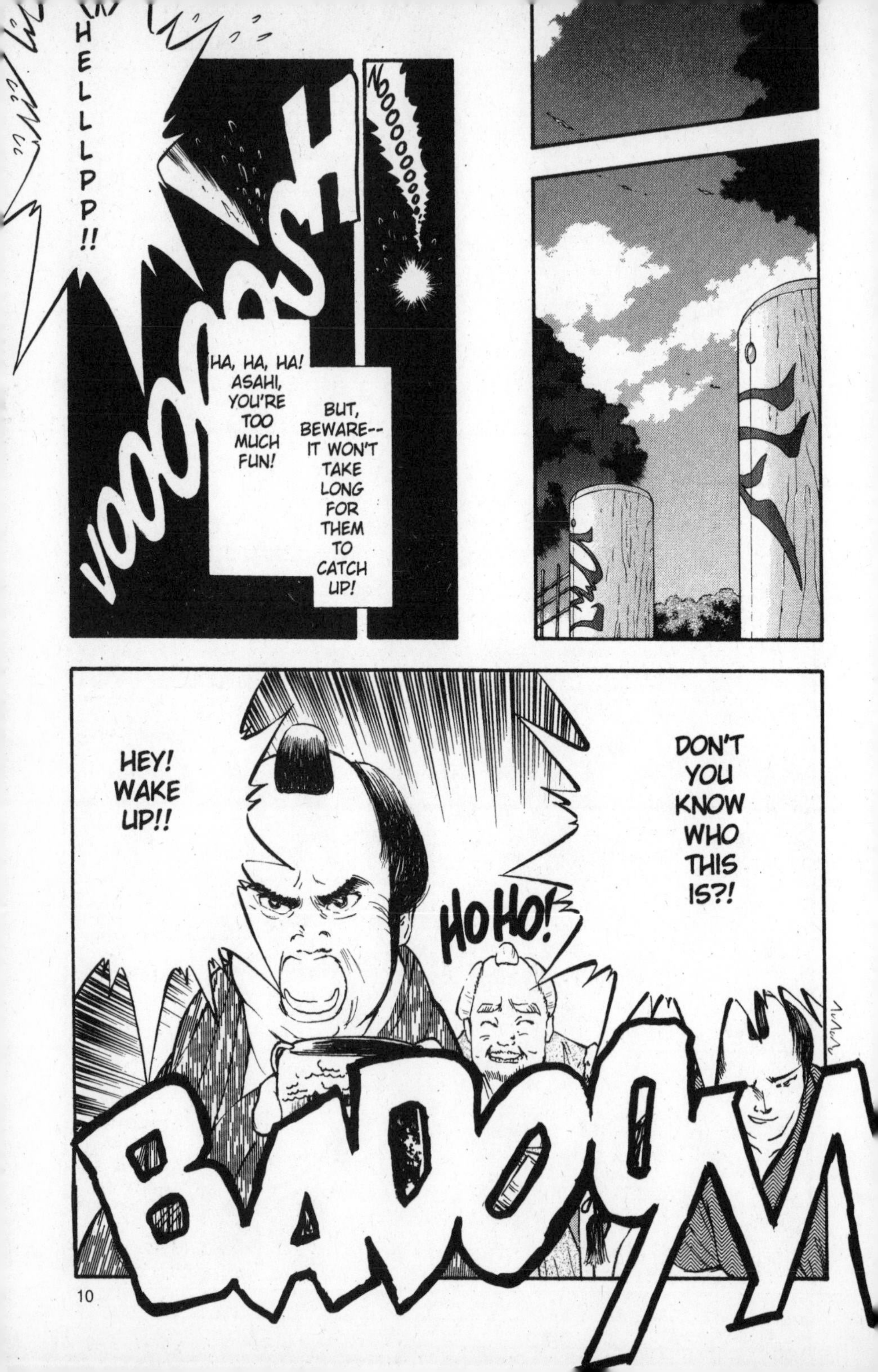
HELLLPPP!!
VOOOOSH
HA, HA, HA! ASAHI, YOU'RE TOO MUCH FUN!
BUT, BEWARE-- IT WON'T TAKE LONG FOR THEM TO CATCH UP!
NOOOOOOOOOO
HEY! WAKE UP!!
HO HO!
DON'T YOU KNOW WHO THIS IS?!
BADOOM

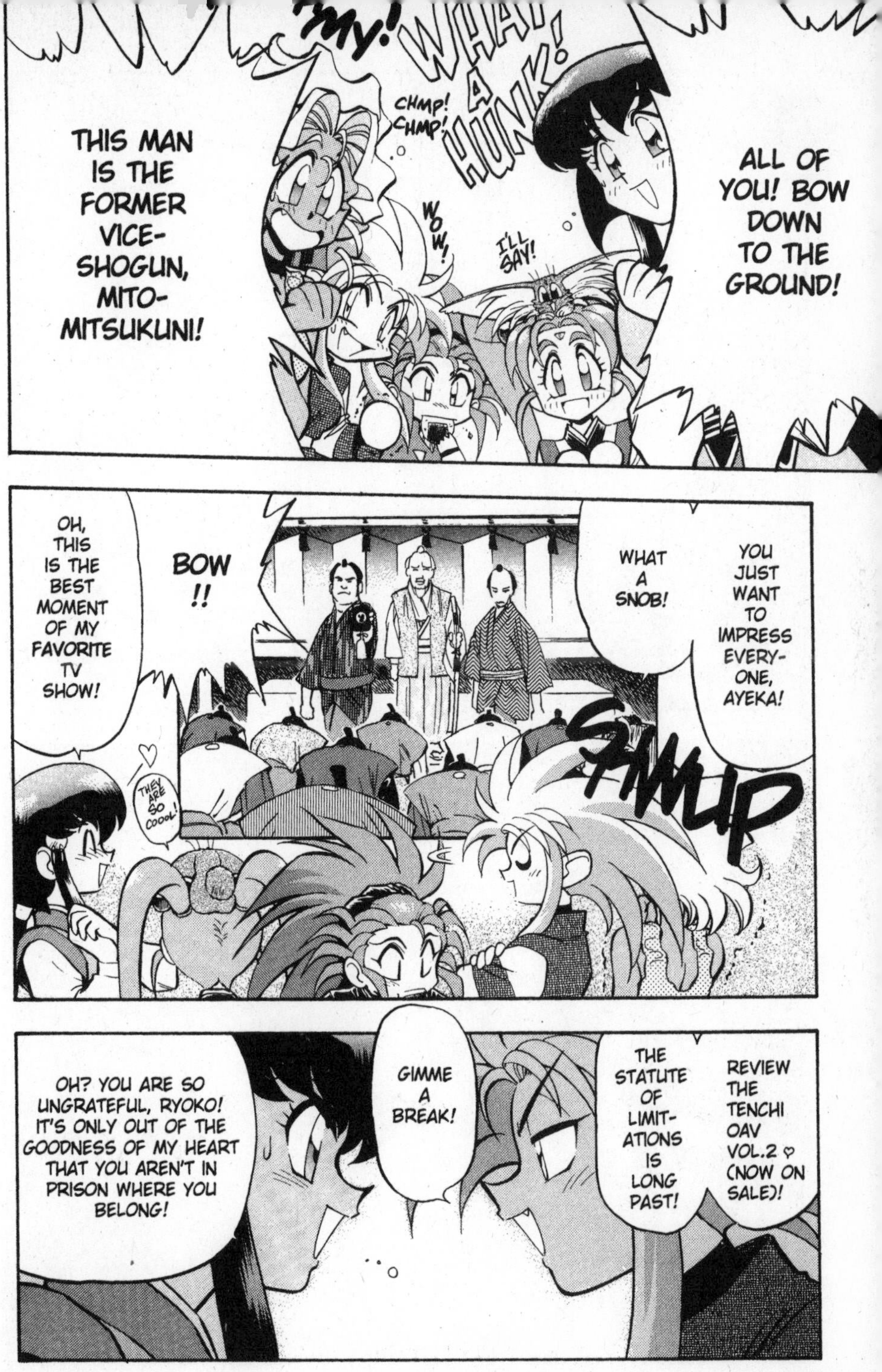
THIS MAN IS THE FORMER VICE-SHOGUN, MITO-MITSUKUNI!
MY!
CHMP! CHMP!
WHAT A HUNK!
WOW!
I'LL SAY!
ALL OF YOU! BOW DOWN TO THE GROUND!
OH, THIS IS THE BEST MOMENT OF MY FAVORITE TV SHOW!
BOW!!
THEY ARE SO COOOL!
WHAT A SNOB!
YOU JUST WANT TO IMPRESS EVERY-ONE, AYEKA!
SMMUP
OH? YOU ARE SO UNGRATEFUL, RYOKO! IT'S ONLY OUT OF THE GOODNESS OF MY HEART THAT YOU AREN'T IN PRISON WHERE YOU BELONG!
GIMME A BREAK!
THE STATUTE OF LIMIT-ATIONS IS LONG PAST!
REVIEW THE TENCHI OAV VOL.2 ♡ (NOW ON SALE)!

ARE YOU GETTING SMART WITH ME?!

OH, YOU TWO! CAN'T WE JUST ENJOY THE SHOW?!

......

LET'S GO TO THE PARK, RYO-OH-KI...

MREOW!

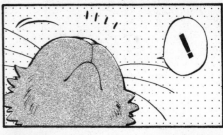

!

HUH? WHAT'S WRONG?

POING!

BOING!

MRROOW!

MYOW MYOW MREOW!

MEOOOWW!!!

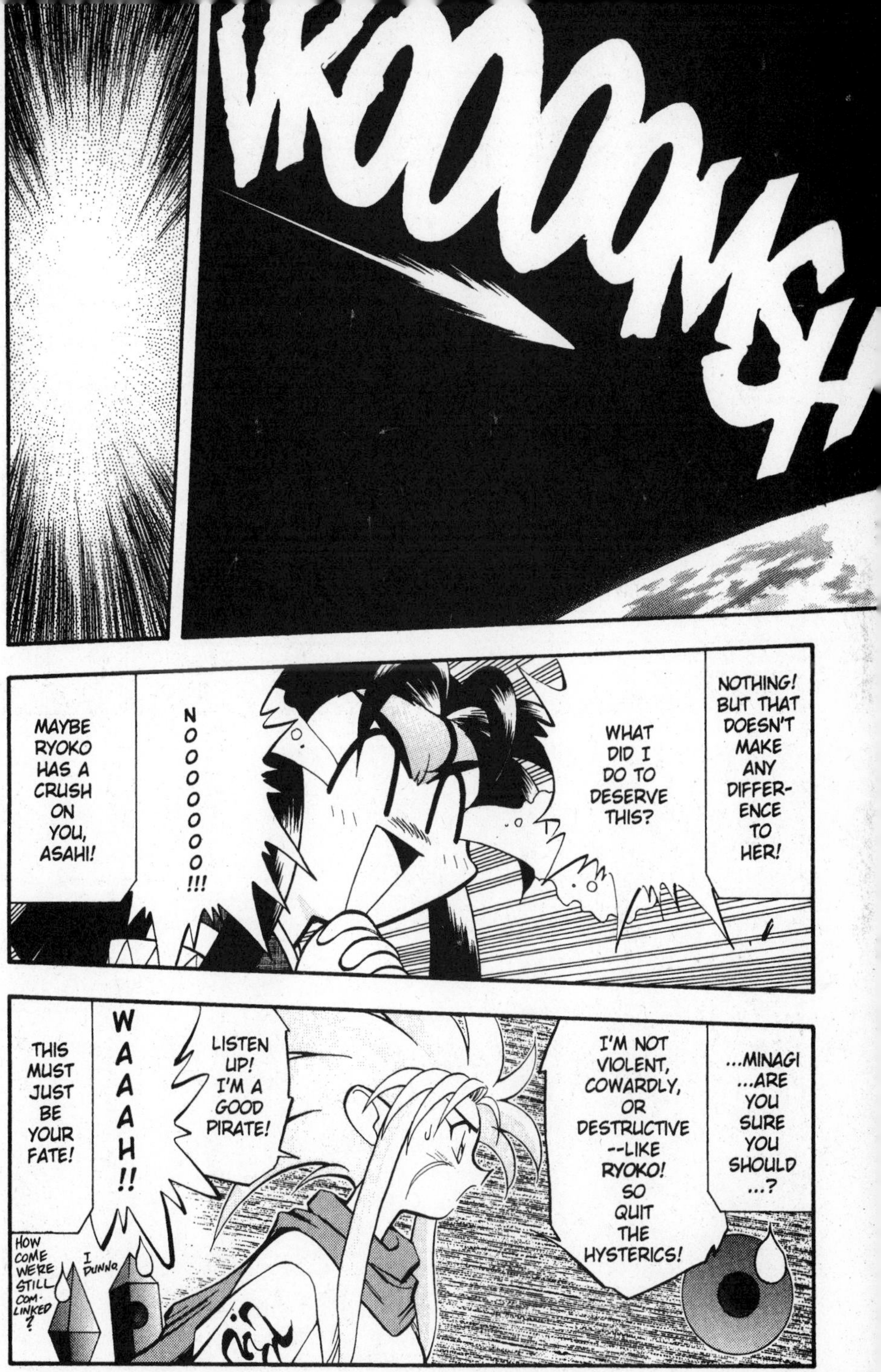
WOOOMSH!
MAYBE RYOKO HAS A CRUSH ON YOU, ASAHI!
NOOOOOOOOO!!!
WHAT DID I DO TO DESERVE THIS?
NOTHING! BUT THAT DOESN'T MAKE ANY DIFFER-ENCE TO HER!
THIS MUST JUST BE YOUR FATE!
WAAAAH!!
LISTEN UP! I'M A GOOD PIRATE!
I'M NOT VIOLENT, COWARDLY, OR DESTRUCTIVE --LIKE RYOKO! SO QUIT THE HYSTERICS!
...MINAGI ...ARE YOU SURE YOU SHOULD ...?
HOW COME WERE STILL COM-LINKED?
I DUNNO.

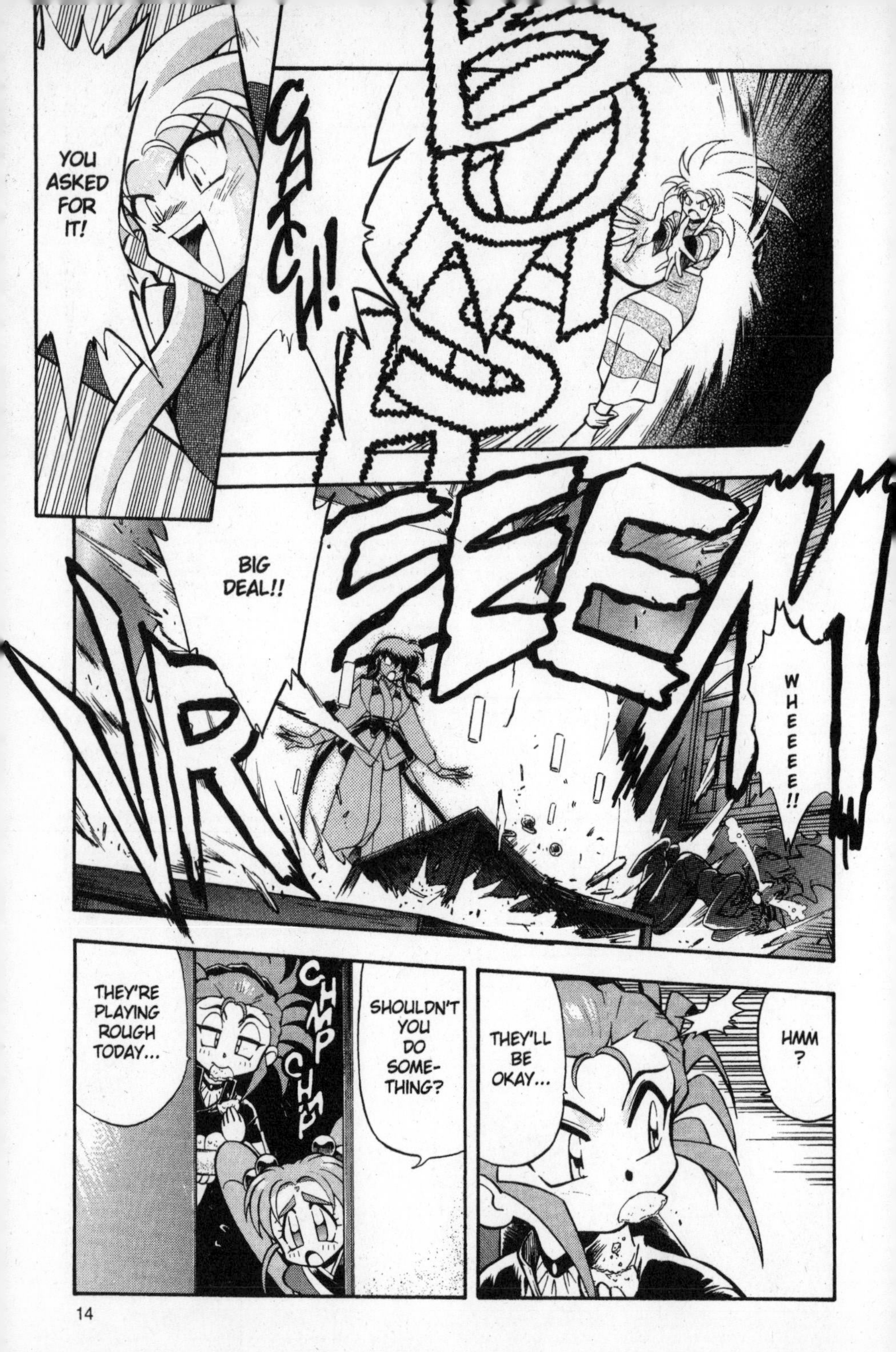
YOU ASKED FOR IT!
CATCH!
BIG DEAL!!
WHEEEEE!!
THEY'RE PLAYING ROUGH TODAY...
CHMP CHMP
SHOULDN'T YOU DO SOME-THING?
THEY'LL BE OKAY...
HMM?

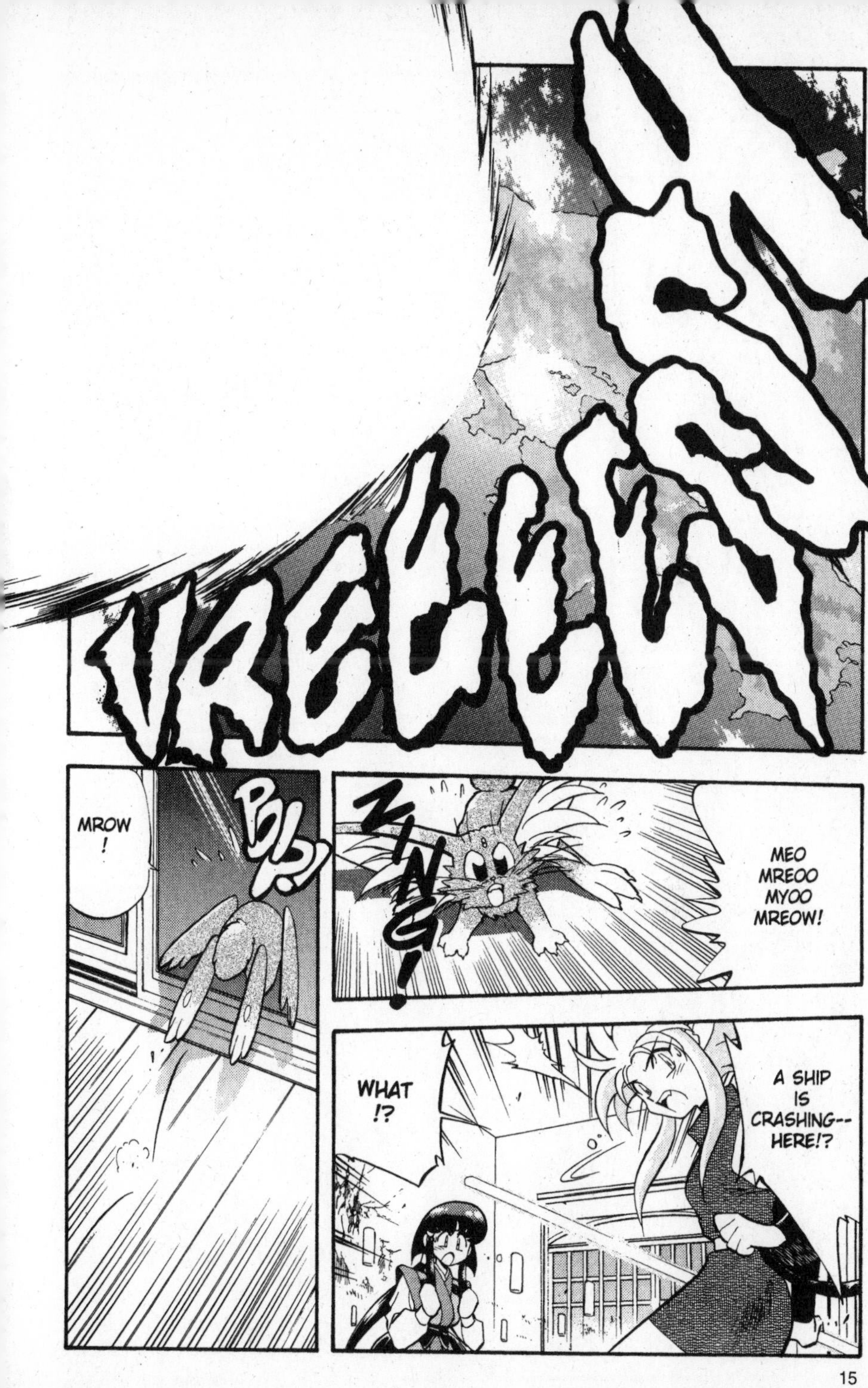
MROW!
MEO MREOO MYOO MREOW!
WHAT!?
A SHIP IS CRASHING--HERE!?

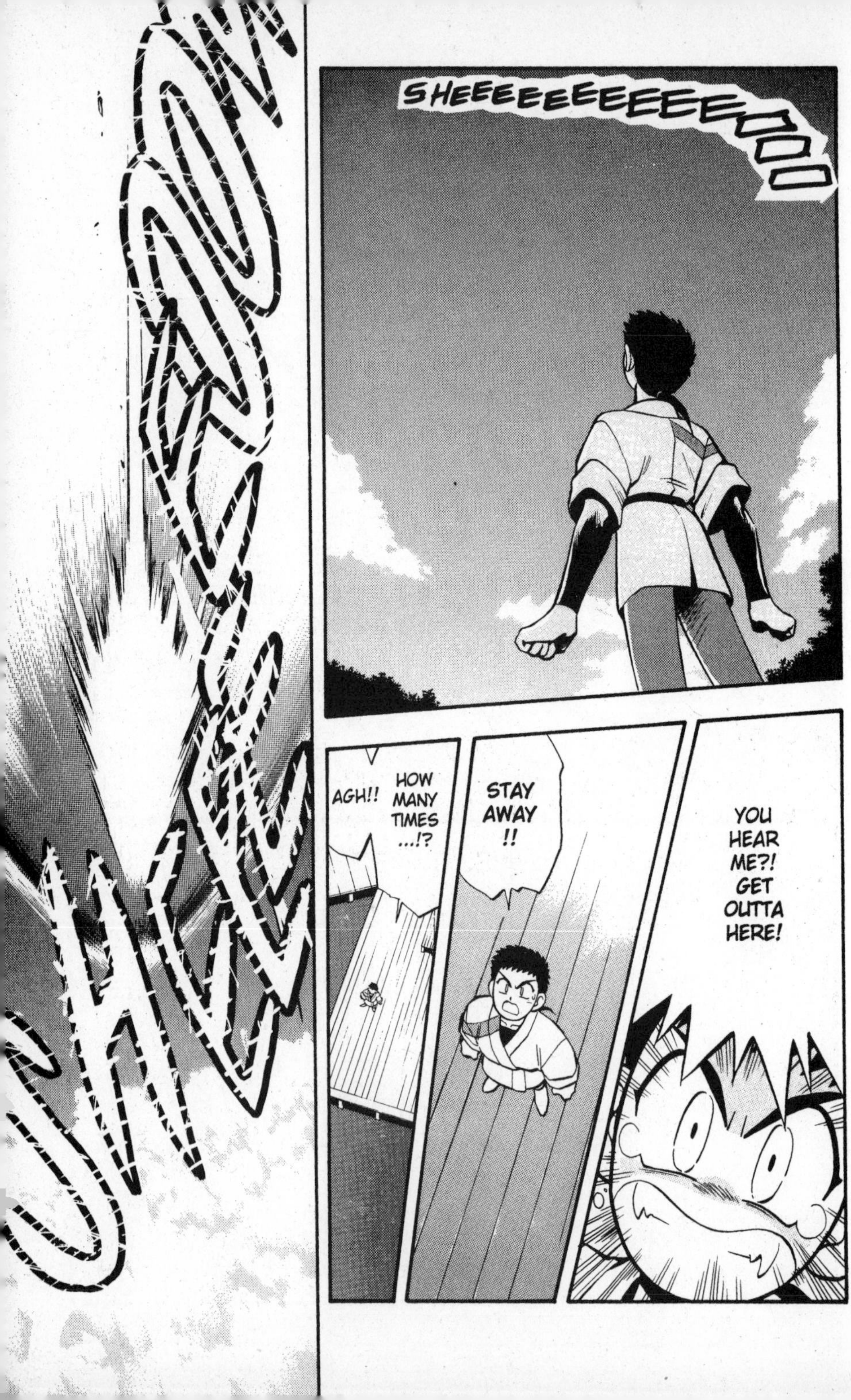
SHEEEEEEEEEEOOO
AGH!!
HOW MANY TIMES ...!?
STAY AWAY !!
YOU HEAR ME?! GET OUTTA HERE!

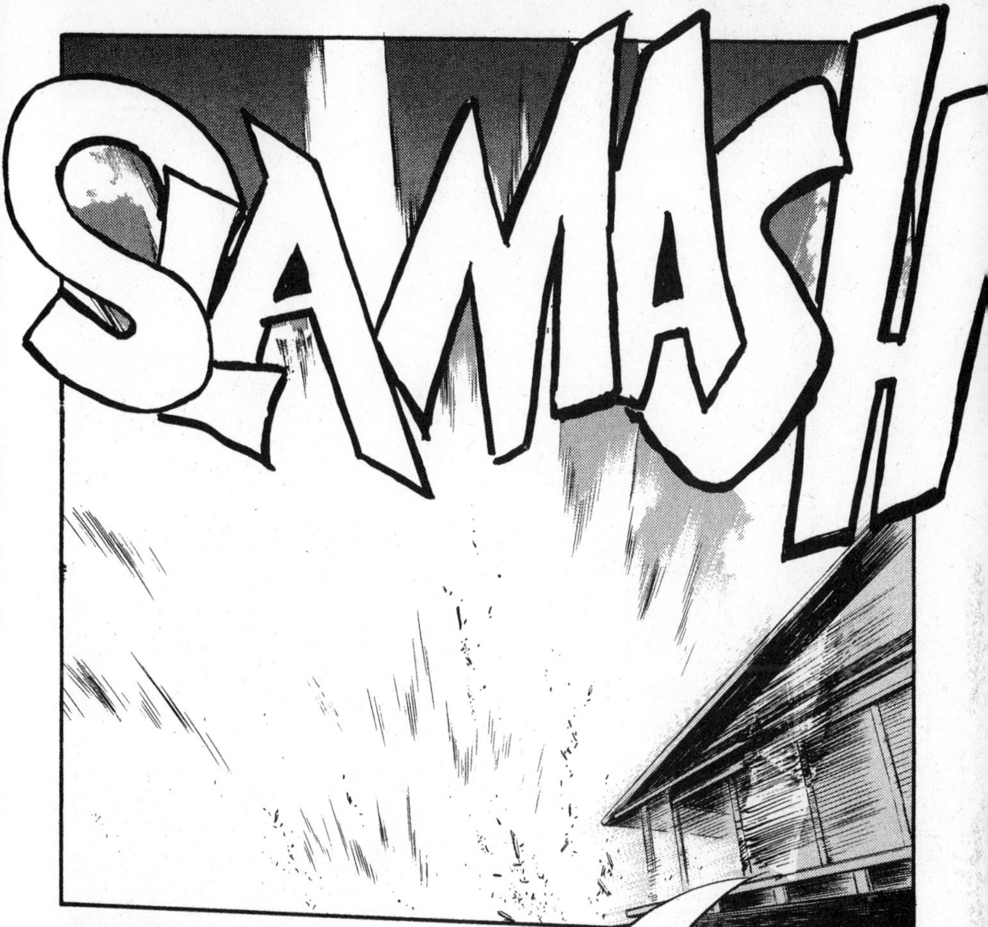
SMASH

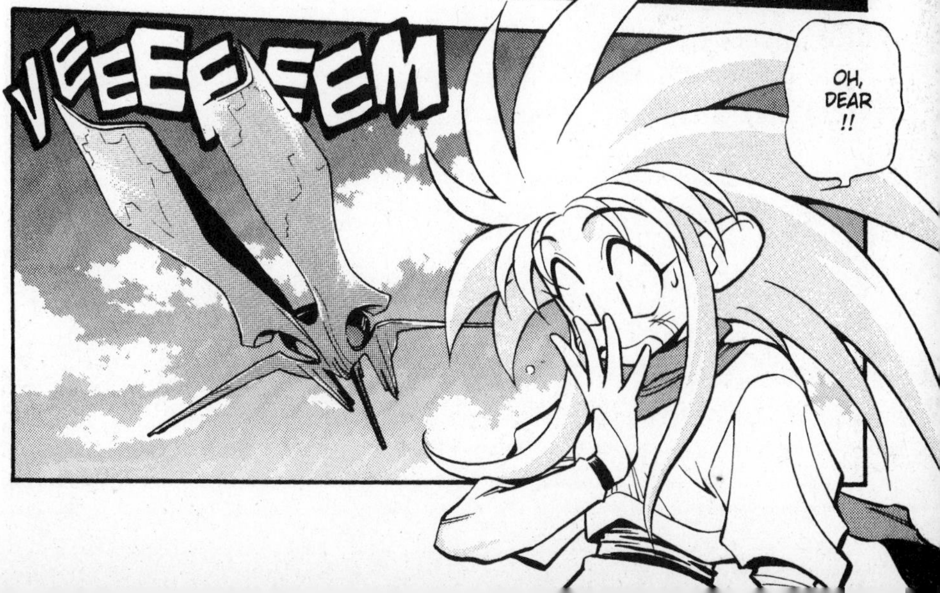
VEEEEEEM
OH, DEAR !!

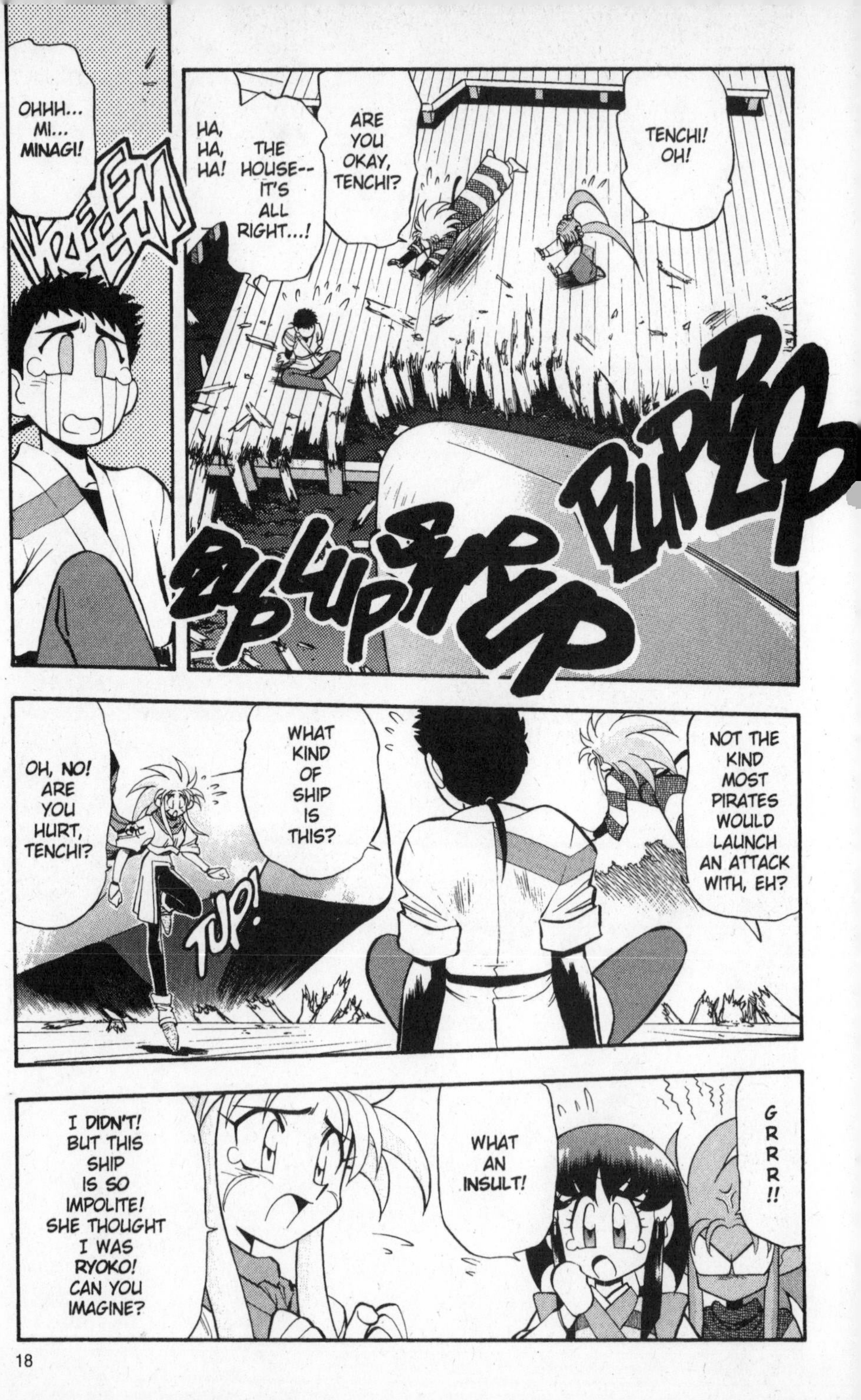
OHHH... MI... MINAGI!
HA, HA, HA! THE HOUSE-- IT'S ALL RIGHT...!
ARE YOU OKAY, TENCHI?
TENCHI! OH!
OH, NO! ARE YOU HURT, TENCHI?
WHAT KIND OF SHIP IS THIS?
TUP!
NOT THE KIND MOST PIRATES WOULD LAUNCH AN ATTACK WITH, EH?
I DIDN'T! BUT THIS SHIP IS SO IMPOLITE! SHE THOUGHT I WAS RYOKO! CAN YOU IMAGINE?
WHAT AN INSULT!
GRRR!!

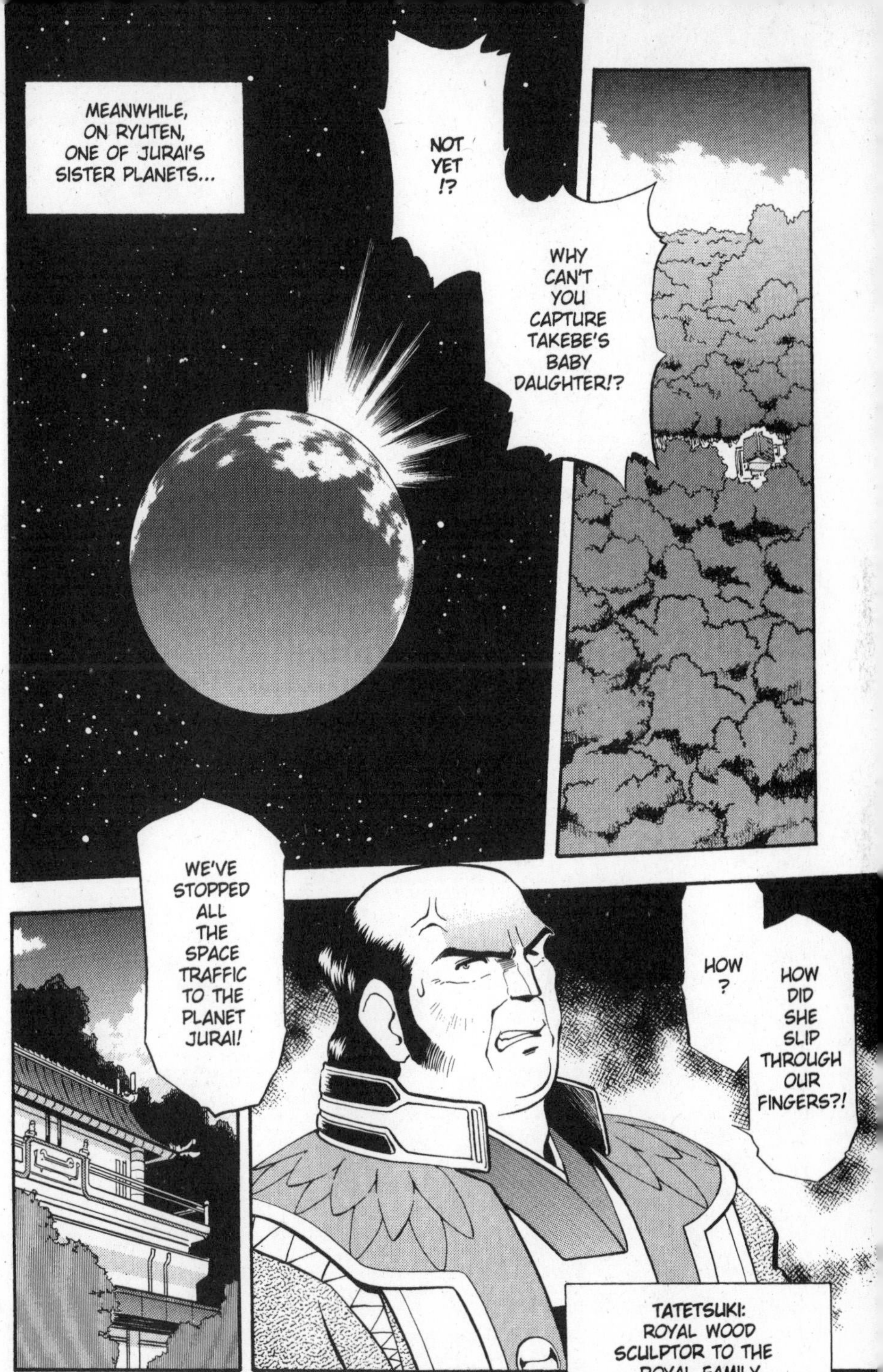
MEANWHILE, ON RYUTEN, ONE OF JURAI'S SISTER PLANETS...
NOT YET !?
WHY CAN'T YOU CAPTURE TAKEBE'S BABY DAUGHTER!?
WE'VE STOPPED ALL THE SPACE TRAFFIC TO THE PLANET JURAI!
HOW ?
HOW DID SHE SLIP THROUGH OUR FINGERS?!
TATETSUKI: ROYAL WOOD SCULPTOR TO THE ROYAL FAMILY OF JURAI...

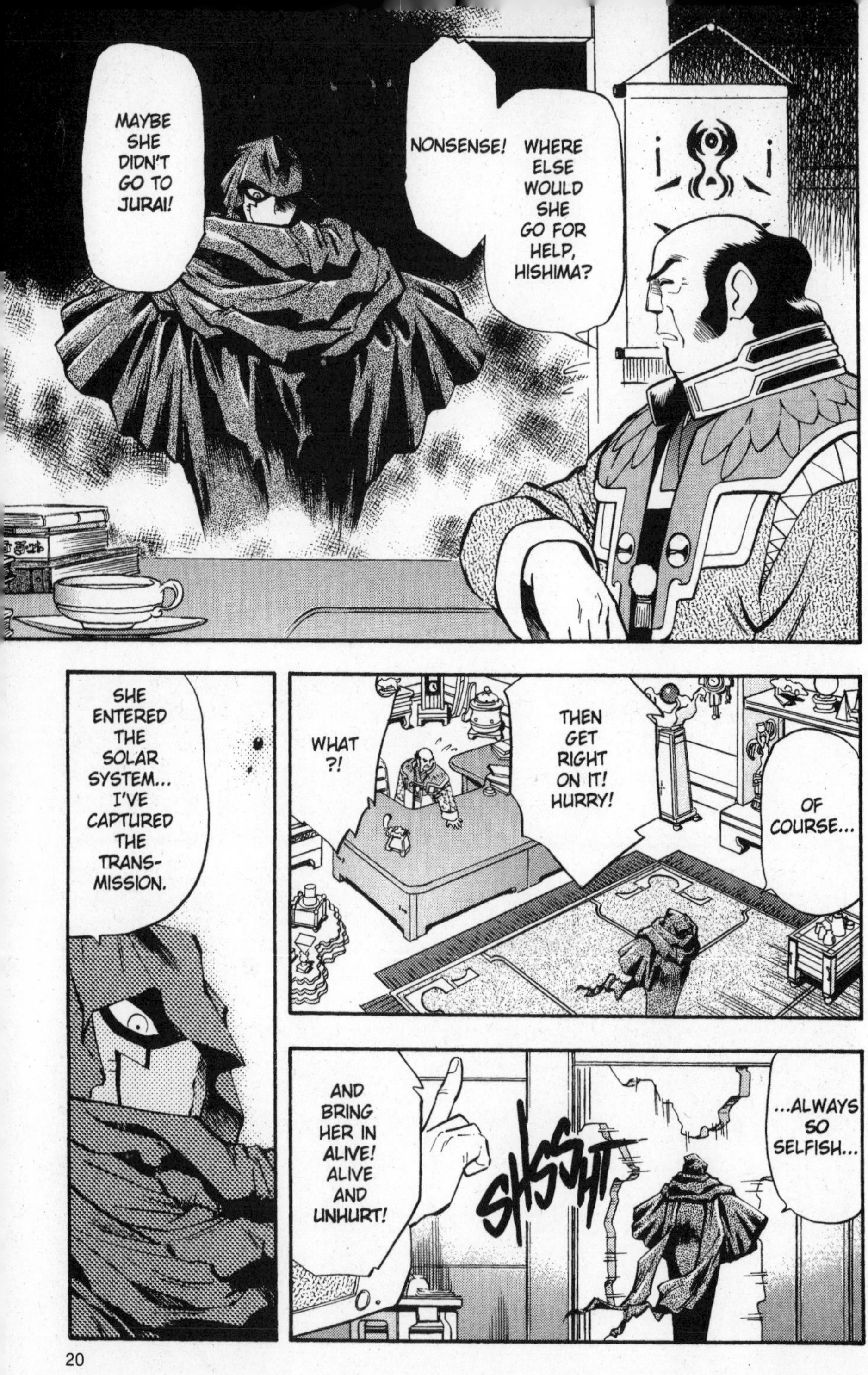
MAYBE SHE DIDN'T GO TO JURAI!
NONSENSE!
WHERE ELSE WOULD SHE GO FOR HELP, HISHIMA?
SHE ENTERED THE SOLAR SYSTEM... I'VE CAPTURED THE TRANS-MISSION.
WHAT?!
THEN GET RIGHT ON IT! HURRY!
OF COURSE...
AND BRING HER IN ALIVE! ALIVE AND UNHURT!
SHSSHT
...ALWAYS SO SELFISH...

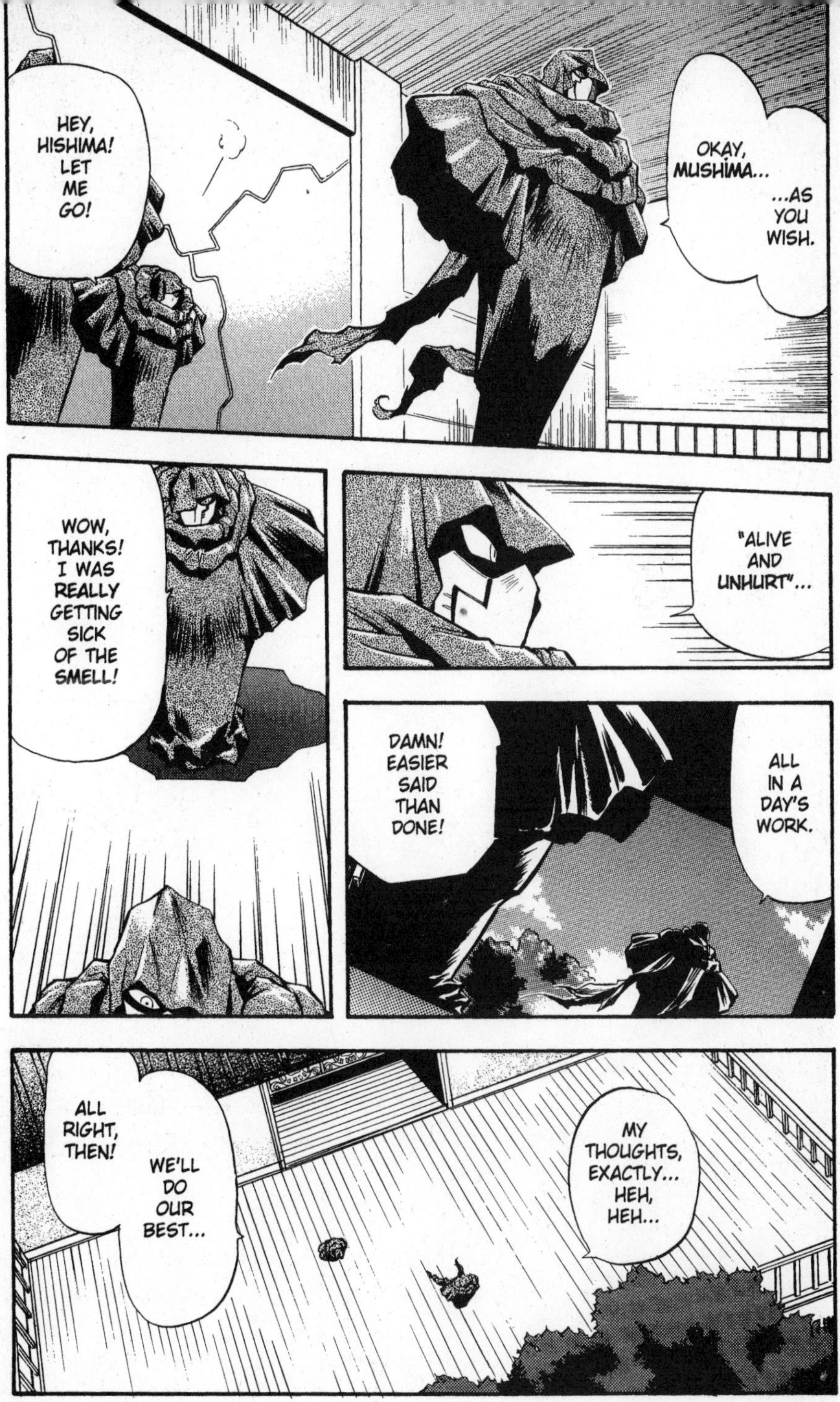
HEY, HISHIMA! LET ME GO!
OKAY, MUSHIMA...
...AS YOU WISH.
WOW, THANKS! I WAS REALLY GETTING SICK OF THE SMELL!
"ALIVE AND UNHURT"...
DAMN! EASIER SAID THAN DONE!
ALL IN A DAY'S WORK.
ALL RIGHT, THEN!
WE'LL DO OUR BEST...
MY THOUGHTS, EXACTLY... HEH, HEH...

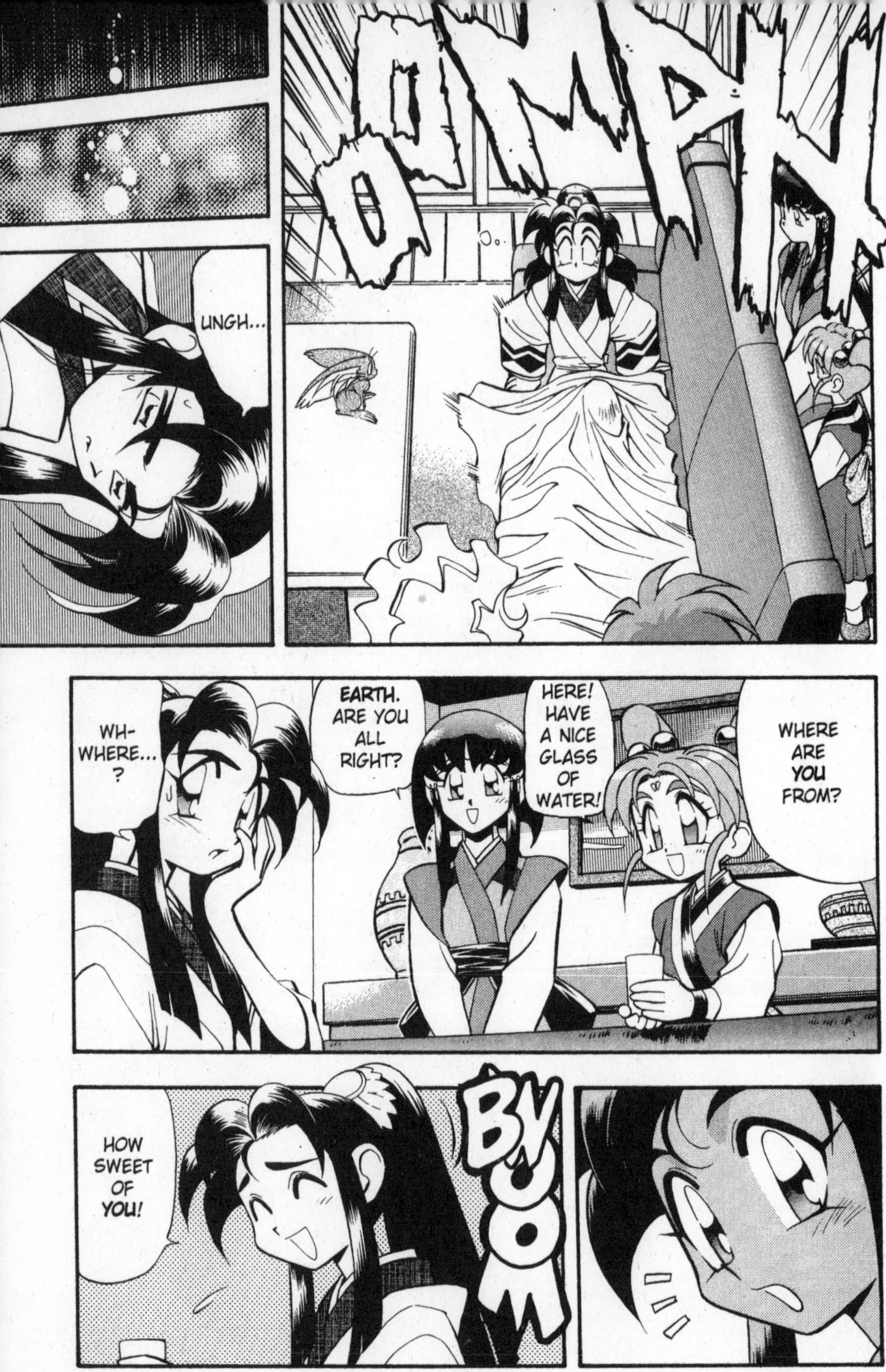
UNGH...
WH- WHERE... ?
EARTH. ARE YOU ALL RIGHT?
HERE! HAVE A NICE GLASS OF WATER!
WHERE ARE YOU FROM?
HOW SWEET OF YOU!

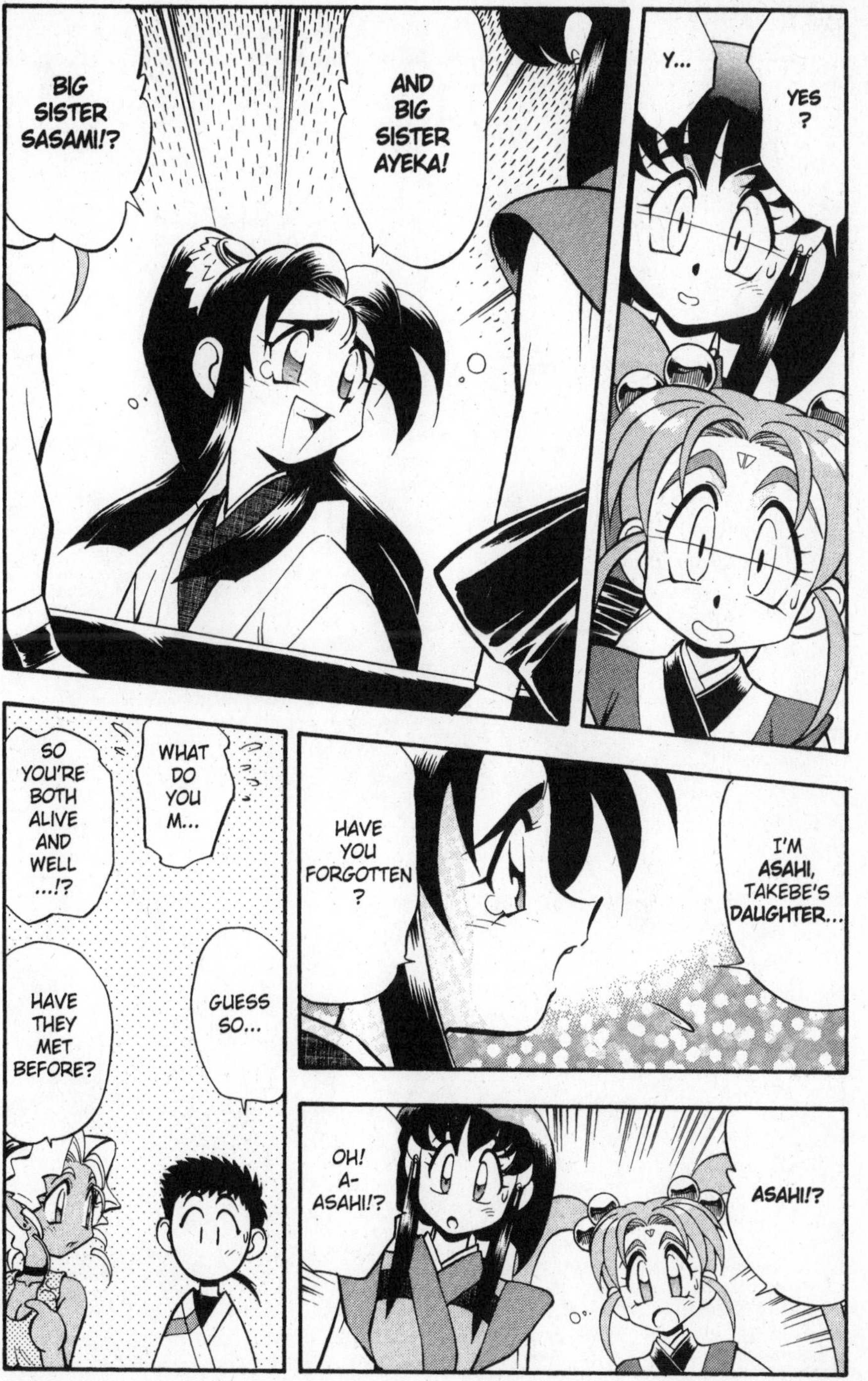
BIG SISTER SASAMI!?
AND BIG SISTER AYEKA!
Y...
YES?
SO YOU'RE BOTH ALIVE AND WELL ...!?
WHAT DO YOU M...
HAVE THEY MET BEFORE?
GUESS SO...
HAVE YOU FORGOTTEN?
I'M ASAHI, TAKEBE'S DAUGHTER...
OH! A-ASAHI!?
ASAHI!?

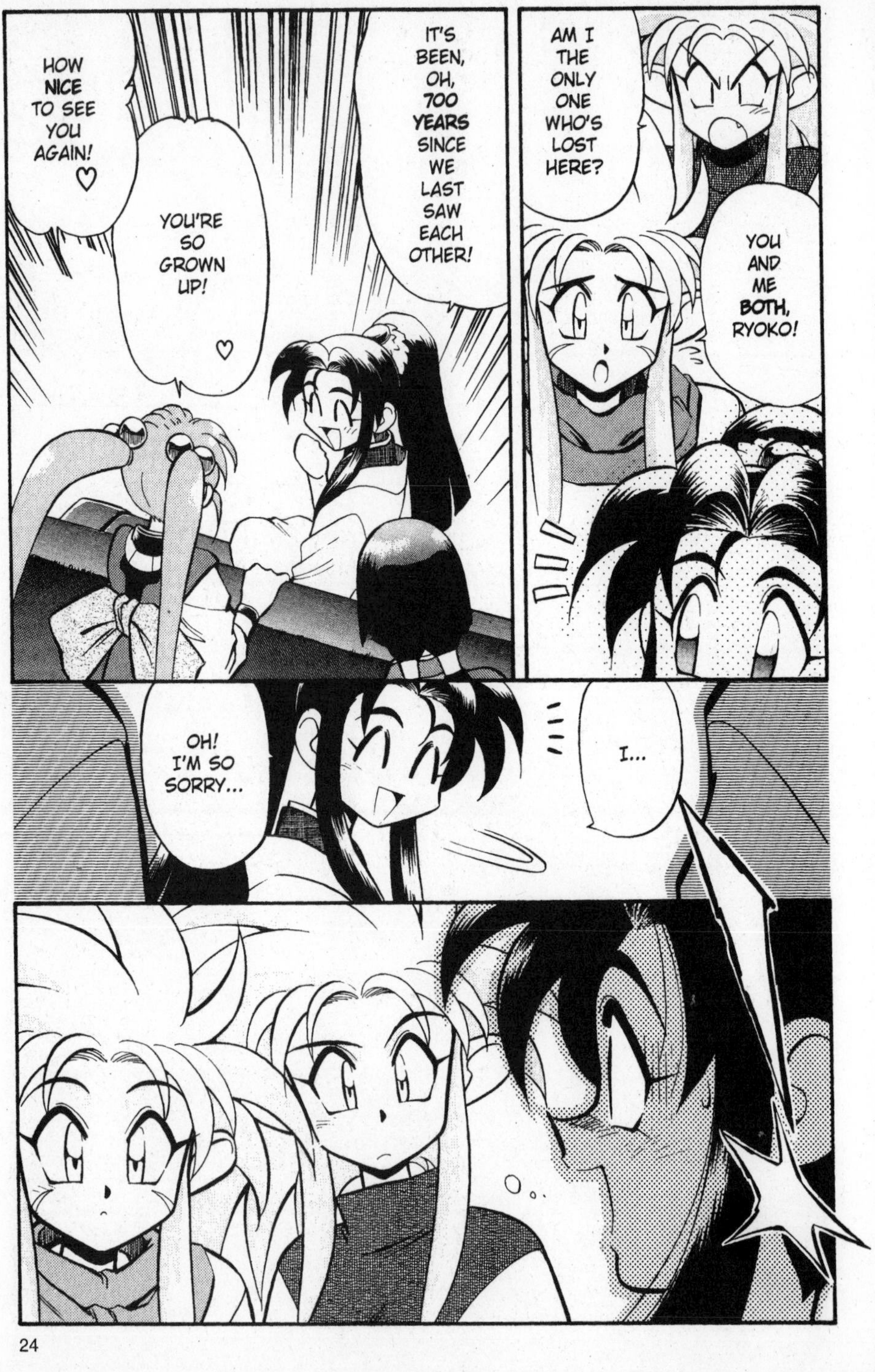
HOW **NICE** TO SEE YOU AGAIN! ♡
YOU'RE SO GROWN UP! ♡
IT'S BEEN, OH, **700 YEARS** SINCE WE LAST SAW EACH OTHER!
AM I THE ONLY ONE WHO'S LOST HERE?
YOU AND ME **BOTH**, RYOKO!
OH! I'M SO SORRY...
I...

? WHAT'S WRONG?

GREAT. SHE FAINTED!

OUT LIKE A LIGHT...

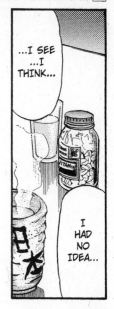

...I SEE ...I THINK...

I HAD NO IDEA...

PLEASE, YOU MUST EXCUSE ME...

SURE-- WHAT- EVER!

SHE'S TALK- ING TO ME, RYOKO!

SO NOW YOU CAN TELL US HOW YOU KNOW THIS GIRL?

SORRY, WASHU! OF COURSE...

TRY SOME LIME GELATIN! IT'S DELISH!

CHMP CHMP

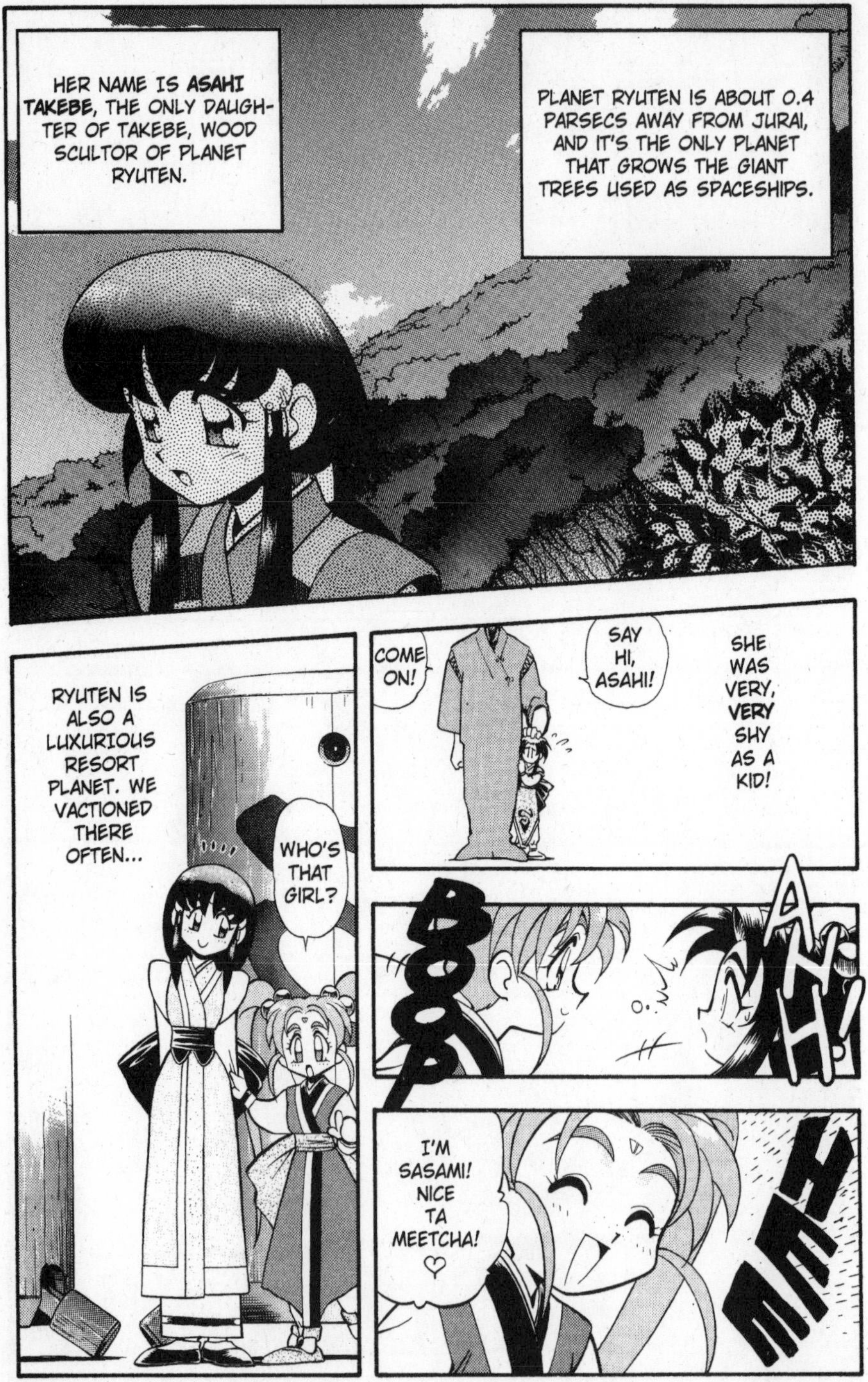
HER NAME IS **ASAHI TAKEBE**, THE ONLY DAUGHTER OF TAKEBE, WOOD SCULTOR OF PLANET RYUTEN.
PLANET RYUTEN IS ABOUT 0.4 PARSECS AWAY FROM JURAI, AND IT'S THE ONLY PLANET THAT GROWS THE GIANT TREES USED AS SPACESHIPS.
RYUTEN IS ALSO A LUXURIOUS RESORT PLANET. WE VACTIONED THERE OFTEN...
WHO'S THAT GIRL?
COME ON!
SAY HI, ASAHI!
SHE WAS VERY, **VERY** SHY AS A KID!
BOOP
AHH!
I'M SASAMI! NICE TA MEETCHA! ♡

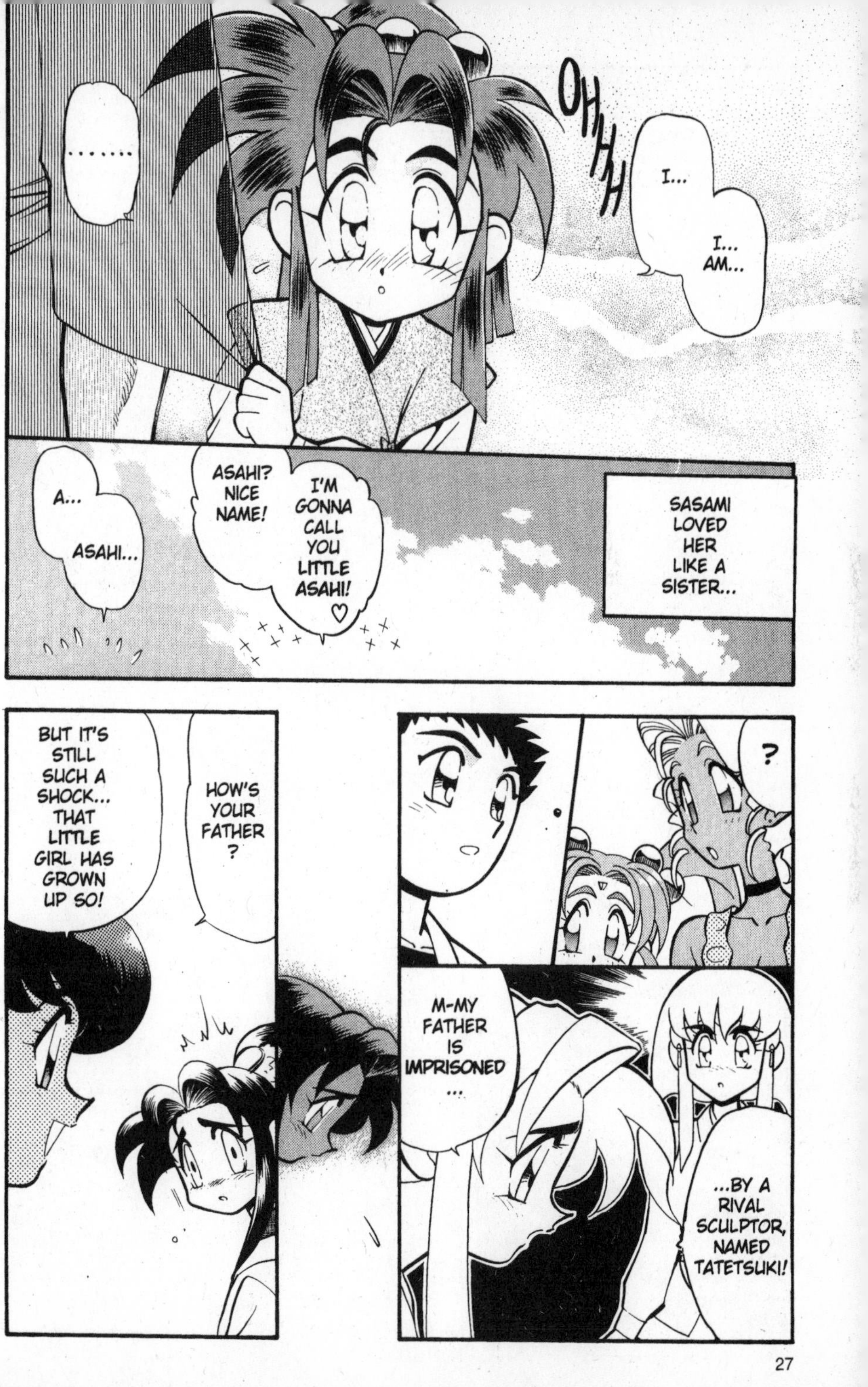
....
OHHHH
I... I... AM...
A... ASAHI...
ASAHI? NICE NAME! I'M GONNA CALL YOU LITTLE ASAHI! ♡
SASAMI LOVED HER LIKE A SISTER...
BUT IT'S STILL SUCH A SHOCK... THAT LITTLE GIRL HAS GROWN UP SO!
HOW'S YOUR FATHER?
?
M-MY FATHER IS IMPRISONED...
...BY A RIVAL SCULPTOR, NAMED TATETSUKI!

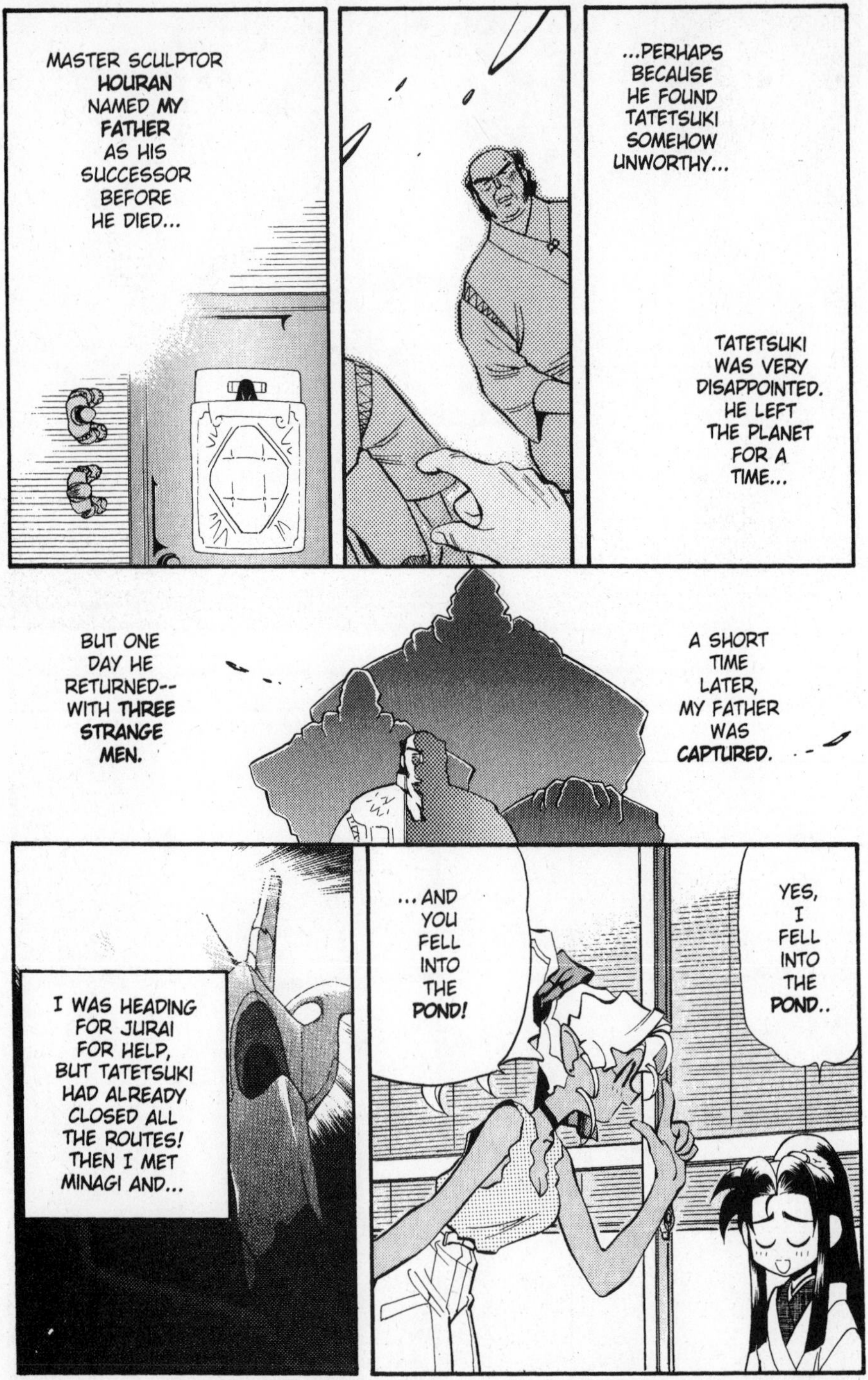
MASTER SCULPTOR HOURAN NAMED MY FATHER AS HIS SUCCESSOR BEFORE HE DIED...
...PERHAPS BECAUSE HE FOUND TATETSUKI SOMEHOW UNWORTHY...
TATETSUKI WAS VERY DISAPPOINTED. HE LEFT THE PLANET FOR A TIME...
BUT ONE DAY HE RETURNED--WITH THREE STRANGE MEN.
A SHORT TIME LATER, MY FATHER WAS CAPTURED.
I WAS HEADING FOR JURAI FOR HELP, BUT TATETSUKI HAD ALREADY CLOSED ALL THE ROUTES! THEN I MET MINAGI AND...
...AND YOU FELL INTO THE POND!
YES, I FELL INTO THE POND..

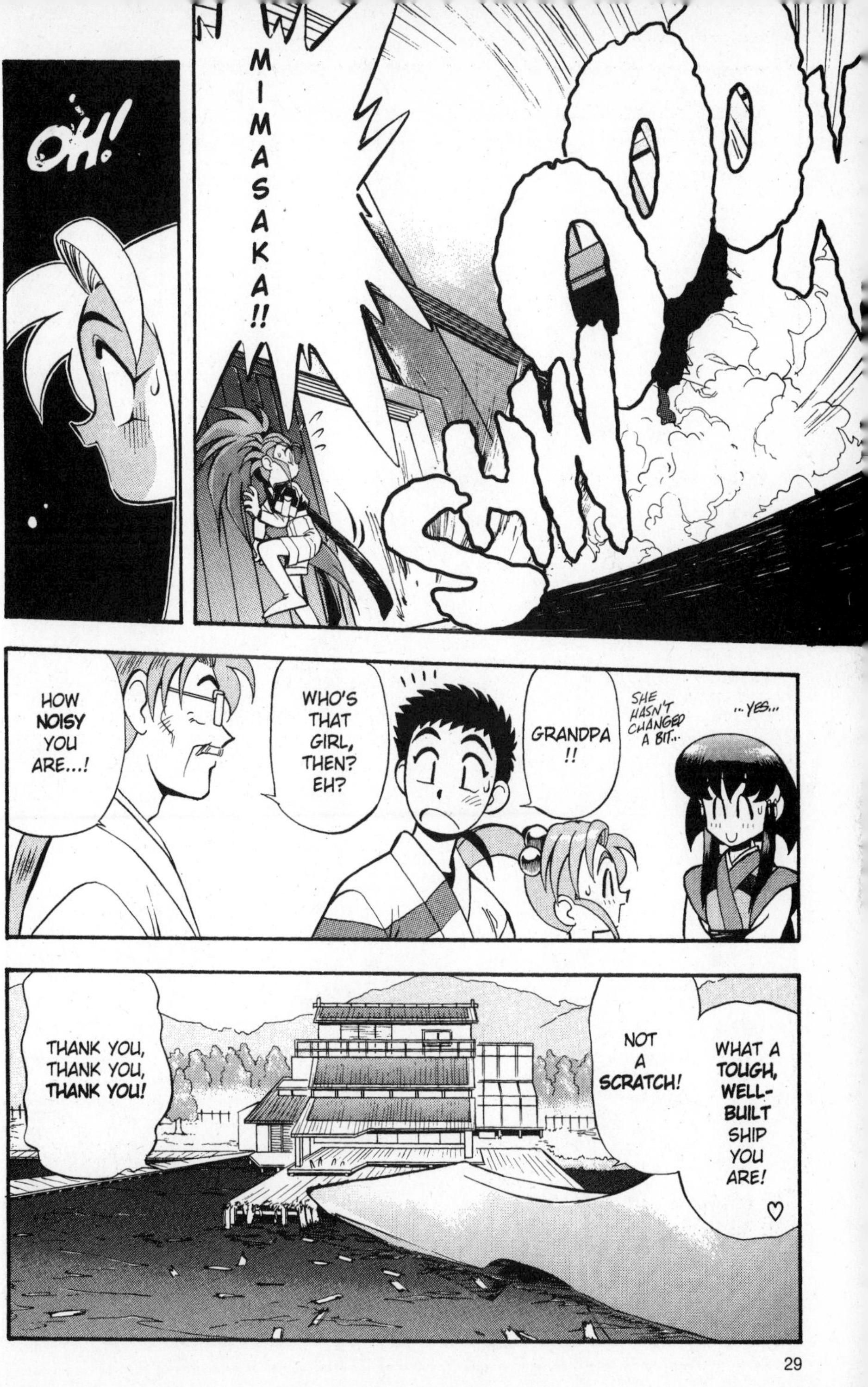
OH!
MIMASAKA!!
HOW NOISY YOU ARE...!
WHO'S THAT GIRL, THEN? EH?
GRANDPA!!
SHE HASN'T CHANGED A BIT...
...YES...
THANK YOU, THANK YOU, THANK YOU!
NOT A SCRATCH!
WHAT A TOUGH, WELL-BUILT SHIP YOU ARE! ♡

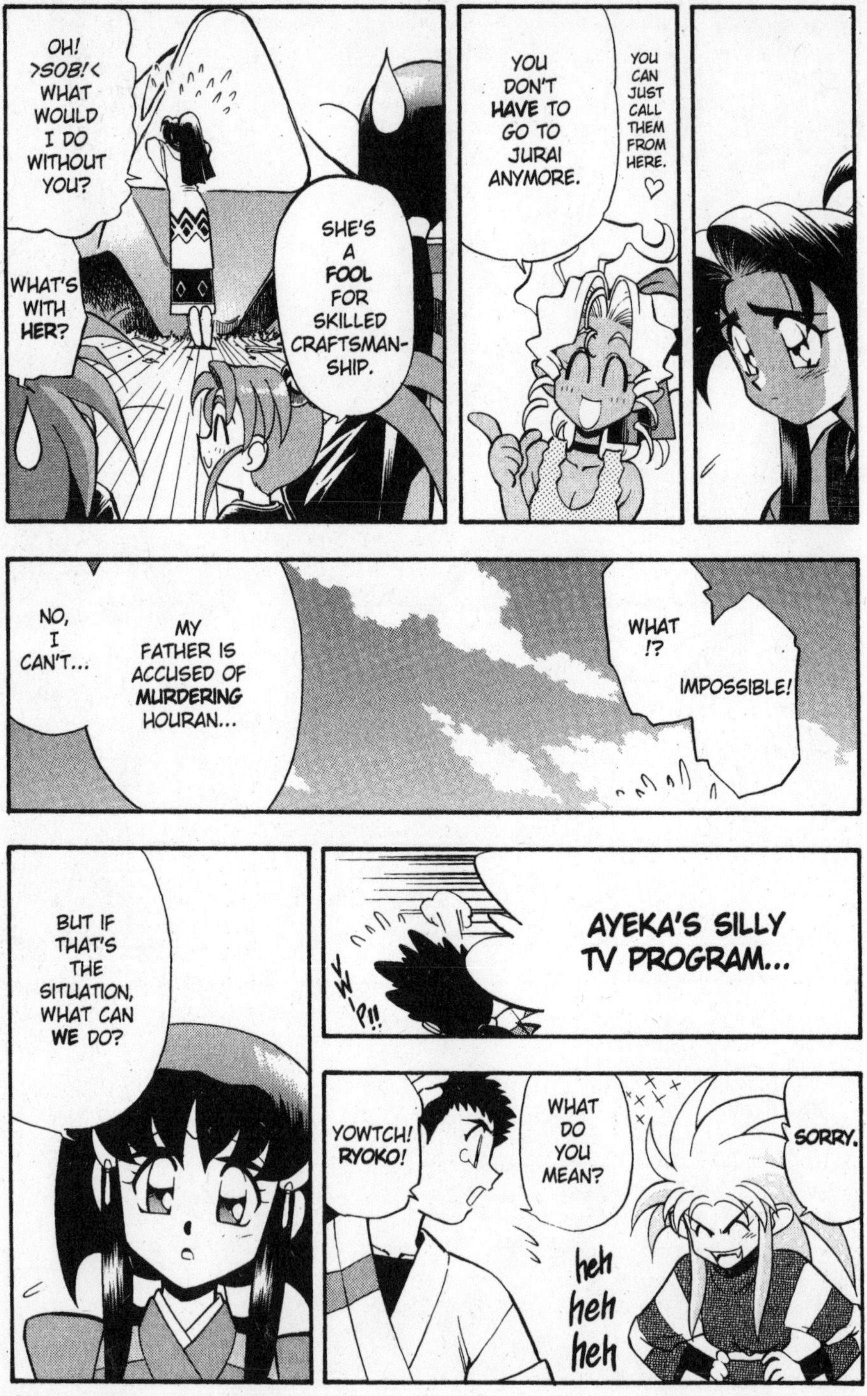

OH! >SOB!< WHAT WOULD I DO WITHOUT YOU?
WHAT'S WITH HER?
SHE'S A FOOL FOR SKILLED CRAFTSMANSHIP.
YOU DON'T HAVE TO GO TO JURAI ANYMORE.
YOU CAN JUST CALL THEM FROM HERE. ♡
NO, I CAN'T...
MY FATHER IS ACCUSED OF MURDERING HOURAN...
WHAT!?
IMPOSSIBLE!
BUT IF THAT'S THE SITUATION, WHAT CAN WE DO?
VWIP!!
AYEKA'S SILLY TV PROGRAM...
YOWTCH! RYOKO!
WHAT DO YOU MEAN?
SORRY.
heh heh heh

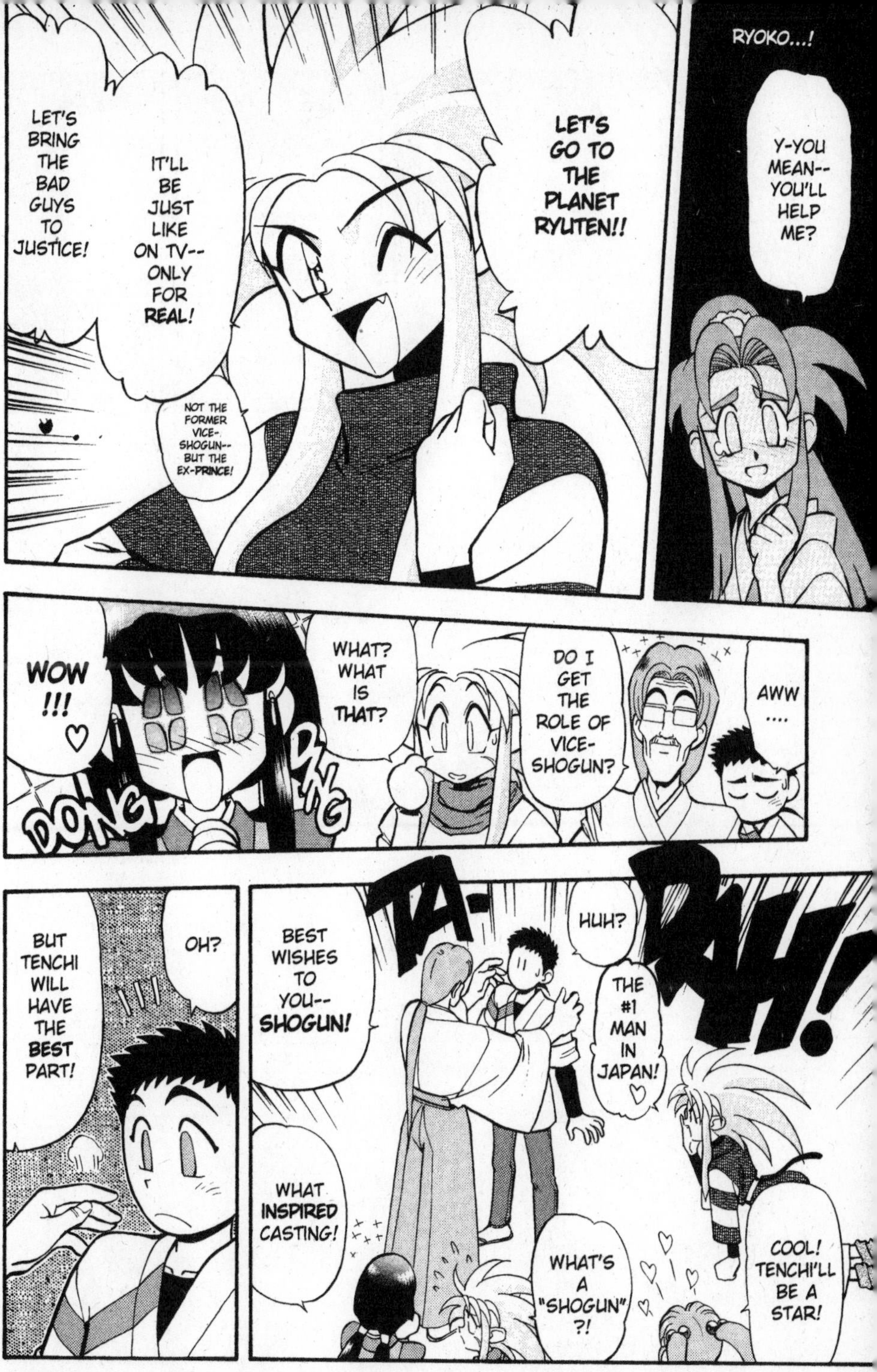
LET'S BRING THE BAD GUYS TO JUSTICE!
IT'LL BE JUST LIKE ON TV-- ONLY FOR REAL!
LET'S GO TO THE PLANET RYUTEN!!
NOT THE FORMER VICE-SHOGUN-- BUT THE EX-PRINCE!
RYOKO...!
Y-YOU MEAN-- YOU'LL HELP ME?
WOW !!! ♡
DONG
DING
WHAT? WHAT IS THAT?
DO I GET THE ROLE OF VICE-SHOGUN?
AWW ....
BUT TENCHI WILL HAVE THE BEST PART!
OH?
TA-
BEST WISHES TO YOU-- SHOGUN!
HUH?
DAH!
THE #1 MAN IN JAPAN! ♡
WHAT INSPIRED CASTING!
WHAT'S A "SHOGUN"?!
COOL! TENCHI'LL BE A STAR!

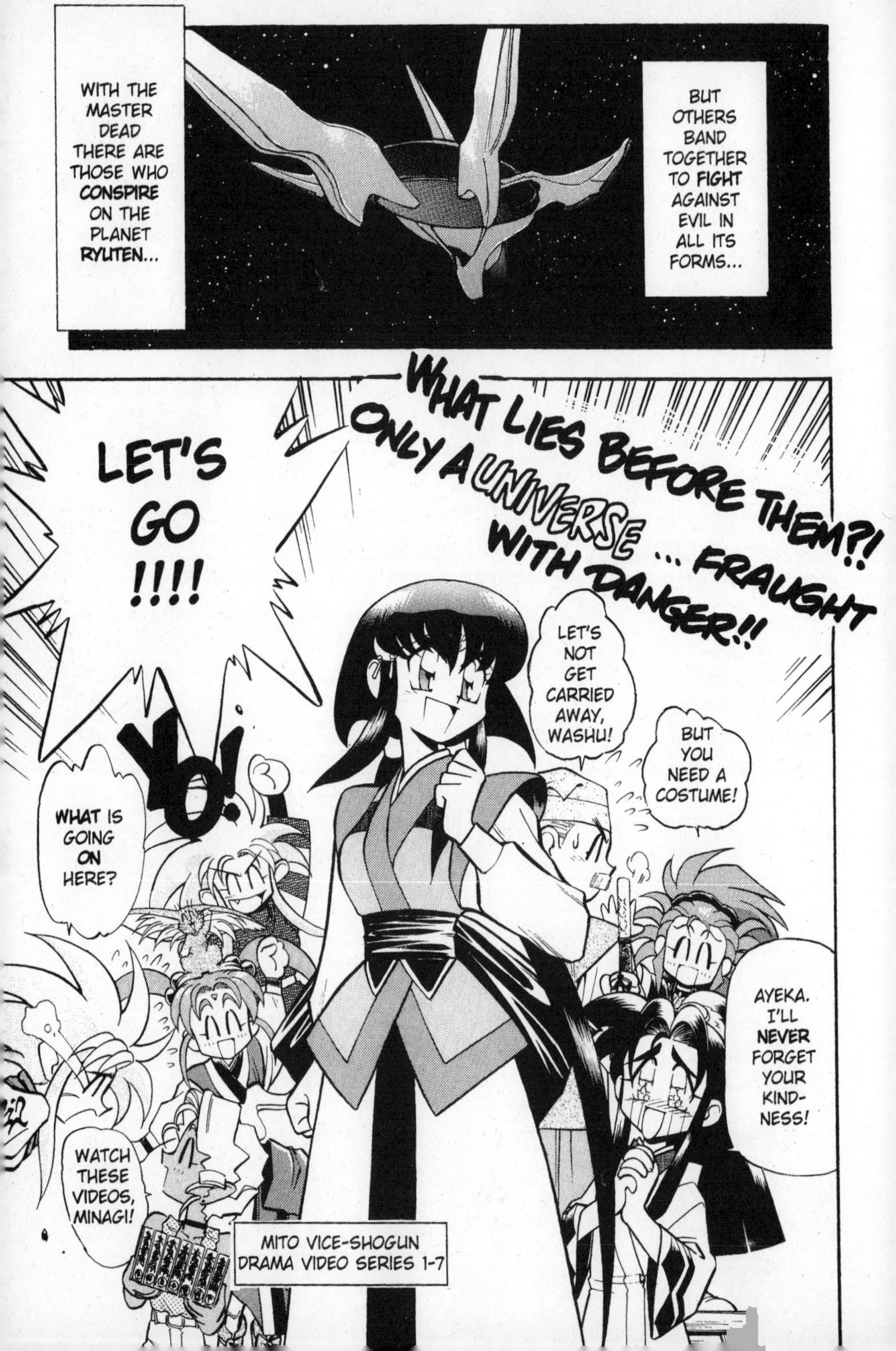
WITH THE MASTER DEAD THERE ARE THOSE WHO CONSPIRE ON THE PLANET RYUTEN...
BUT OTHERS BAND TOGETHER TO FIGHT AGAINST EVIL IN ALL ITS FORMS...
LET'S GO !!!!
YO!
WHAT LIES BEFORE THEM?!
ONLY A UNIVERSE ... FRAUGHT WITH DANGER!!
LET'S NOT GET CARRIED AWAY, WASHU!
BUT YOU NEED A COSTUME!
WHAT IS GOING ON HERE?
AYEKA. I'LL NEVER FORGET YOUR KINDNESS!
WATCH THESE VIDEOS, MINAGI!
MITO VICE-SHOGUN DRAMA VIDEO SERIES 1-7

Tales of Tenchi #2

ALLERGIC REACTION

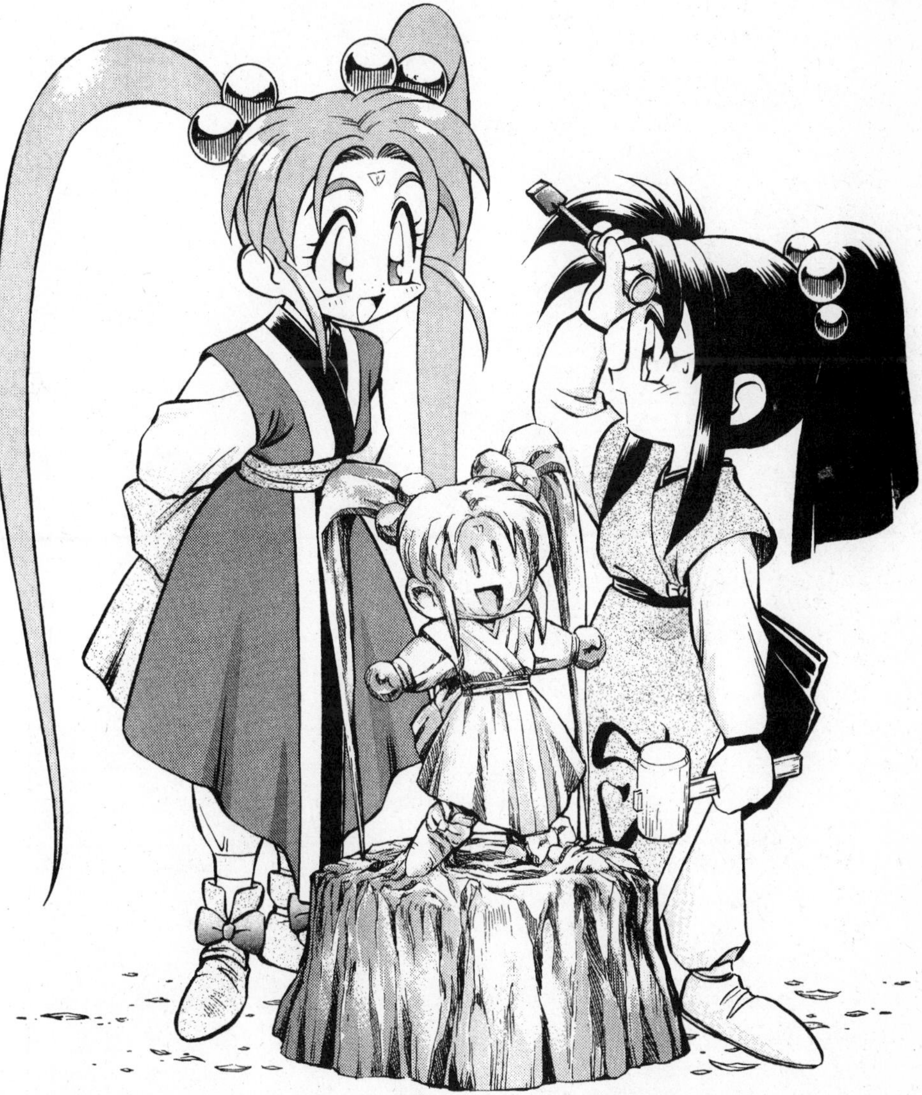

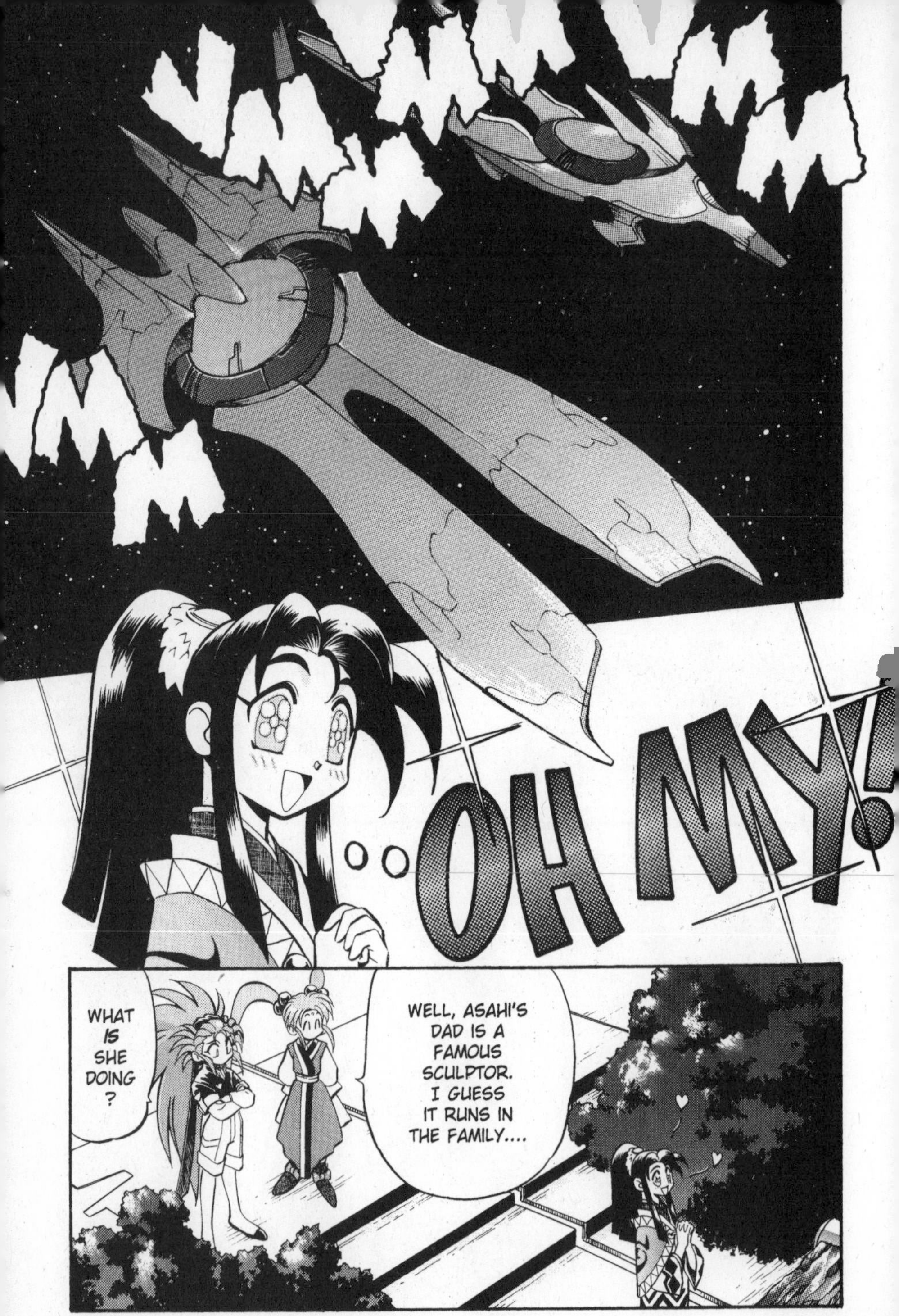
..OH MY!
WHAT IS SHE DOING?
WELL, ASAHI'S DAD IS A FAMOUS SCULPTOR. I GUESS IT RUNS IN THE FAMILY....

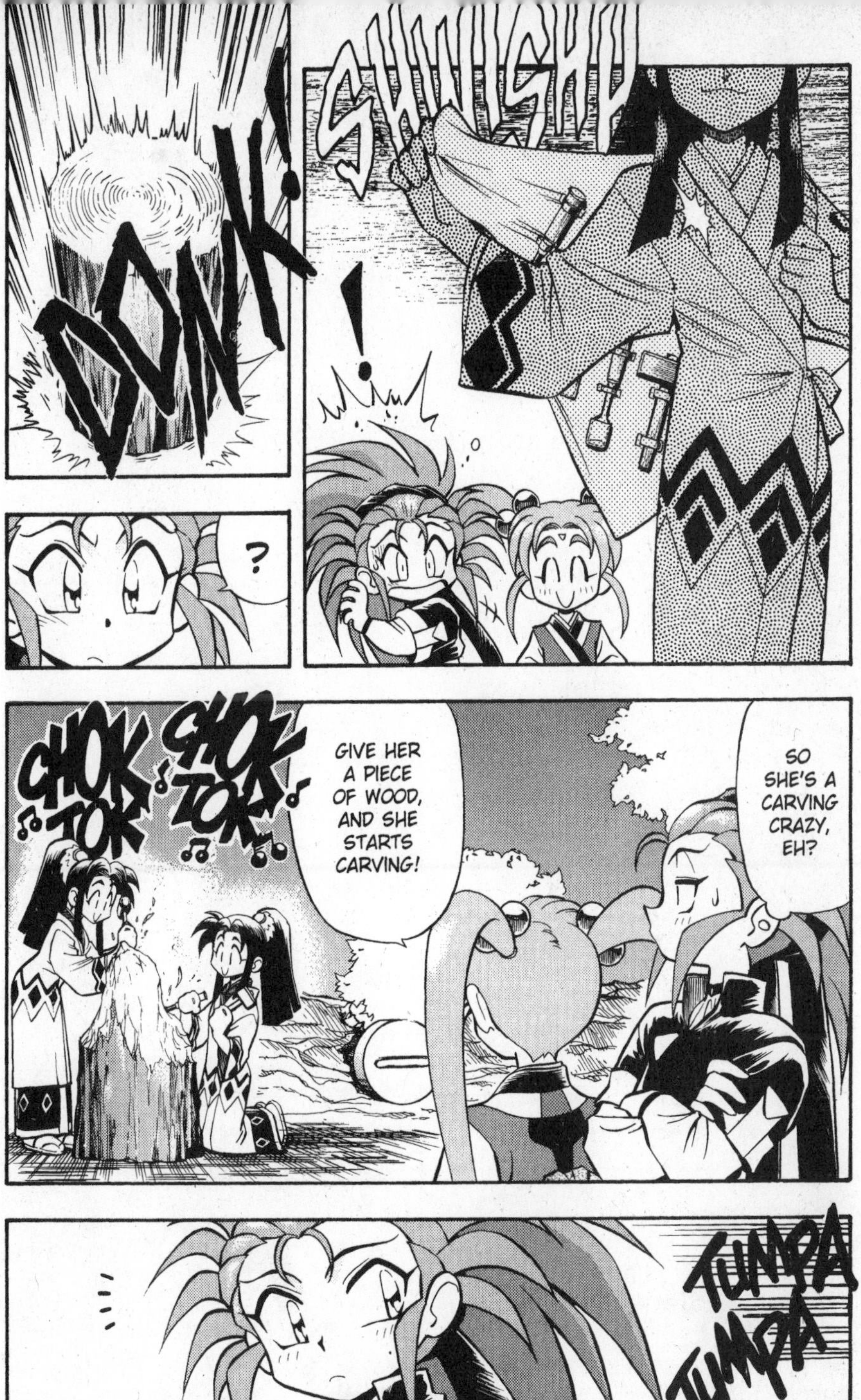
DONK!
SWUSHP
!
?
CHOK TOK
CHOK TOK
GIVE HER A PIECE OF WOOD, AND SHE STARTS CARVING!
SO SHE'S A CARVING CRAZY, EH?
TUMPA TUMPA

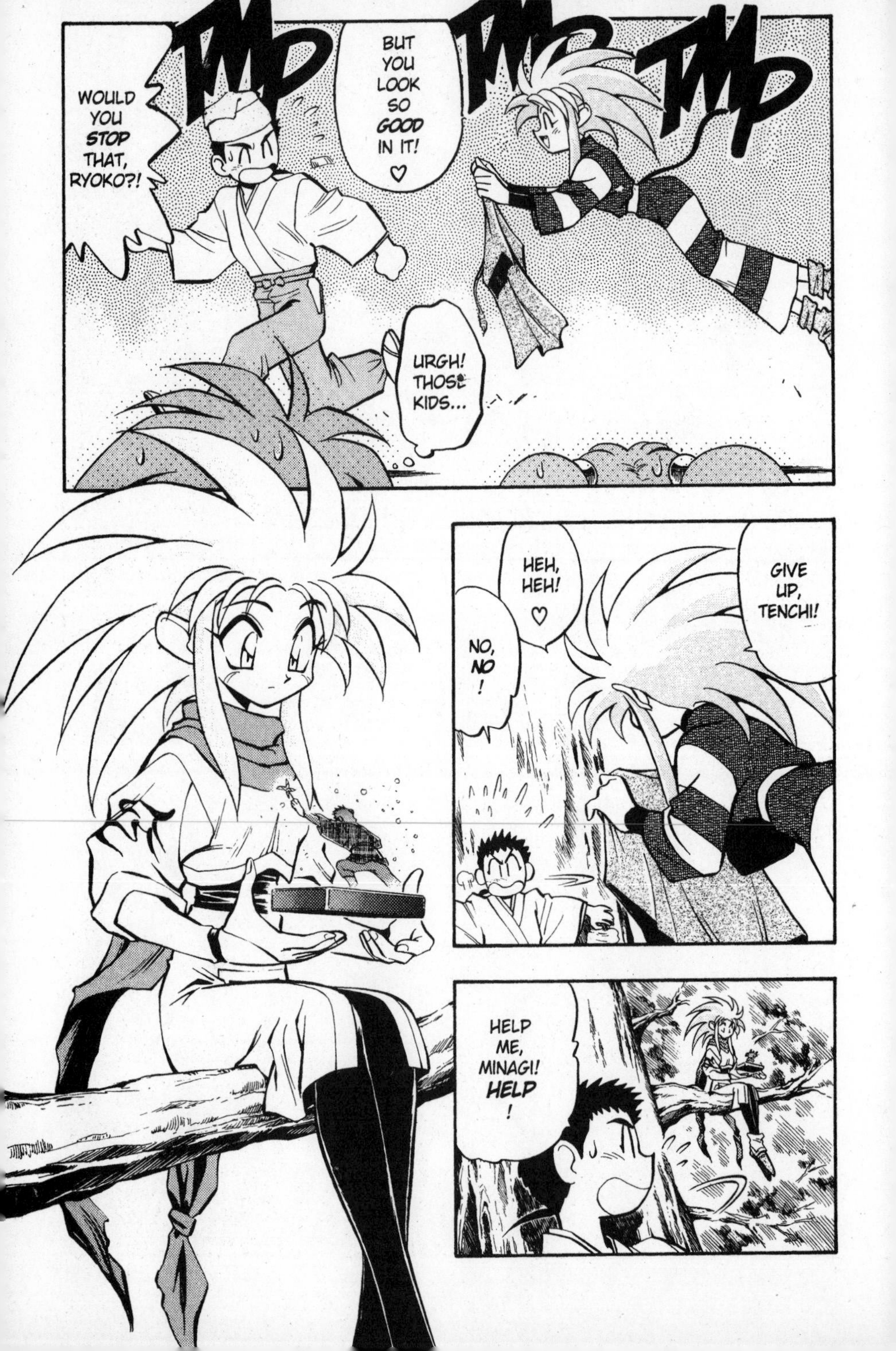
TMP
WOULD YOU STOP THAT, RYOKO?!
BUT YOU LOOK SO GOOD IN IT! ♡
TMP
TMP
URGH! THOSE KIDS...
HEH, HEH! ♡
NO, NO!
GIVE UP, TENCHI!
HELP ME, MINAGI! HELP!

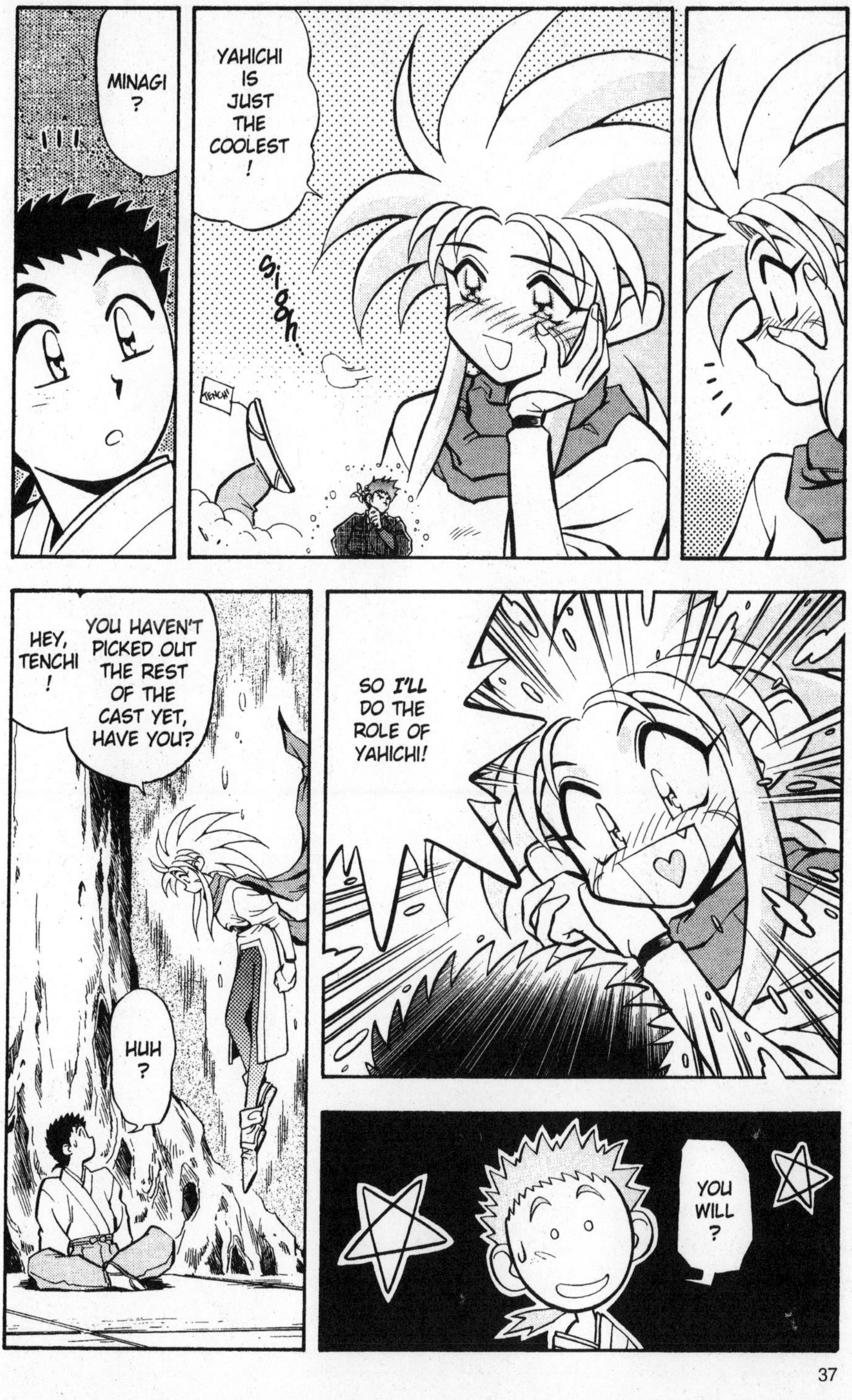
MINAGI ?
YAHICHI IS JUST THE COOLEST !
SIGGH...
TENCHI
HEY, TENCHI !
YOU HAVEN'T PICKED OUT THE REST OF THE CAST YET, HAVE YOU?
HUH ?
SO I'LL DO THE ROLE OF YAHICHI!
YOU WILL ?

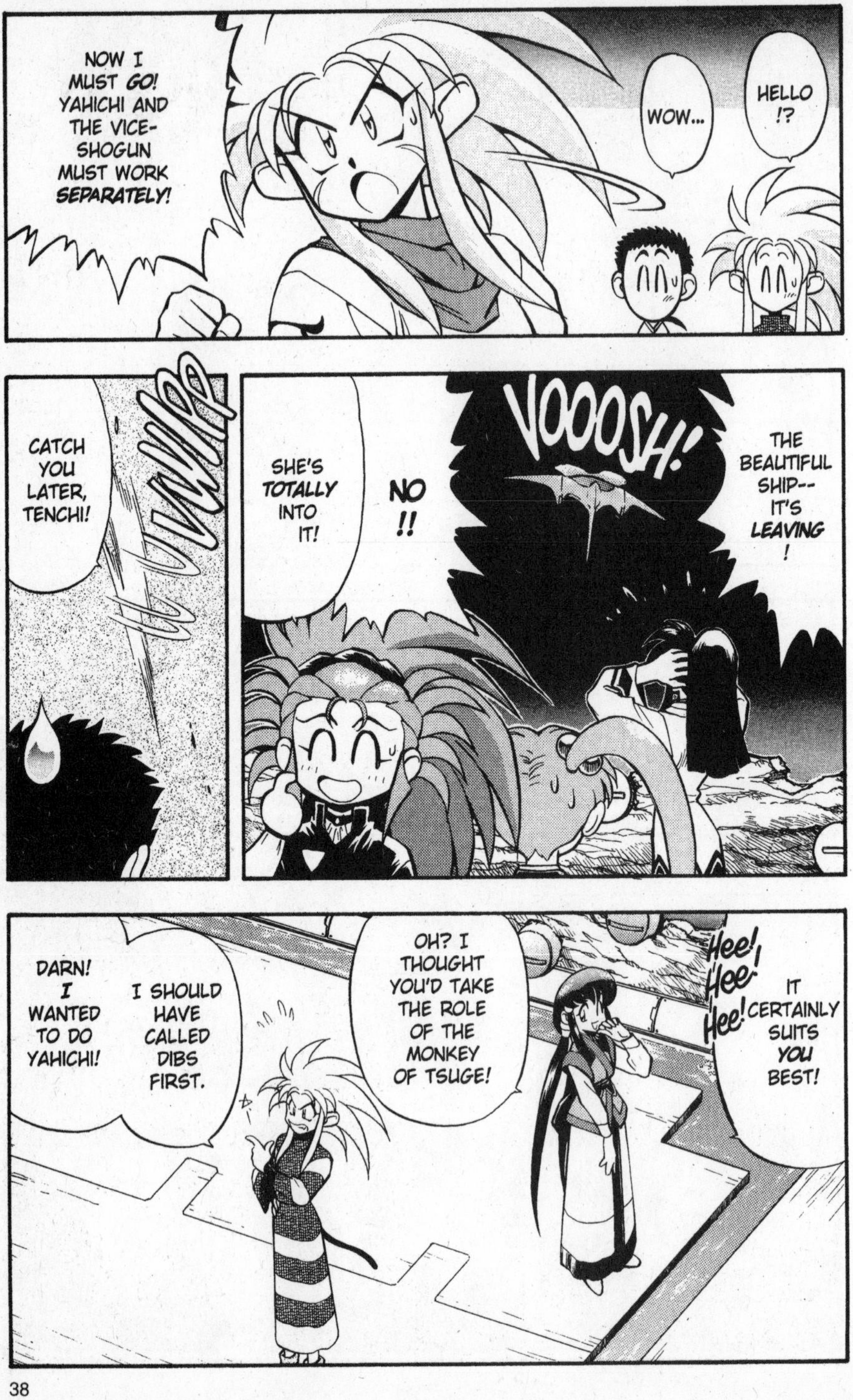
NOW I MUST *GO!* YAHICHI AND THE VICE-SHOGUN MUST WORK *SEPARATELY!*
WOW...
HELLO !?
CATCH YOU LATER, TENCHI!
SHE'S *TOTALLY* INTO IT!
NO !!
VOOOSH!
THE BEAUTIFUL SHIP-- IT'S *LEAVING* !
DARN! *I* WANTED TO DO YAHICHI!
I SHOULD HAVE CALLED DIBS FIRST.
OH? I THOUGHT YOU'D TAKE THE ROLE OF THE MONKEY OF TSUGE!
Hee! Hee! Hee!
IT CERTAINLY SUITS *YOU* BEST!

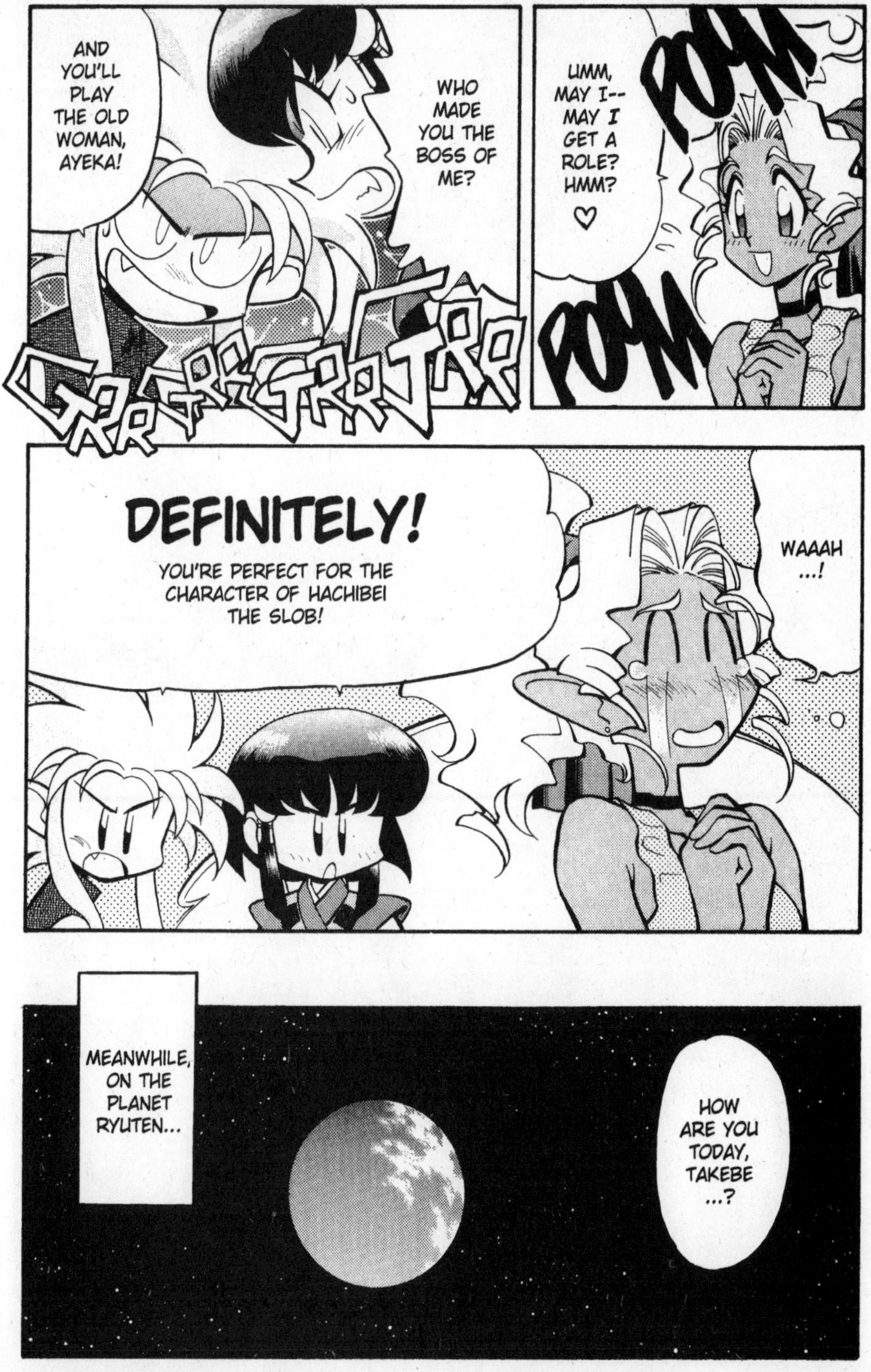
AND YOU'LL PLAY THE OLD WOMAN, AYEKA!
WHO MADE YOU THE BOSS OF ME?
UMM, MAY I-- MAY I GET A ROLE? HMM? ♡
POM
POM
DEFINITELY!
YOU'RE PERFECT FOR THE CHARACTER OF HACHIBEI THE SLOB!
WAAAH ...!
MEANWHILE, ON THE PLANET RYUTEN...
HOW ARE YOU TODAY, TAKEBE ...?

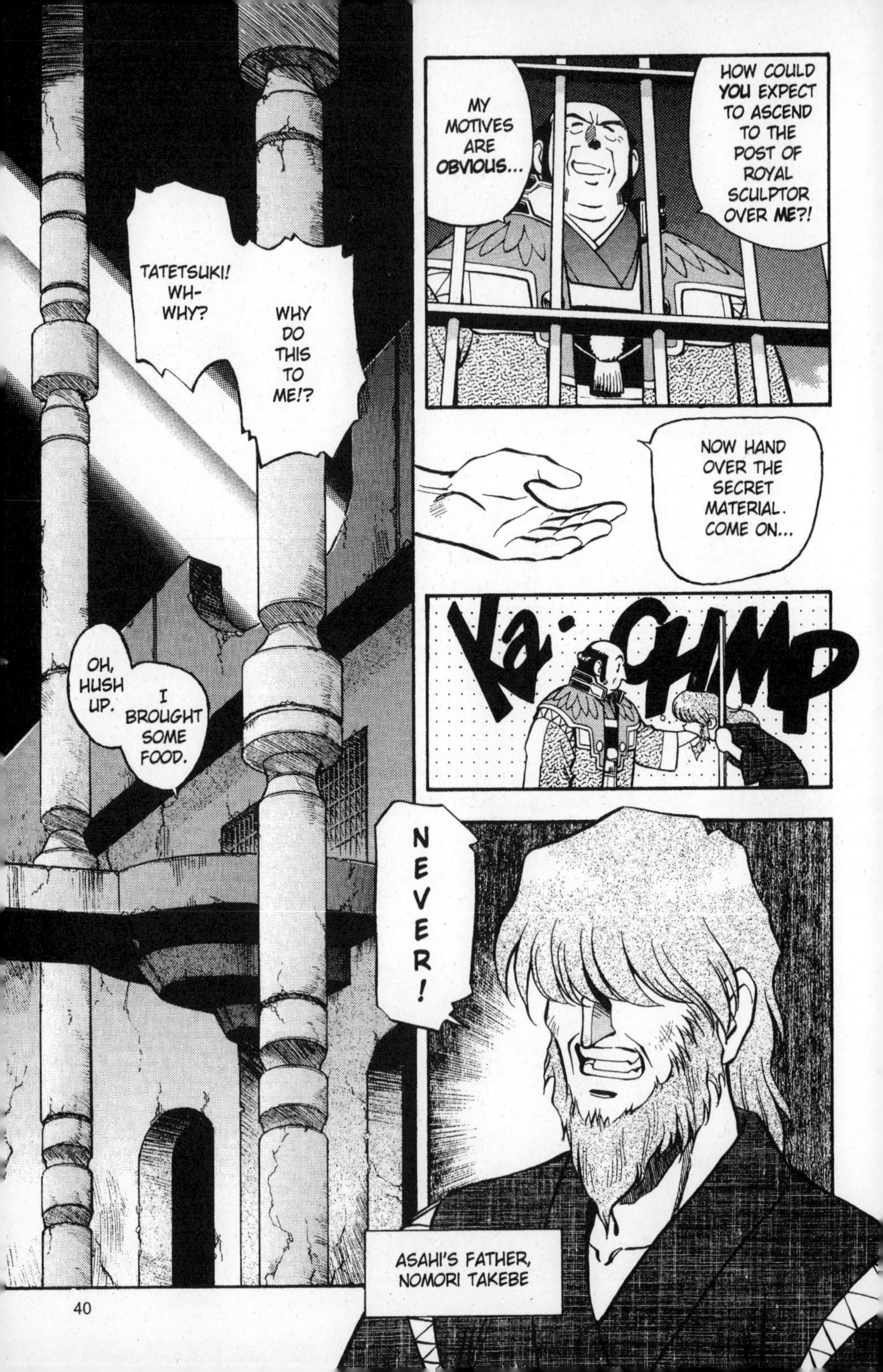
TATETSUKI! WH- WHY?
WHY DO THIS TO ME!?
OH, HUSH UP.
I BROUGHT SOME FOOD.
MY MOTIVES ARE OBVIOUS...
HOW COULD YOU EXPECT TO ASCEND TO THE POST OF ROYAL SCULPTOR OVER ME?!
NOW HAND OVER THE SECRET MATERIAL. COME ON...
KA-CHUMP
NEVER!
ASAHI'S FATHER, NOMORI TAKEBE

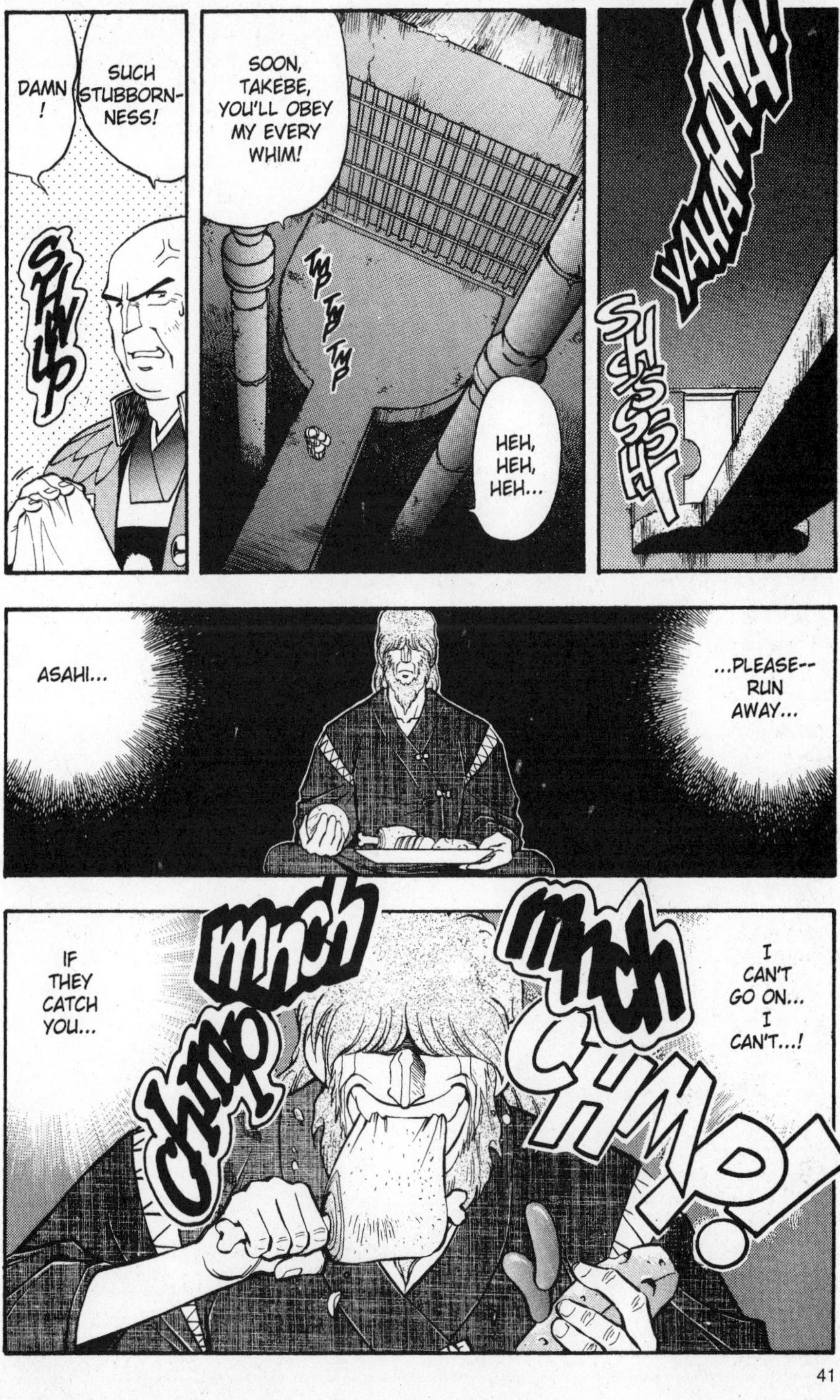
DAMN!
SUCH STUBBORNNESS!
SHWUP
SOON, TAKEBE, YOU'LL OBEY MY EVERY WHIM!
TMP TMP TMP
HEH, HEH, HEH...
YAHAHAHA!
SHSSSHT
ASAHI...
...PLEASE--RUN AWAY...
IF THEY CATCH YOU...
mnch chmp
mnch CHMP!
I CAN'T GO ON... I CAN'T...!

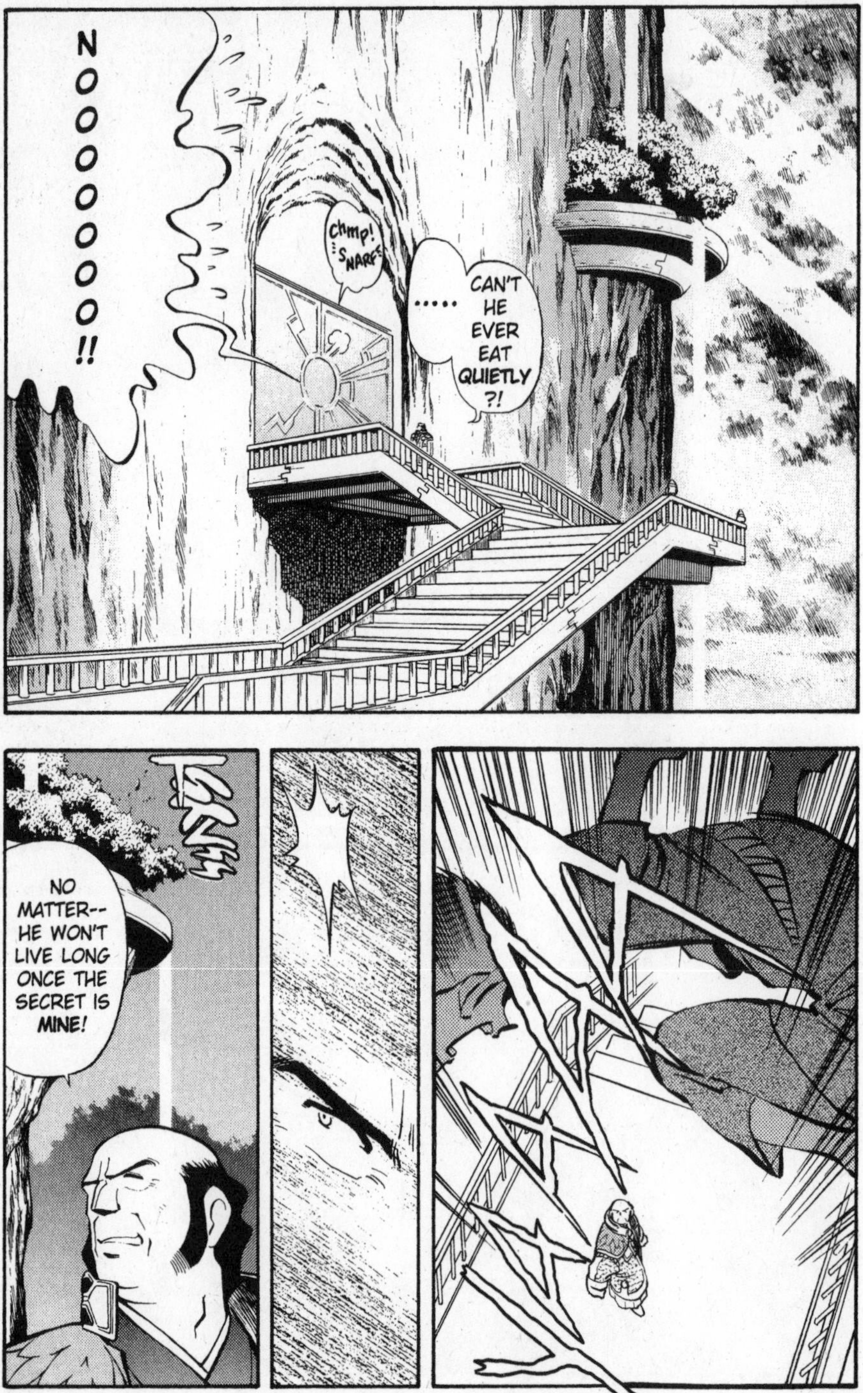
NOOOOOOO!!
Chmp! SNARF
..... CAN'T HE EVER EAT QUIETLY ?!
TSK
NO MATTER-- HE WON'T LIVE LONG ONCE THE SECRET IS MINE!

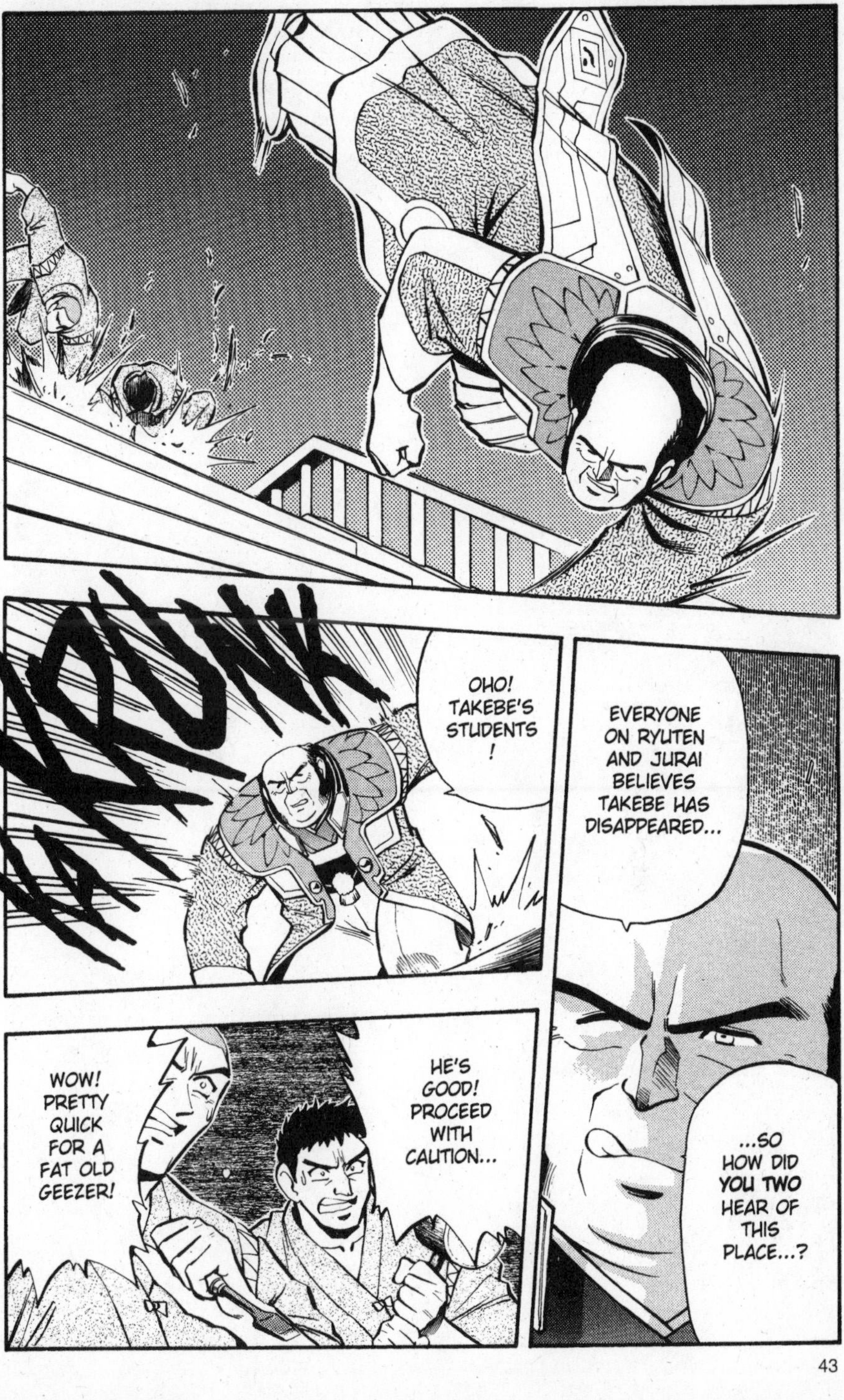
KA KRUNK
OHO! TAKEBE'S STUDENTS!
WOW! PRETTY QUICK FOR A FAT OLD GEEZER!
HE'S GOOD! PROCEED WITH CAUTION...
EVERYONE ON RYUTEN AND JURAI BELIEVES TAKEBE HAS DISAPPEARED...
...SO HOW DID YOU TWO HEAR OF THIS PLACE...?

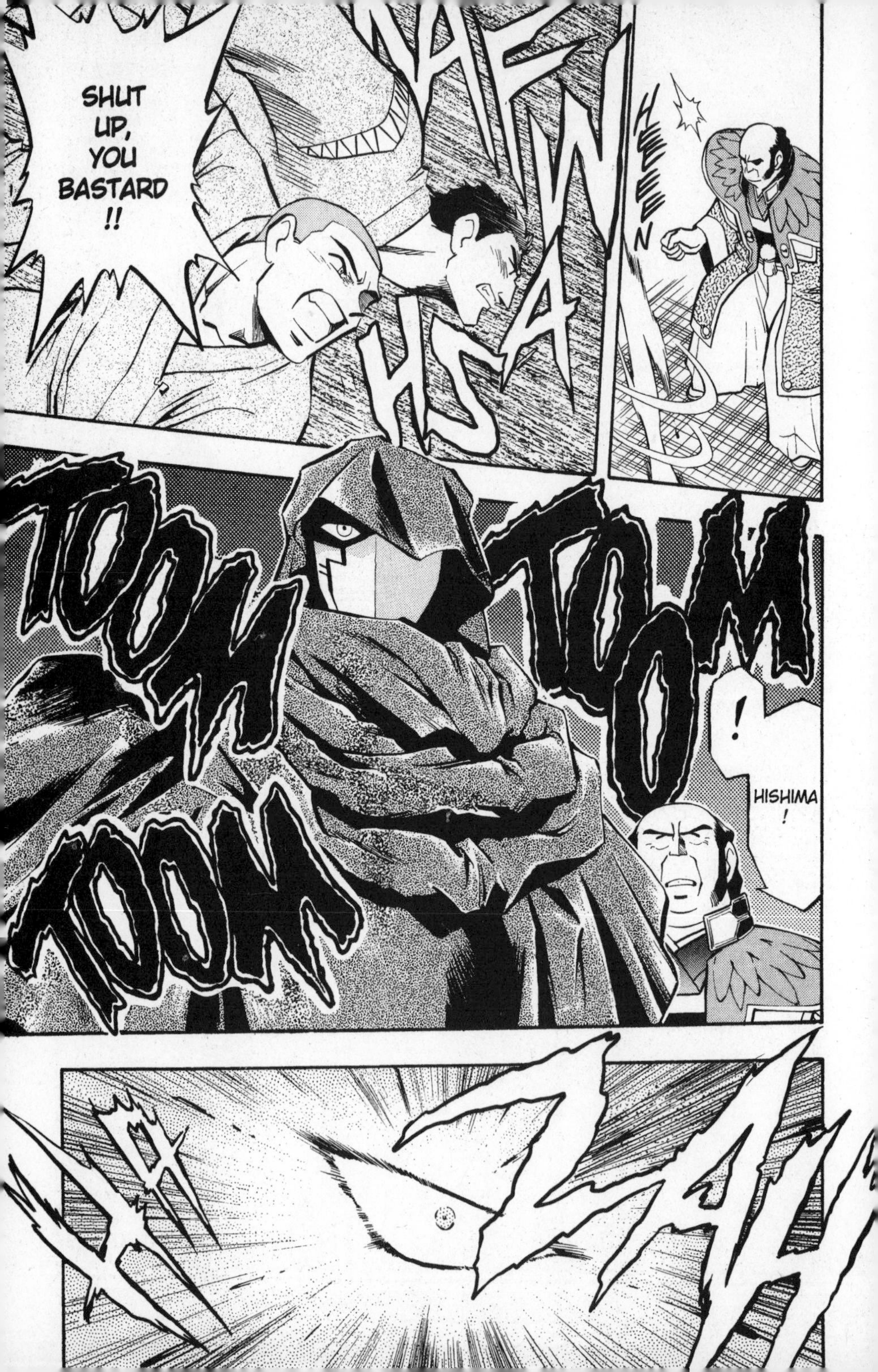
SHUT UP, YOU BASTARD !!
TOOM TOOM
TOOM TOOM
!
HISHIMA !

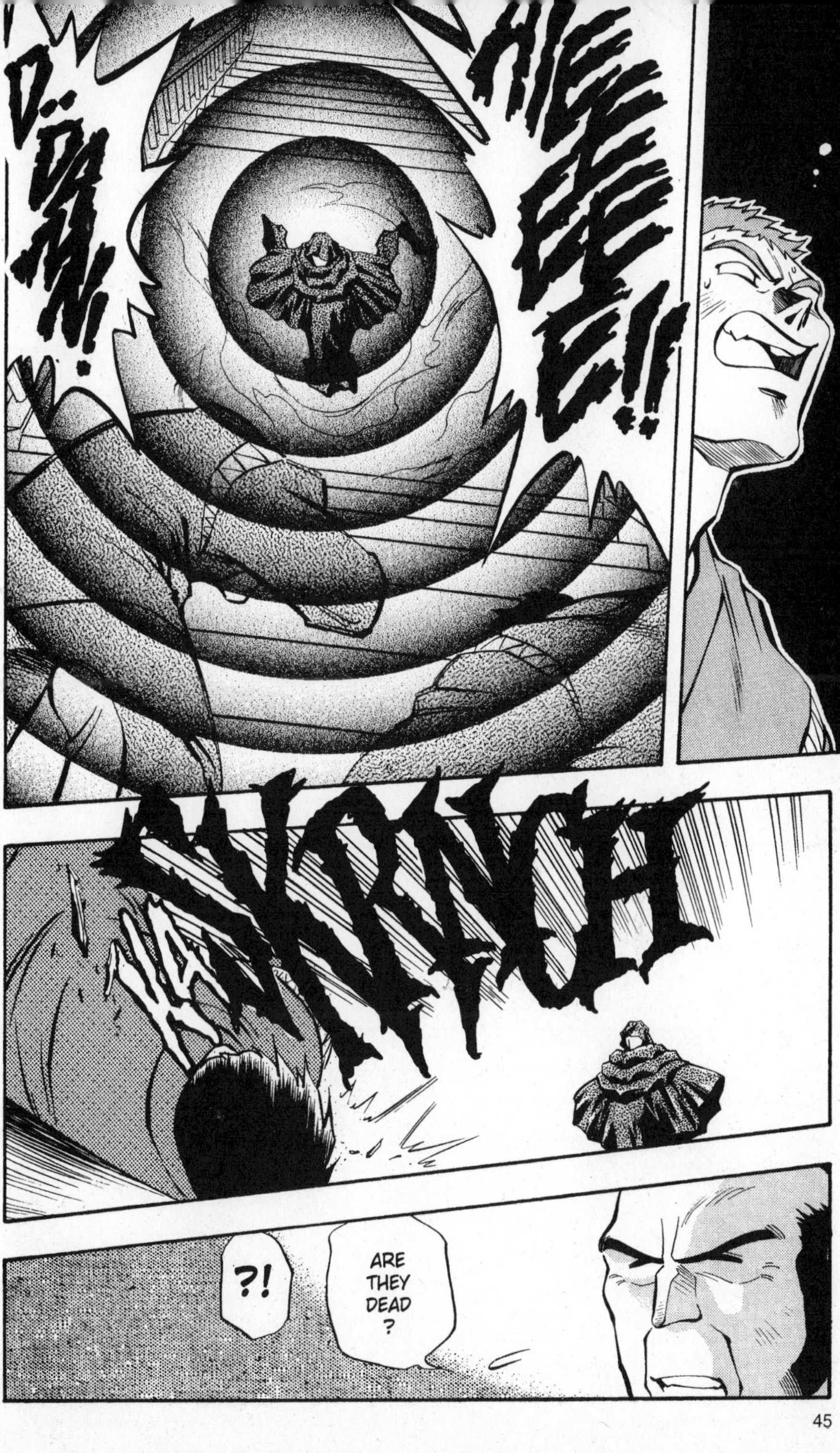
?!
ARE THEY DEAD?

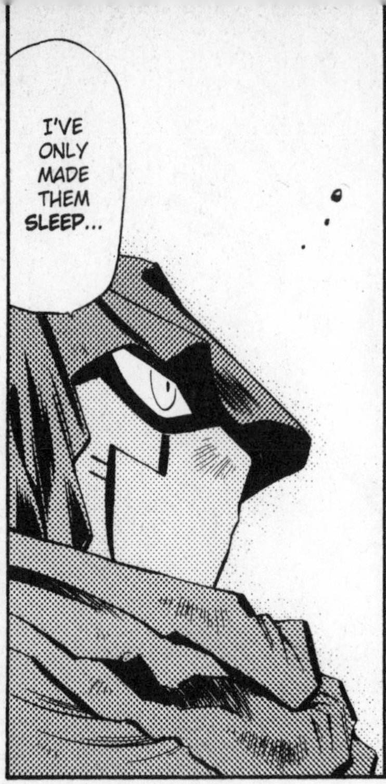
I'VE ONLY MADE THEM SLEEP...
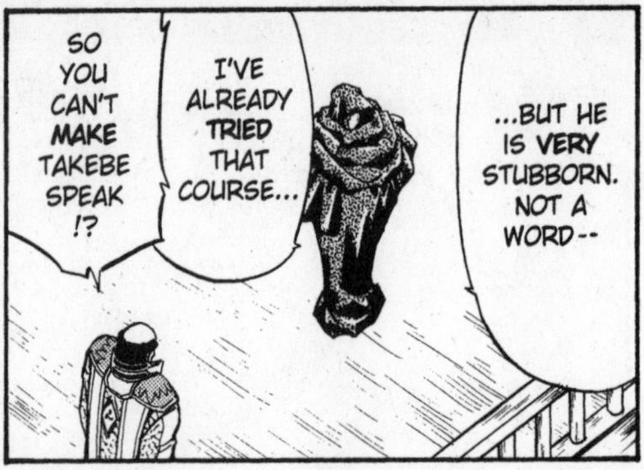
SO YOU CAN'T MAKE TAKEBE SPEAK !?
I'VE ALREADY TRIED THAT COURSE...
...BUT HE IS VERY STUBBORN. NOT A WORD--
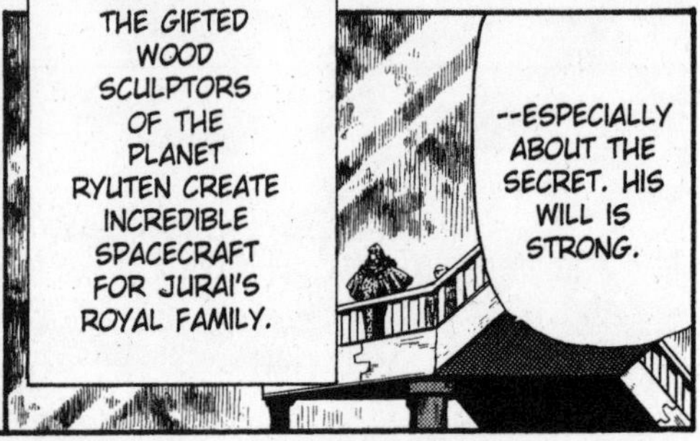
THE GIFTED WOOD SCULPTORS OF THE PLANET RYUTEN CREATE INCREDIBLE SPACECRAFT FOR JURAI'S ROYAL FAMILY.
--ESPECIALLY ABOUT THE SECRET. HIS WILL IS STRONG.

OF ALL THE CRAFTSPEOPLE, THE SCULPTORS ARE GIVEN THE GREATEST POWER...

... AND TATETSUKI DESPERATELY WANTS THEIR PRIVILEGED INFORMATION!

HIS GOAL: TO SUCCEED HOURAN AS THE HOU FAMILY'S MASTER SCULPTOR-- AND TO DO SO, HE MUST ACQUIRE TAKEBE'S SECRETS!

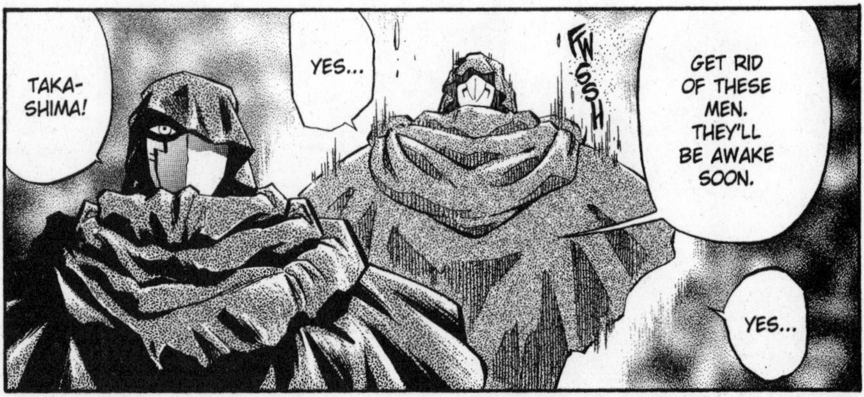
TAKA-SHIMA!
YES...
FWSSH
GET RID OF THESE MEN. THEY'LL BE AWAKE SOON.
YES...

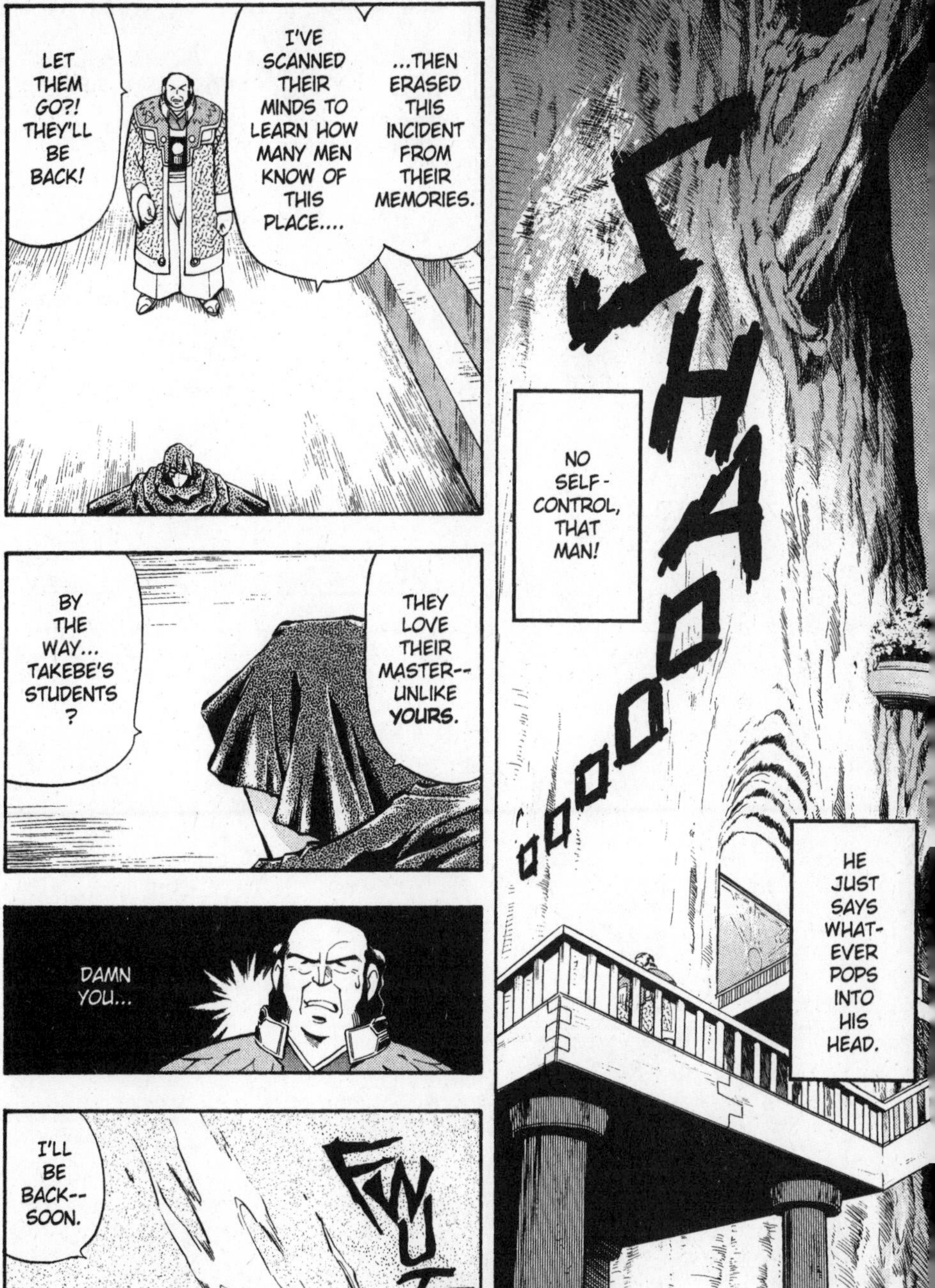
LET THEM GO?! THEY'LL BE BACK!
I'VE SCANNED THEIR MINDS TO LEARN HOW MANY MEN KNOW OF THIS PLACE....
...THEN ERASED THIS INCIDENT FROM THEIR MEMORIES.
BY THE WAY... TAKEBE'S STUDENTS?
THEY LOVE THEIR MASTER--UNLIKE YOURS.
DAMN YOU...
I'LL BE BACK--SOON.
FWUTTT
NO SELF-CONTROL, THAT MAN!
HE JUST SAYS WHATEVER POPS INTO HIS HEAD.

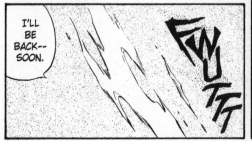

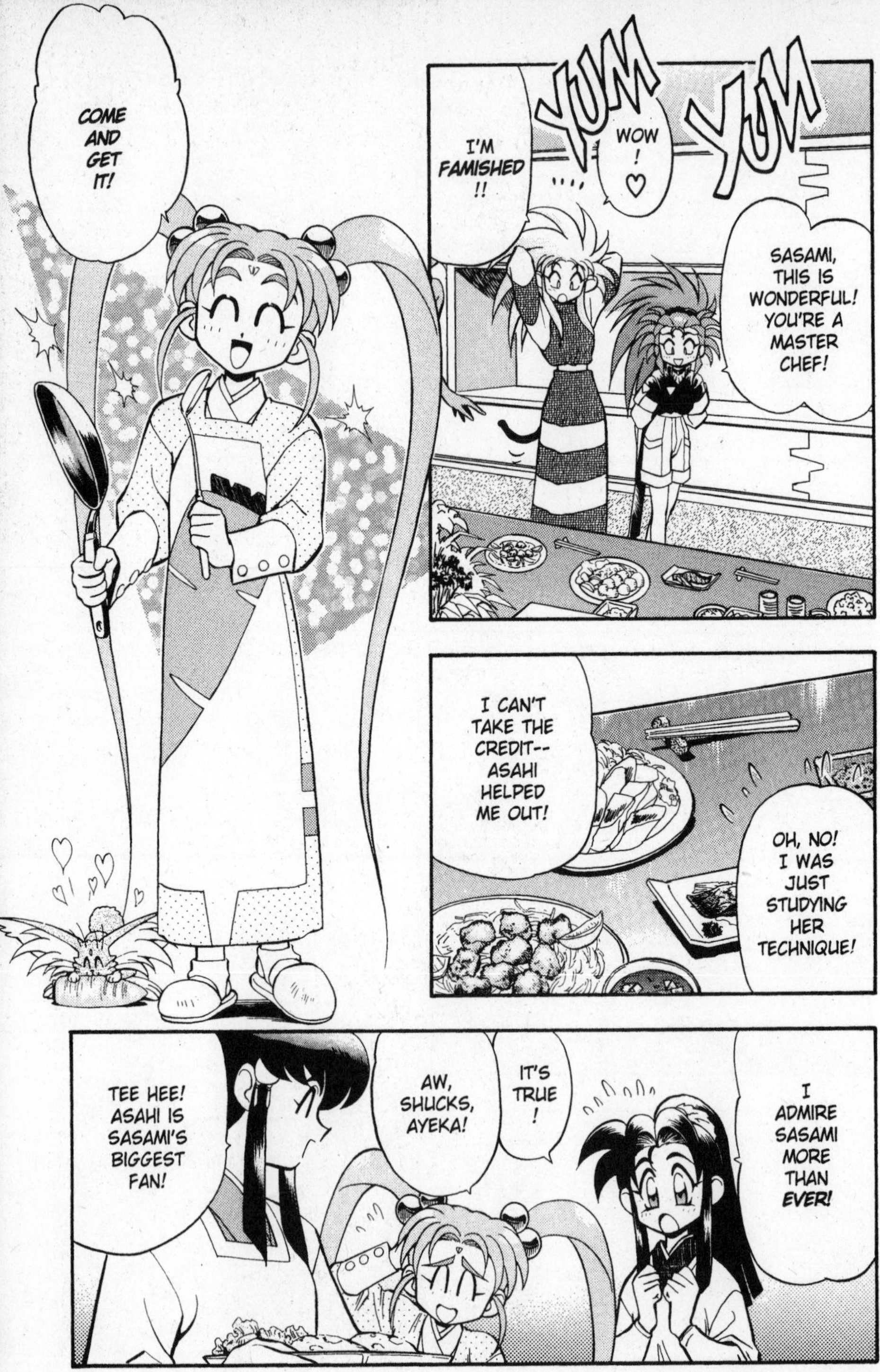

COME AND GET IT!
I'M FAMISHED!!
YUM
WOW! ♥
YUM
SASAMI, THIS IS WONDERFUL! YOU'RE A MASTER CHEF!
I CAN'T TAKE THE CREDIT-- ASAHI HELPED ME OUT!
OH, NO! I WAS JUST STUDYING HER TECHNIQUE!
TEE HEE! ASAHI IS SASAMI'S BIGGEST FAN!
AW, SHUCKS, AYEKA!
IT'S TRUE!
I ADMIRE SASAMI MORE THAN EVER!

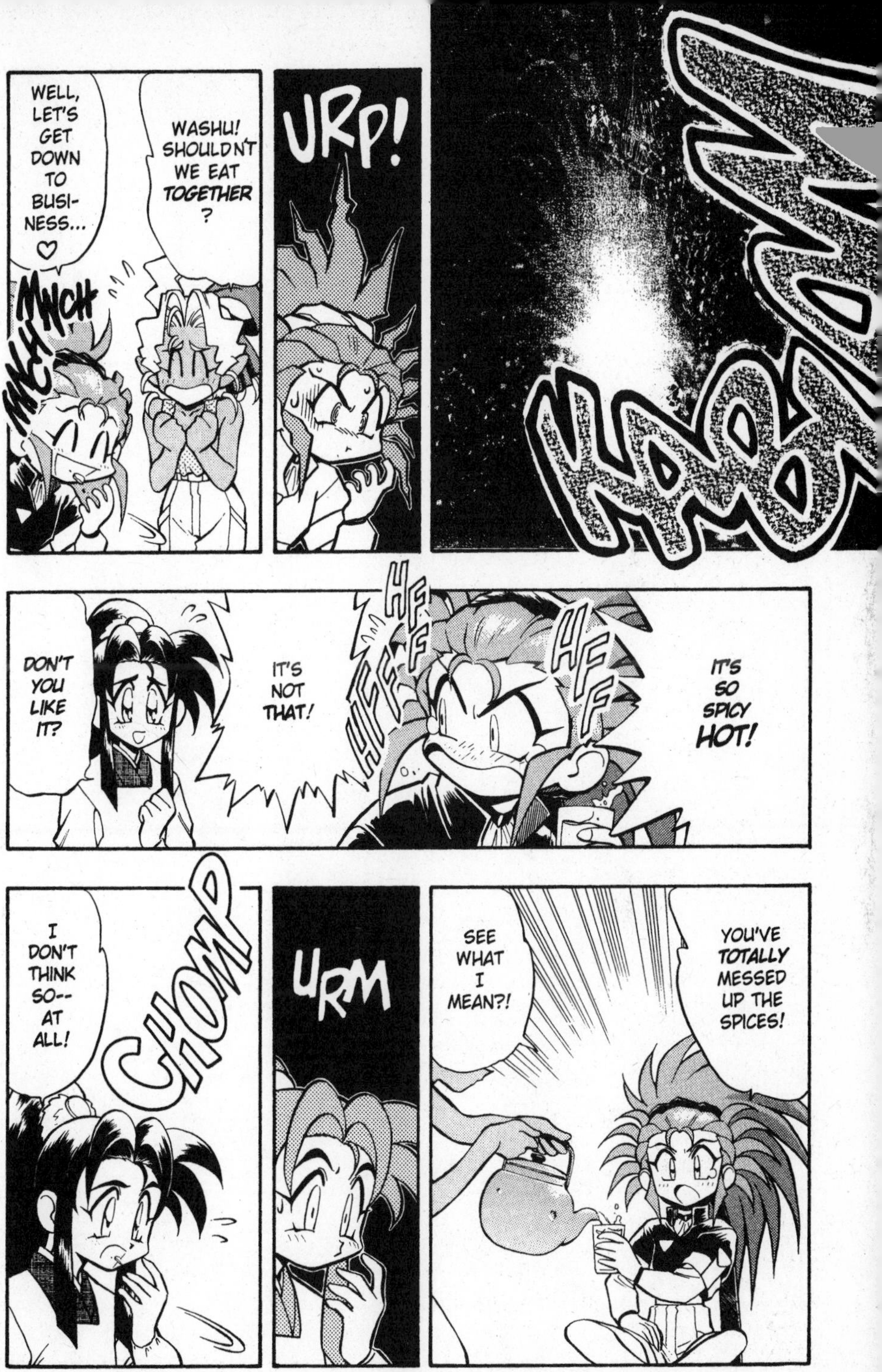

WELL, LET'S GET DOWN TO BUSINESS... ♡
WASHU! SHOULDN'T WE EAT TOGETHER?
MNCH MNCH MNCH
URP!
KABOOM
DON'T YOU LIKE IT?
IT'S NOT THAT!
HFF HFF HFF
IT'S SO SPICY HOT!
I DON'T THINK SO-- AT ALL!
CHOMP
URM
SEE WHAT I MEAN?!
YOU'VE TOTALLY MESSED UP THE SPICES!

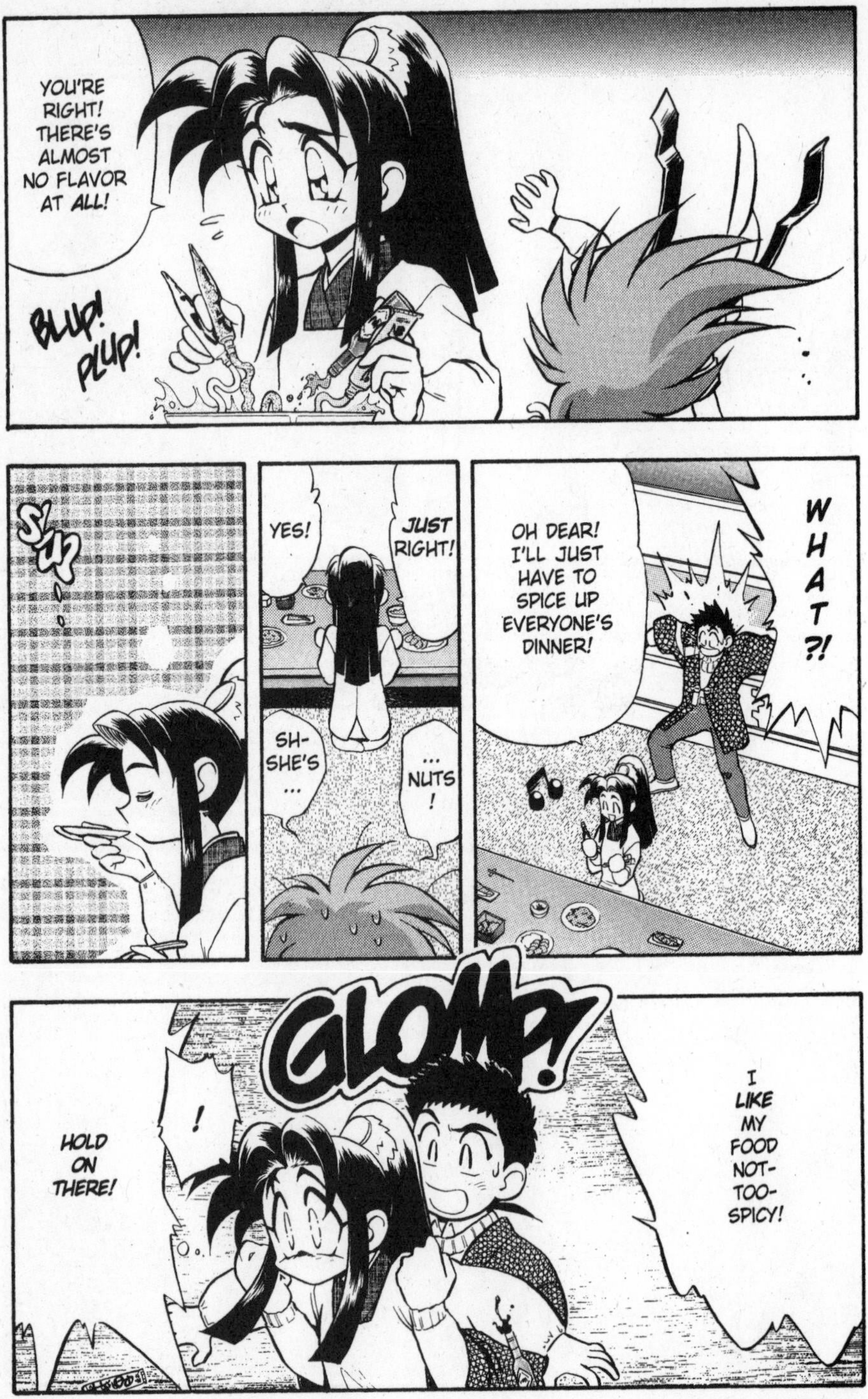
YOU'RE RIGHT! THERE'S ALMOST NO FLAVOR AT ALL!
BLUP! PLUP!
SLUP
YES!
JUST RIGHT!
SH-SHE'S ...
... NUTS!
OH DEAR! I'LL JUST HAVE TO SPICE UP EVERYONE'S DINNER!
WHAT?!
GLOMP!
HOLD ON THERE!
!
I LIKE MY FOOD NOT-TOO-SPICY!

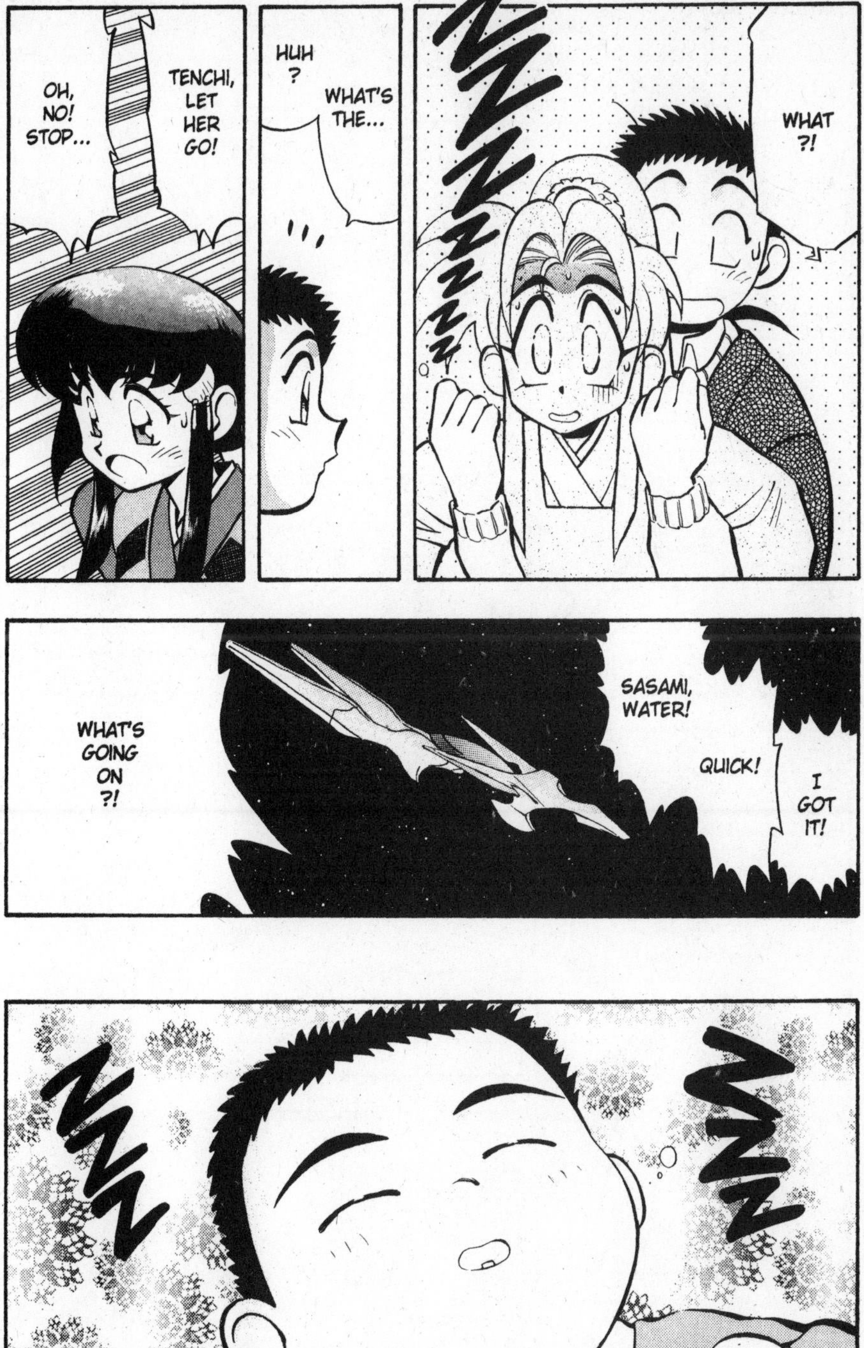
OH, NO! STOP...
TENCHI, LET HER GO!
HUH ?
WHAT'S THE...
WHAT ?!
WHAT'S GOING ON ?!
SASAMI, WATER!
QUICK!
I GOT IT!

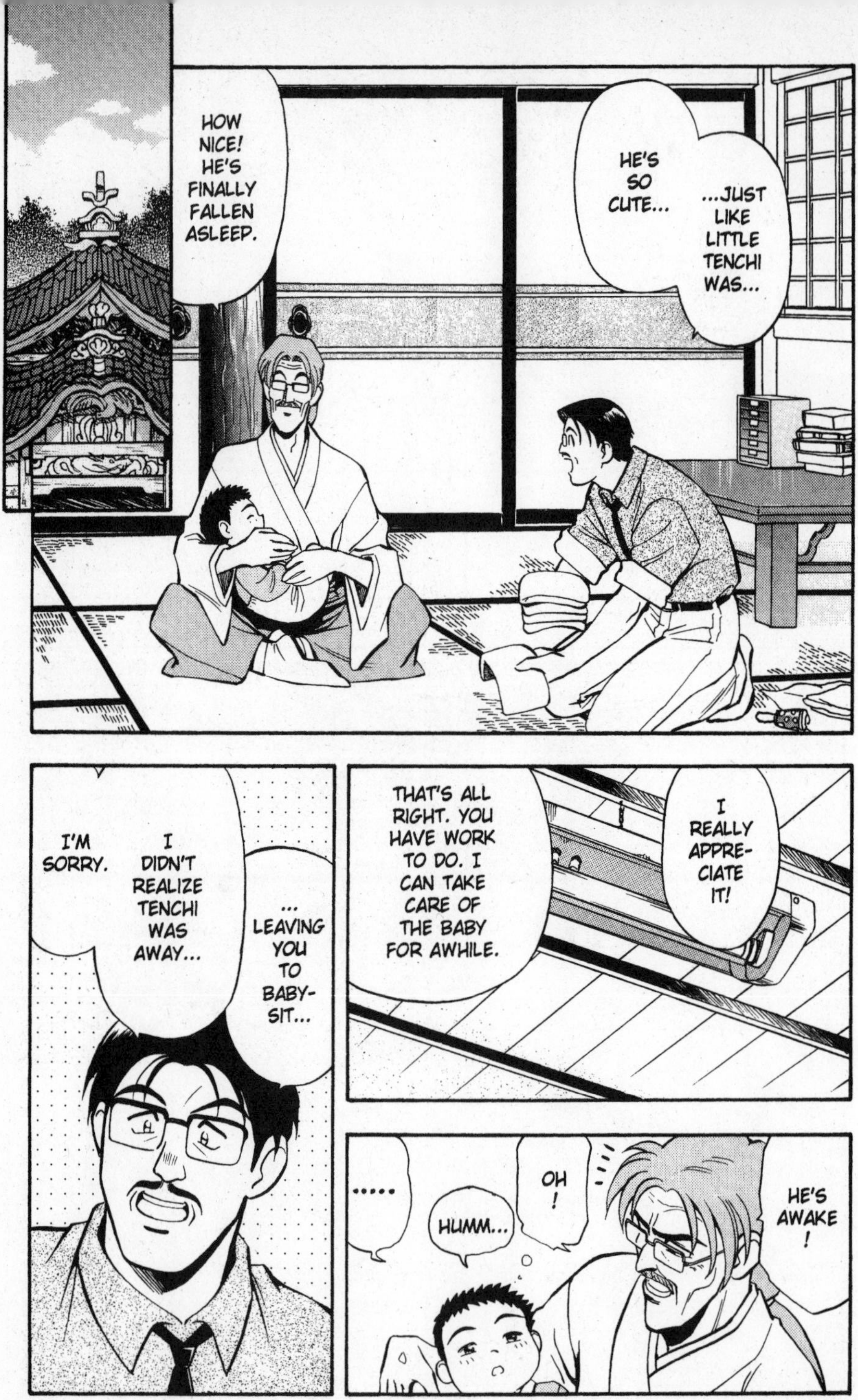
HOW NICE! HE'S FINALLY FALLEN ASLEEP.
HE'S SO CUTE...
...JUST LIKE LITTLE TENCHI WAS...
I'M SORRY.
I DIDN'T REALIZE TENCHI WAS AWAY...
...LEAVING YOU TO BABY-SIT...
THAT'S ALL RIGHT. YOU HAVE WORK TO DO. I CAN TAKE CARE OF THE BABY FOR AWHILE.
I REALLY APPRE-CIATE IT!
.....
HUMM...
OH!
HE'S AWAKE!

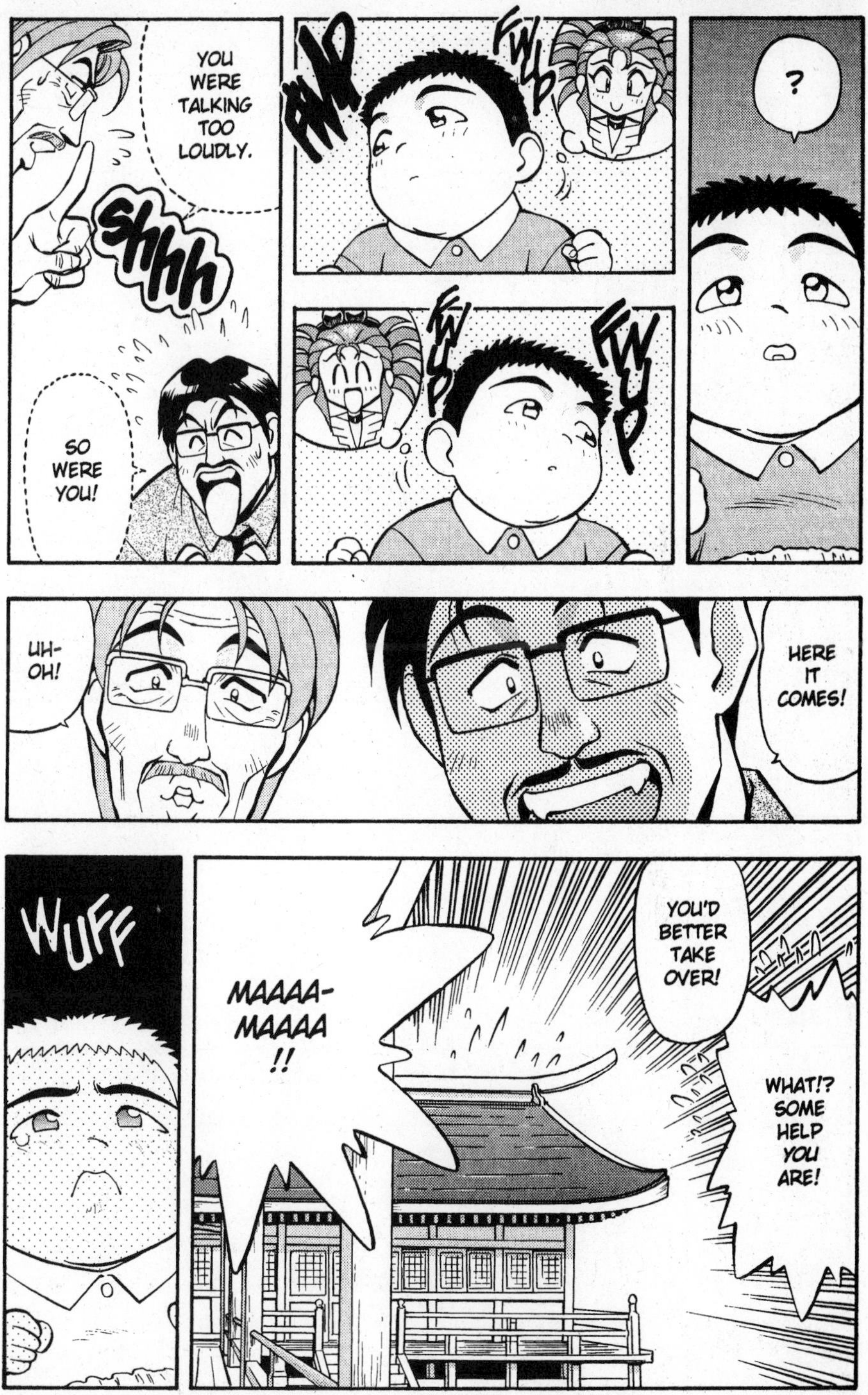
YOU WERE TALKING TOO LOUDLY.
SHHH
SO WERE YOU!
FWIP
FWUP
FWUP
FWUP
?
UH-OH!
HERE IT COMES!
WUFF
MAAAA-MAAAA !!
YOU'D BETTER TAKE OVER!
WHAT!? SOME HELP YOU ARE!

ASAHI'S FATHER LOVES HIS FAMILY...

WHEN HER MOTHER DIED, ASAHI WAS ALL HE HAD LEFT. HE--HE SMOTHERED HER, IN A WAY.

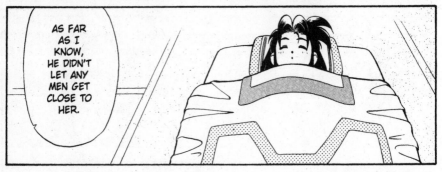

AS FAR AS I KNOW, HE DIDN'T LET ANY MEN GET CLOSE TO HER.

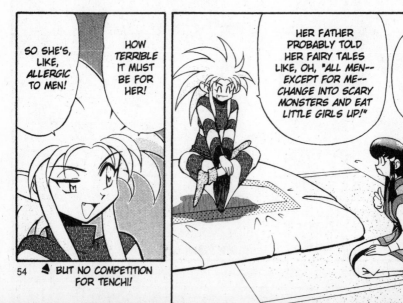

SO SHE'S, LIKE, ALLERGIC TO MEN!

HOW TERRIBLE IT MUST BE FOR HER!

HER FATHER PROBABLY TOLD HER FAIRY TALES LIKE, OH, "ALL MEN--EXCEPT FOR ME--CHANGE INTO SCARY MONSTERS AND EAT LITTLE GIRLS UP!"

DON'T BE MEAN, RYOKO!

54 ♣ BUT NO COMPETITION FOR TENCHI!

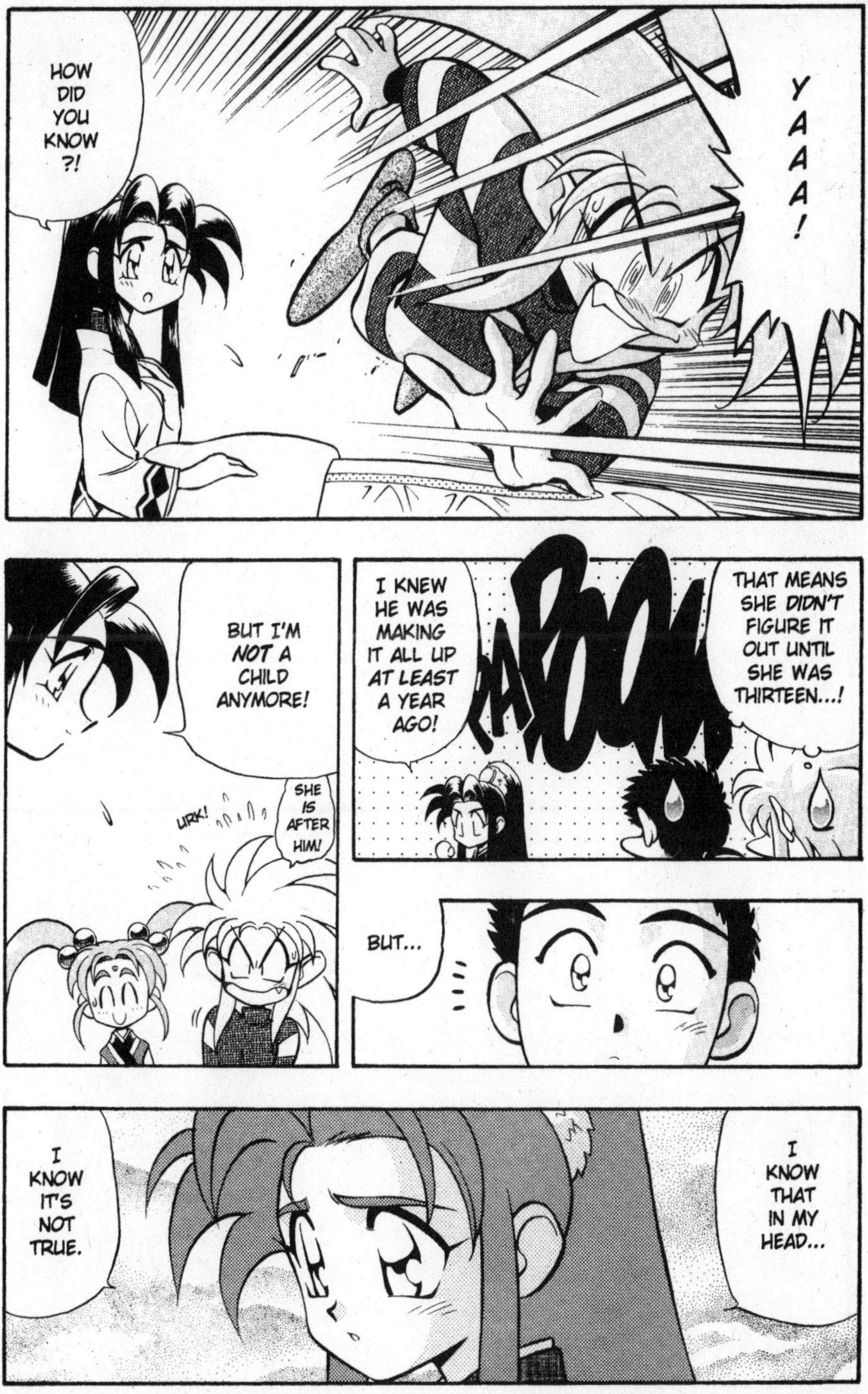
HOW DID YOU KNOW ?!
YAAAA!
BUT I'M NOT A CHILD ANYMORE!
URK!
SHE IS AFTER HIM!
I KNEW HE WAS MAKING IT ALL UP AT LEAST A YEAR AGO!
PABOOM
THAT MEANS SHE DIDN'T FIGURE IT OUT UNTIL SHE WAS THIRTEEN...!
BUT...
I KNOW IT'S NOT TRUE.
I KNOW THAT IN MY HEAD...

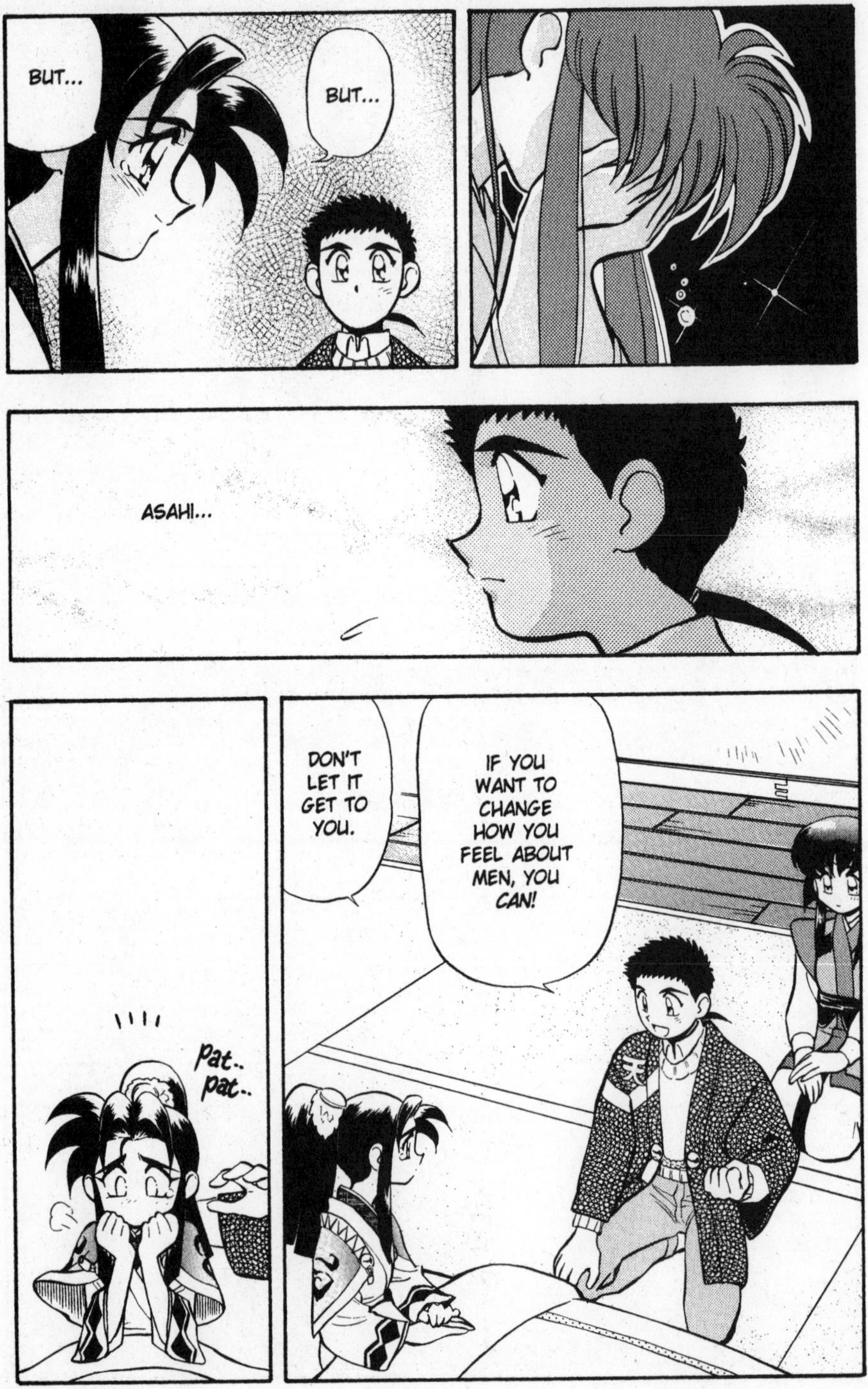
BUT...
BUT...
ASAHI...
DON'T LET IT GET TO YOU.
IF YOU WANT TO CHANGE HOW YOU FEEL ABOUT MEN, YOU CAN!
pat.. pat..

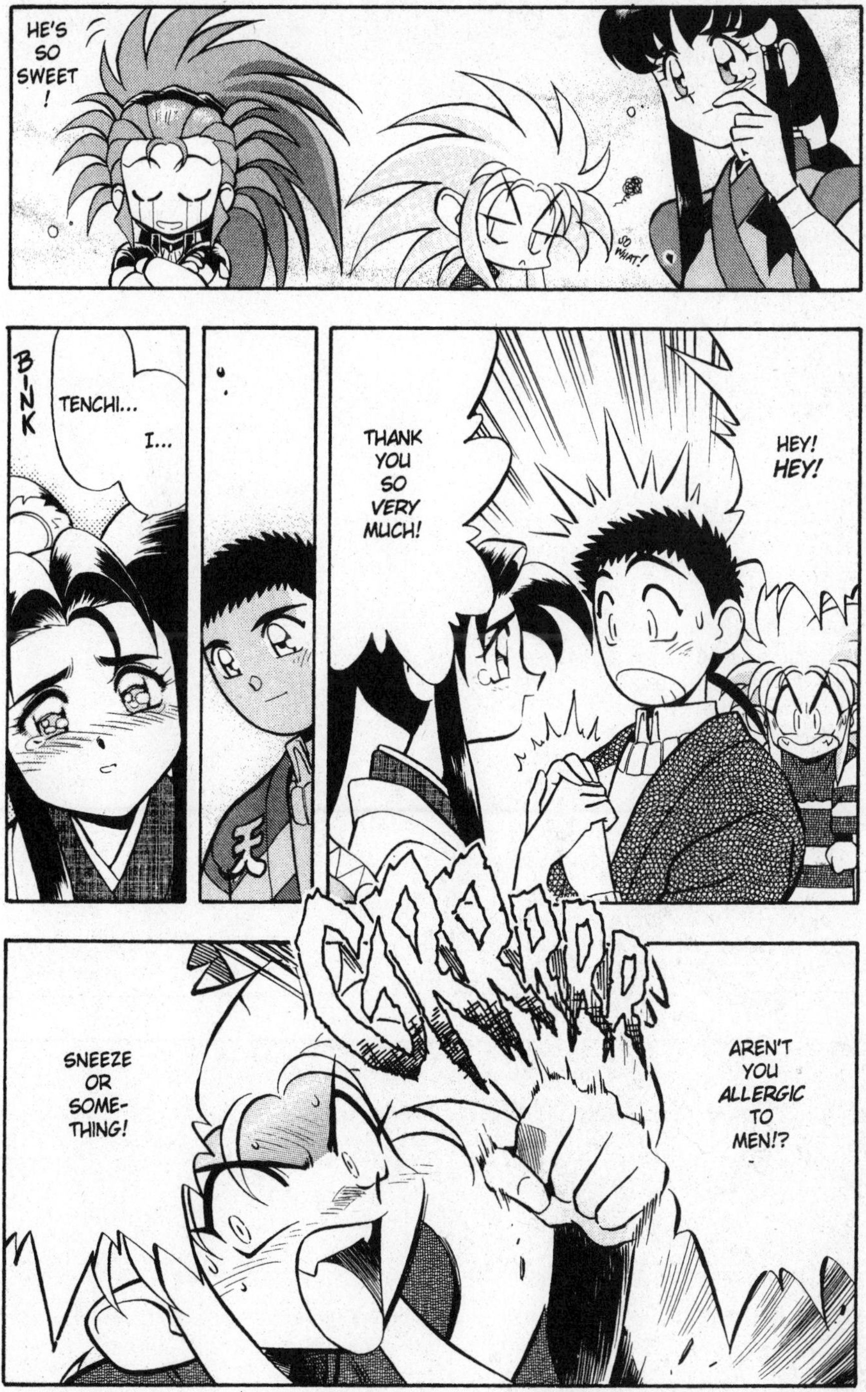
HE'S SO SWEET!
SO WHAT!
BINK
TENCHI... I...
THANK YOU SO VERY MUCH!
HEY! HEY!
SNEEZE OR SOME-THING!
AREN'T YOU ALLERGIC TO MEN!?

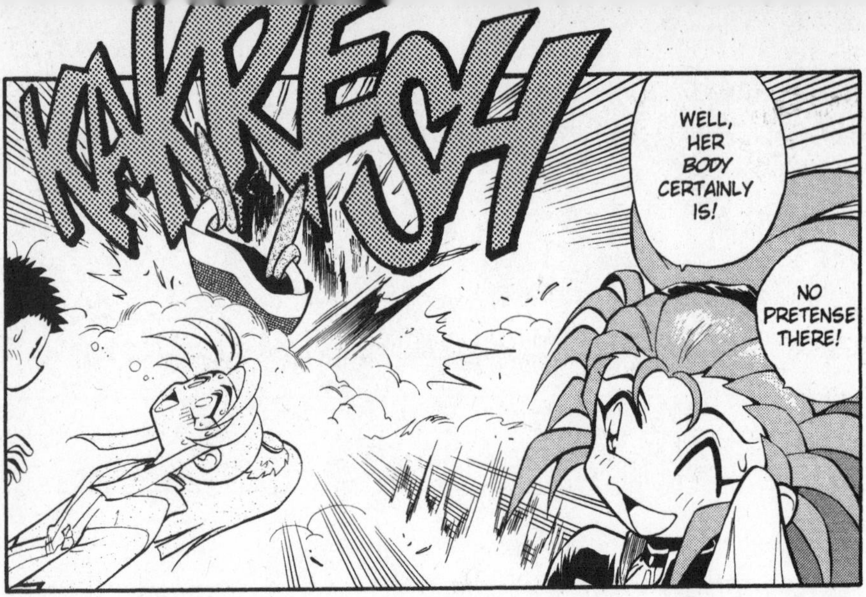
KAKRECH
WELL, HER BODY CERTAINLY IS!
NO PRETENSE THERE!

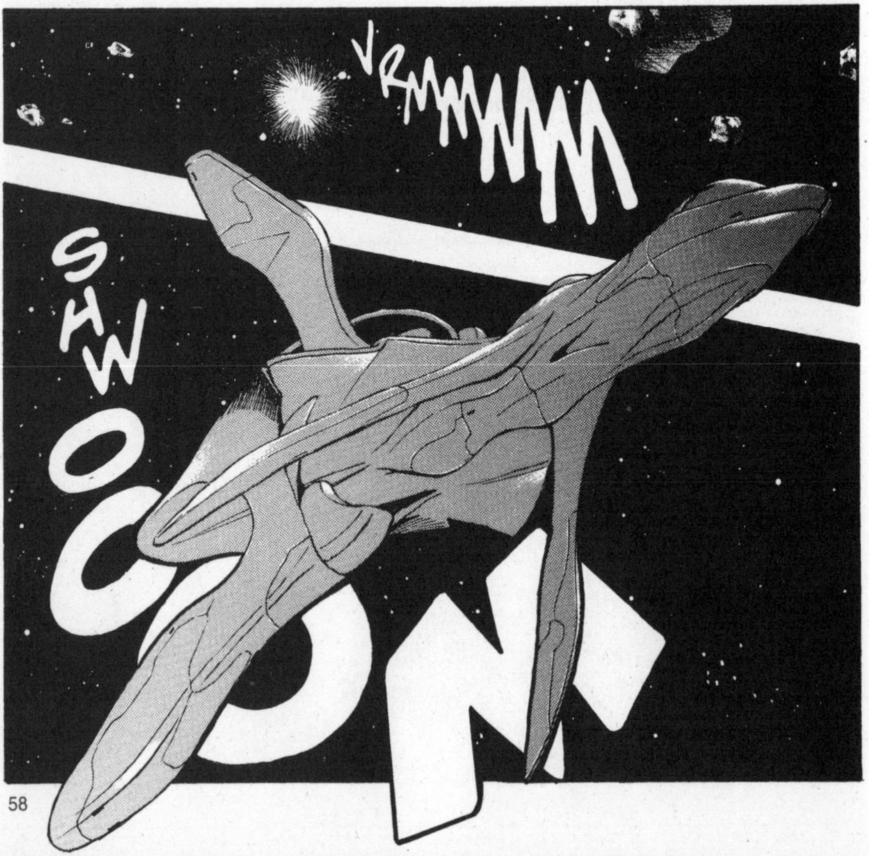
VRMMMM
SHWOOM

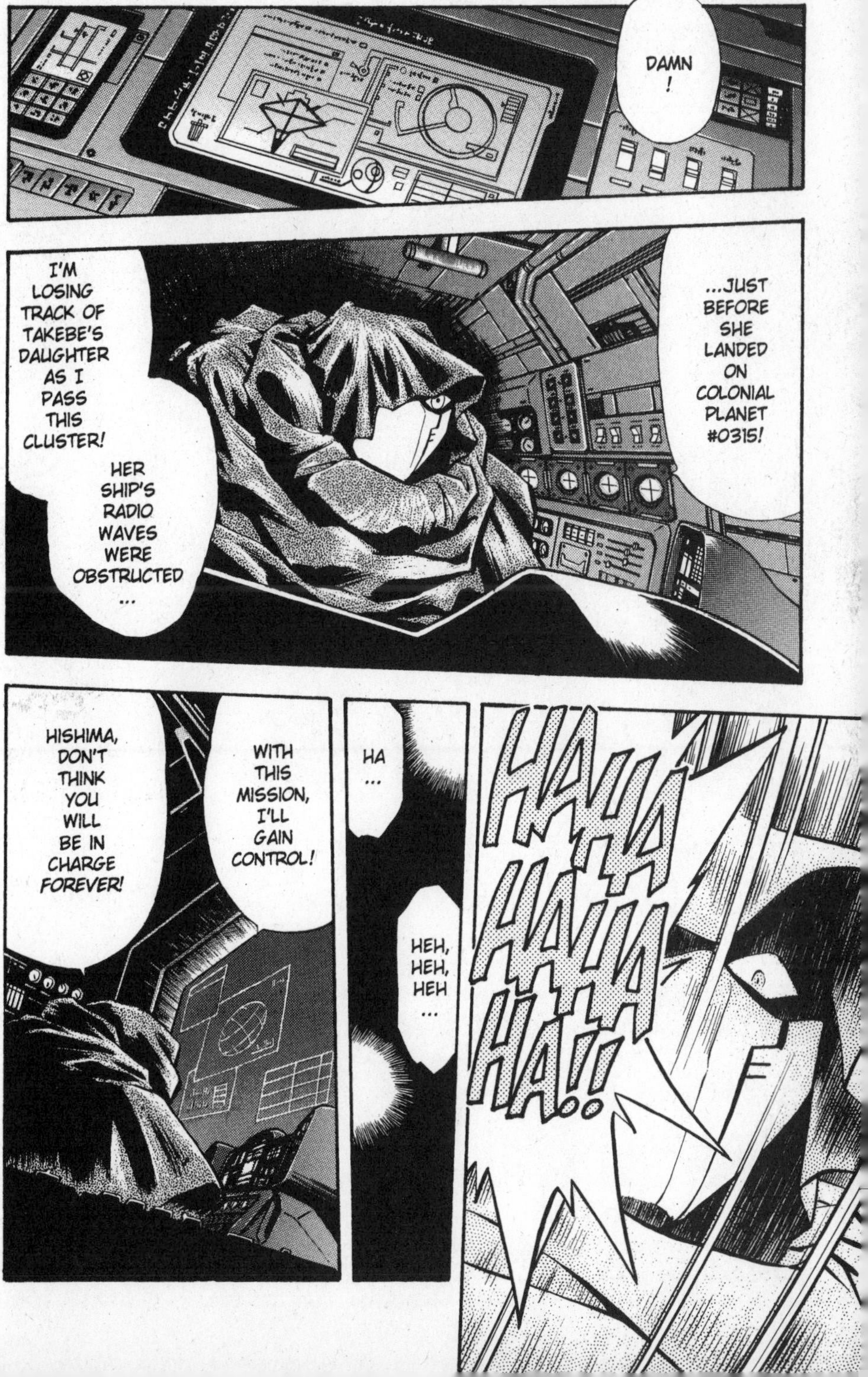
DAMN!
I'M LOSING TRACK OF TAKEBE'S DAUGHTER AS I PASS THIS CLUSTER!
HER SHIP'S RADIO WAVES WERE OBSTRUCTED...
...JUST BEFORE SHE LANDED ON COLONIAL PLANET #0315!
HISHIMA, DON'T THINK YOU WILL BE IN CHARGE FOREVER!
WITH THIS MISSION, I'LL GAIN CONTROL!
HA...
HEH, HEH, HEH...
HAHAHAHAHAHA!!

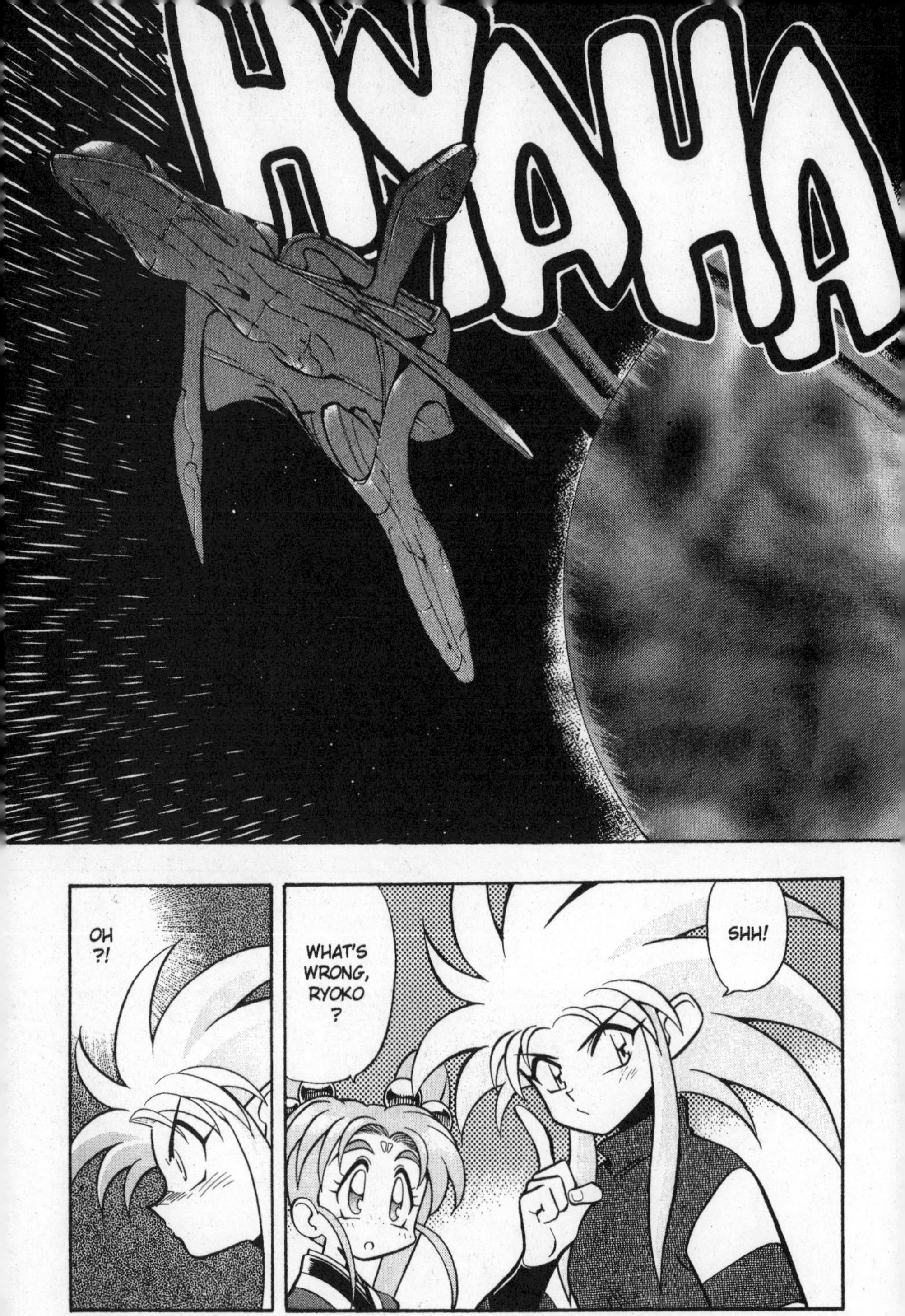
HAHAHA
OH ?!
WHAT'S WRONG, RYOKO ?
SHH!

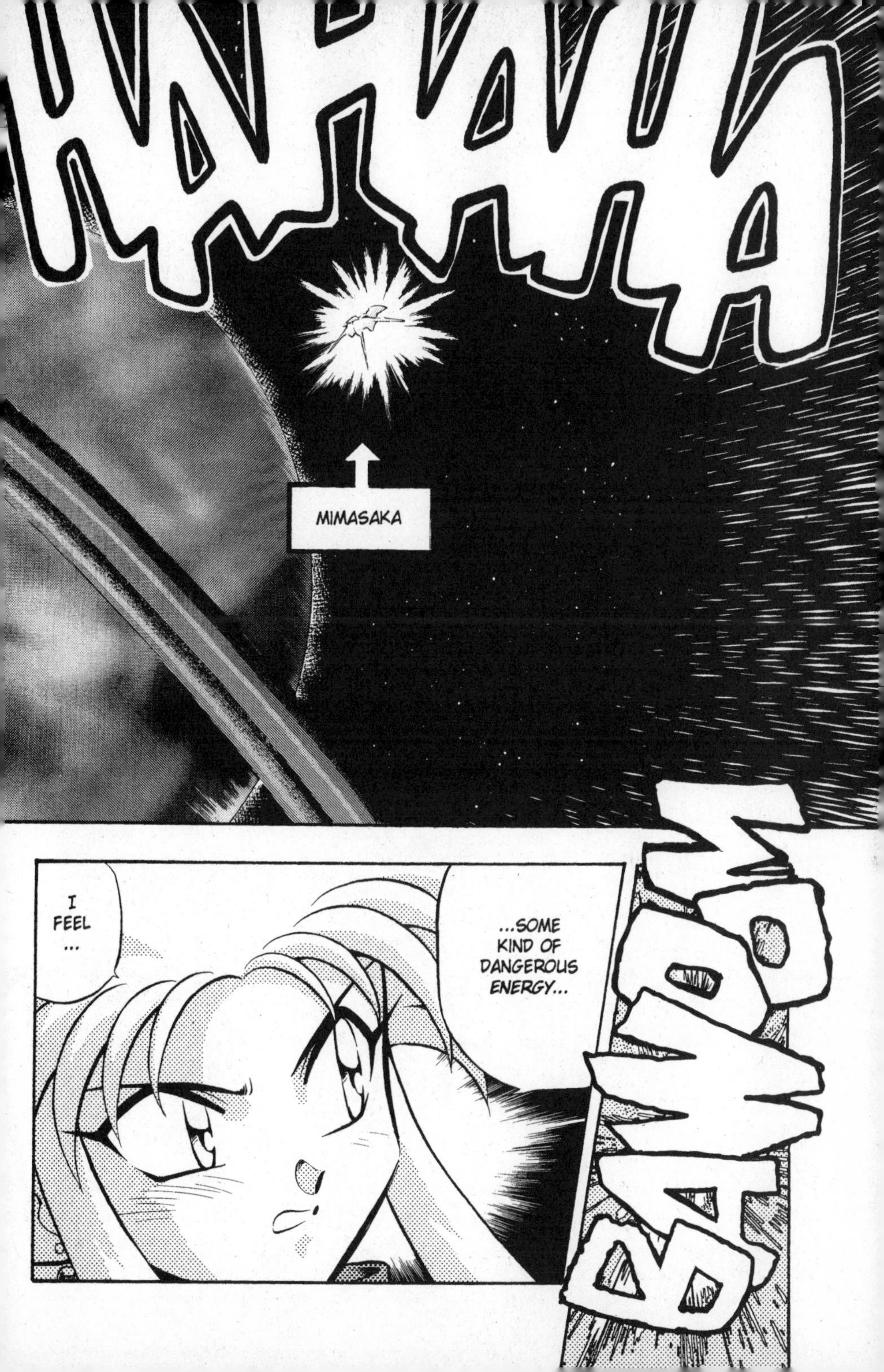
MIMASAKA
I FEEL ...
...SOME KIND OF DANGEROUS ENERGY...

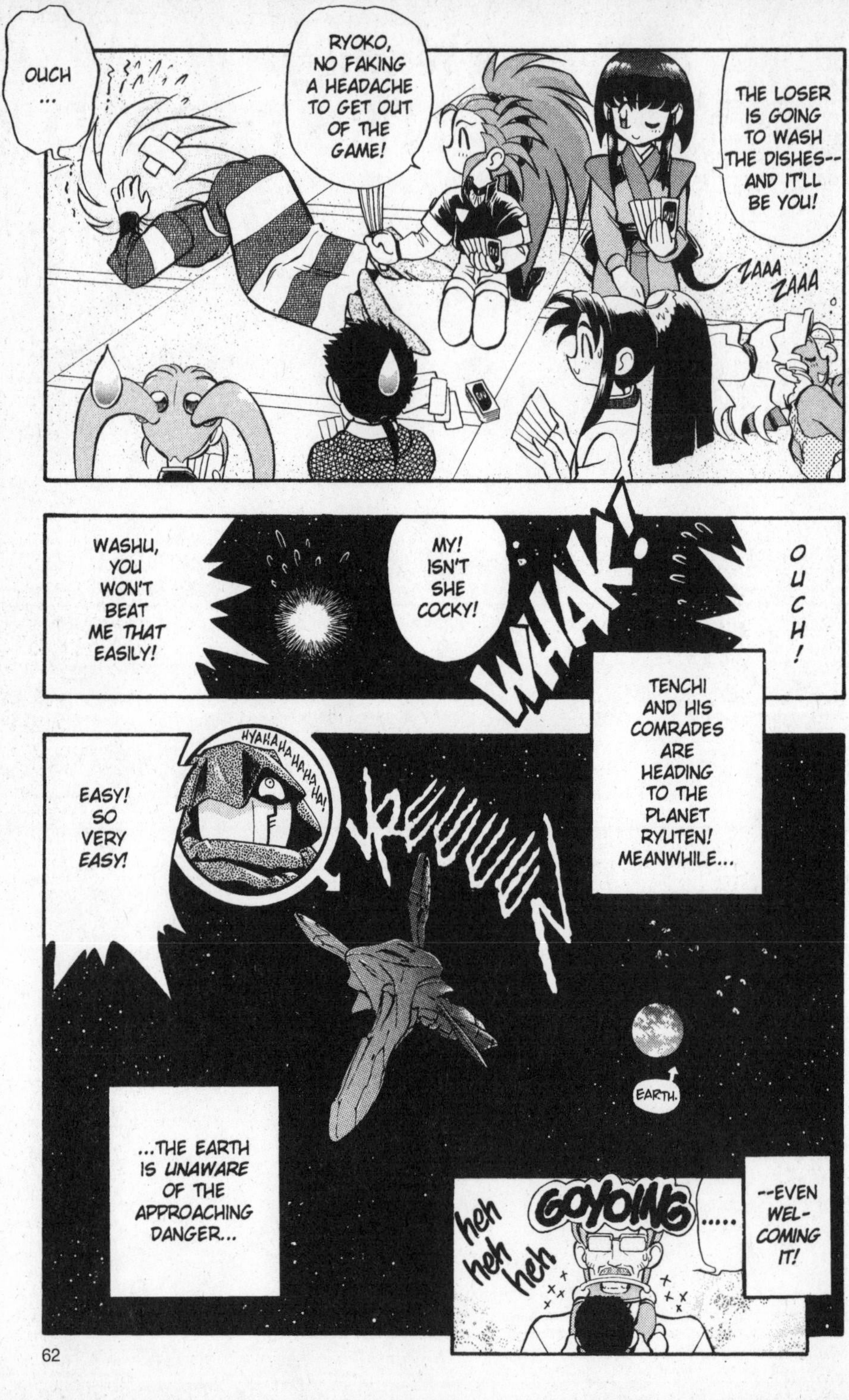
OUCH ...
RYOKO, NO FAKING A HEADACHE TO GET OUT OF THE GAME!
THE LOSER IS GOING TO WASH THE DISHES-- AND IT'LL BE YOU!
ZAAA ZAAA
WASHU, YOU WON'T BEAT ME THAT EASILY!
MY! ISN'T SHE COCKY!
WHAK!
OUCH!
TENCHI AND HIS COMRADES ARE HEADING TO THE PLANET RYUTEN! MEANWHILE...
HYAHAHAHAHAHA!
EASY! SO VERY EASY!
EARTH.
...THE EARTH IS *UNAWARE* OF THE APPROACHING DANGER...
heh heh heh
GOYOING
.....
--EVEN WEL-COMING IT!

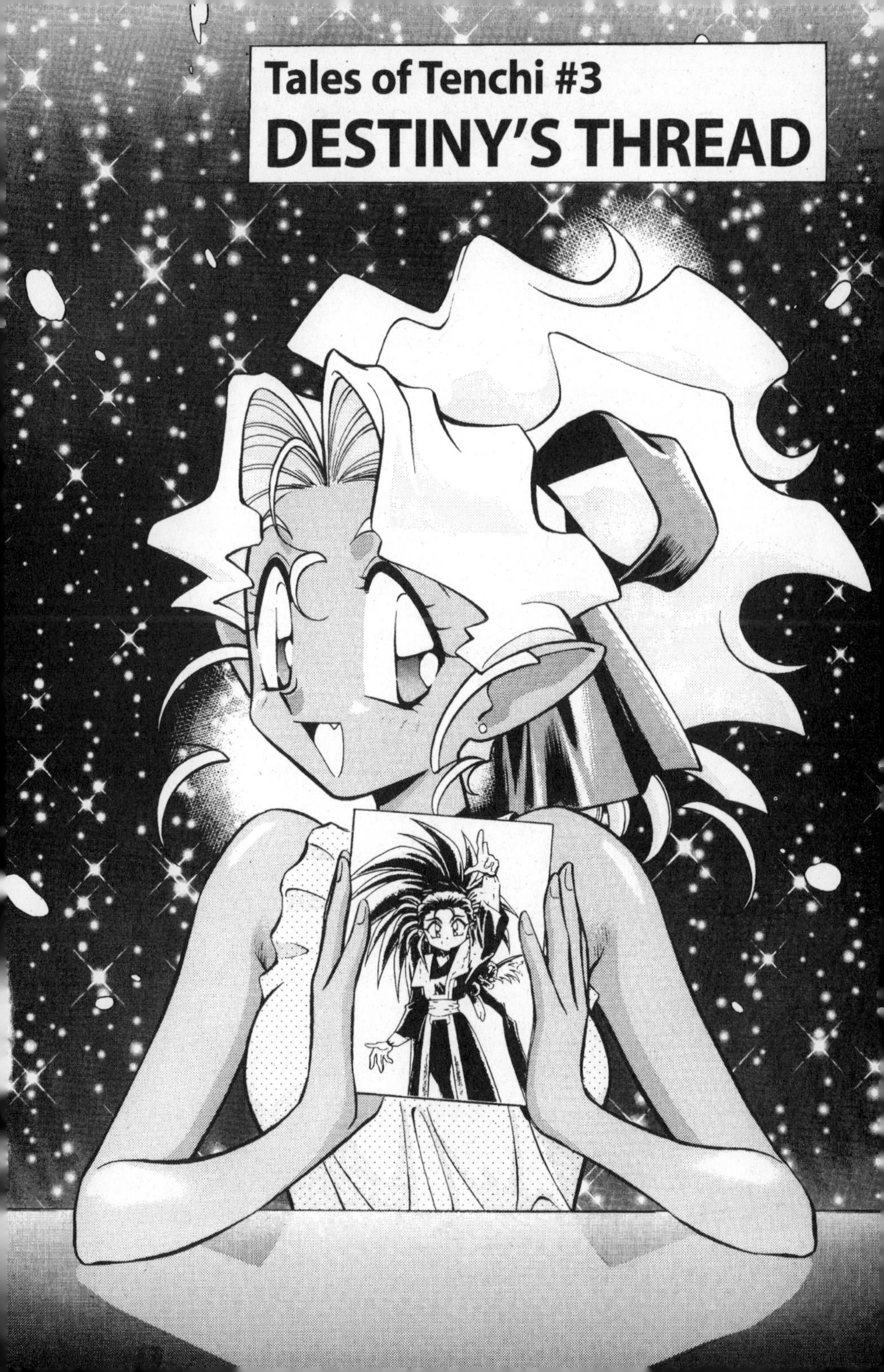
Tales of Tenchi #3
DESTINY'S THREAD

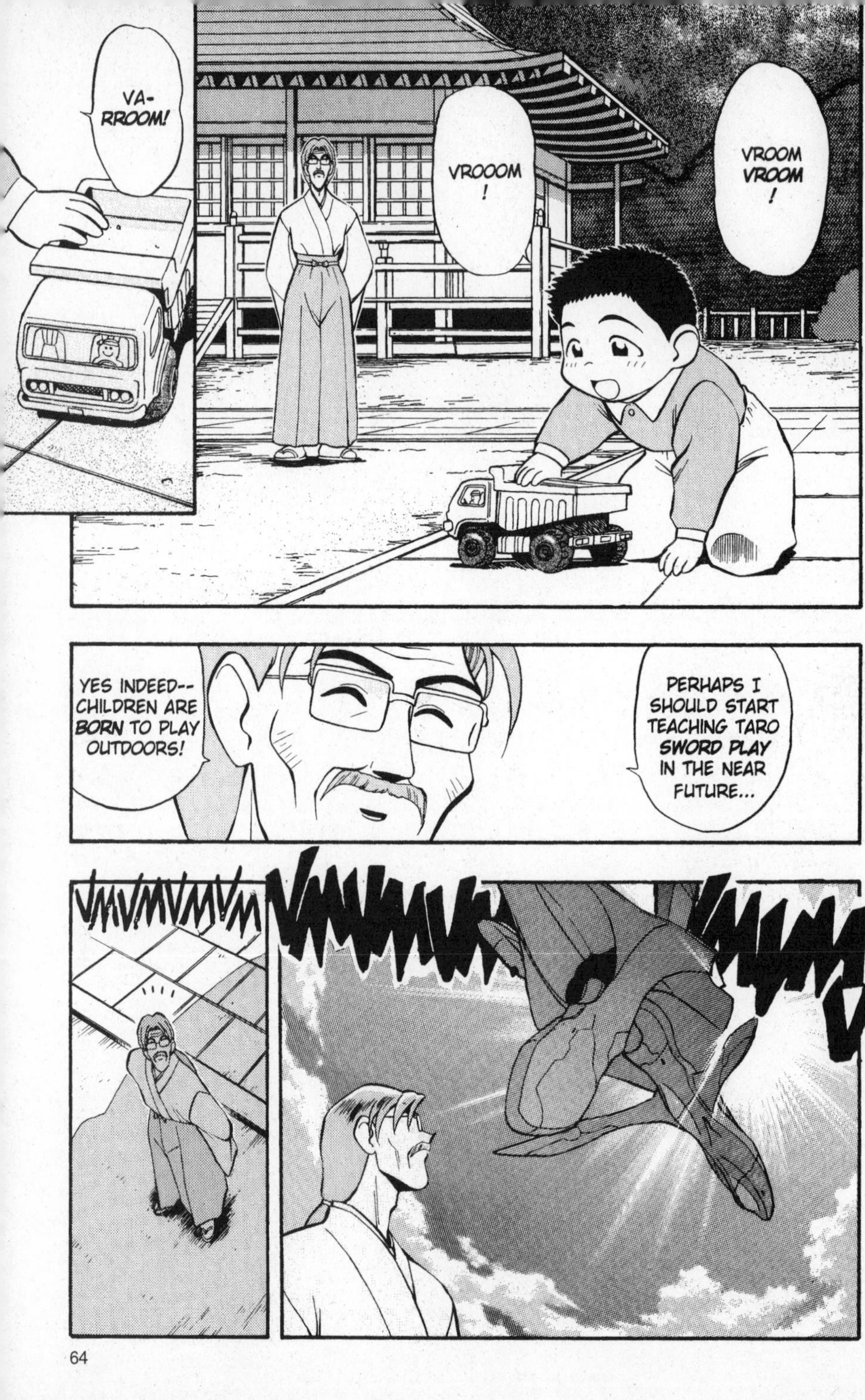
VA-RROOM!
VROOOM!
VROOM VROOM!
YES INDEED-- CHILDREN ARE BORN TO PLAY OUTDOORS!
PERHAPS I SHOULD START TEACHING TARO SWORD PLAY IN THE NEAR FUTURE...

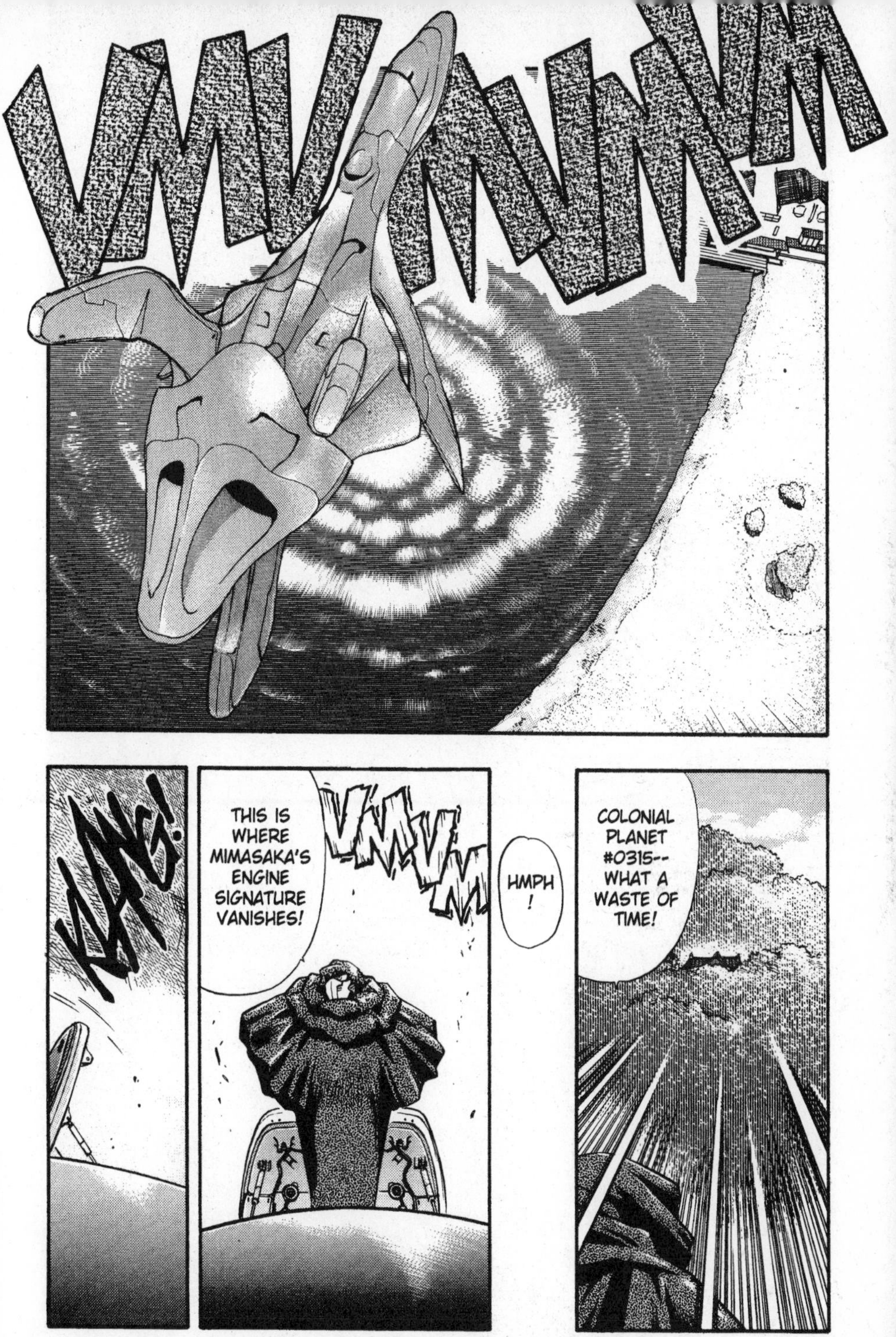
KANG!
THIS IS WHERE MIMASAKA'S ENGINE SIGNATURE VANISHES!
VMVM
HMPH!
COLONIAL PLANET #0315--WHAT A WASTE OF TIME!

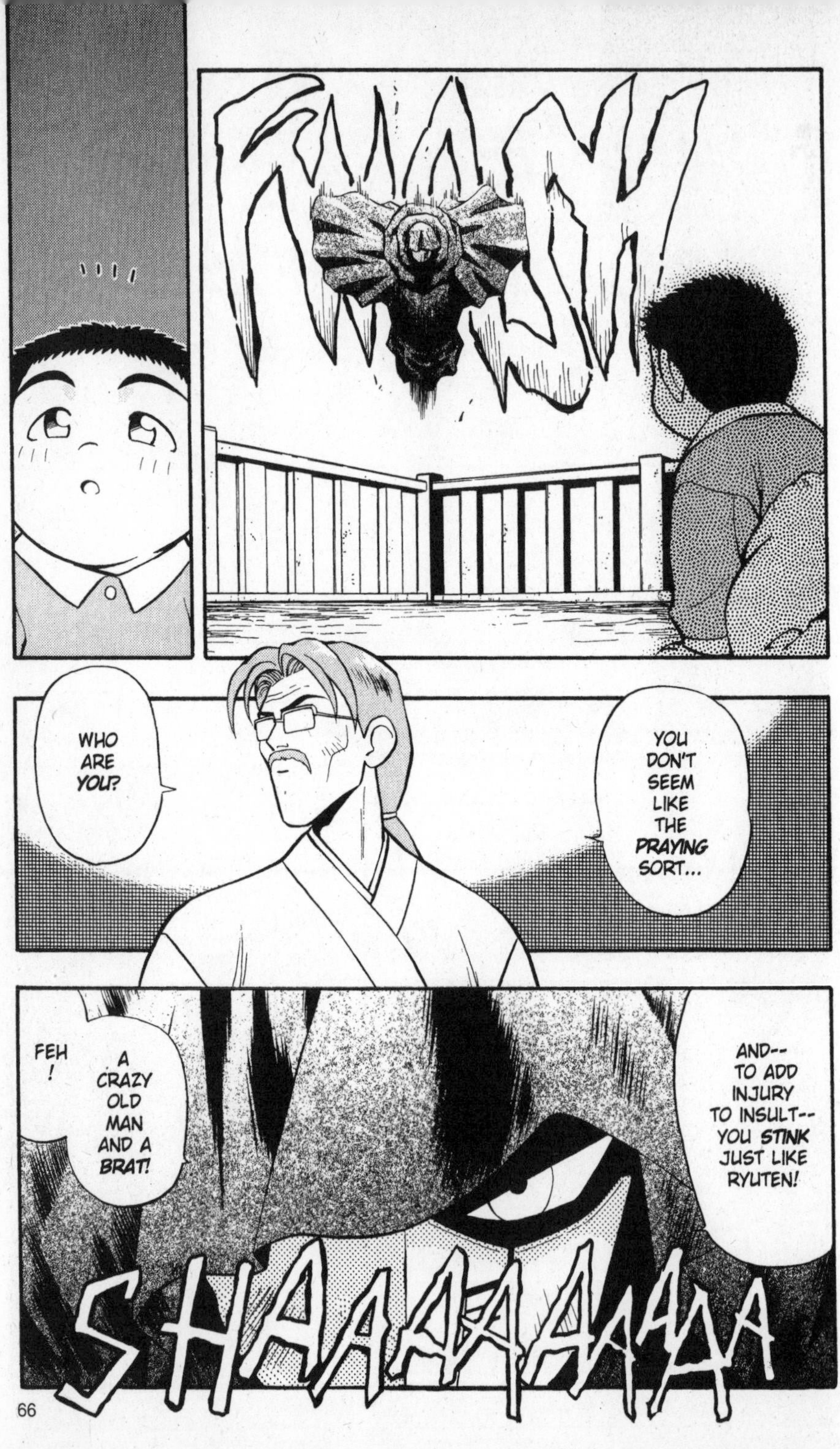

FWASH!
WHO ARE YOU?
YOU DON'T SEEM LIKE THE PRAYING SORT...
FEH!
A CRAZY OLD MAN AND A BRAT!
AND-- TO ADD INJURY TO INSULT-- YOU STINK JUST LIKE RYUTEN!
SHAAAAAAAA

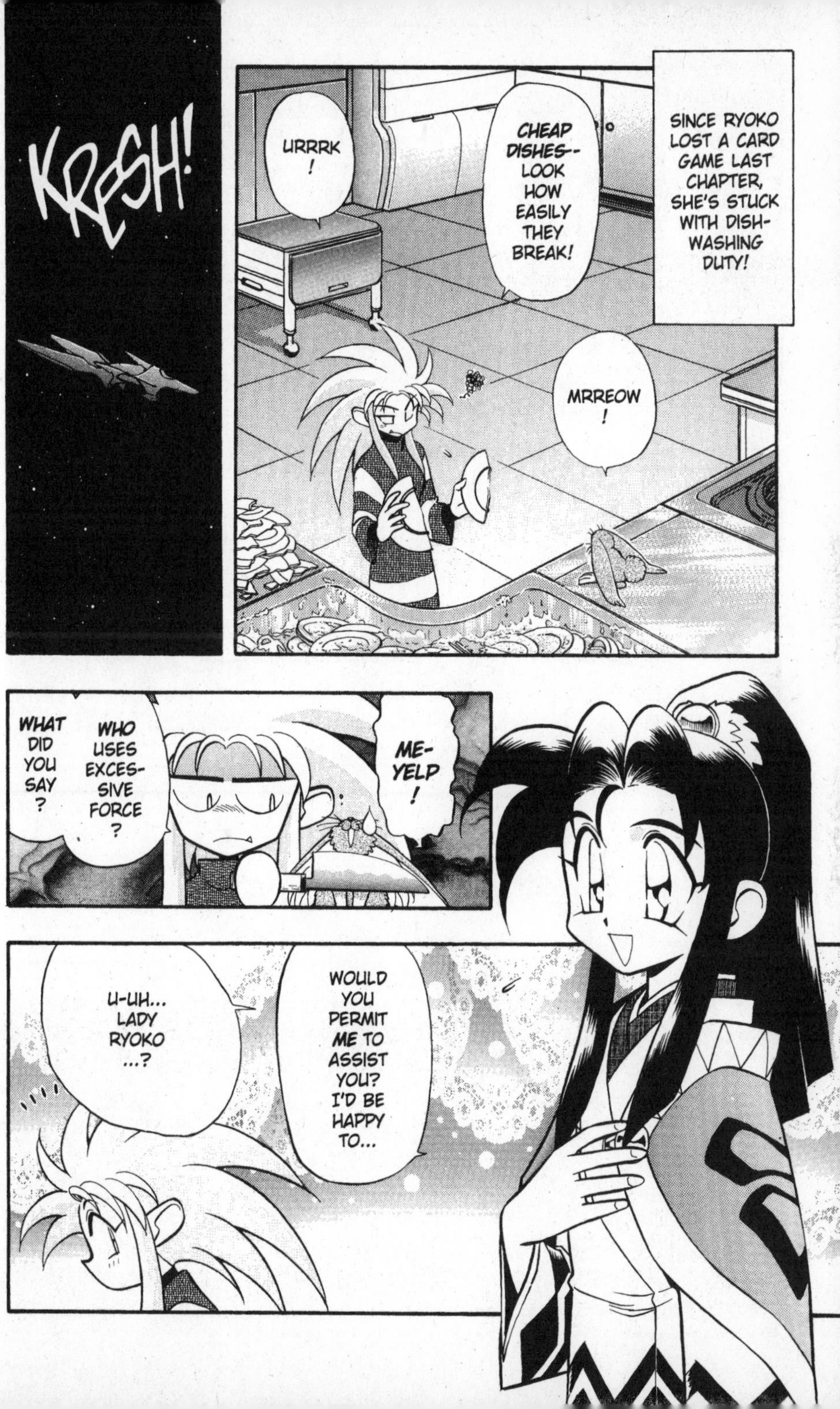
KRESH!
URRRK!
CHEAP DISHES--LOOK HOW EASILY THEY BREAK!
SINCE RYOKO LOST A CARD GAME LAST CHAPTER, SHE'S STUCK WITH DISH-WASHING DUTY!
MRREOW!
WHAT DID YOU SAY?
WHO USES EXCES-SIVE FORCE?
ME-YELP!
U-UH... LADY RYOKO...?
WOULD YOU PERMIT ME TO ASSIST YOU? I'D BE HAPPY TO...

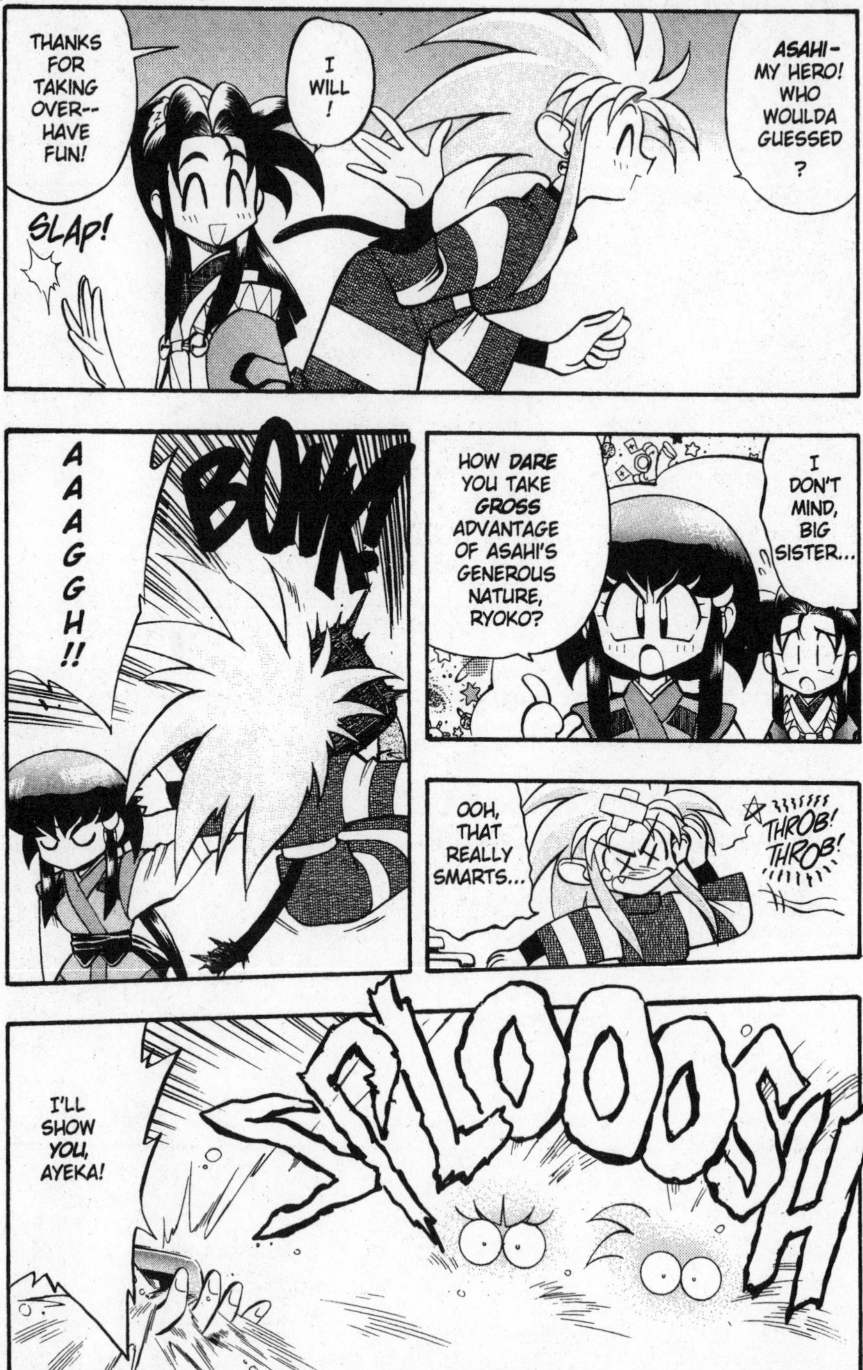
THANKS FOR TAKING OVER-- HAVE FUN!
I WILL!
ASAHI- MY HERO! WHO WOULDA GUESSED?
SLAP!
AAAAGGH!!
BONK!
HOW DARE YOU TAKE GROSS ADVANTAGE OF ASAHI'S GENEROUS NATURE, RYOKO?
I DON'T MIND, BIG SISTER...
OOH, THAT REALLY SMARTS...
THROB! THROB!
I'LL SHOW YOU, AYEKA!
SPLOOOSH

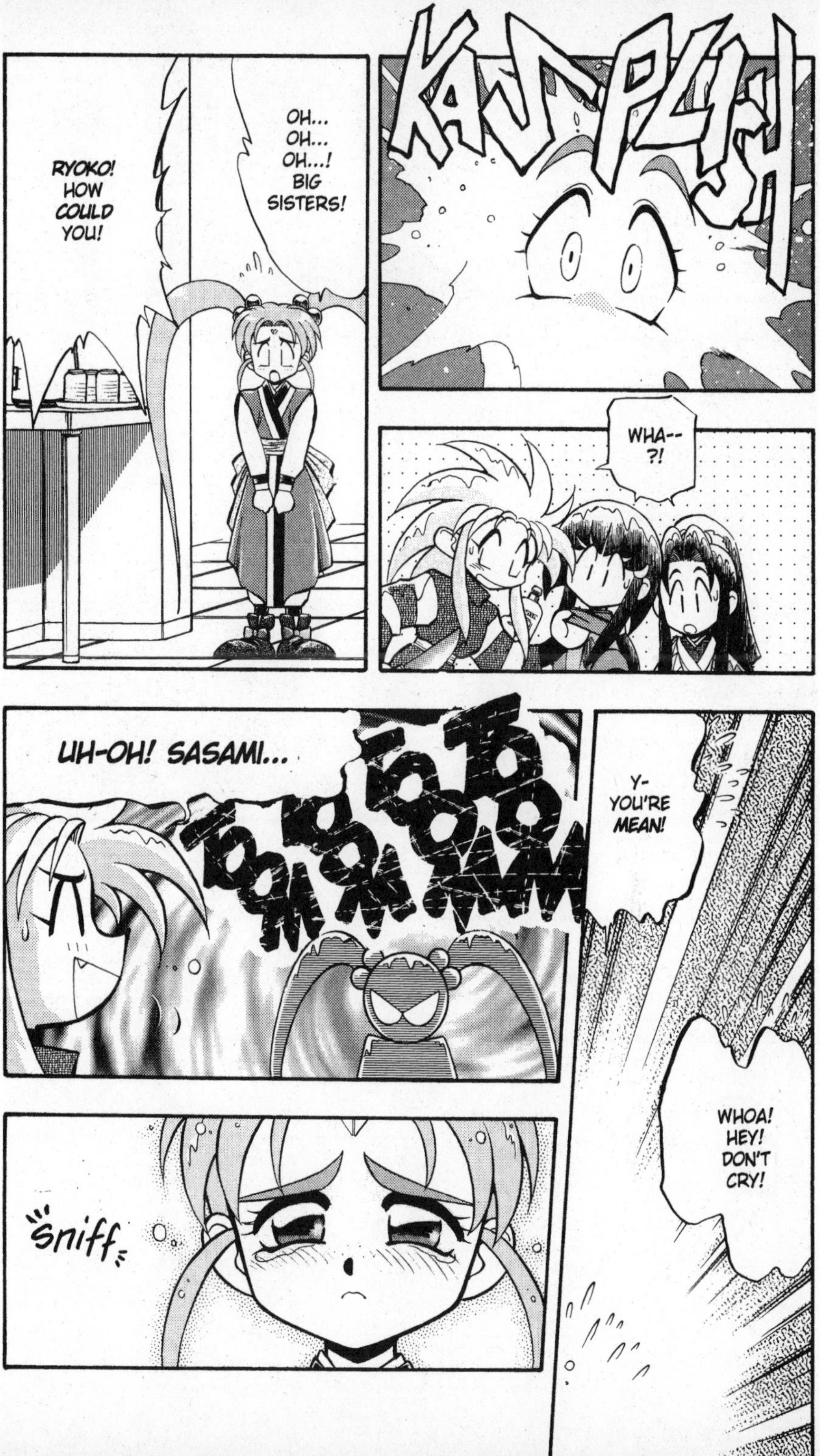
RYOKO! HOW COULD YOU!
OH... OH... OH...! BIG SISTERS!
KASPLASH
WHA-- ?!
UH-OH! SASAMI...
sniff
Y- YOU'RE MEAN!
WHOA! HEY! DON'T CRY!

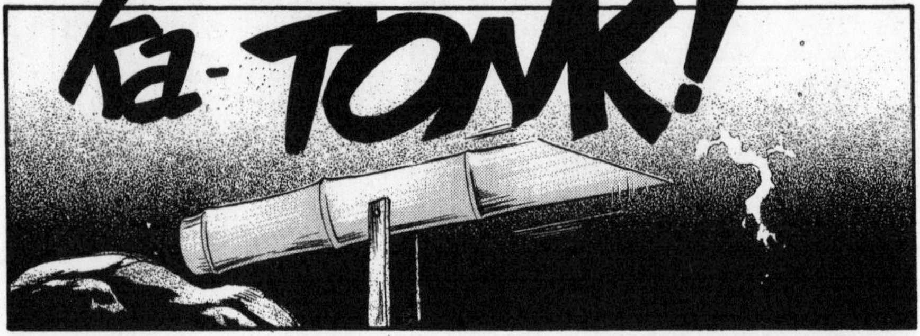
ka-TONK!

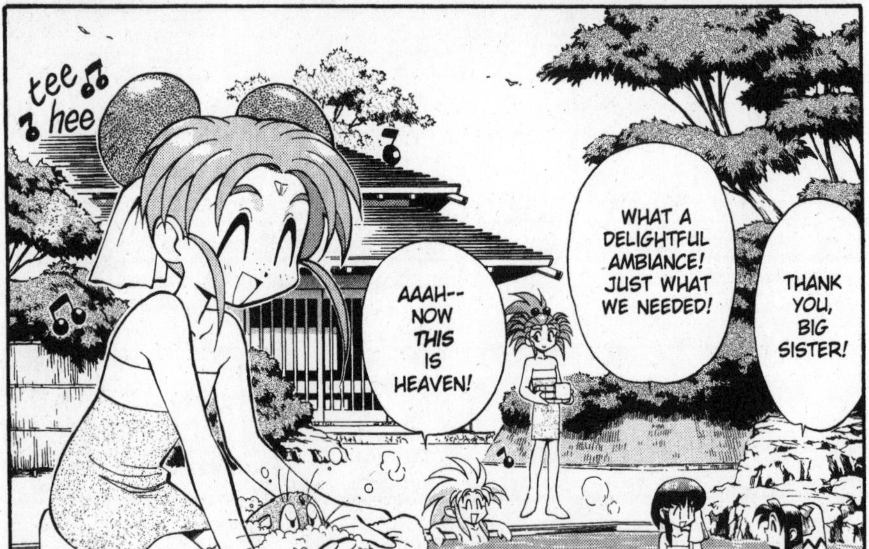
tee hee
AAAH-- NOW THIS IS HEAVEN!
WHAT A DELIGHTFUL AMBIANCE! JUST WHAT WE NEEDED!
THANK YOU, BIG SISTER!

SHE HAS REGAINED HER SUNNY DISPOSITION!

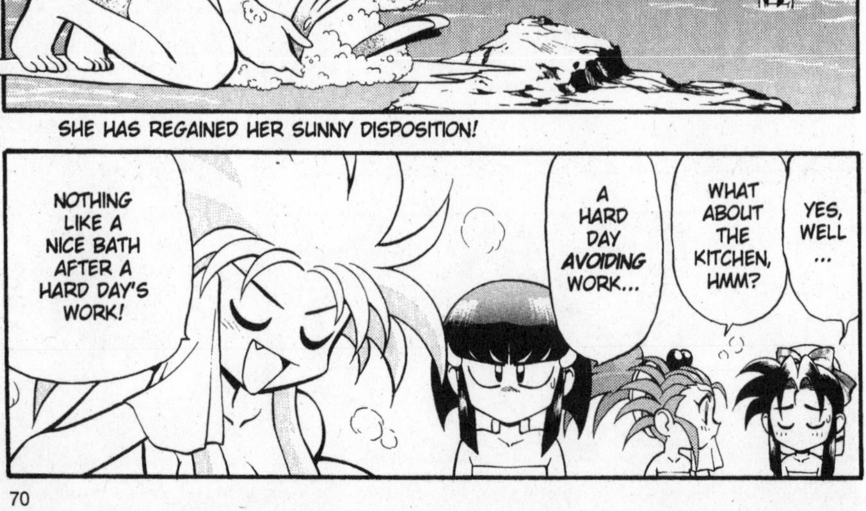
NOTHING LIKE A NICE BATH AFTER A HARD DAY'S WORK!
A HARD DAY AVOIDING WORK...
WHAT ABOUT THE KITCHEN, HMM?
YES, WELL ...

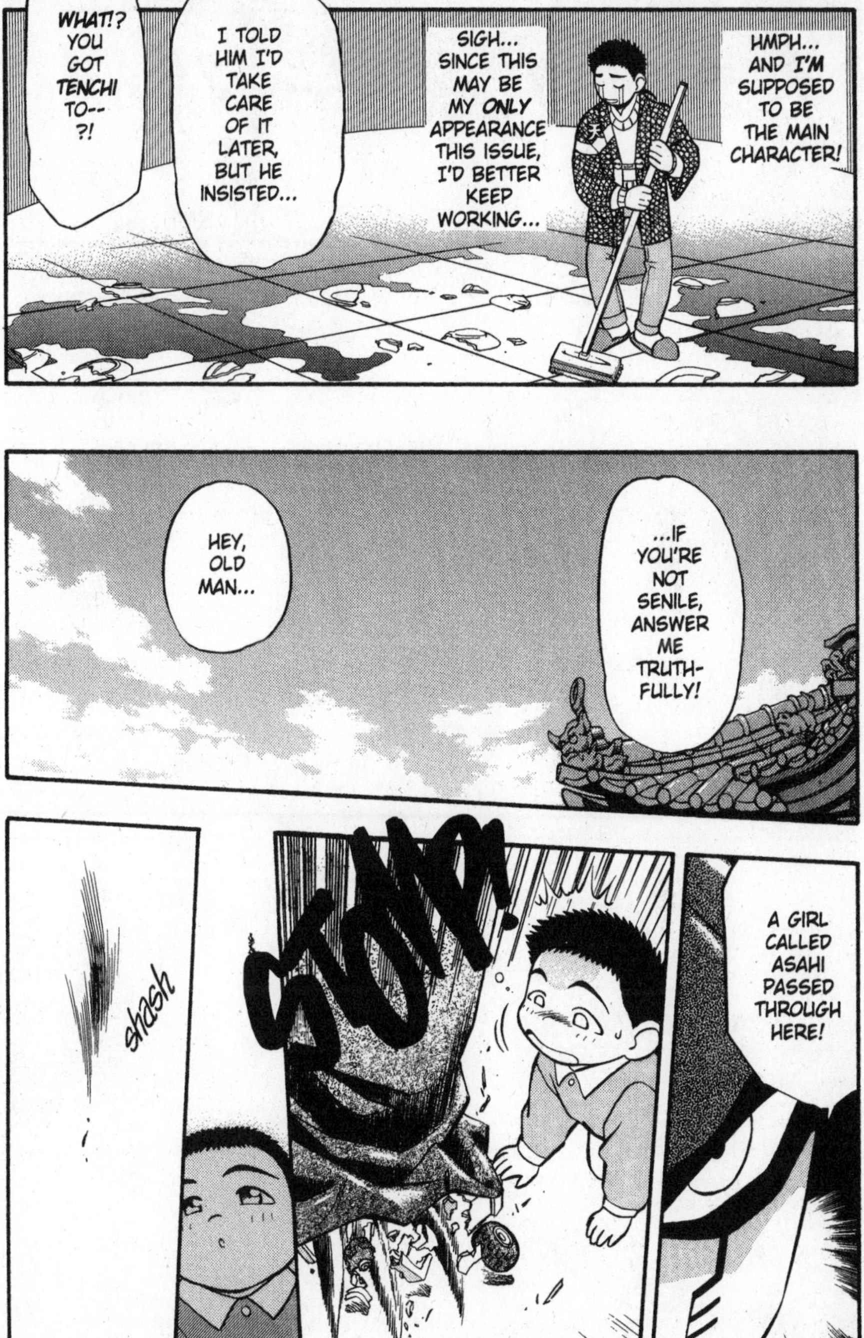
WHAT!? YOU GOT TENCHI TO--?!
I TOLD HIM I'D TAKE CARE OF IT LATER, BUT HE INSISTED...
SIGH... SINCE THIS MAY BE MY ONLY APPEARANCE THIS ISSUE, I'D BETTER KEEP WORKING...
HMPH... AND I'M SUPPOSED TO BE THE MAIN CHARACTER!
HEY, OLD MAN...
...IF YOU'RE NOT SENILE, ANSWER ME TRUTH-FULLY!
shash
STOMP!
A GIRL CALLED ASAHI PASSED THROUGH HERE!

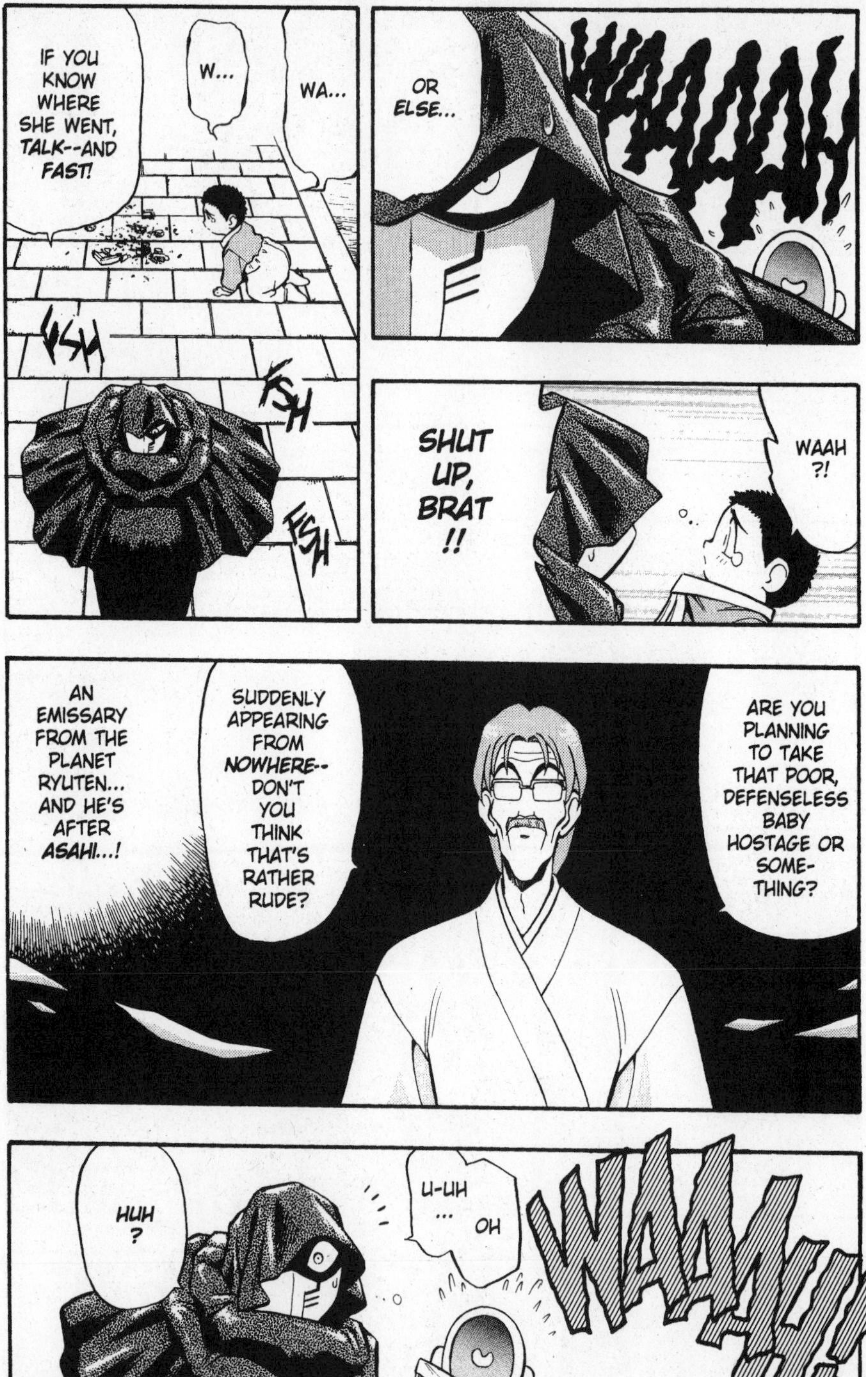
IF YOU KNOW WHERE SHE WENT, TALK--AND FAST!
W...
WA...
VSH
FSH
FSH
OR ELSE...
WAAAH
SHUT UP, BRAT!!
WAAH?!
AN EMISSARY FROM THE PLANET RYUTEN... AND HE'S AFTER ASAHI...!
SUDDENLY APPEARING FROM NOWHERE--DON'T YOU THINK THAT'S RATHER RUDE?
ARE YOU PLANNING TO TAKE THAT POOR, DEFENSELESS BABY HOSTAGE OR SOME-THING?
HUH?
U-UH... OH
WAAAAH!!

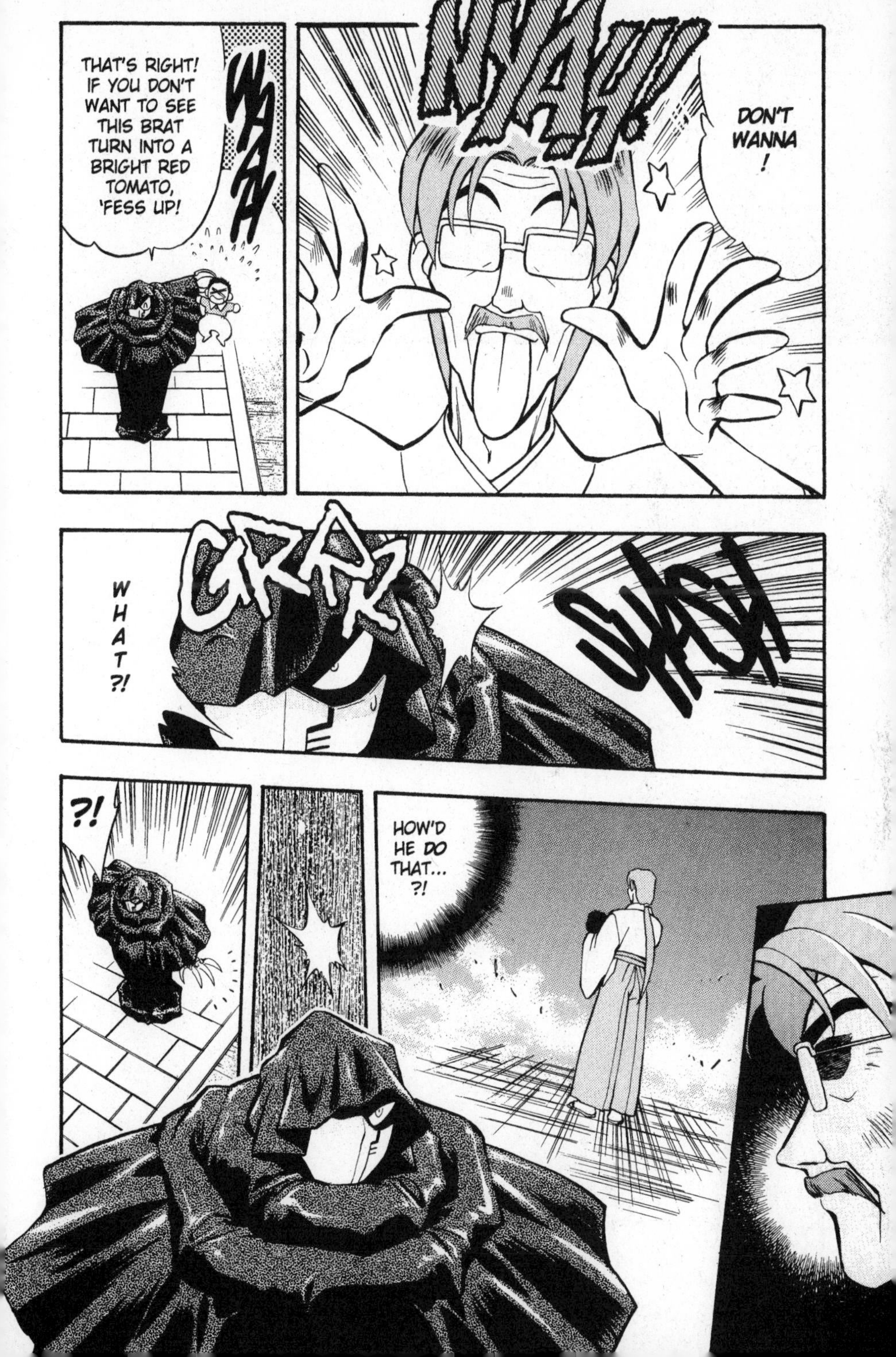
THAT'S RIGHT! IF YOU DON'T WANT TO SEE THIS BRAT TURN INTO A BRIGHT RED TOMATO, 'FESS UP!
NYAH!!
DON'T WANNA!
WHAT?!
?!
HOW'D HE DO THAT...?!

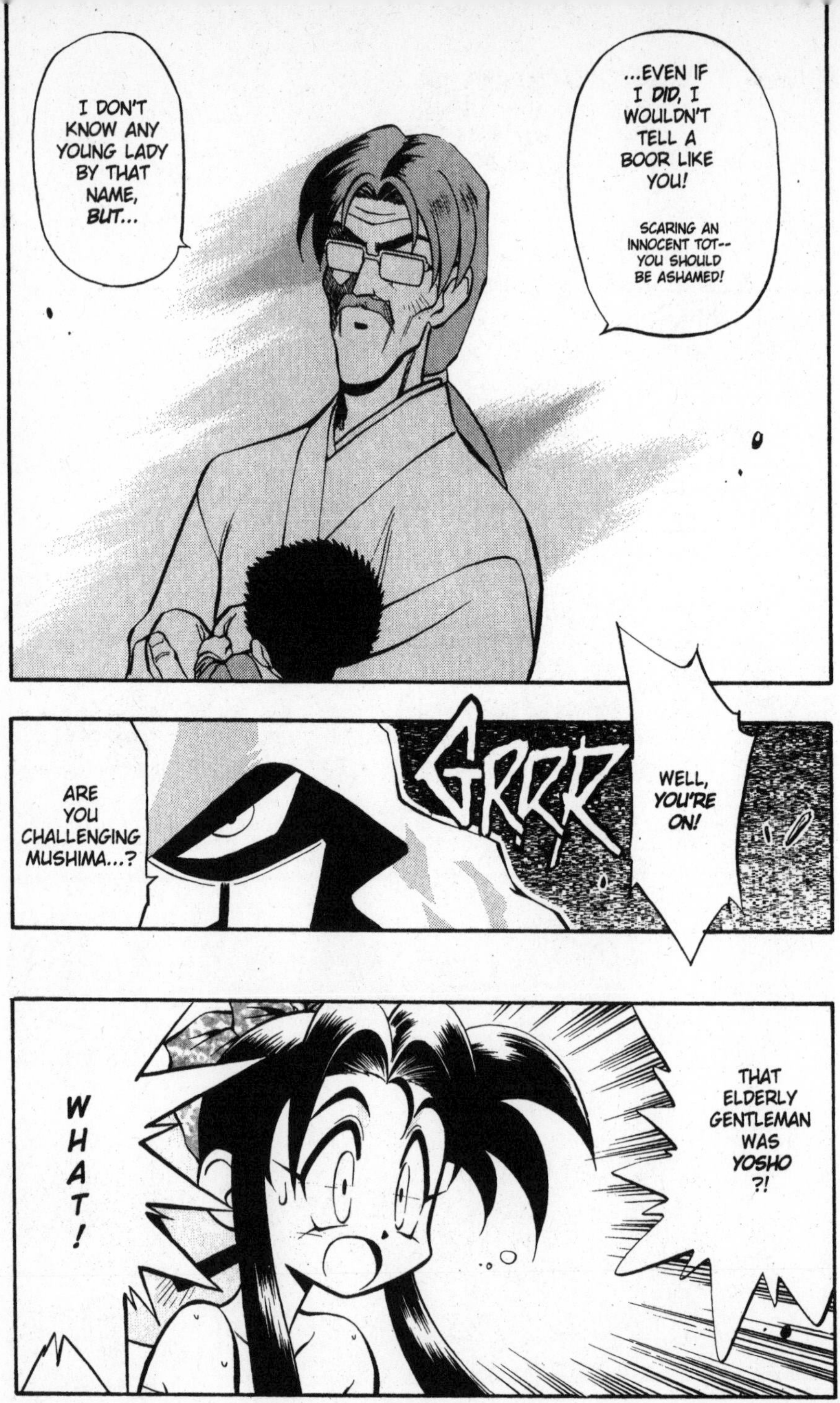
I DON'T KNOW ANY YOUNG LADY BY THAT NAME, *BUT...*
...EVEN IF I *DID*, I WOULDN'T TELL A BOOR LIKE YOU!
SCARING AN INNOCENT TOT-- YOU SHOULD BE ASHAMED!
ARE YOU CHALLENGING MUSHIMA...?
GRRR
WELL, *YOU'RE ON!*
WHAT!
THAT ELDERLY GENTLEMAN WAS *YOSHO* ?!

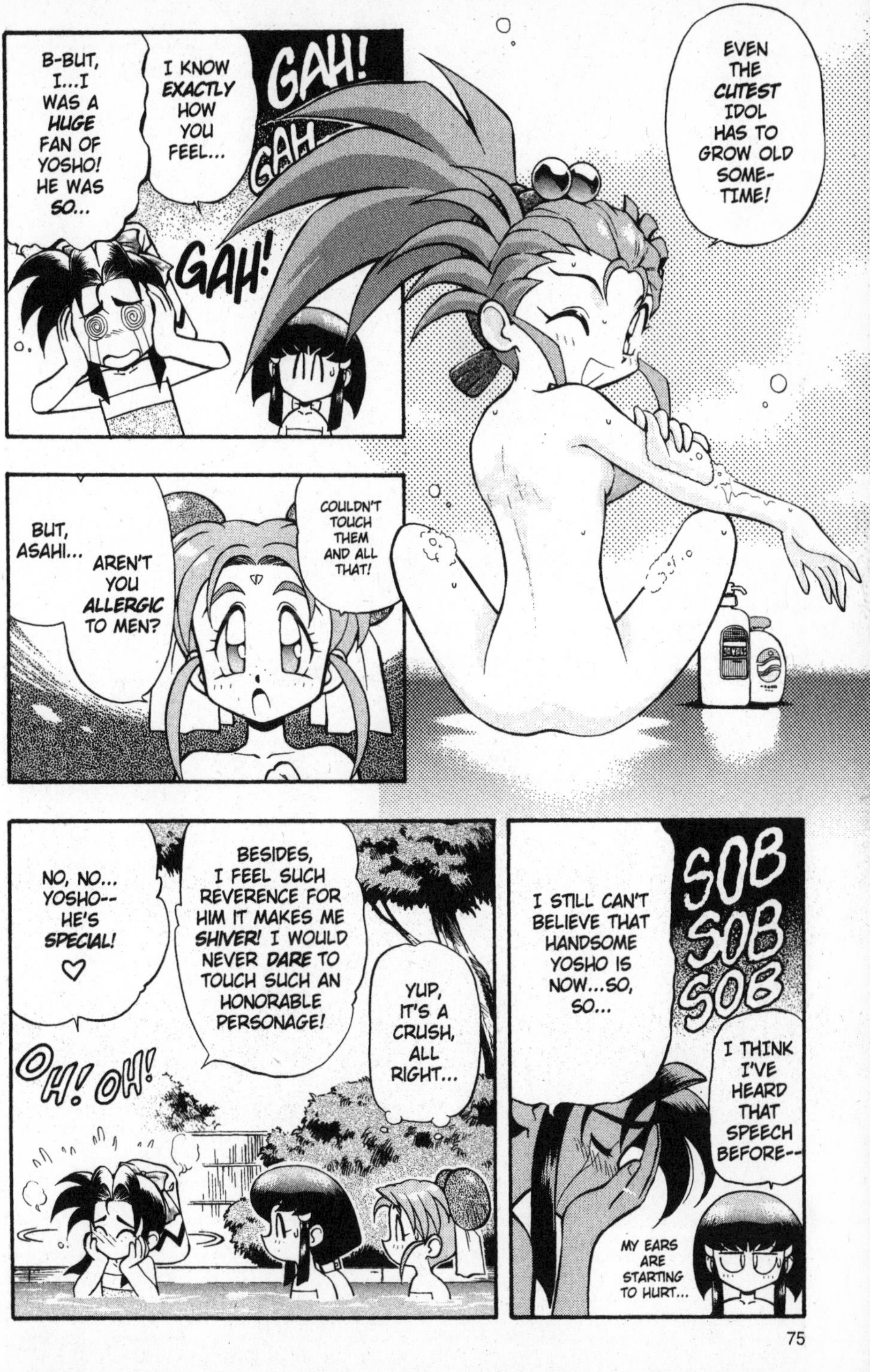
B-BUT, I...I WAS A HUGE FAN OF YOSHO! HE WAS SO...
I KNOW EXACTLY HOW YOU FEEL...
GAH! GAH GAH!
EVEN THE CUTEST IDOL HAS TO GROW OLD SOME-TIME!
BUT, ASAHI...
AREN'T YOU ALLERGIC TO MEN?
COULDN'T TOUCH THEM AND ALL THAT!
NO, NO... YOSHO-- HE'S SPECIAL! ♡
BESIDES, I FEEL SUCH REVERENCE FOR HIM IT MAKES ME SHIVER! I WOULD NEVER DARE TO TOUCH SUCH AN HONORABLE PERSONAGE!
YUP, IT'S A CRUSH, ALL RIGHT...
OH! OH!
I STILL CAN'T BELIEVE THAT HANDSOME YOSHO IS NOW...SO, SO...
SOB SOB SOB
I THINK I'VE HEARD THAT SPEECH BEFORE--
MY EARS ARE STARTING TO HURT...

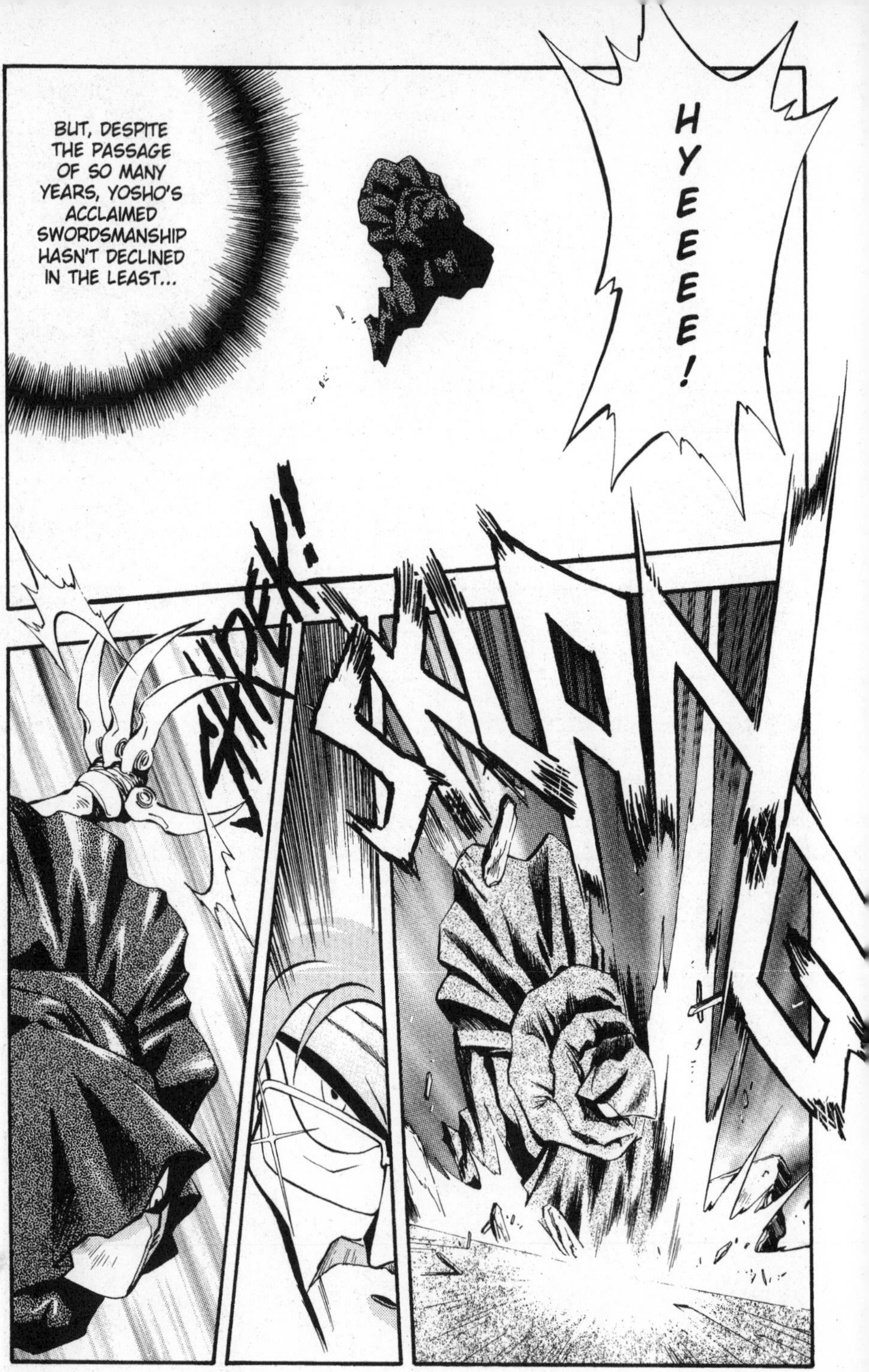
BUT, DESPITE THE PASSAGE OF SO MANY YEARS, YOSHO'S ACCLAIMED SWORDSMANSHIP HASN'T DECLINED IN THE LEAST...
HYEEEEE!
SHREK!

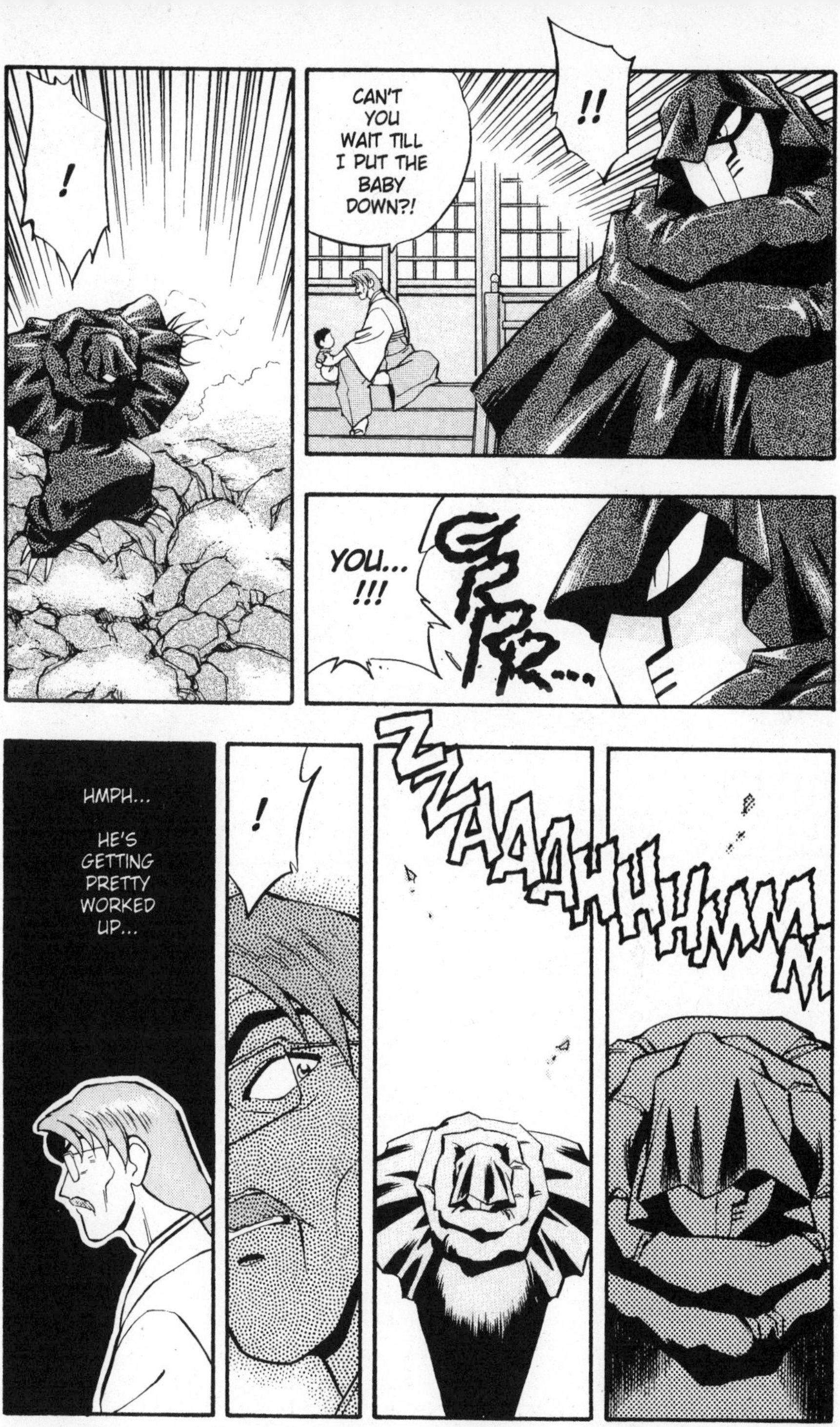
!
CAN'T YOU WAIT TILL I PUT THE BABY DOWN?!
!!
YOU... !!!
GRRR...
HMPH... HE'S GETTING PRETTY WORKED UP...
!
NNAAAHHHMMM

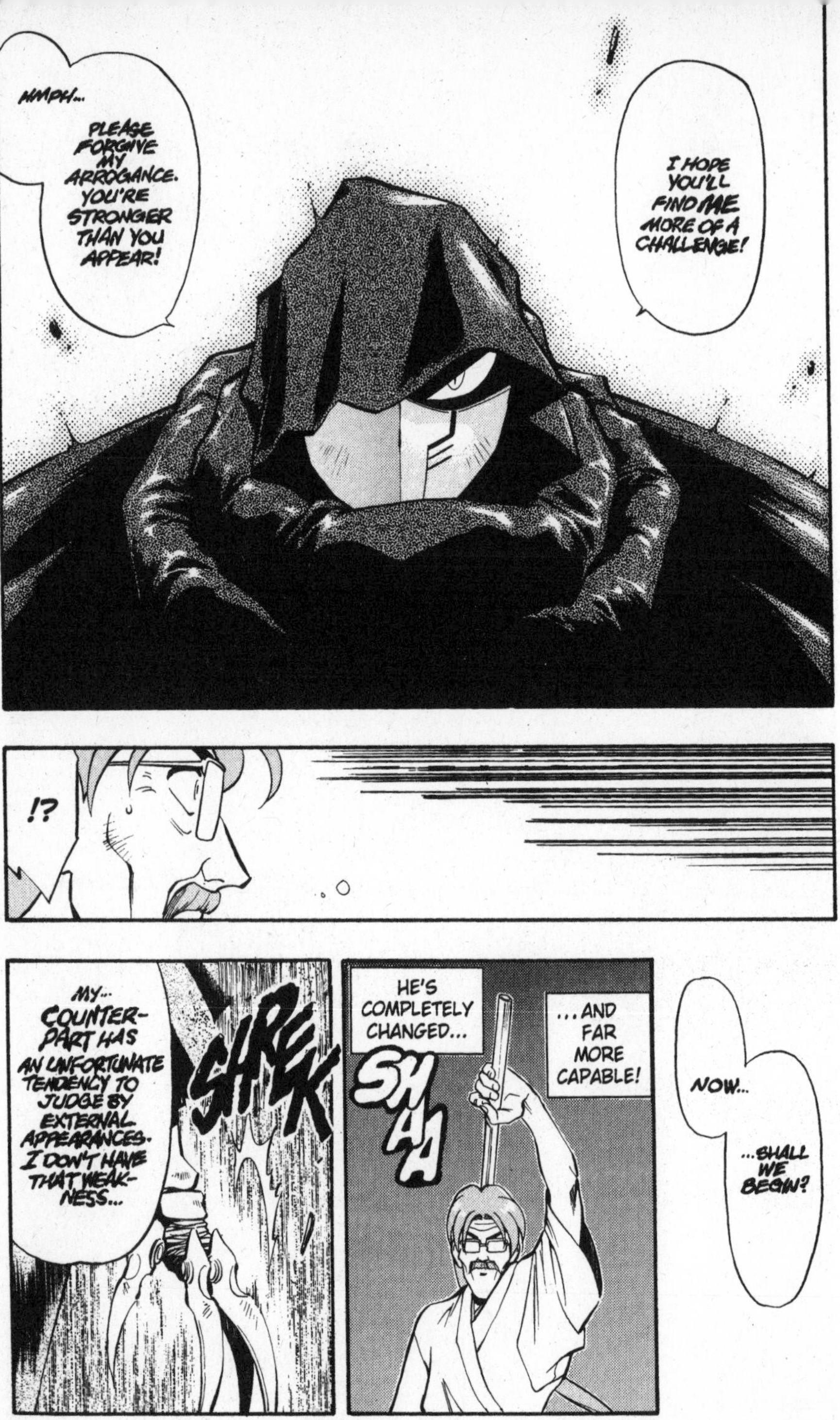
HMPH... PLEASE FORGIVE MY ARROGANCE. YOU'RE STRONGER THAN YOU APPEAR!
I HOPE YOU'LL FIND ME MORE OF A CHALLENGE!
!?
MY... COUNTER-PART HAS AN UNFORTUNATE TENDENCY TO JUDGE BY EXTERNAL APPEARANCES. I DON'T HAVE THAT WEAK-NESS...
SHREK
HE'S COMPLETELY CHANGED...
SHAA
...AND FAR MORE CAPABLE!
NOW...
...SHALL WE BEGIN?

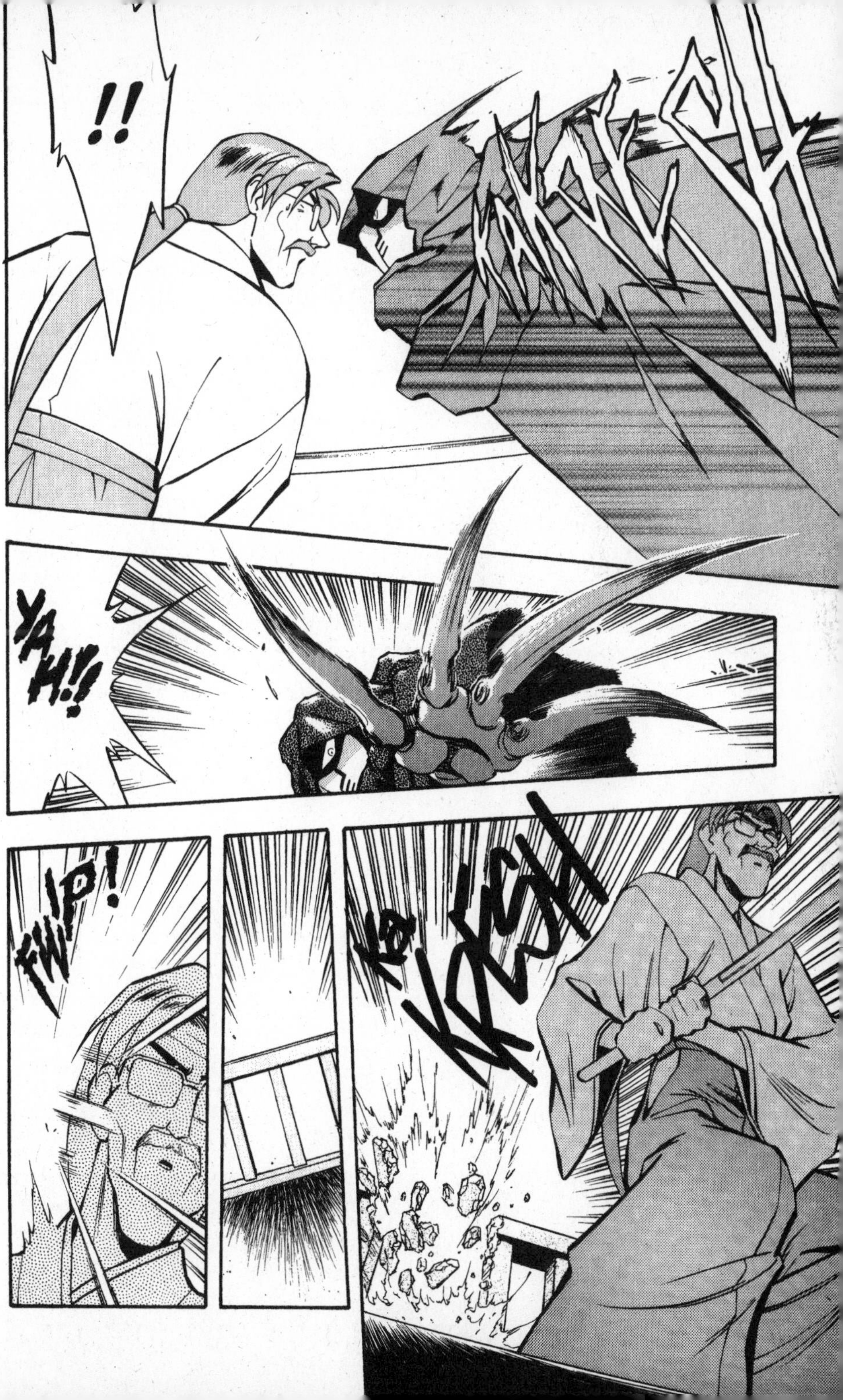
!!
KASHAK
YAAH!!
FWIP!
KRASH

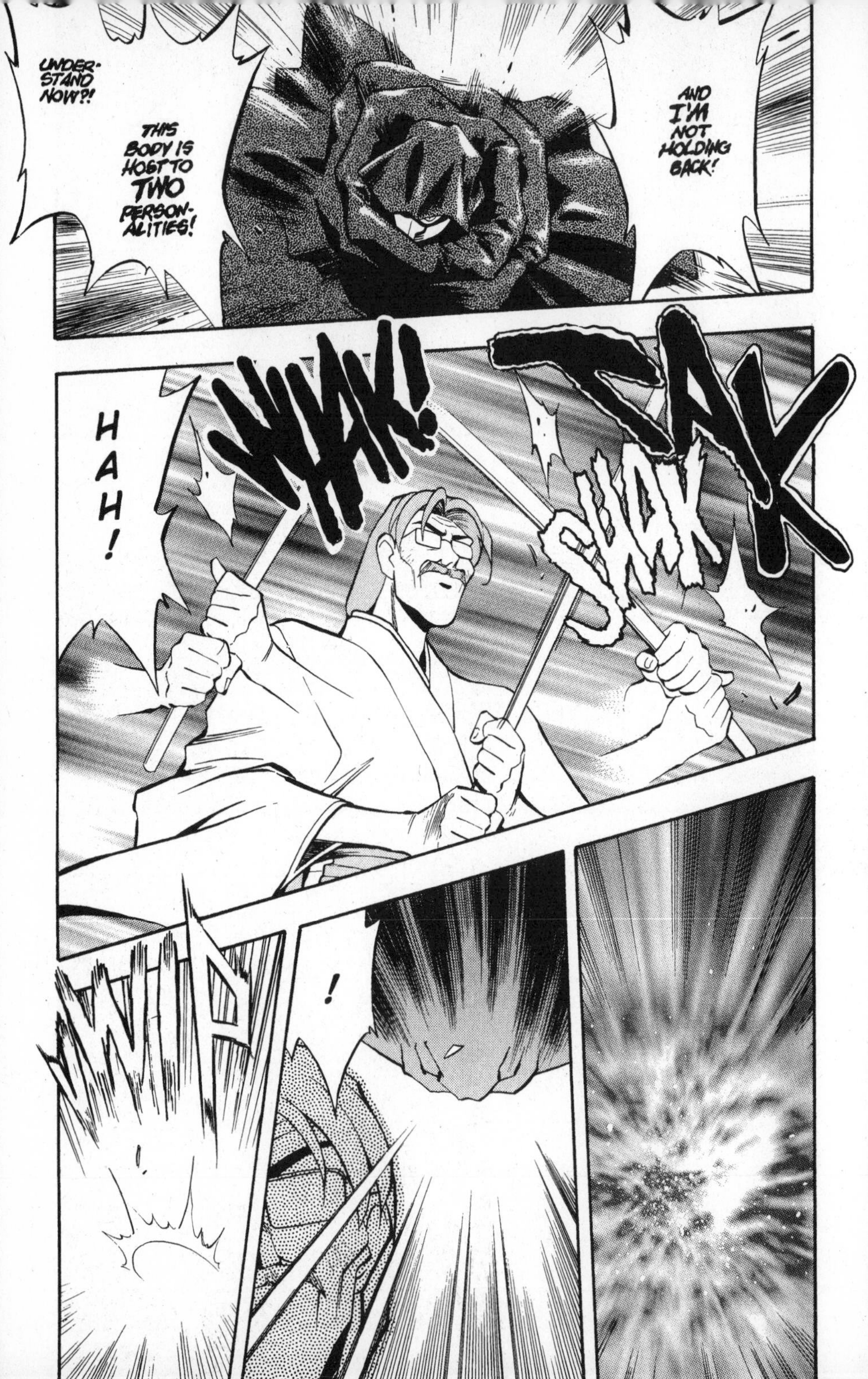
UNDER-STAND NOW?!
THIS BODY IS HOST TO TWO PERSON-ALITIES!
AND I'M NOT HOLDING BACK!
HAH!
WHAK!
TAK
SHAK
WHAP
!

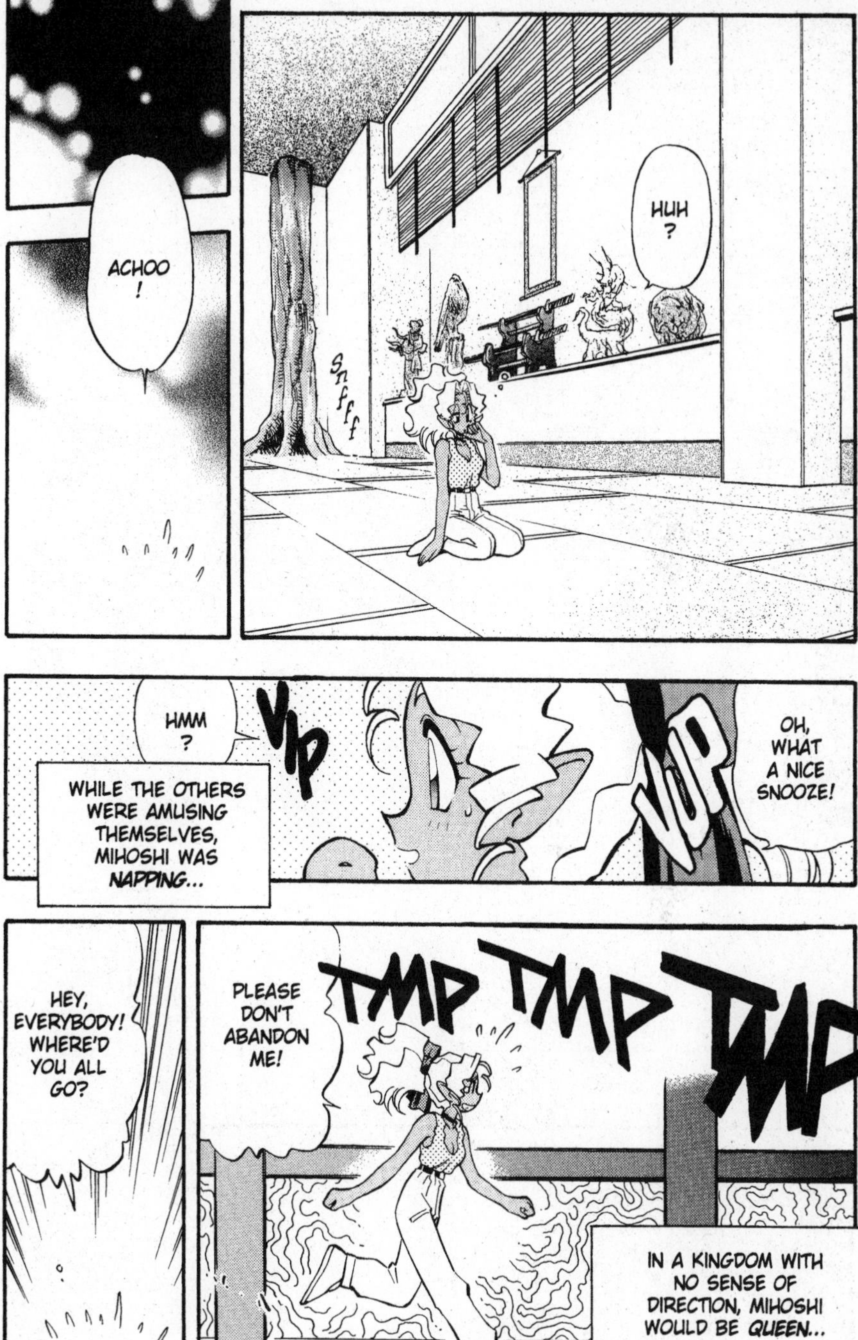
ACHOO!
HUH?
Snfff
HMM?
WHILE THE OTHERS WERE AMUSING THEMSELVES, MIHOSHI WAS *NAPPING*...
VIP
VUP
OH, WHAT A NICE SNOOZE!
HEY, EVERYBODY! WHERE'D YOU ALL GO?
PLEASE DON'T ABANDON ME!
TMP TMP TMP
IN A KINGDOM WITH NO SENSE OF DIRECTION, MIHOSHI WOULD BE *QUEEN*...

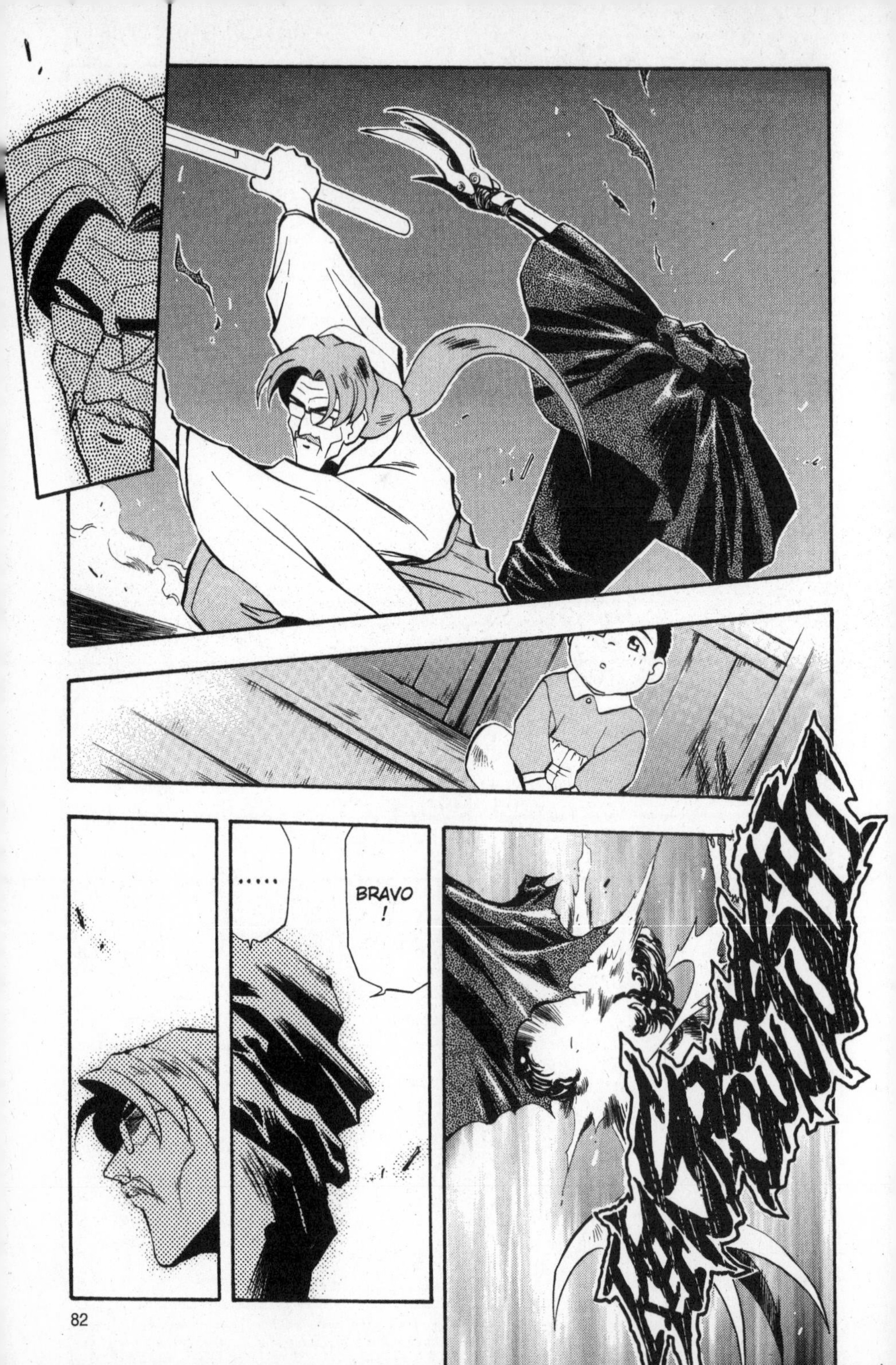
.....
BRAVO
!

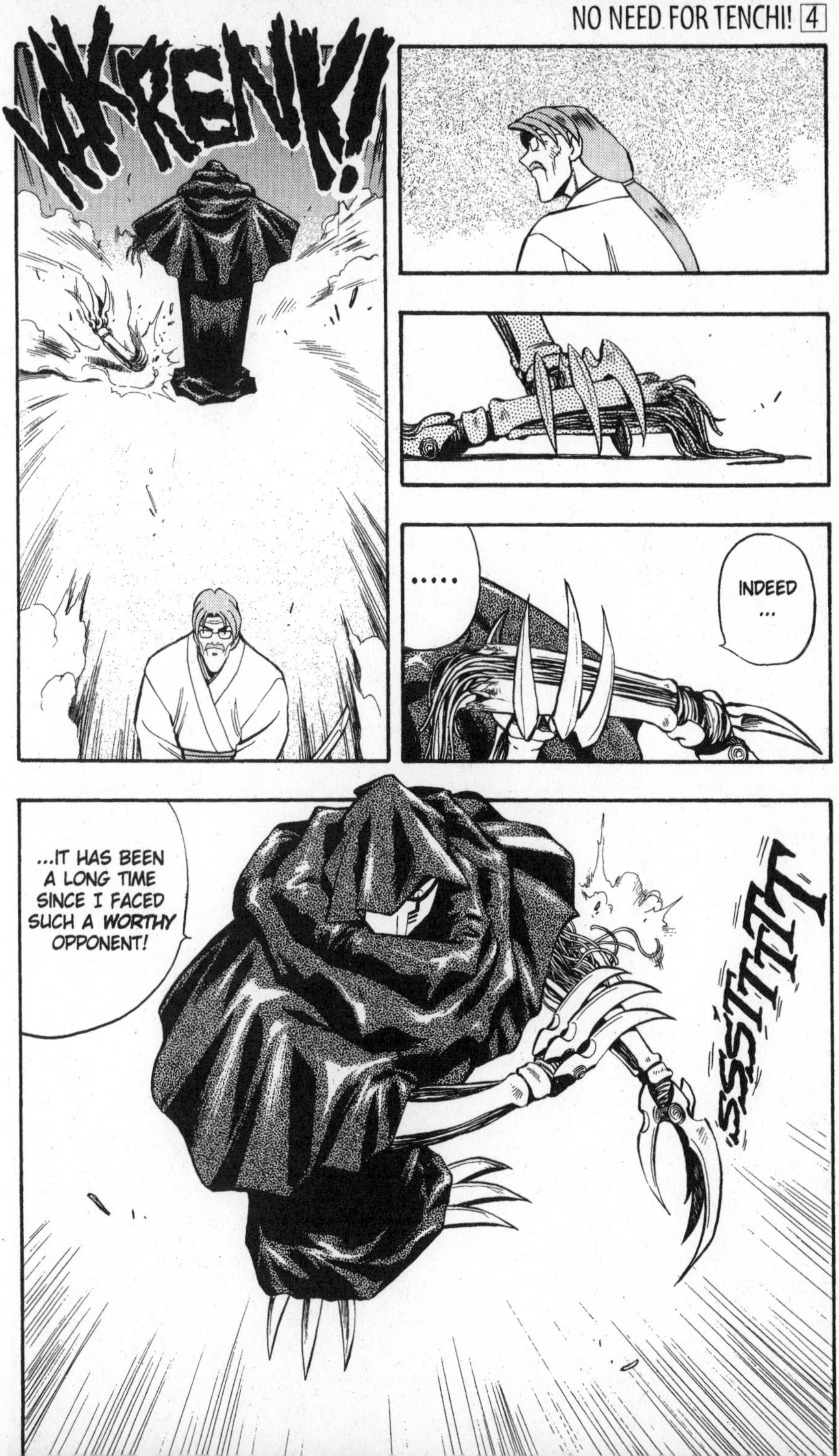
KA-KRENK!
.....
INDEED ...
...IT HAS BEEN A LONG TIME SINCE I FACED SUCH A WORTHY OPPONENT!
SSTTTT

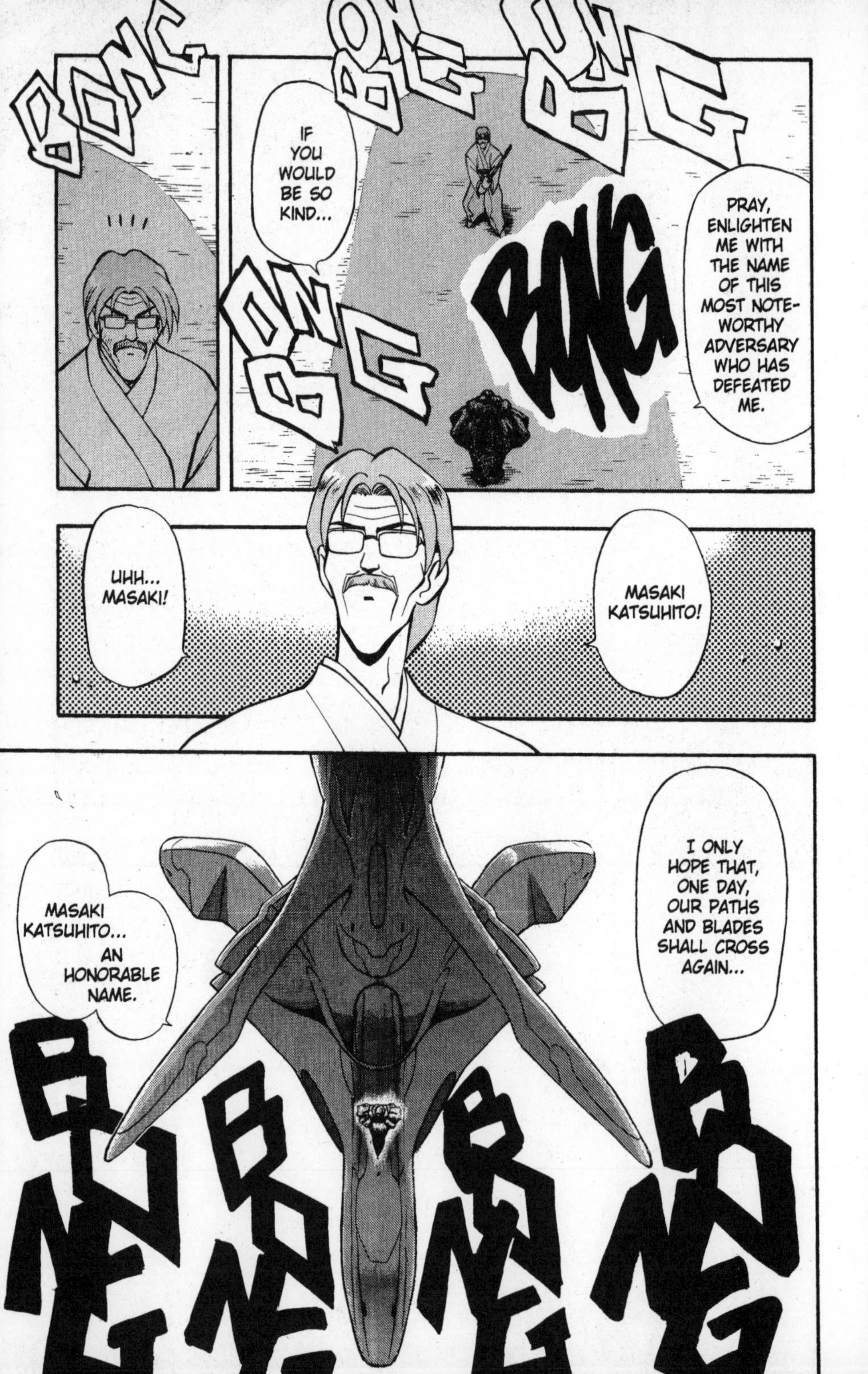
IF YOU WOULD BE SO KIND...
BONG
PRAY, ENLIGHTEN ME WITH THE NAME OF THIS MOST NOTE-WORTHY ADVERSARY WHO HAS DEFEATED ME.
UHH... MASAKI!
MASAKI KATSUHITO!
MASAKI KATSUHITO... AN HONORABLE NAME.
I ONLY HOPE THAT, ONE DAY, OUR PATHS AND BLADES SHALL CROSS AGAIN...

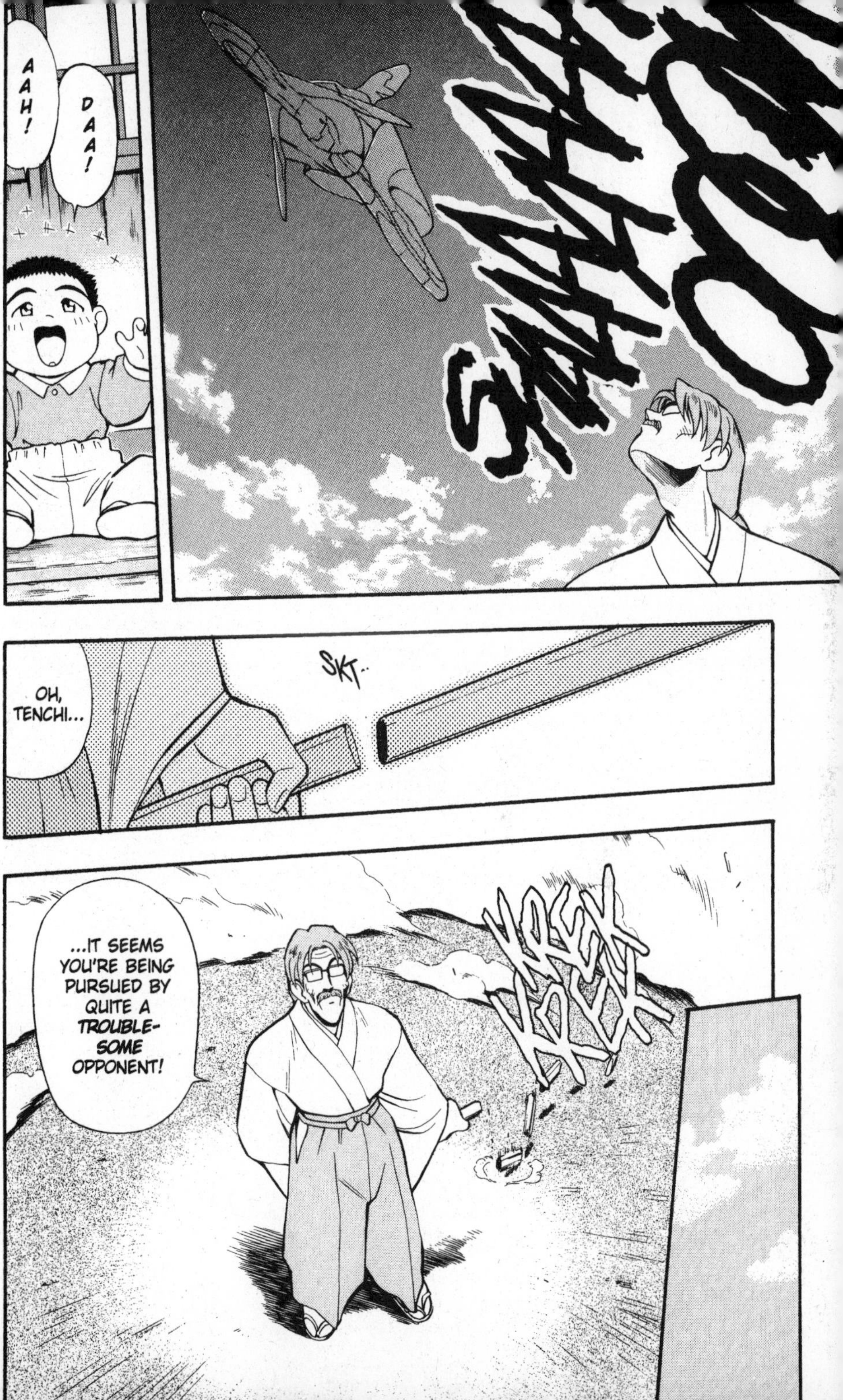
AAH!
DAA!
SKT..
OH, TENCHI...
...IT SEEMS YOU'RE BEING PURSUED BY QUITE A TROUBLE-SOME OPPONENT!

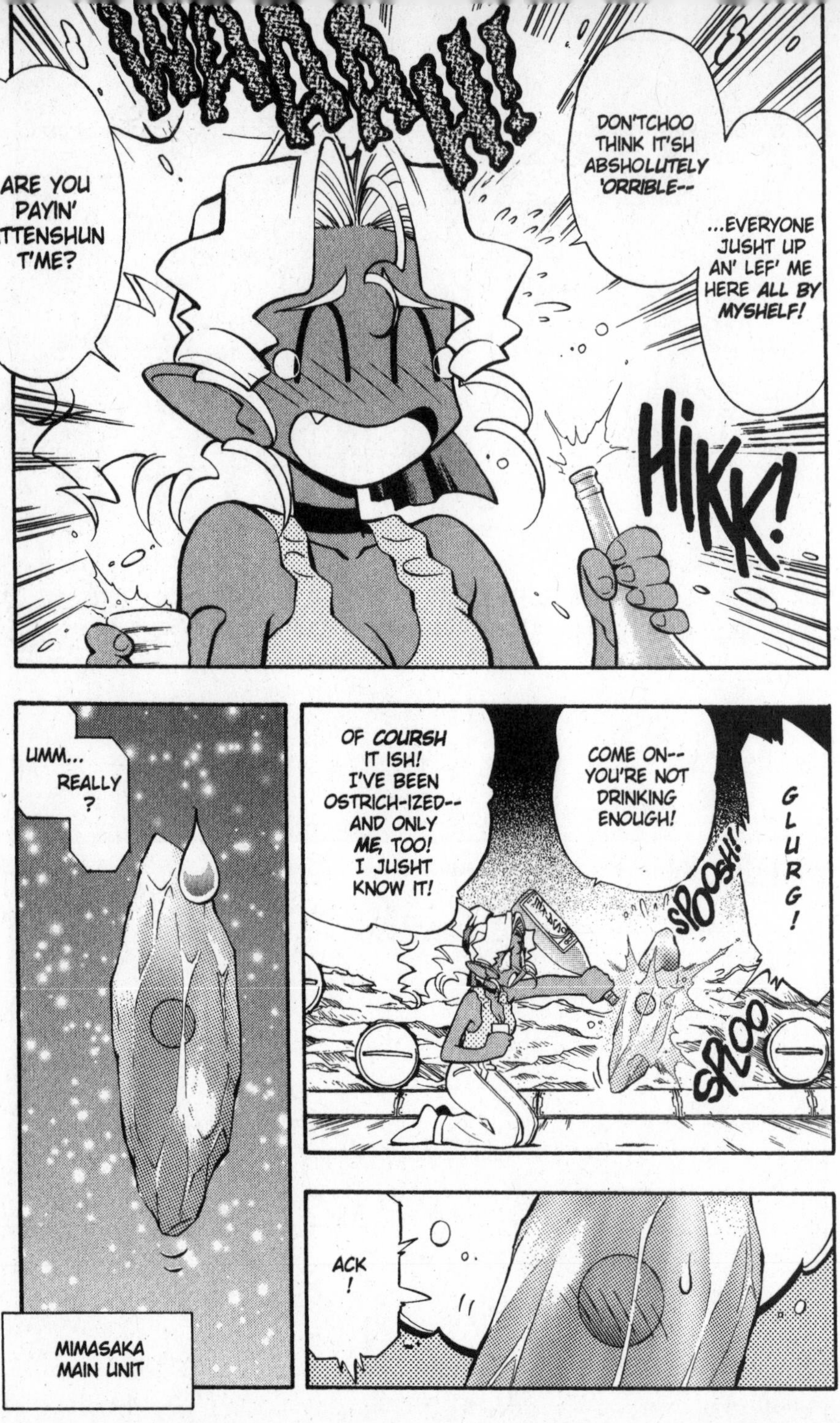
WAAAAH!
ARE YOU PAYIN' ATTENSHUN T'ME?
DON'TCHOO THINK IT'SH ABSHOLUTELY 'ORRIBLE--
...EVERYONE JUSHT UP AN' LEF' ME HERE ALL BY MYSHELF!
HIKK!
UMM... REALLY?
MIMASAKA MAIN UNIT
OF COURSH IT ISH! I'VE BEEN OSTRICH-IZED-- AND ONLY ME, TOO! I JUSHT KNOW IT!
COME ON-- YOU'RE NOT DRINKING ENOUGH!
SPOOSH!
GLURG!
SPLOO
ACK!

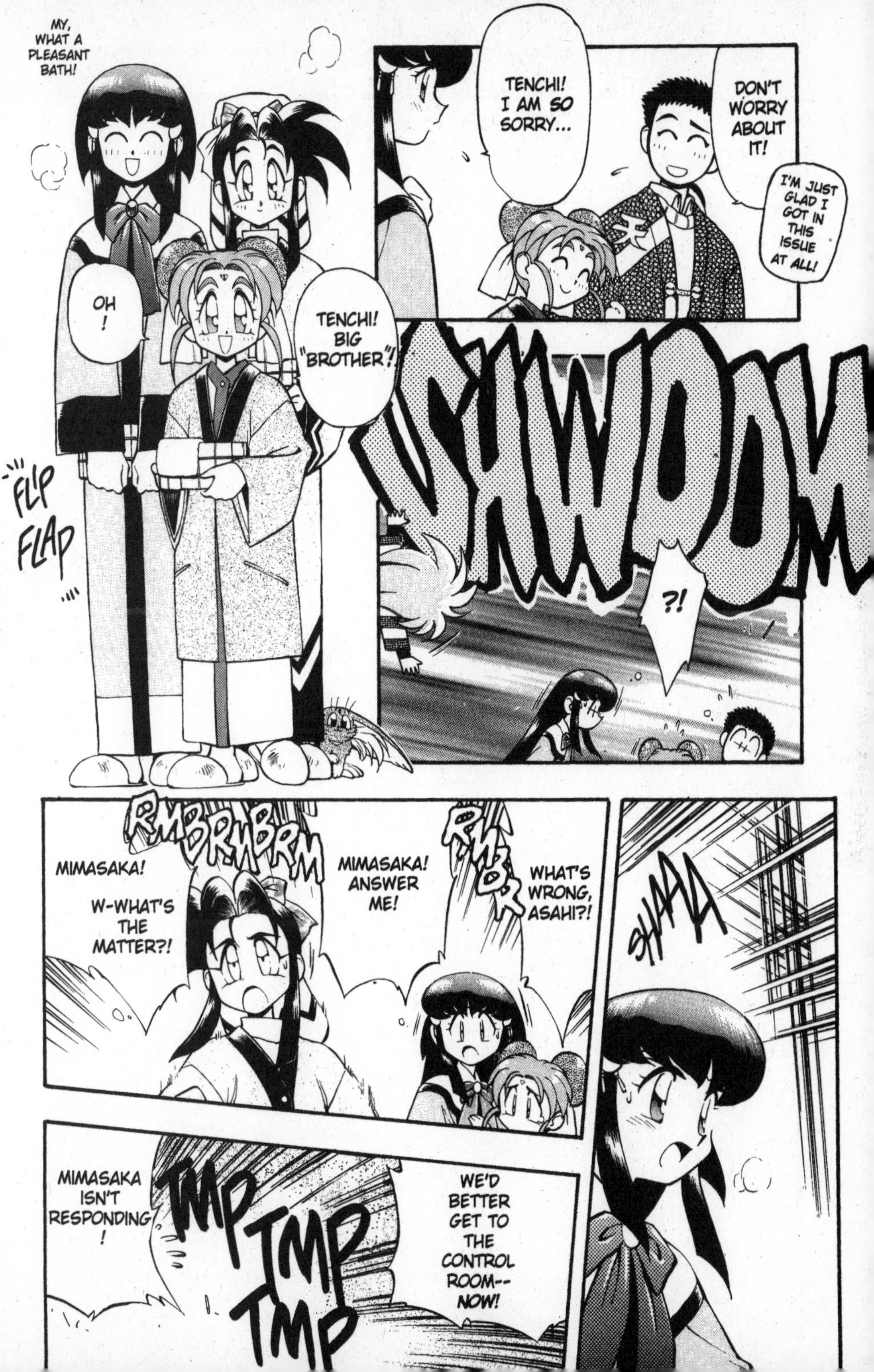
MY, WHAT A PLEASANT BATH!
OH!
TENCHI! BIG "BROTHER"!
FLIP FLAP
TENCHI! I AM SO SORRY...
DON'T WORRY ABOUT IT!
I'M JUST GLAD I GOT IN THIS ISSUE AT ALL!
SHWOOM
?!
RMBRMBRM
MIMASAKA!
W-WHAT'S THE MATTER?!
MIMASAKA! ANSWER ME!
RMB
WHAT'S WRONG, ASAHI?!
MIMASAKA ISN'T RESPONDING!
TMP TMP TMP
WE'D BETTER GET TO THE CONTROL ROOM-- NOW!
SHAAA

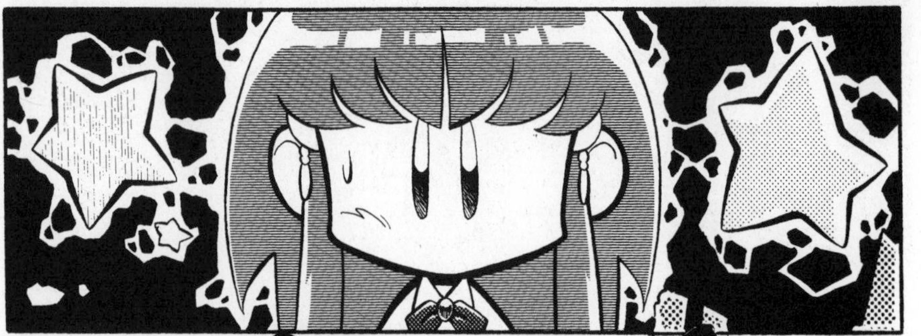

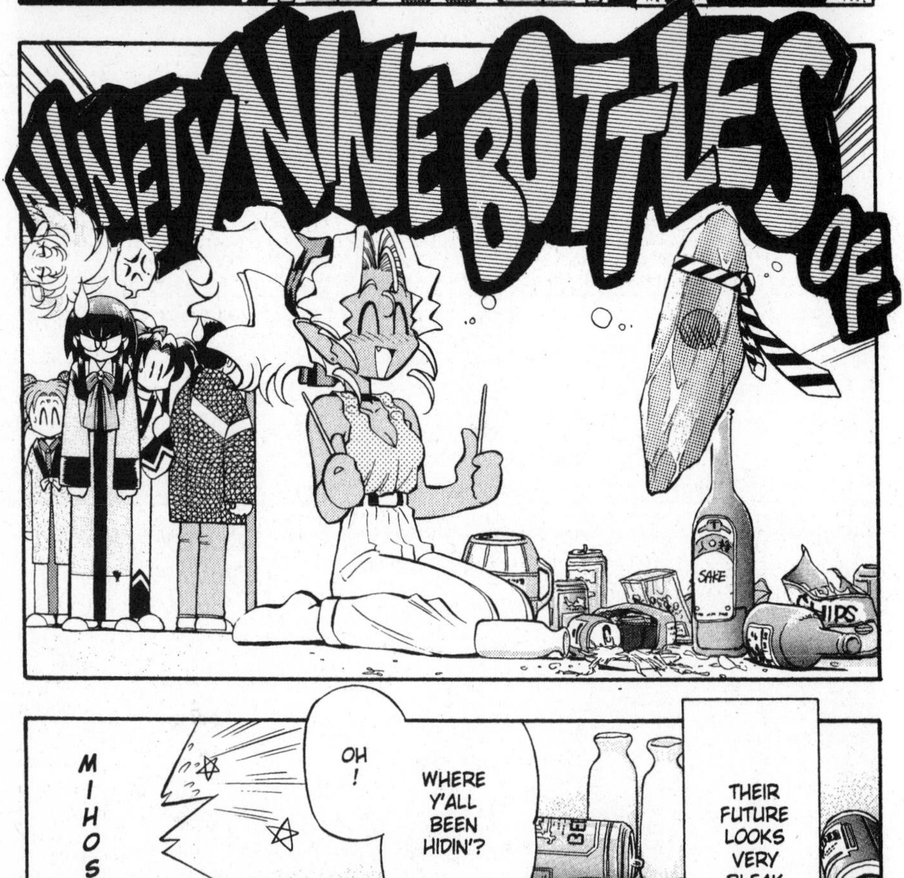
NINETY NINE BOTTLES OF.
SAKE
CHIPS

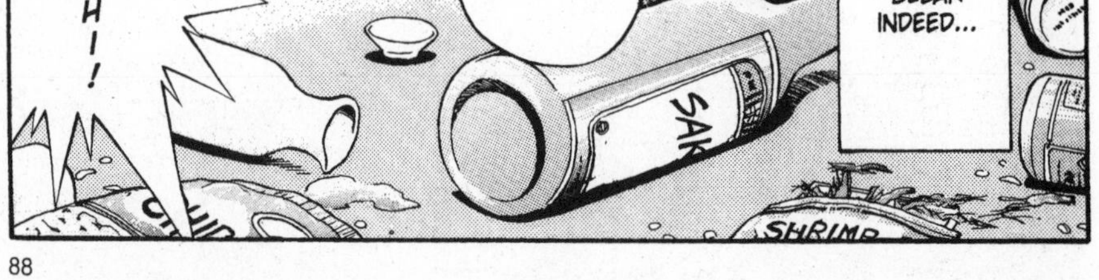
MIHOSHI!
OH!
WHERE Y'ALL BEEN HIDIN'?
THEIR FUTURE LOOKS VERY BLEAK INDEED...
SAK
SHRIMP

Tales of Tenchi #4

TYRANNY'S TORMENT

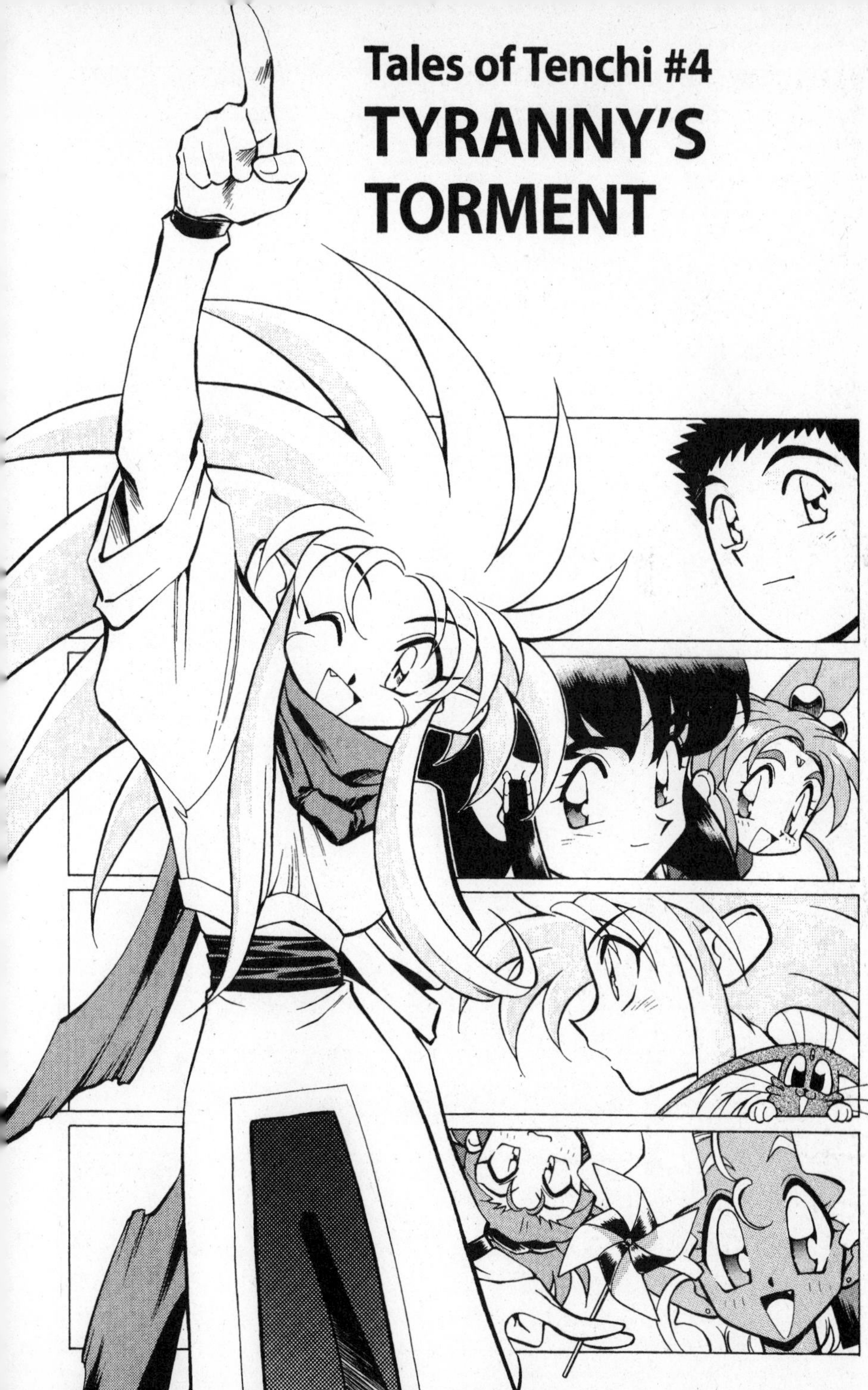

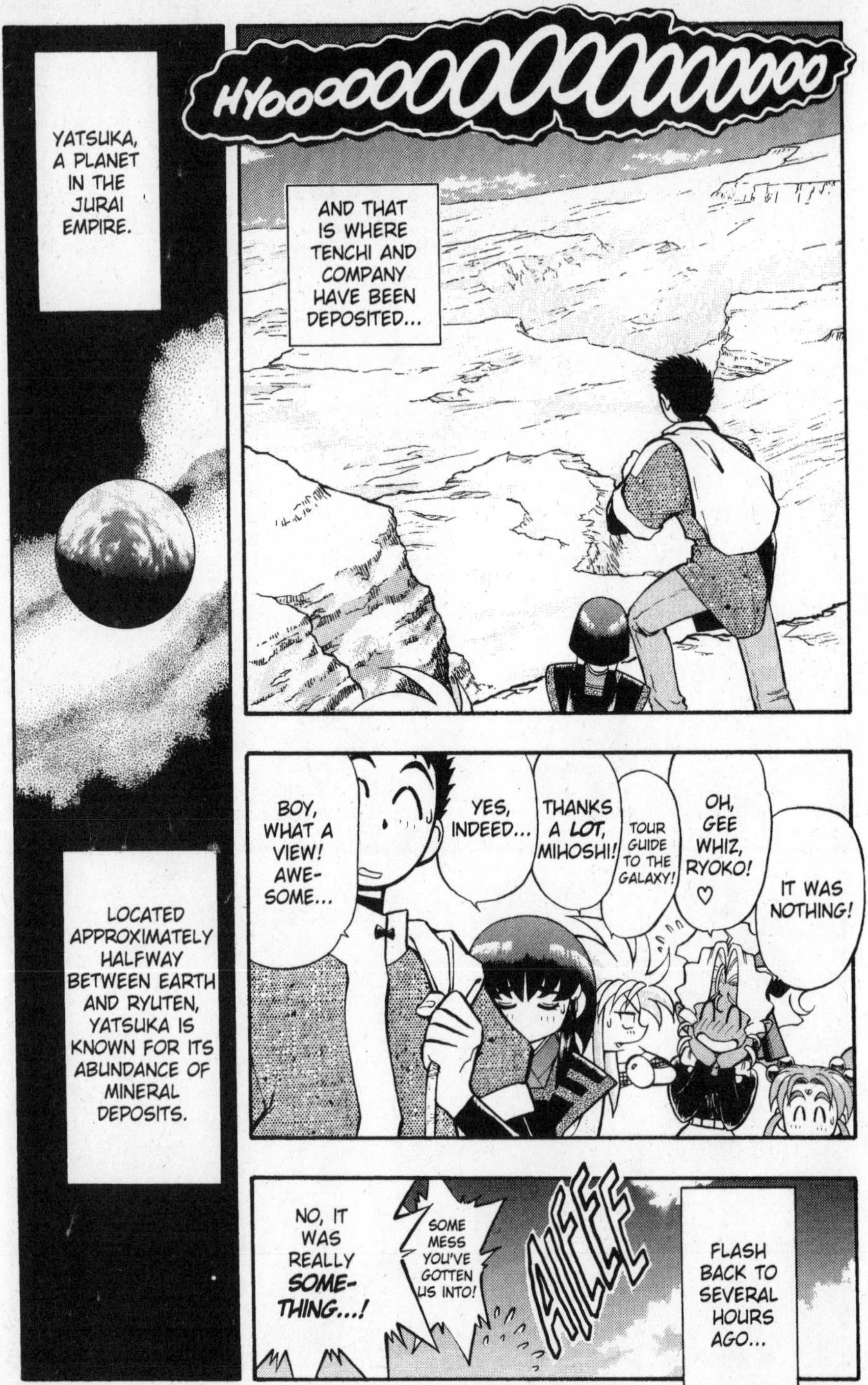
YATSUKA, A PLANET IN THE JURAI EMPIRE.
LOCATED APPROXIMATELY HALFWAY BETWEEN EARTH AND RYUTEN, YATSUKA IS KNOWN FOR ITS ABUNDANCE OF MINERAL DEPOSITS.
HYOOOOOOOOOOOOOOOOO
AND THAT IS WHERE TENCHI AND COMPANY HAVE BEEN DEPOSITED...
BOY, WHAT A VIEW! AWE-SOME...
YES, INDEED...
THANKS A **LOT**, MIHOSHI!
TOUR GUIDE TO THE GALAXY!
OH, GEE WHIZ, RYOKO! ♡
IT WAS NOTHING!
NO, IT WAS REALLY **SOME-THING...!**
SOME MESS YOU'VE GOTTEN US INTO!
AIEEE
FLASH BACK TO SEVERAL HOURS AGO...

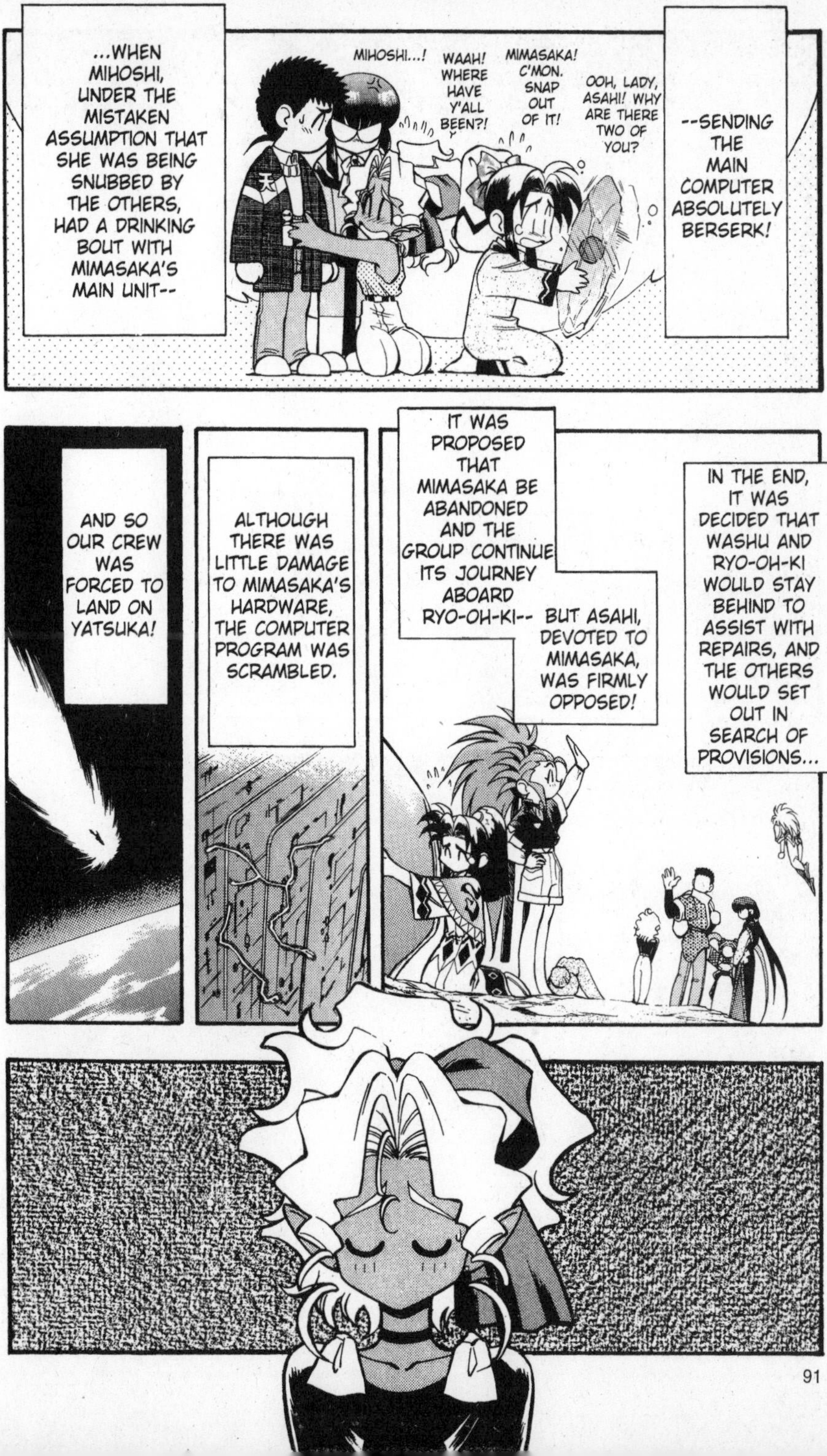
...WHEN MIHOSHI, UNDER THE MISTAKEN ASSUMPTION THAT SHE WAS BEING SNUBBED BY THE OTHERS, HAD A DRINKING BOUT WITH MIMASAKA'S MAIN UNIT--
MIHOSHI...!
WAAH! WHERE HAVE Y'ALL BEEN?!
MIMASAKA! C'MON. SNAP OUT OF IT!
OOH, LADY, ASAHI! WHY ARE THERE TWO OF YOU?
--SENDING THE MAIN COMPUTER ABSOLUTELY BERSERK!
AND SO OUR CREW WAS FORCED TO LAND ON YATSUKA!
ALTHOUGH THERE WAS LITTLE DAMAGE TO MIMASAKA'S HARDWARE, THE COMPUTER PROGRAM WAS SCRAMBLED.
IT WAS PROPOSED THAT MIMASAKA BE ABANDONED AND THE GROUP CONTINUE ITS JOURNEY ABOARD RYO-OH-KI--
BUT ASAHI, DEVOTED TO MIMASAKA, WAS FIRMLY OPPOSED!
IN THE END, IT WAS DECIDED THAT WASHU AND RYO-OH-KI WOULD STAY BEHIND TO ASSIST WITH REPAIRS, AND THE OTHERS WOULD SET OUT IN SEARCH OF PROVISIONS...

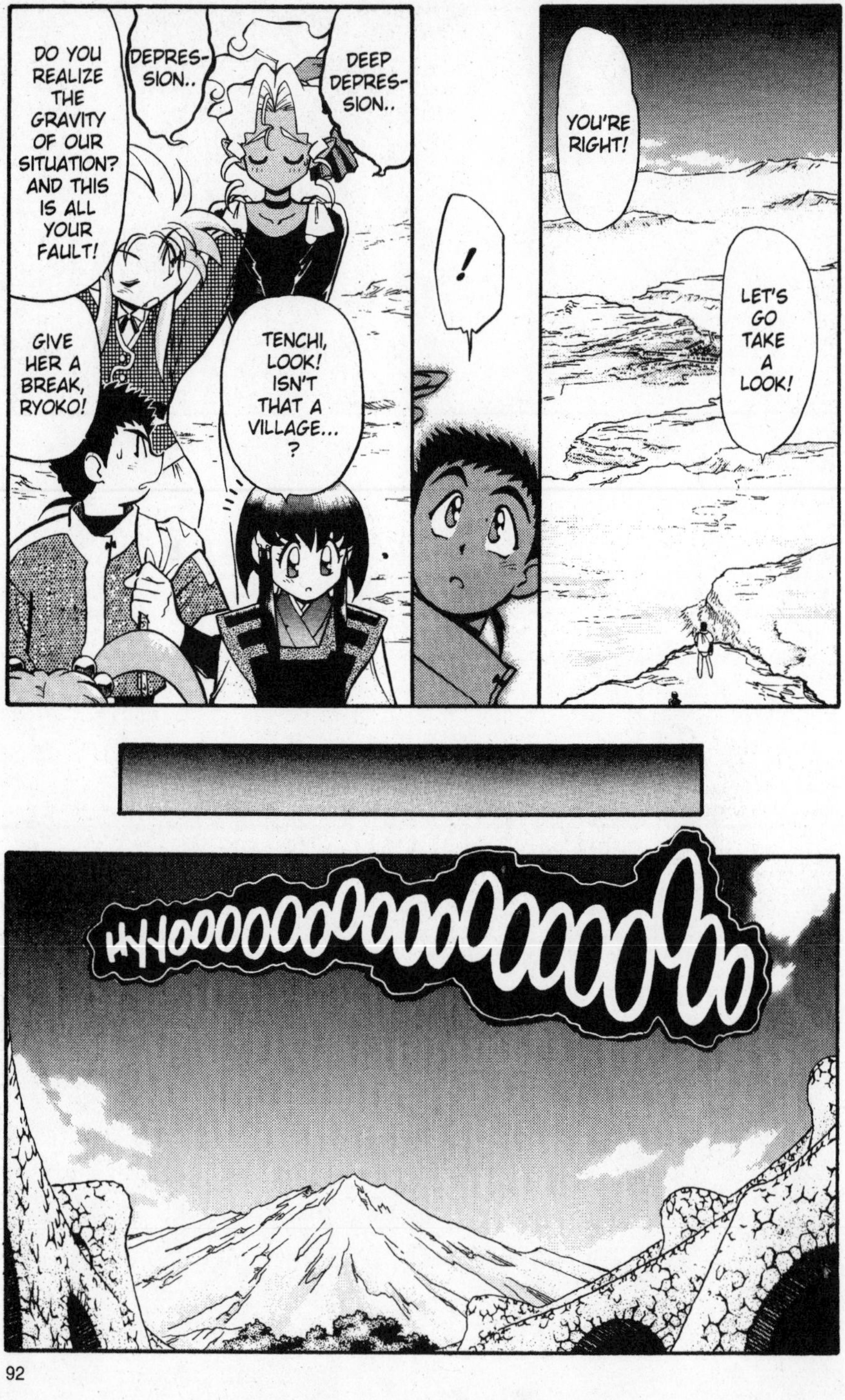
DO YOU REALIZE THE GRAVITY OF OUR SITUATION? AND THIS IS ALL YOUR FAULT!
DEPRES-SION..
DEEP DEPRES-SION..
GIVE HER A BREAK, RYOKO!
TENCHI, LOOK! ISN'T THAT A VILLAGE...?
!
YOU'RE RIGHT!
LET'S GO TAKE A LOOK!
HYYOOOOOOOOOOOOOOOOO

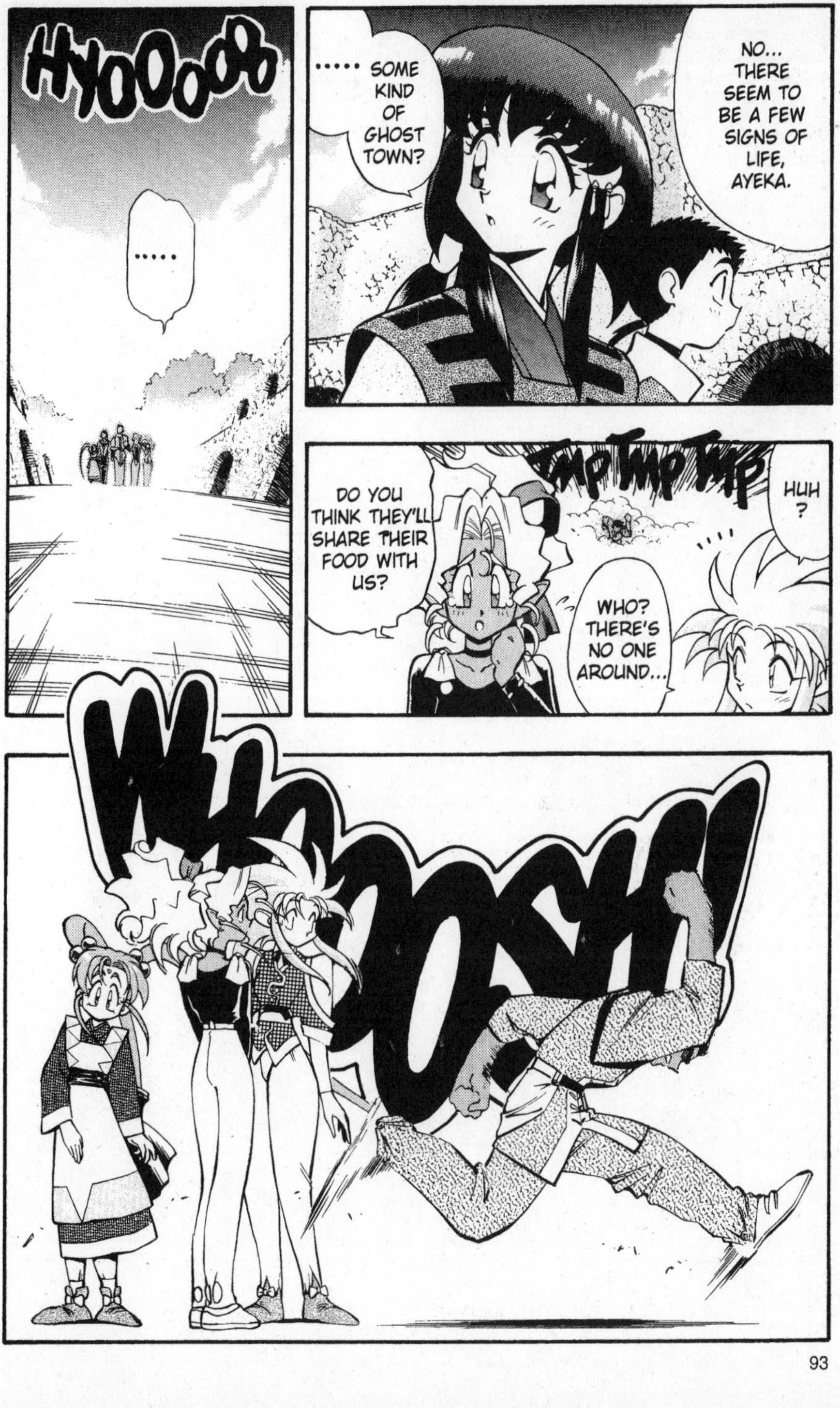
HYOOOOO
.....
..... SOME KIND OF GHOST TOWN?
NO... THERE SEEM TO BE A FEW SIGNS OF LIFE, AYEKA.
DO YOU THINK THEY'LL SHARE THEIR FOOD WITH US?
TMP TMP TMP
HUH?
WHO? THERE'S NO ONE AROUND...
WHOOSH!

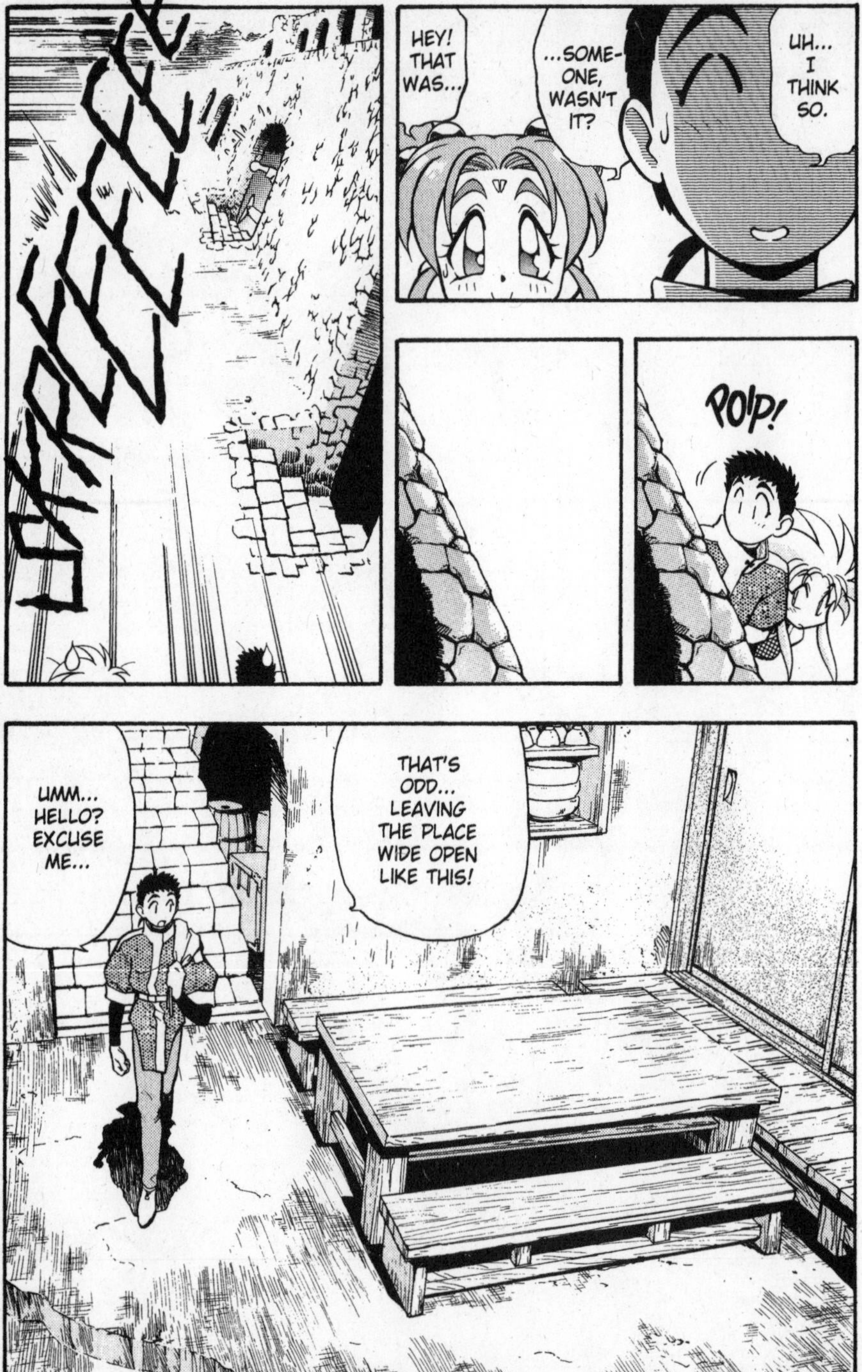
HEY! THAT WAS...
...SOME-ONE, WASN'T IT?
UH... I THINK SO.
POP!
UMM... HELLO? EXCUSE ME...
THAT'S ODD... LEAVING THE PLACE WIDE OPEN LIKE THIS!

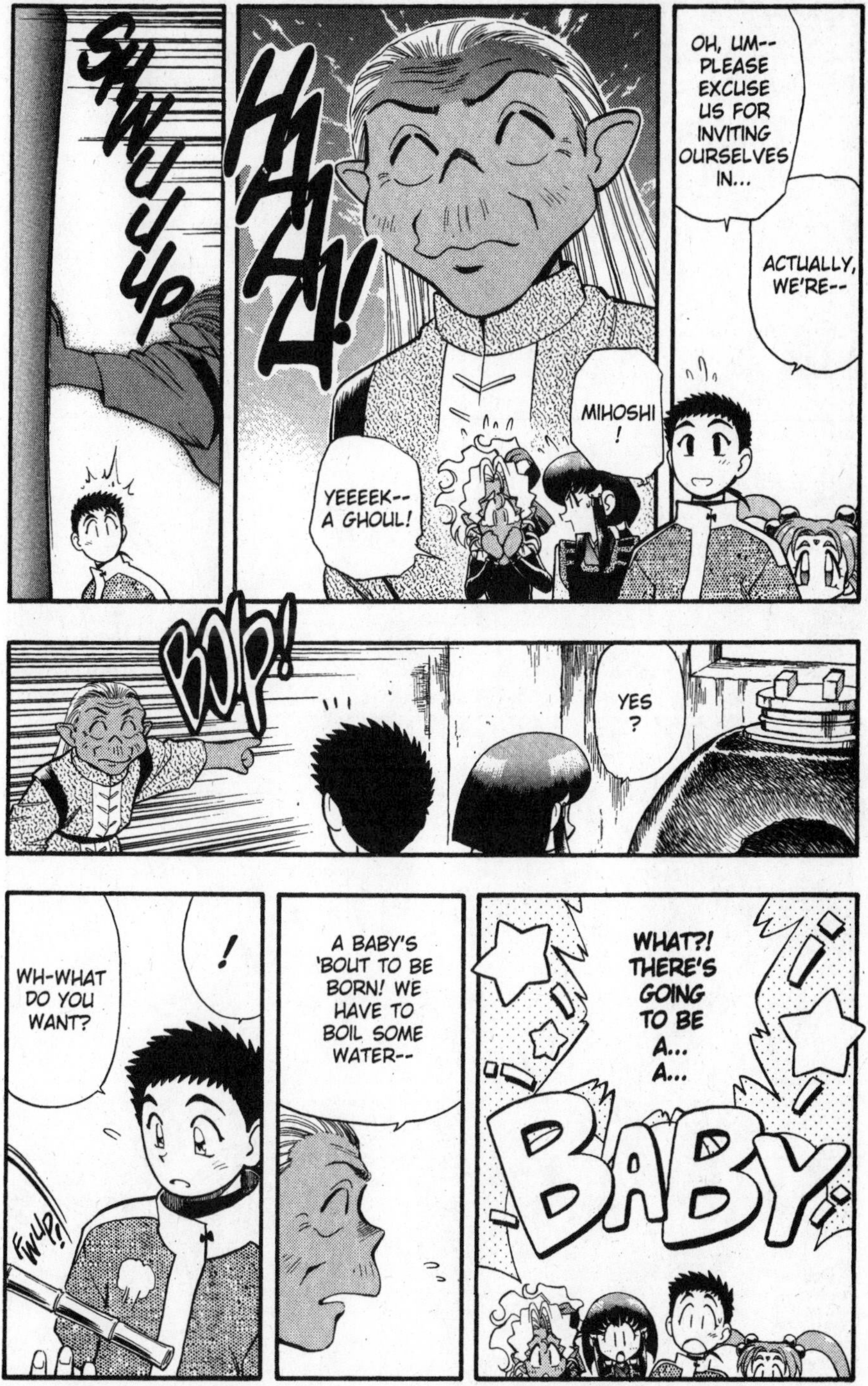
SHWUUUP
HAAA!
YEEEEK-- A GHOUL!
MIHOSHI!
OH, UM-- PLEASE EXCUSE US FOR INVITING OURSELVES IN...
ACTUALLY, WE'RE--
BOP!
YES?
WH-WHAT DO YOU WANT?
!
FWUP!
A BABY'S 'BOUT TO BE BORN! WE HAVE TO BOIL SOME WATER--
WHAT?! THERE'S GOING TO BE A... A...
BABY!

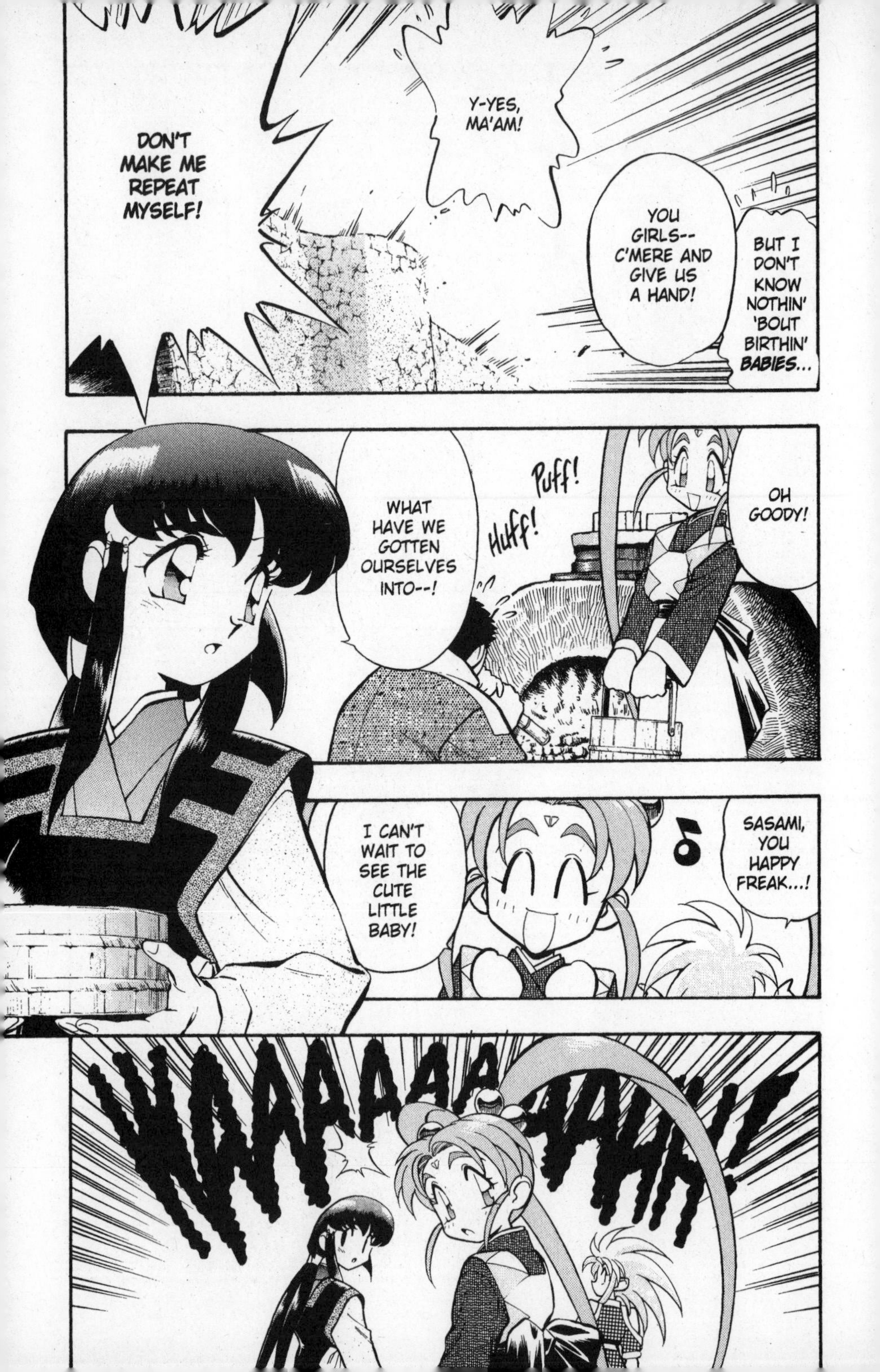
DON'T MAKE ME REPEAT MYSELF!
Y-YES, MA'AM!
YOU GIRLS-- C'MERE AND GIVE US A HAND!
BUT I DON'T KNOW NOTHIN' 'BOUT BIRTHIN' BABIES...
WHAT HAVE WE GOTTEN OURSELVES INTO--!
Puff!
Huff!
OH GOODY!
I CAN'T WAIT TO SEE THE CUTE LITTLE BABY!
SASAMI, YOU HAPPY FREAK...!
WAAAAAAAHH!

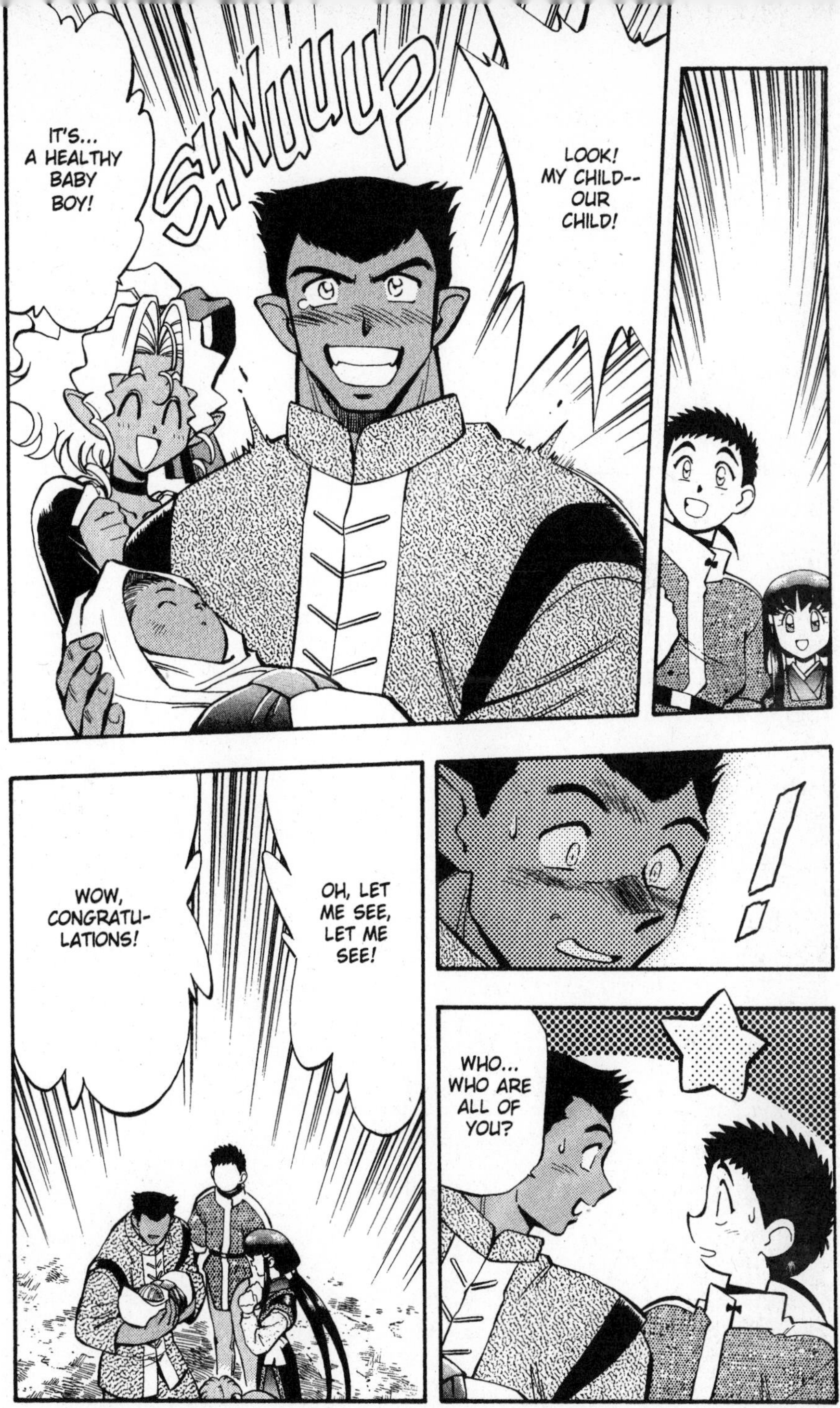
IT'S... A HEALTHY BABY BOY!
SHWUUUP
LOOK! MY CHILD-- OUR CHILD!
WOW, CONGRATU-LATIONS!
OH, LET ME SEE, LET ME SEE!
!
WHO... WHO ARE ALL OF YOU?

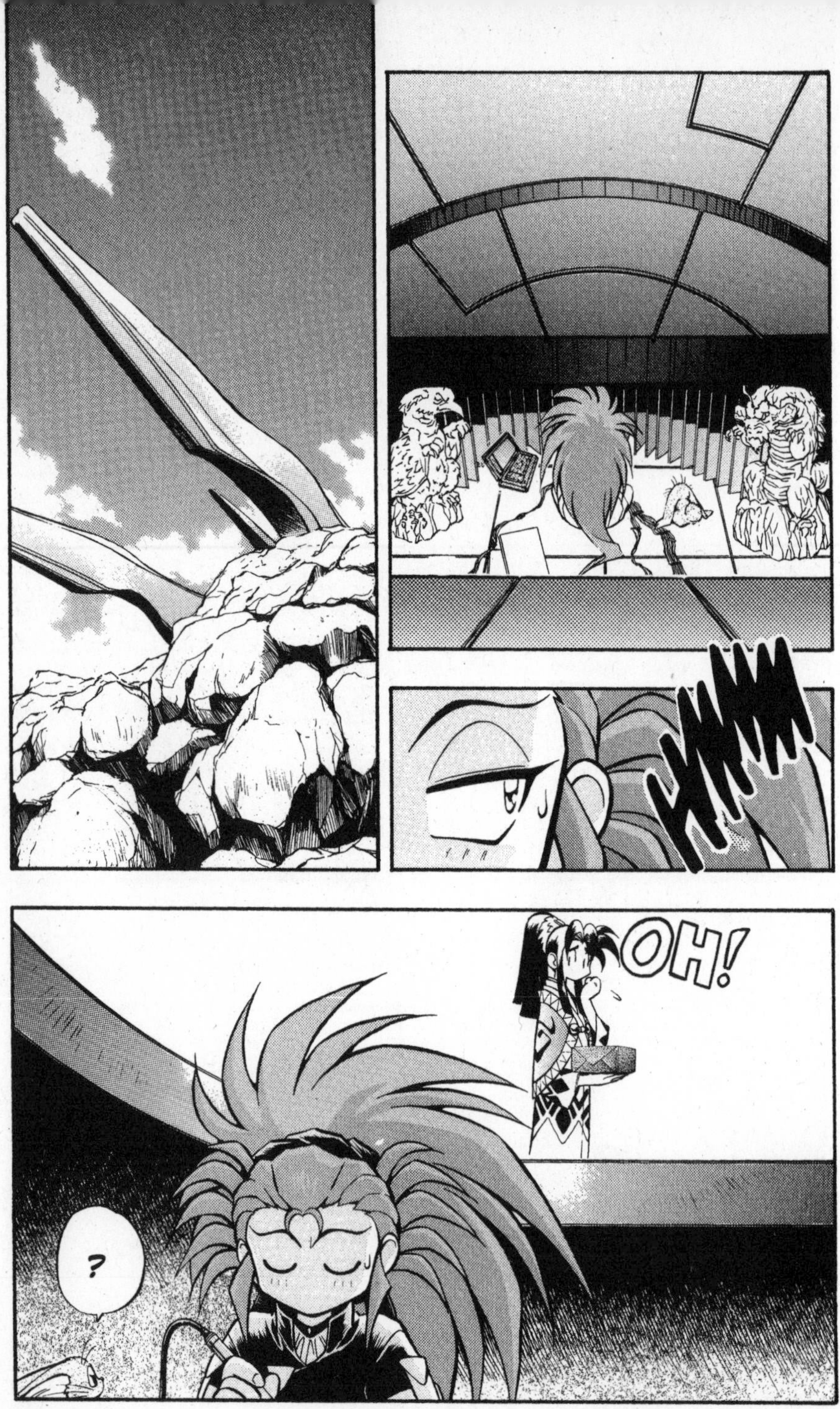
HMMM
OH!
?

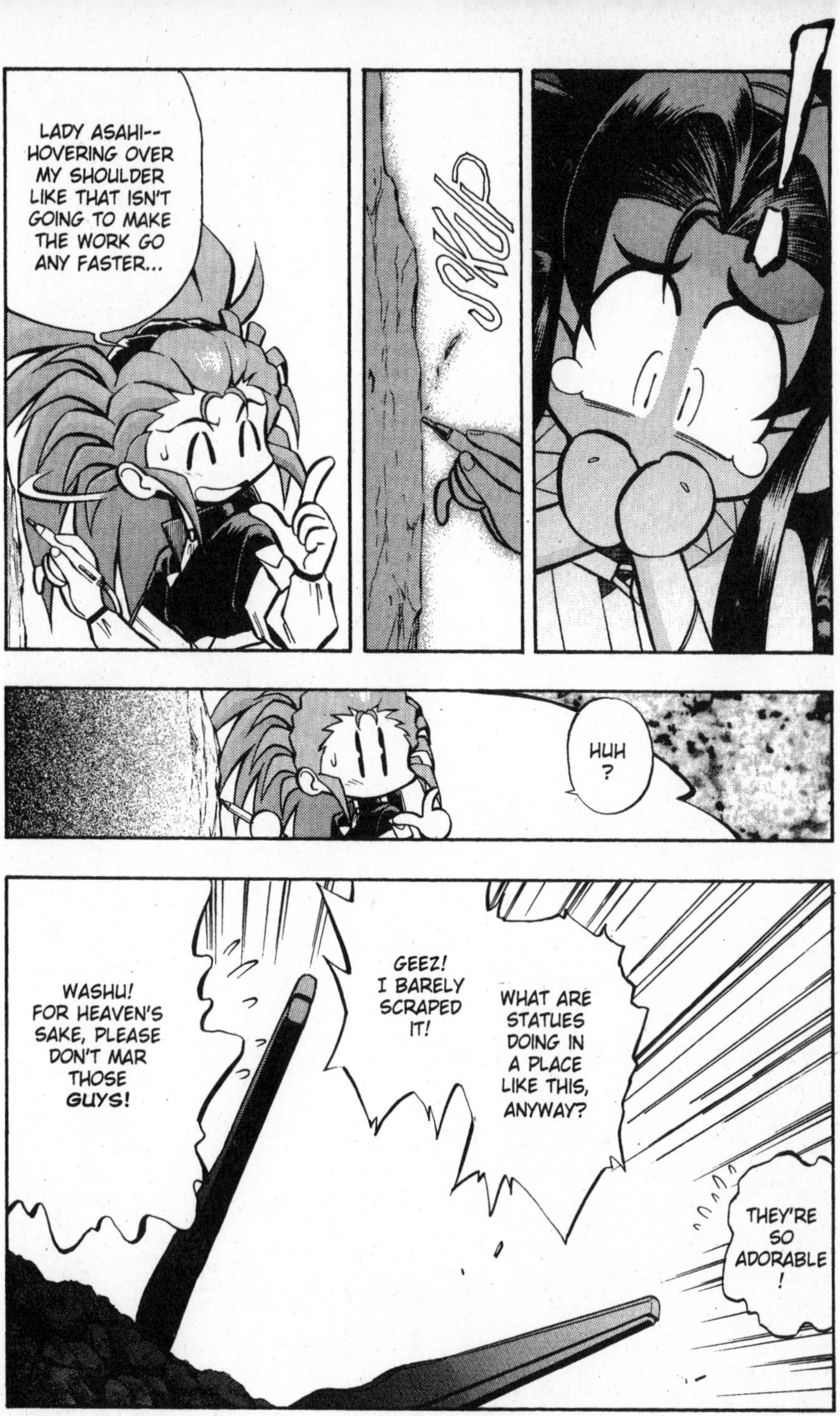
LADY ASAHI-- HOVERING OVER MY SHOULDER LIKE THAT ISN'T GOING TO MAKE THE WORK GO ANY FASTER...
SKLIP
HUH ?
WASHU! FOR HEAVEN'S SAKE, PLEASE DON'T MAR THOSE GUYS!
GEEZ! I BARELY SCRAPED IT!
WHAT ARE STATUES DOING IN A PLACE LIKE THIS, ANYWAY?
THEY'RE SO ADORABLE !

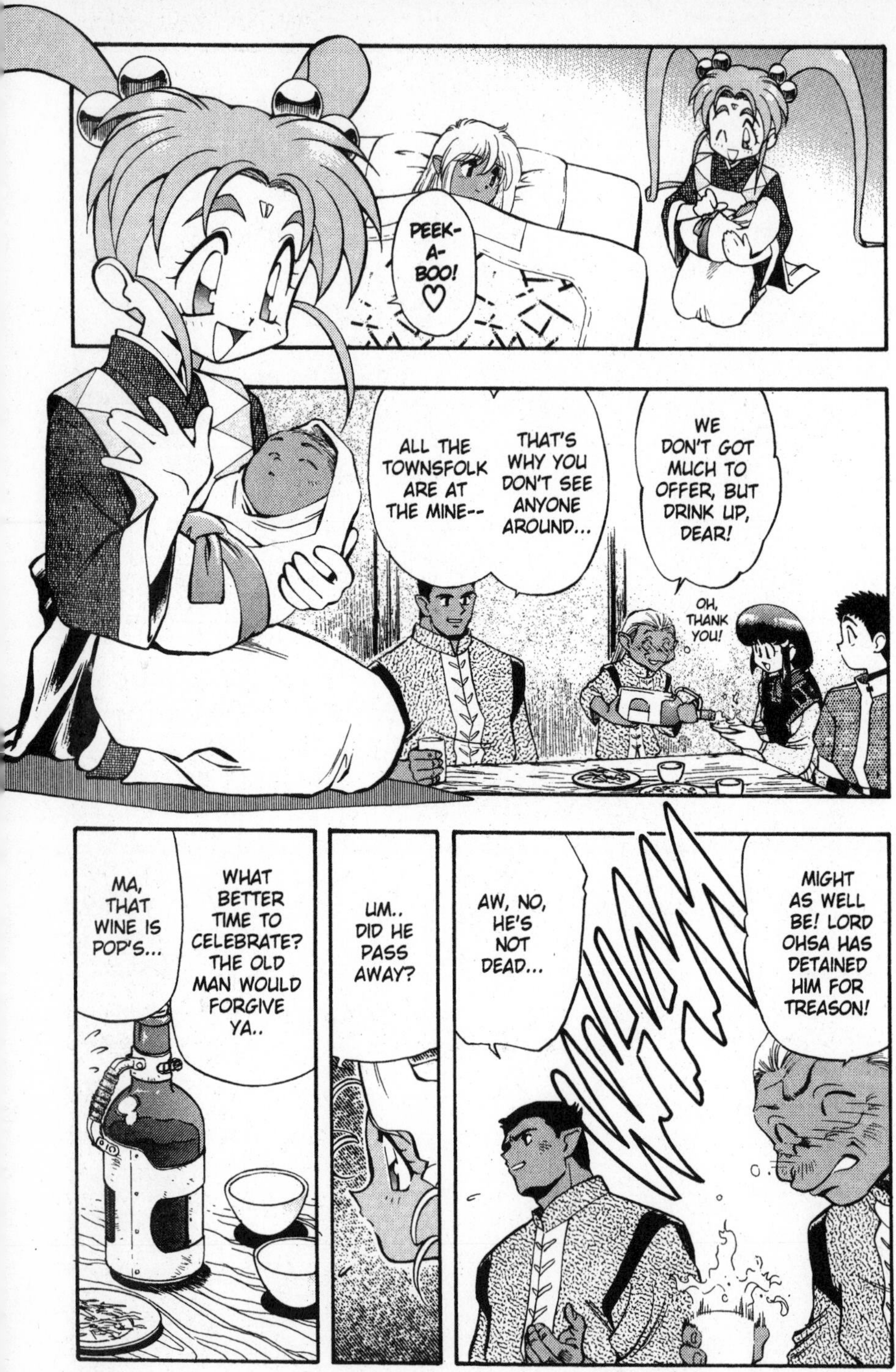
PEEK-A-BOO! ♡
ALL THE TOWNSFOLK ARE AT THE MINE--
THAT'S WHY YOU DON'T SEE ANYONE AROUND...
WE DON'T GOT MUCH TO OFFER, BUT DRINK UP, DEAR!
OH, THANK YOU!
MA, THAT WINE IS POP'S...
WHAT BETTER TIME TO CELEBRATE? THE OLD MAN WOULD FORGIVE YA..
UM.. DID HE PASS AWAY?
AW, NO, HE'S NOT DEAD...
MIGHT AS WELL BE! LORD OHSA HAS DETAINED HIM FOR TREASON!

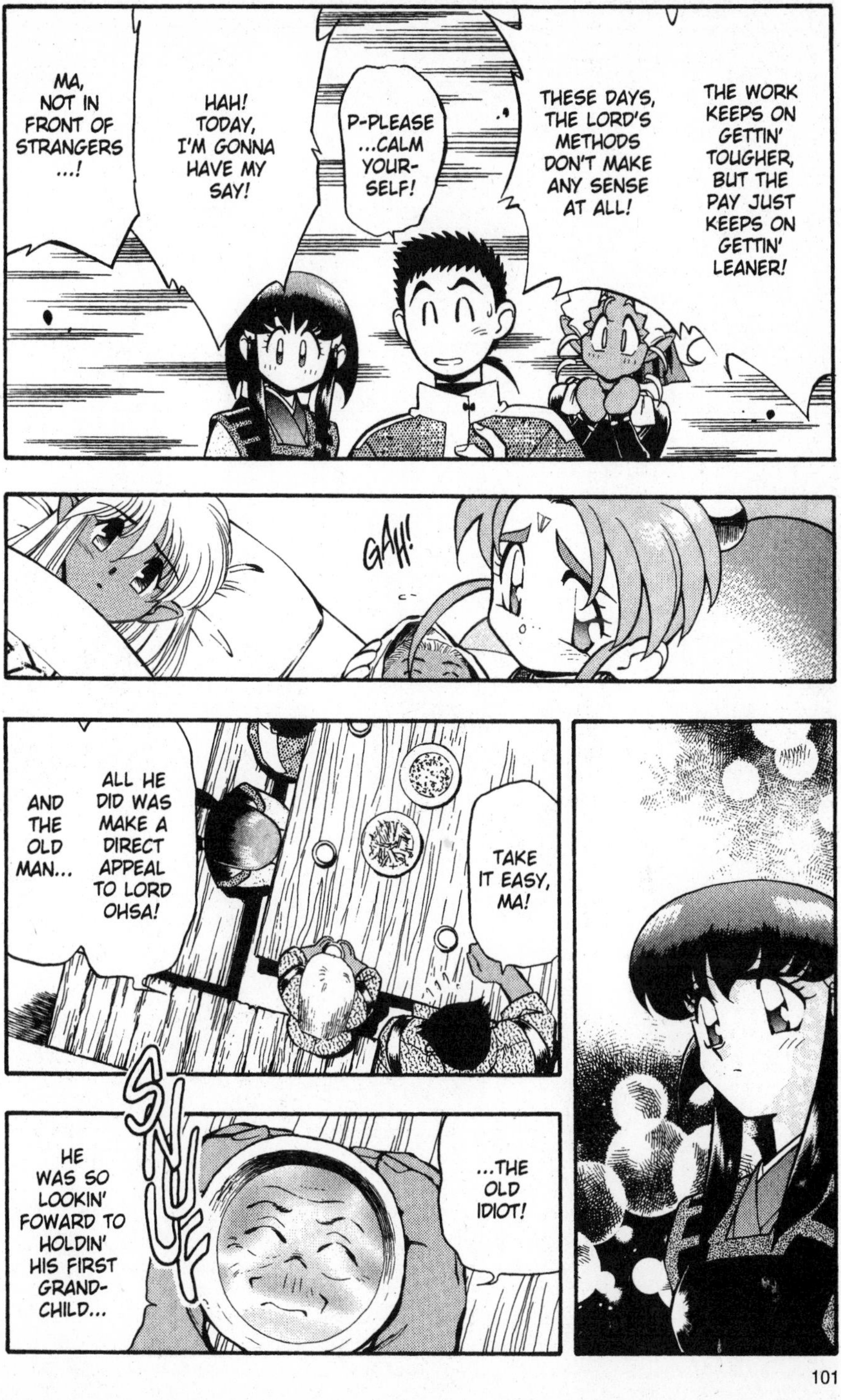
MA, NOT IN FRONT OF STRANGERS ...!
HAH! TODAY, I'M GONNA HAVE MY SAY!
P-PLEASE ...CALM YOURSELF!
THESE DAYS, THE LORD'S METHODS DON'T MAKE ANY SENSE AT ALL!
THE WORK KEEPS ON GETTIN' TOUGHER, BUT THE PAY JUST KEEPS ON GETTIN' LEANER!
GAH!
AND THE OLD MAN...
ALL HE DID WAS MAKE A DIRECT APPEAL TO LORD OHSA!
TAKE IT EASY, MA!
HE WAS SO LOOKIN' FOWARD TO HOLDIN' HIS FIRST GRAND-CHILD...
SNIFF
...THE OLD IDIOT!

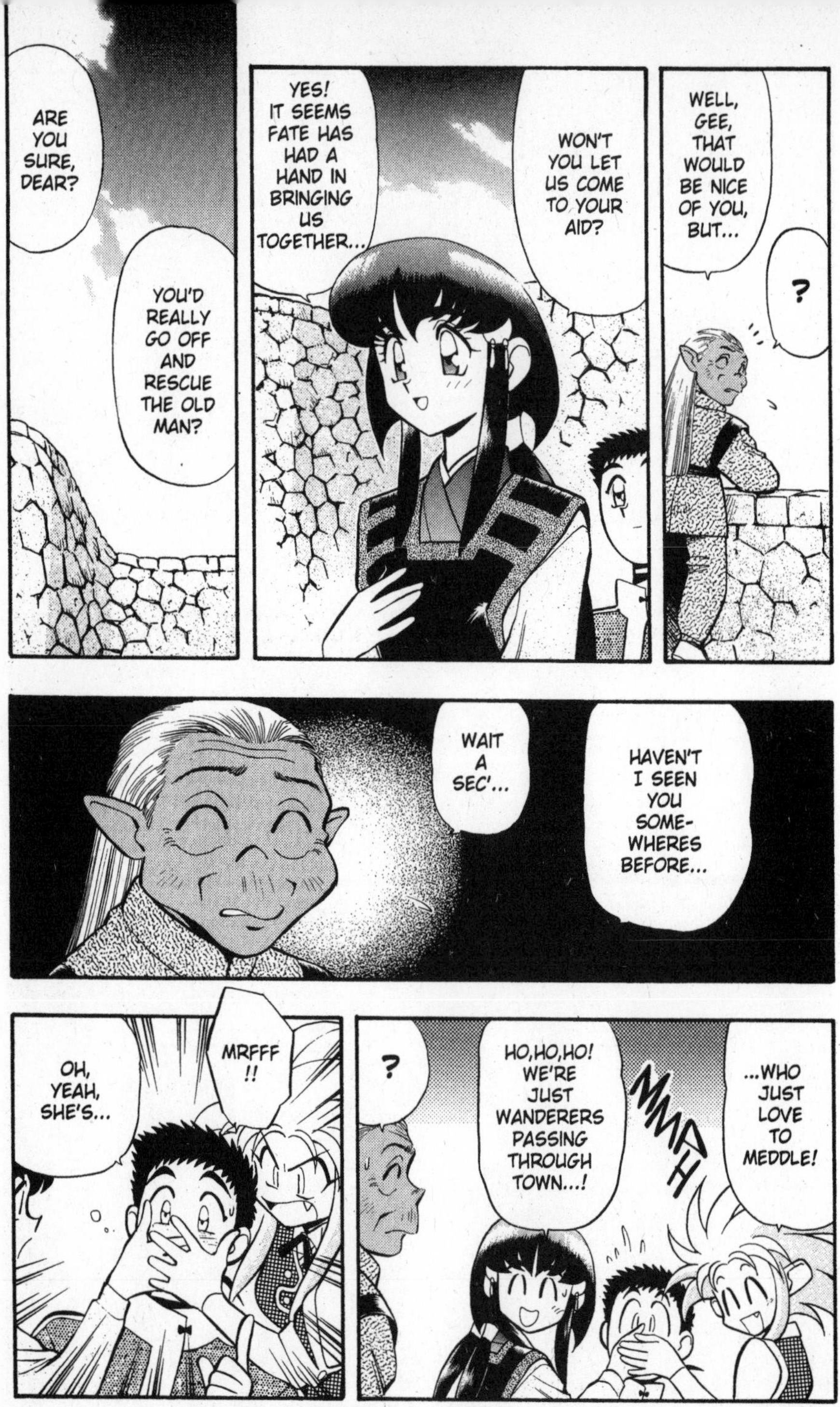
ARE YOU SURE, DEAR?
YOU'D REALLY GO OFF AND RESCUE THE OLD MAN?
YES! IT SEEMS FATE HAS HAD A HAND IN BRINGING US TOGETHER...
WON'T YOU LET US COME TO YOUR AID?
WELL, GEE, THAT WOULD BE NICE OF YOU, BUT...
?
WAIT A SEC'...
HAVEN'T I SEEN YOU SOME-WHERES BEFORE...
OH, YEAH, SHE'S...
MRFFF !!
?
HO,HO,HO! WE'RE JUST WANDERERS PASSING THROUGH TOWN...!
MMPH
...WHO JUST LOVE TO MEDDLE!

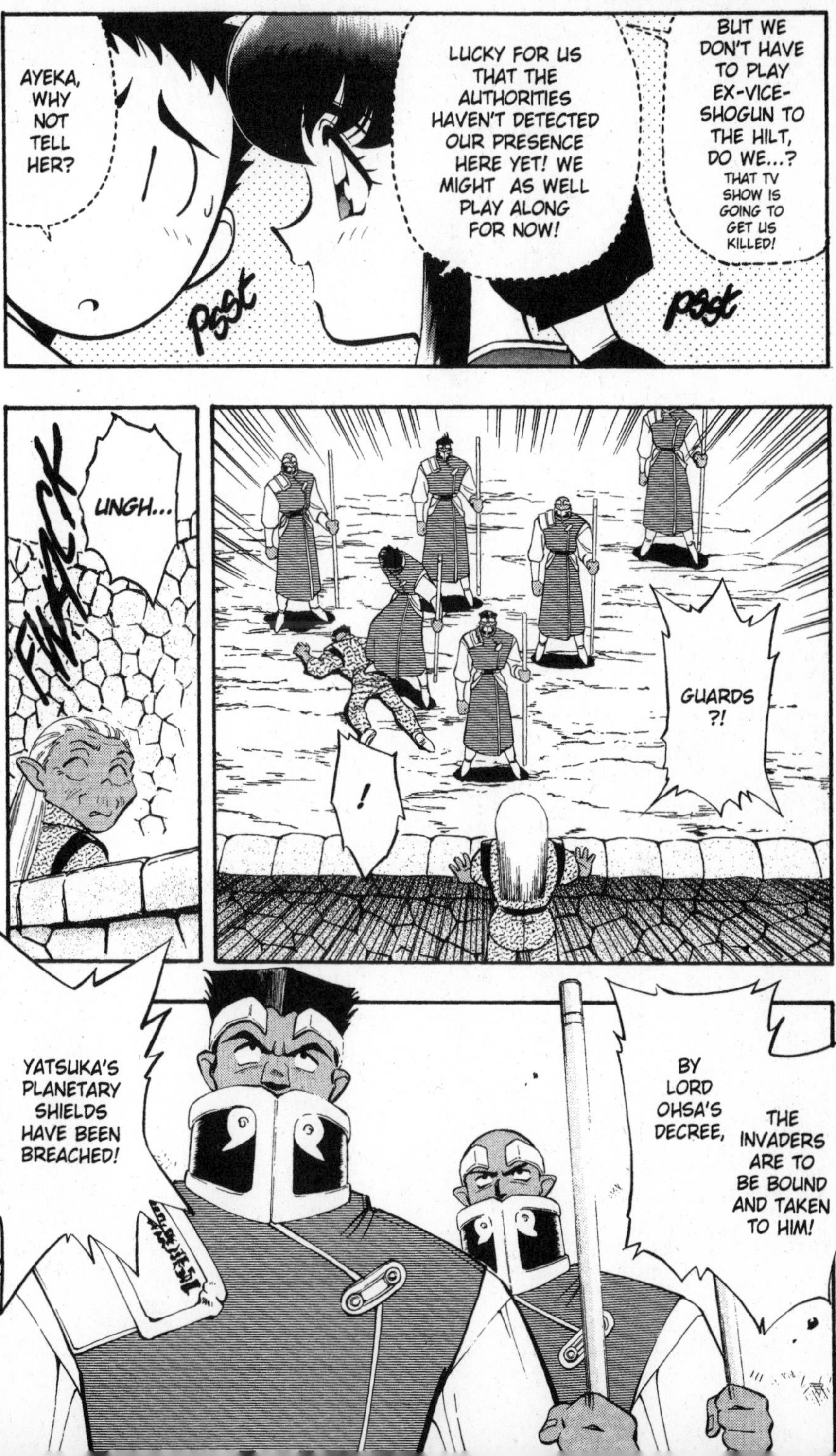
AYEKA, WHY NOT TELL HER?
LUCKY FOR US THAT THE AUTHORITIES HAVEN'T DETECTED OUR PRESENCE HERE YET! WE MIGHT AS WELL PLAY ALONG FOR NOW!
BUT WE DON'T HAVE TO PLAY EX-VICE-SHOGUN TO THE HILT, DO WE...?
THAT TV SHOW IS GOING TO GET US KILLED!
psst
psst
FWACK
UNGH...
GUARDS ?!
!
YATSUKA'S PLANETARY SHIELDS HAVE BEEN BREACHED!
BY LORD OHSA'S DECREE,
THE INVADERS ARE TO BE BOUND AND TAKEN TO HIM!

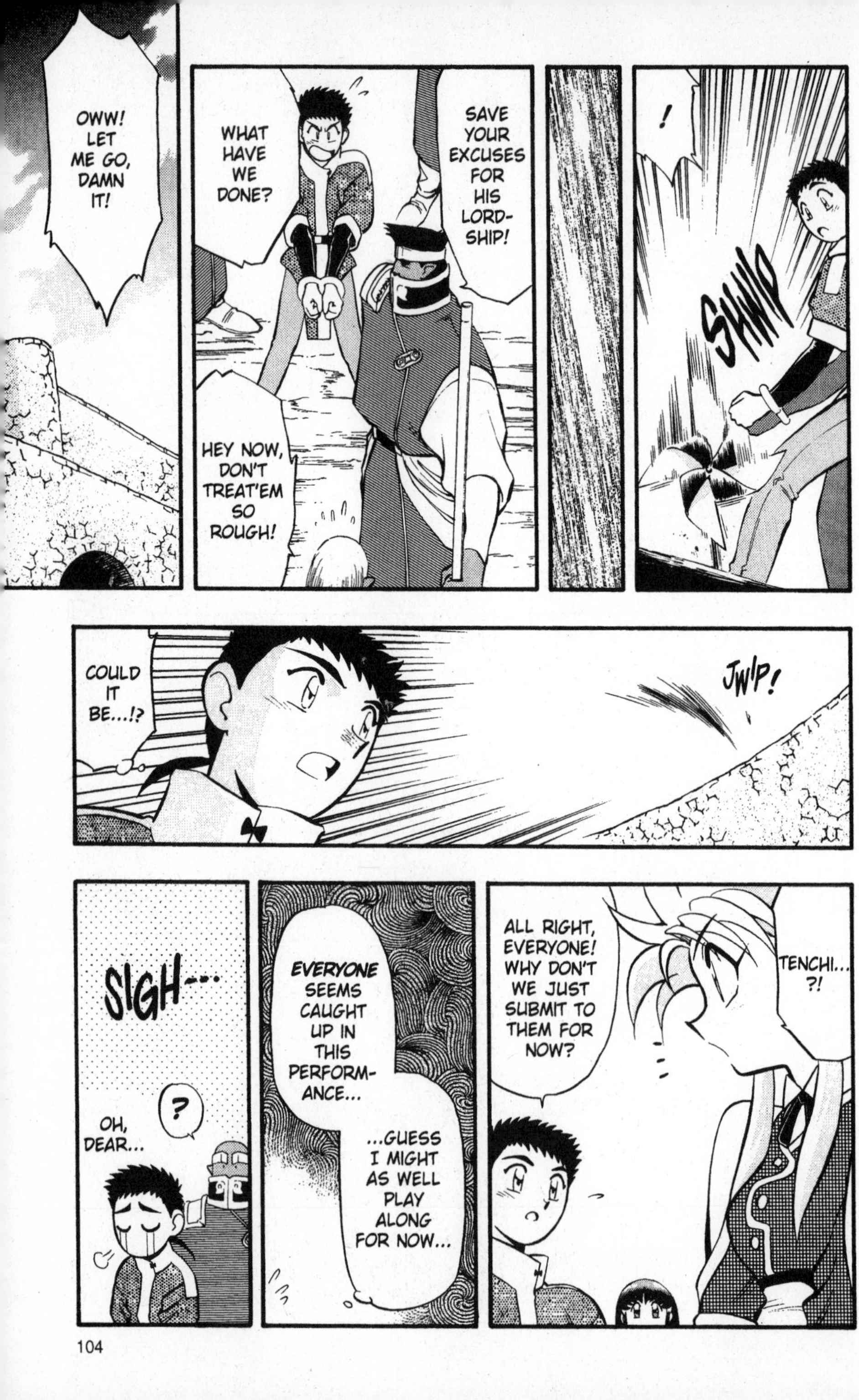
OWW! LET ME GO, DAMN IT!
WHAT HAVE WE DONE?
SAVE YOUR EXCUSES FOR HIS LORDSHIP!
HEY NOW, DON'T TREAT'EM SO ROUGH!
!
SHWIP
COULD IT BE...!?
JWIP!
SIGH...
OH, DEAR...
?
EVERYONE SEEMS CAUGHT UP IN THIS PERFORMANCE...
...GUESS I MIGHT AS WELL PLAY ALONG FOR NOW...
ALL RIGHT, EVERYONE! WHY DON'T WE JUST SUBMIT TO THEM FOR NOW?
TENCHI...?!

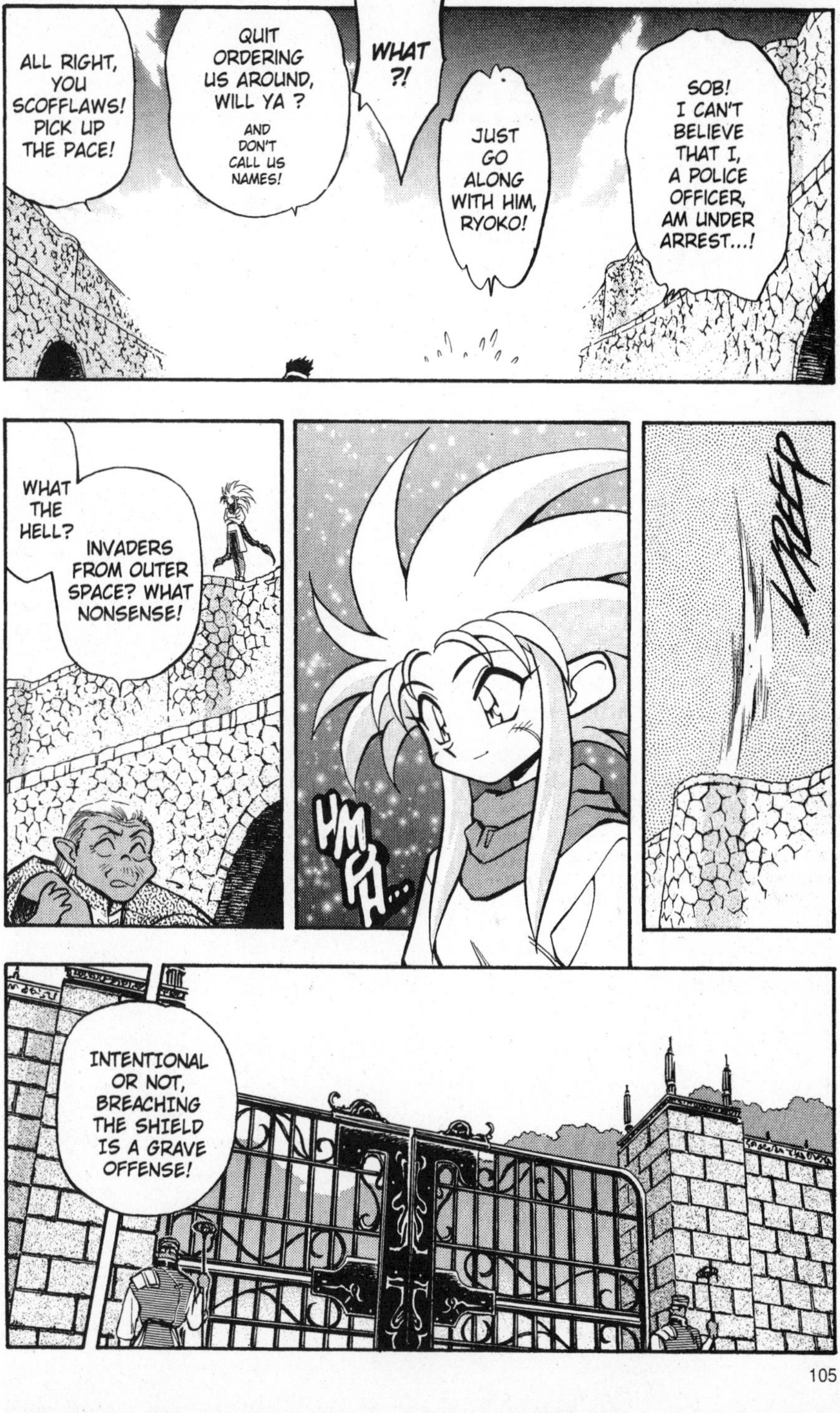
ALL RIGHT, YOU SCOFFLAWS! PICK UP THE PACE!
QUIT ORDERING US AROUND, WILL YA ?
AND DON'T CALL US NAMES!
WHAT ?!
JUST GO ALONG WITH HIM, RYOKO!
SOB! I CAN'T BELIEVE THAT I, A POLICE OFFICER, AM UNDER ARREST...!
WHAT THE HELL?
INVADERS FROM OUTER SPACE? WHAT NONSENSE!
INTENTIONAL OR NOT, BREACHING THE SHIELD IS A GRAVE OFFENSE!

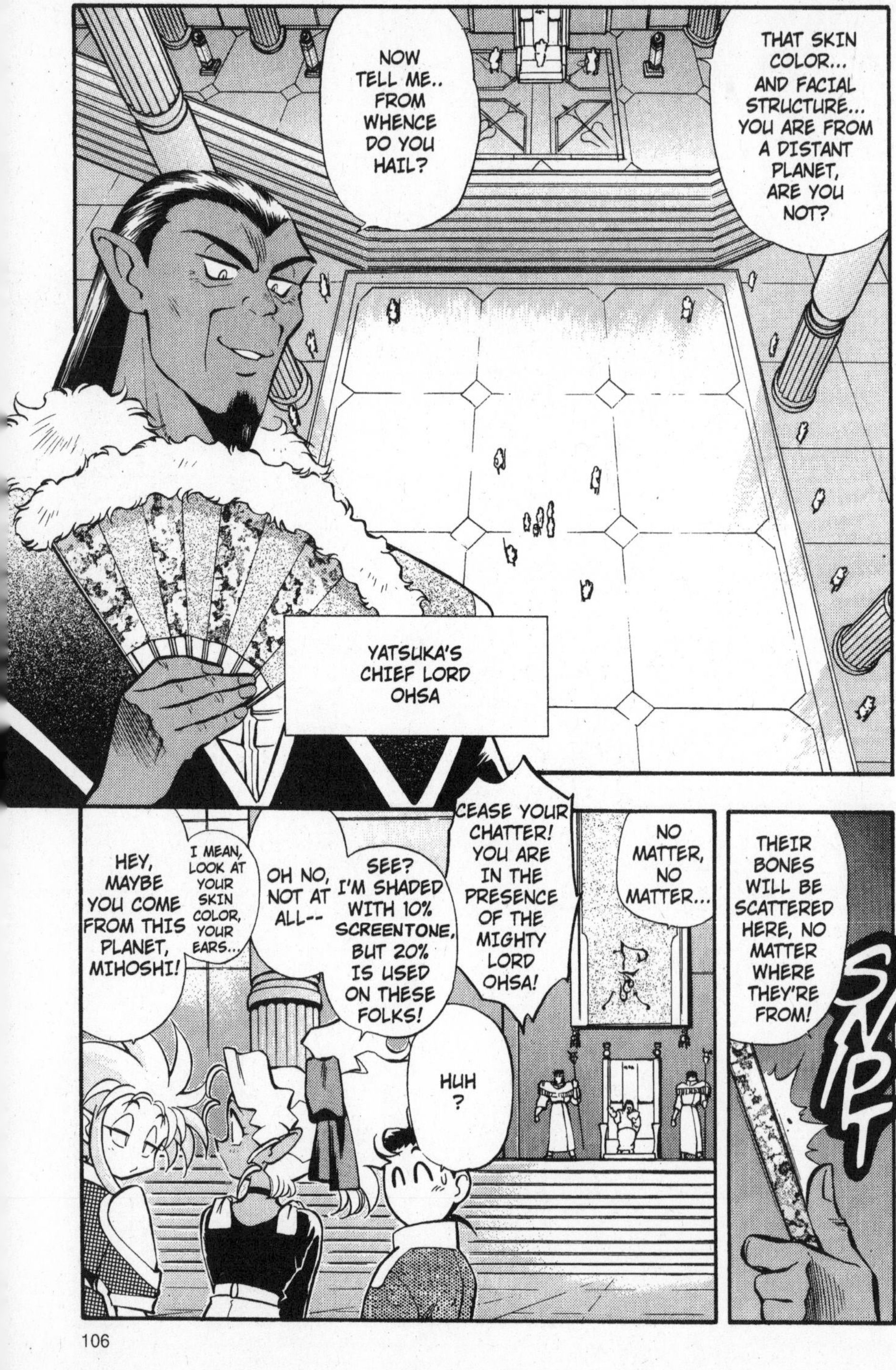
NOW TELL ME.. FROM WHENCE DO YOU HAIL?
THAT SKIN COLOR... AND FACIAL STRUCTURE... YOU ARE FROM A DISTANT PLANET, ARE YOU NOT?
YATSUKA'S CHIEF LORD OHSA
HEY, MAYBE YOU COME FROM THIS PLANET, MIHOSHI!
I MEAN, LOOK AT YOUR SKIN COLOR, YOUR EARS...
OH NO, NOT AT ALL--
SEE? I'M SHADED WITH 10% SCREENTONE, BUT 20% IS USED ON THESE FOLKS!
HUH ?
CEASE YOUR CHATTER! YOU ARE IN THE PRESENCE OF THE MIGHTY LORD OHSA!
NO MATTER, NO MATTER...
THEIR BONES WILL BE SCATTERED HERE, NO MATTER WHERE THEY'RE FROM!
SNAP

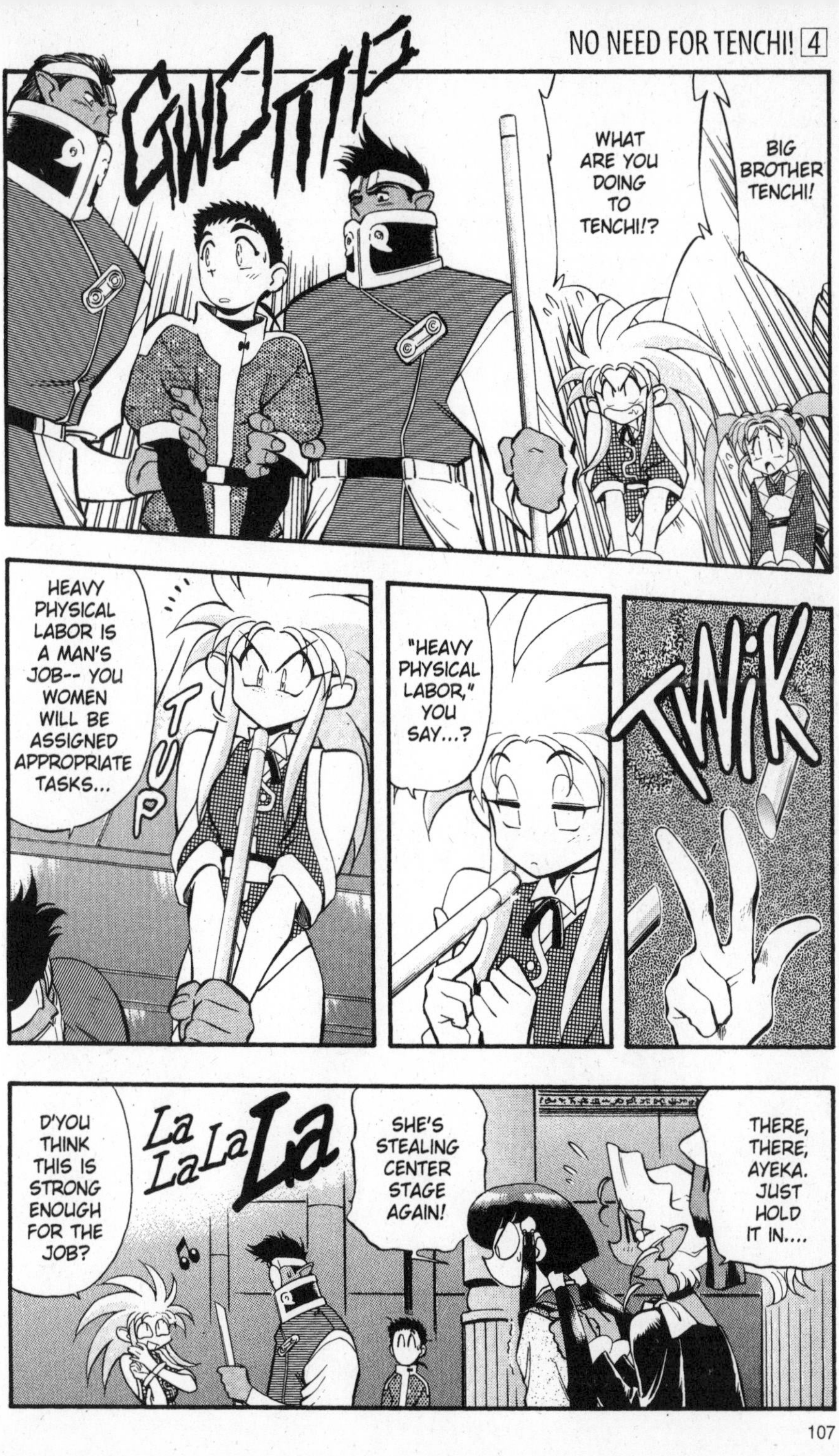
GWOMMP
WHAT ARE YOU DOING TO TENCHI!?
BIG BROTHER TENCHI!
HEAVY PHYSICAL LABOR IS A MAN'S JOB-- YOU WOMEN WILL BE ASSIGNED APPROPRIATE TASKS...
TUP
"HEAVY PHYSICAL LABOR," YOU SAY...?
TWIK
D'YOU THINK THIS IS STRONG ENOUGH FOR THE JOB?
La La La La
SHE'S STEALING CENTER STAGE AGAIN!
THERE, THERE, AYEKA. JUST HOLD IT IN....

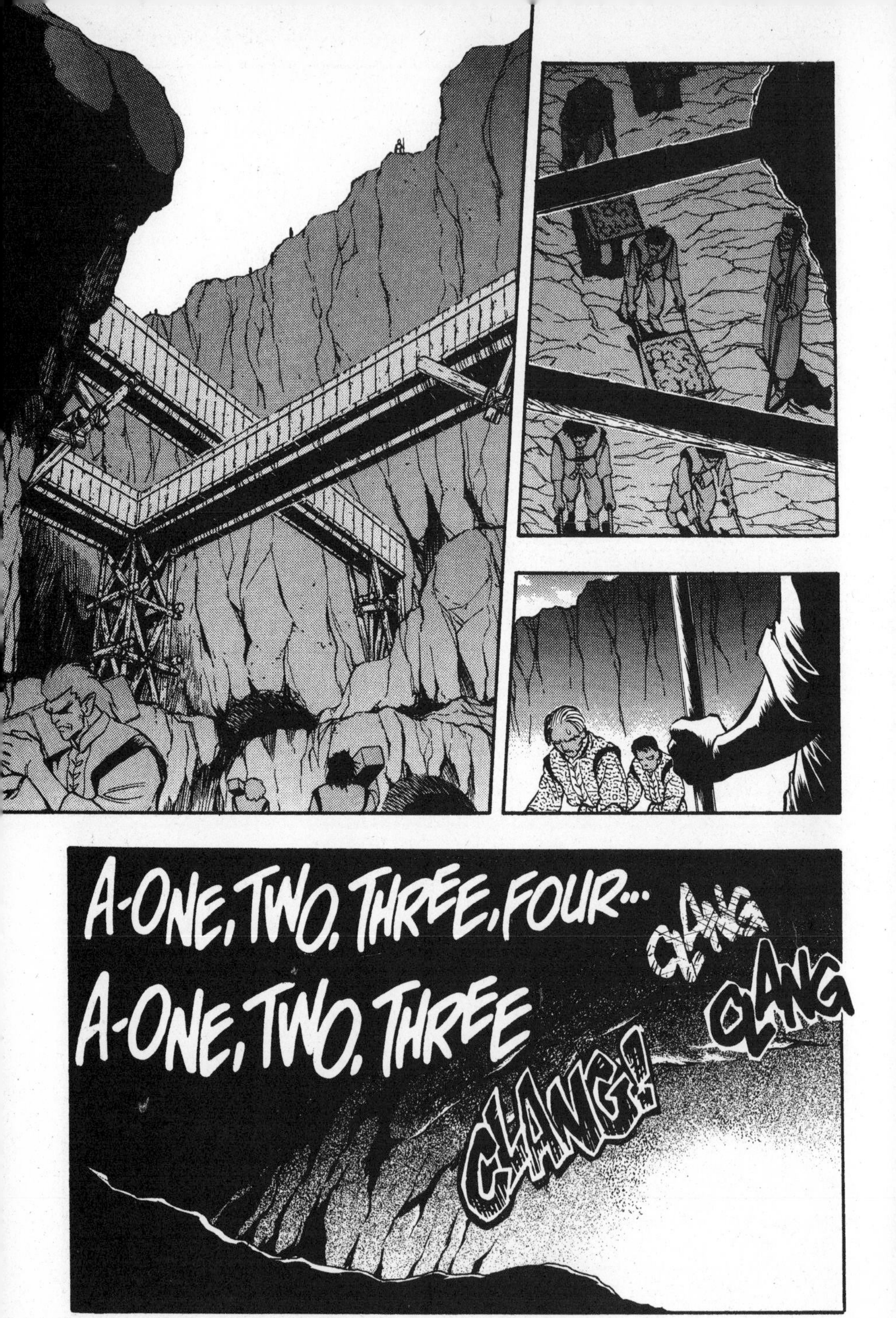
A-ONE, TWO, THREE, FOUR...
A-ONE, TWO, THREE
CLANG
CLANG
CLANG!

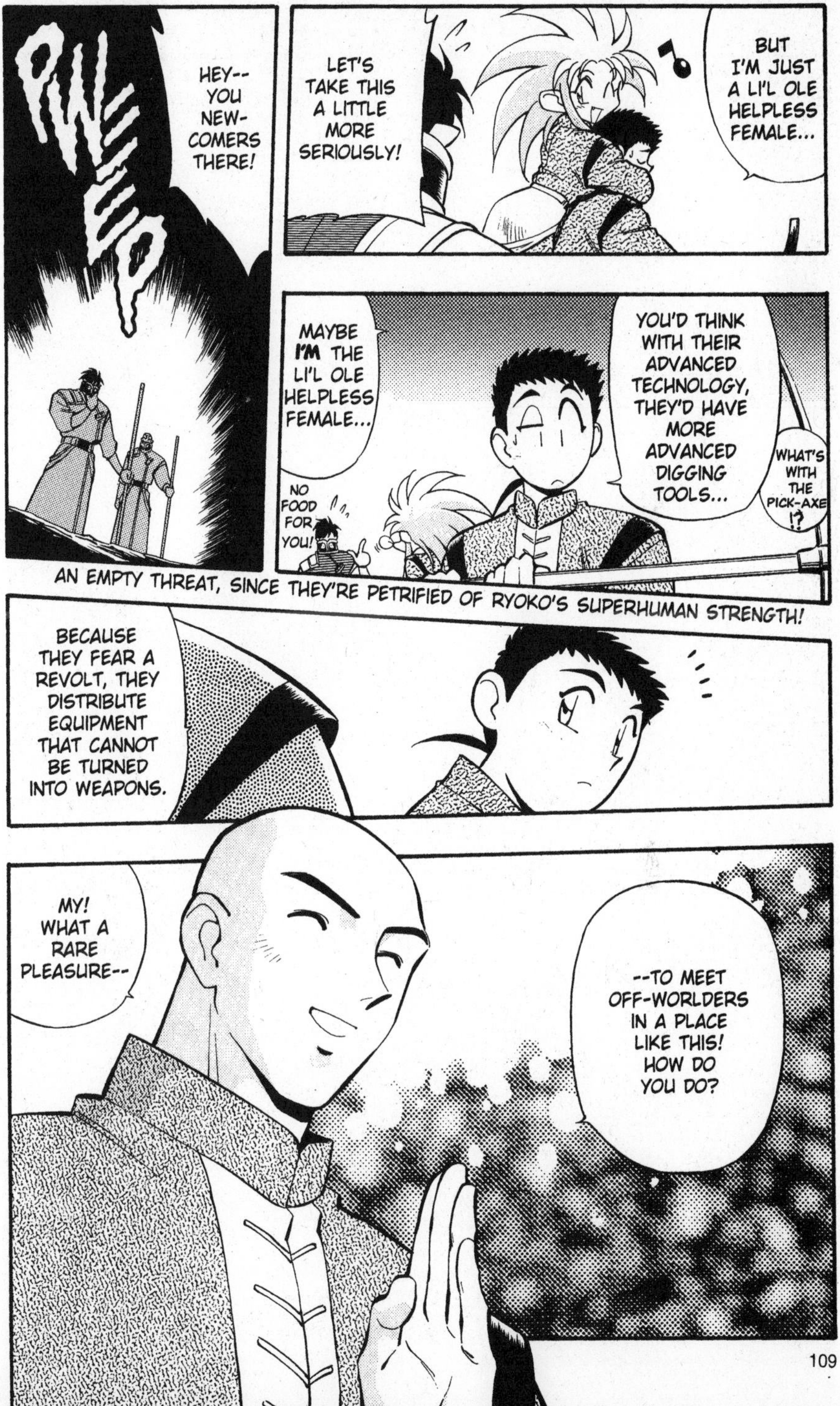

PWEEP
HEY-- YOU NEW-COMERS THERE!
LET'S TAKE THIS A LITTLE MORE SERIOUSLY!
BUT I'M JUST A LI'L OLE HELPLESS FEMALE...
MAYBE I'M THE LI'L OLE HELPLESS FEMALE...
NO FOOD FOR YOU!
YOU'D THINK WITH THEIR ADVANCED TECHNOLOGY, THEY'D HAVE MORE ADVANCED DIGGING TOOLS...
WHAT'S WITH THE PICK-AXE !?
AN EMPTY THREAT, SINCE THEY'RE PETRIFIED OF RYOKO'S SUPERHUMAN STRENGTH!
BECAUSE THEY FEAR A REVOLT, THEY DISTRIBUTE EQUIPMENT THAT CANNOT BE TURNED INTO WEAPONS.
MY! WHAT A RARE PLEASURE--
--TO MEET OFF-WORLDERS IN A PLACE LIKE THIS! HOW DO YOU DO?

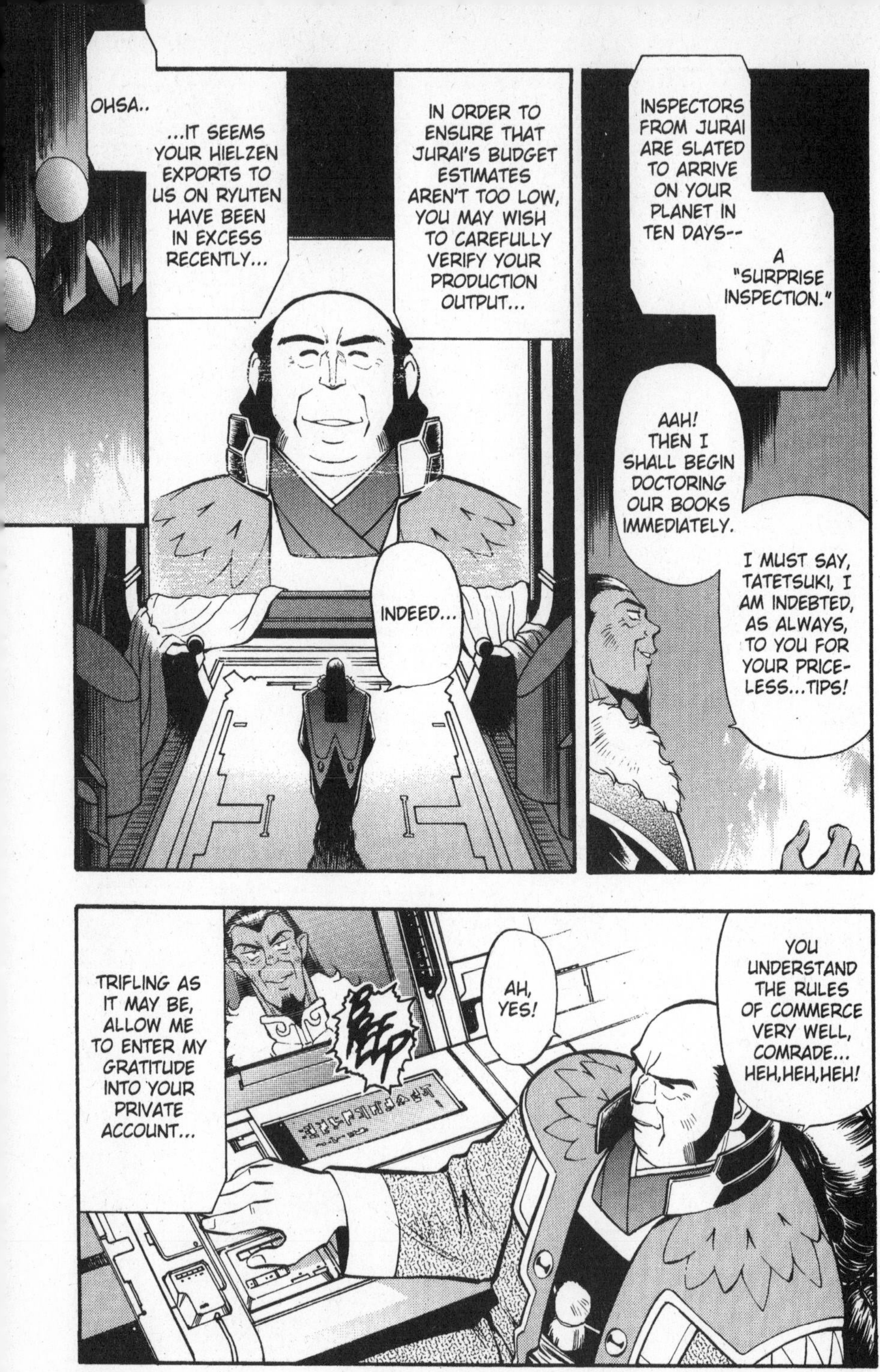
OHSA..
...IT SEEMS YOUR HIELZEN EXPORTS TO US ON RYUTEN HAVE BEEN IN EXCESS RECENTLY...
IN ORDER TO ENSURE THAT JURAI'S BUDGET ESTIMATES AREN'T TOO LOW, YOU MAY WISH TO CAREFULLY VERIFY YOUR PRODUCTION OUTPUT...
INDEED...
INSPECTORS FROM JURAI ARE SLATED TO ARRIVE ON YOUR PLANET IN TEN DAYS--
A "SURPRISE INSPECTION."
AAH! THEN I SHALL BEGIN DOCTORING OUR BOOKS IMMEDIATELY.
I MUST SAY, TATETSUKI, I AM INDEBTED, AS ALWAYS, TO YOU FOR YOUR PRICE-LESS...TIPS!
TRIFLING AS IT MAY BE, ALLOW ME TO ENTER MY GRATITUDE INTO YOUR PRIVATE ACCOUNT...
BEEP
AH, YES!
YOU UNDERSTAND THE RULES OF COMMERCE VERY WELL, COMRADE... HEH,HEH,HEH!

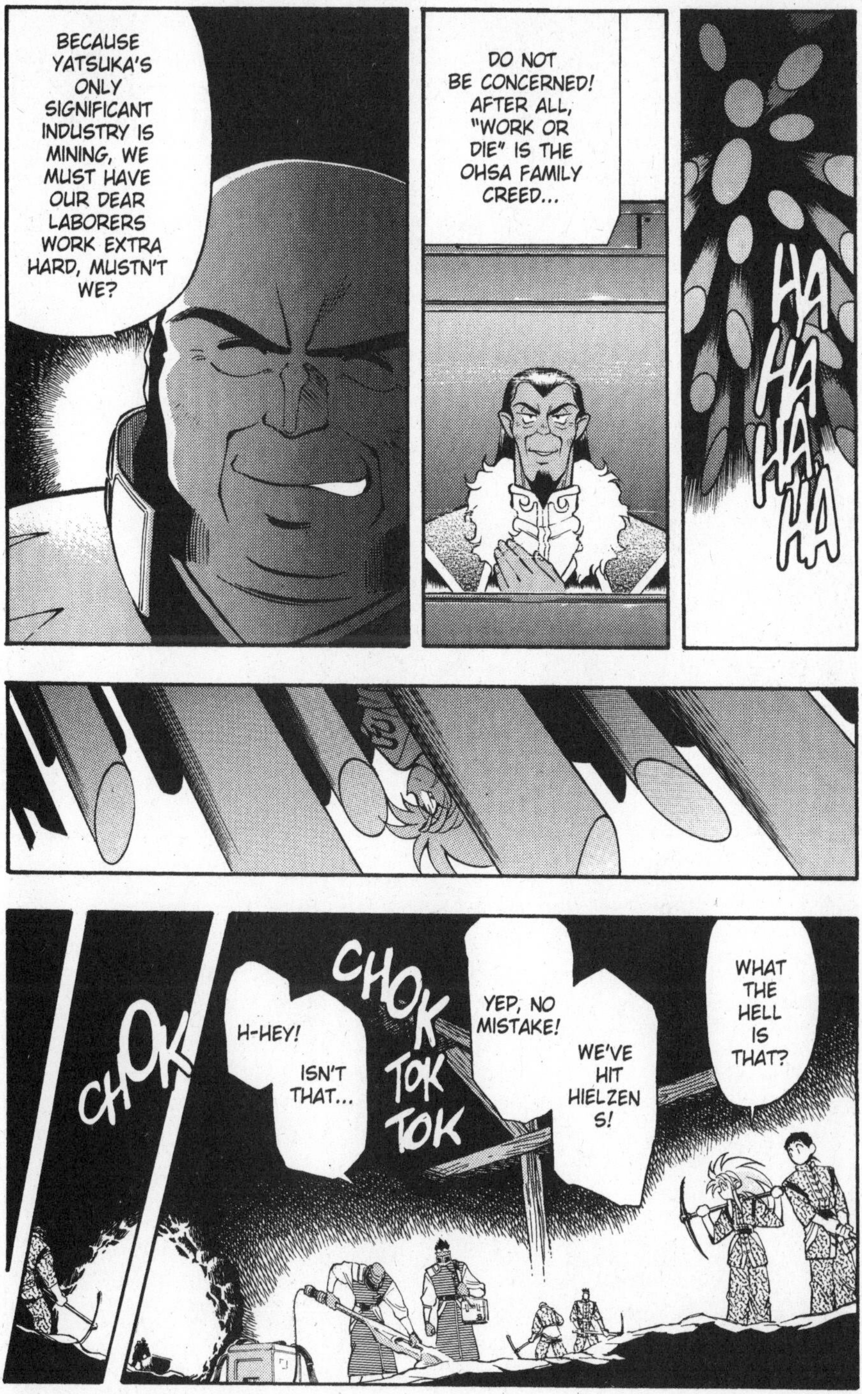
BECAUSE YATSUKA'S ONLY SIGNIFICANT INDUSTRY IS MINING, WE MUST HAVE OUR DEAR LABORERS WORK EXTRA HARD, MUSTN'T WE?
DO NOT BE CONCERNED! AFTER ALL, "WORK OR DIE" IS THE OHSA FAMILY CREED...
HA HA HA HA HA
CHOK
H-HEY!
ISN'T THAT...
CHOK TOK TOK
YEP, NO MISTAKE!
WE'VE HIT HIELZENS!
WHAT THE HELL IS THAT?

THE ORE WE'RE MINING IS A SEMI-PRECIOUS METAL KNOWN IN THE MINERAL TRADE AS "HIELZEN"...

OH, IT'S YOU, GOHGEI!

ON RARE OCCASIONS, A VEIN OF ULTRA-RICH, HIGH PURITY HIELZEN ORE IS DISCOVERED-- HIELZEN SUPER!

THAT'S THE HIELZEN S THEY'RE TALKING ABOUT?

CORRECT.

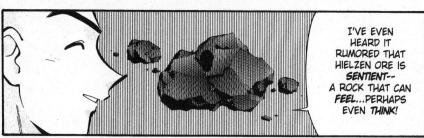

I'VE EVEN HEARD IT RUMORED THAT HIELZEN ORE IS *SENTIENT*-- A ROCK THAT CAN *FEEL*...PERHAPS EVEN *THINK*!

HMMM...THIS GOHGEI SAID HE WAS A MONK-IN-TRAINING...SO WHAT'S HE DOING IN A PLACE LIKE THIS?

HOW DOES IT LOOK?

DAMN! THIS ROCK'S GOING TO BE TROUBLE-SOME!

WE COULD GO AT IT FOR THREE DAYS STRAIGHT AND STILL NOT REACH THAT VEIN!

WHERE IS THE ROCK BARRIER THINNEST?

RIGHT AROUND HERE...

YOU DON'T MEAN YOU'RE GOING TO TRY PUNCHING THROUGH TO THE ORE!? THAT ROCK IS TWO METERS THICK!

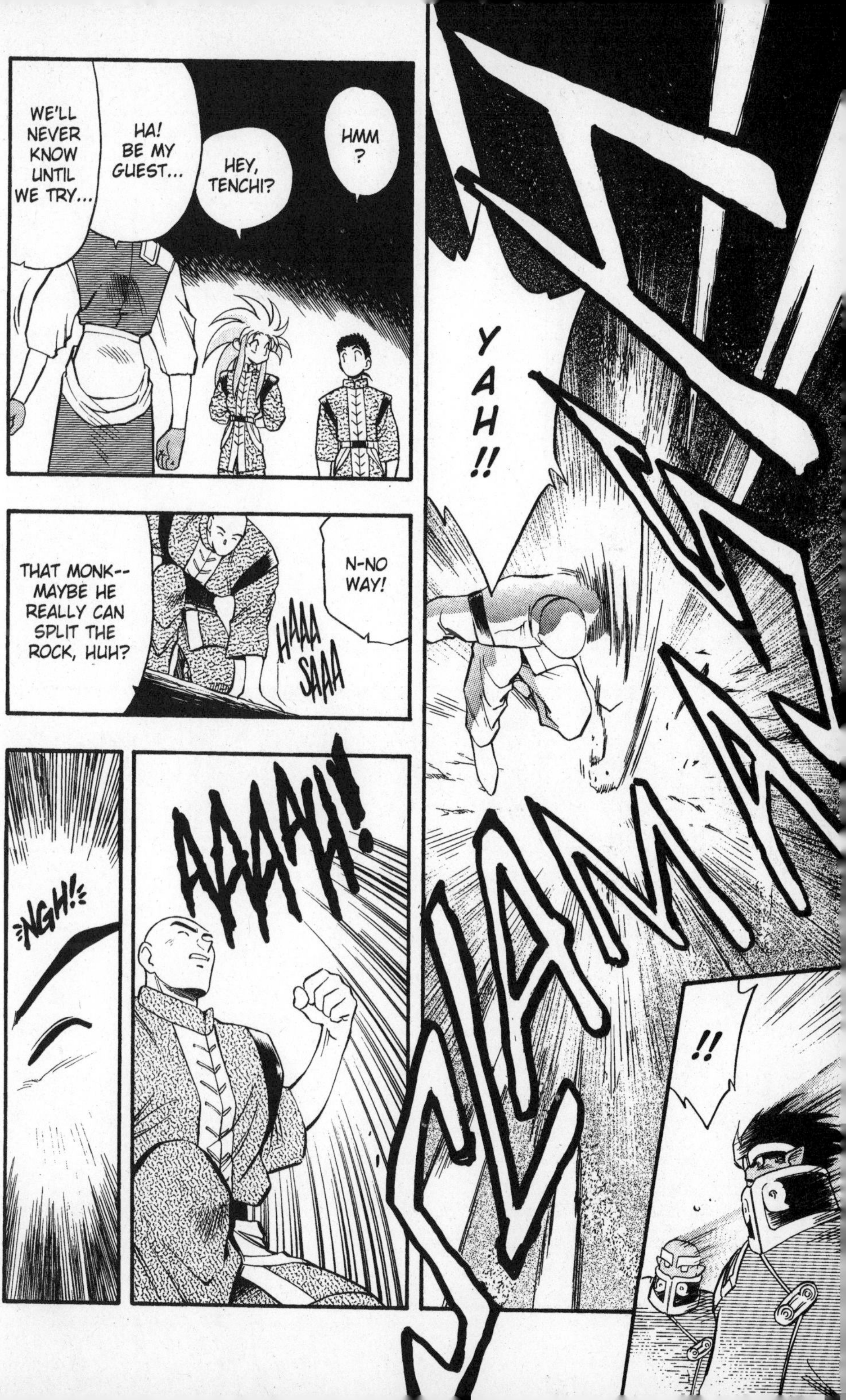
WE'LL NEVER KNOW UNTIL WE TRY...
HA! BE MY GUEST...
HEY, TENCHI?
HMM?
THAT MONK-- MAYBE HE REALLY CAN SPLIT THE ROCK, HUH?
HAAA SAAA
N-NO WAY!
NGH!!
AAAAH!
YAH!!
!!

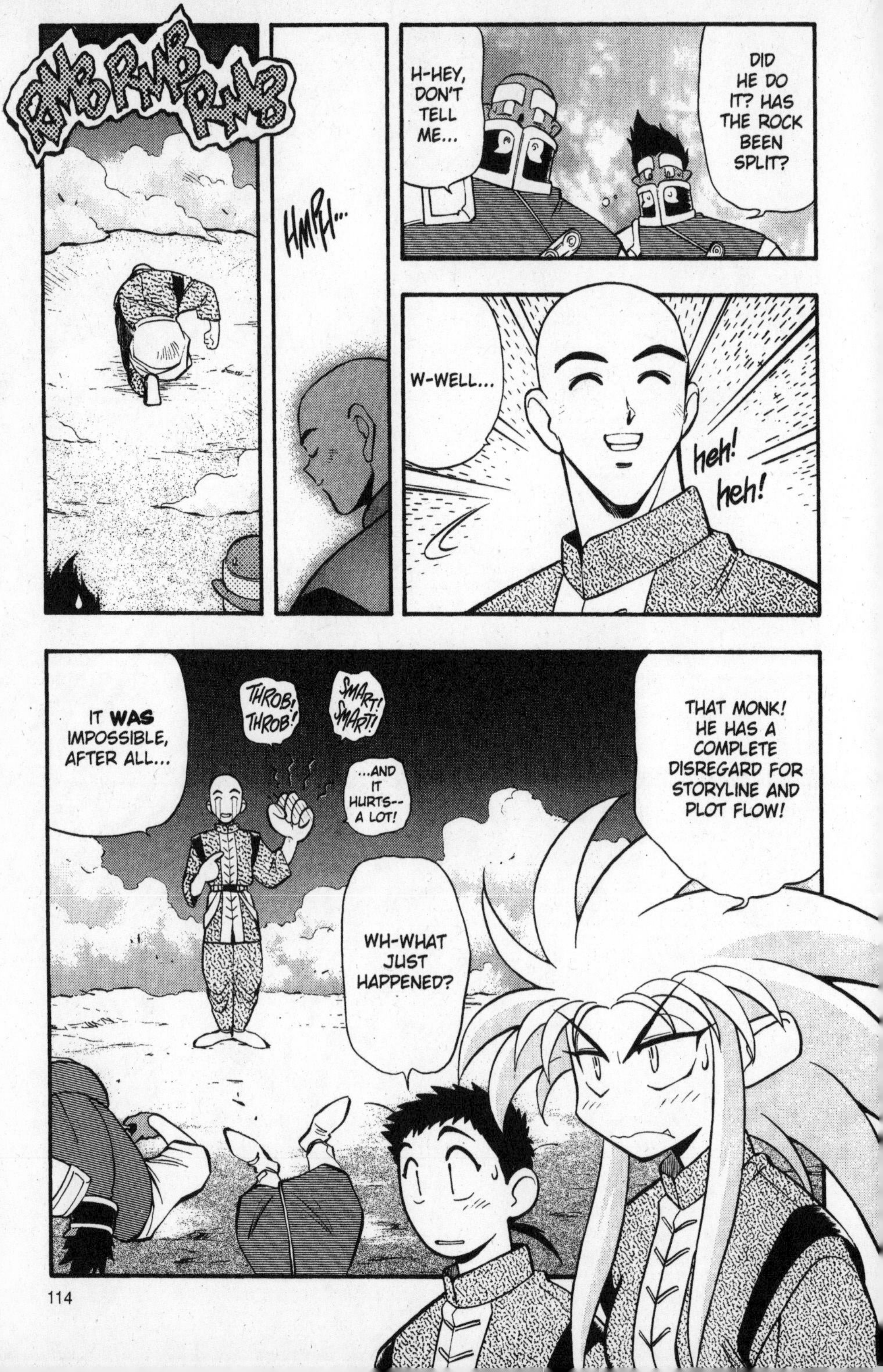

RUMB RUMB RUMB
HMPH...
H-HEY, DON'T TELL ME...
DID HE DO IT? HAS THE ROCK BEEN SPLIT?
W-WELL...
heh! heh!
IT **WAS** IMPOSSIBLE, AFTER ALL...
THROB! THROB!
SMART! SMART!
...AND IT HURTS-- A LOT!
WH-WHAT JUST HAPPENED?
THAT MONK! HE HAS A COMPLETE DISREGARD FOR STORYLINE AND PLOT FLOW!

Tales of Tenchi #5

TRUE HEARTS

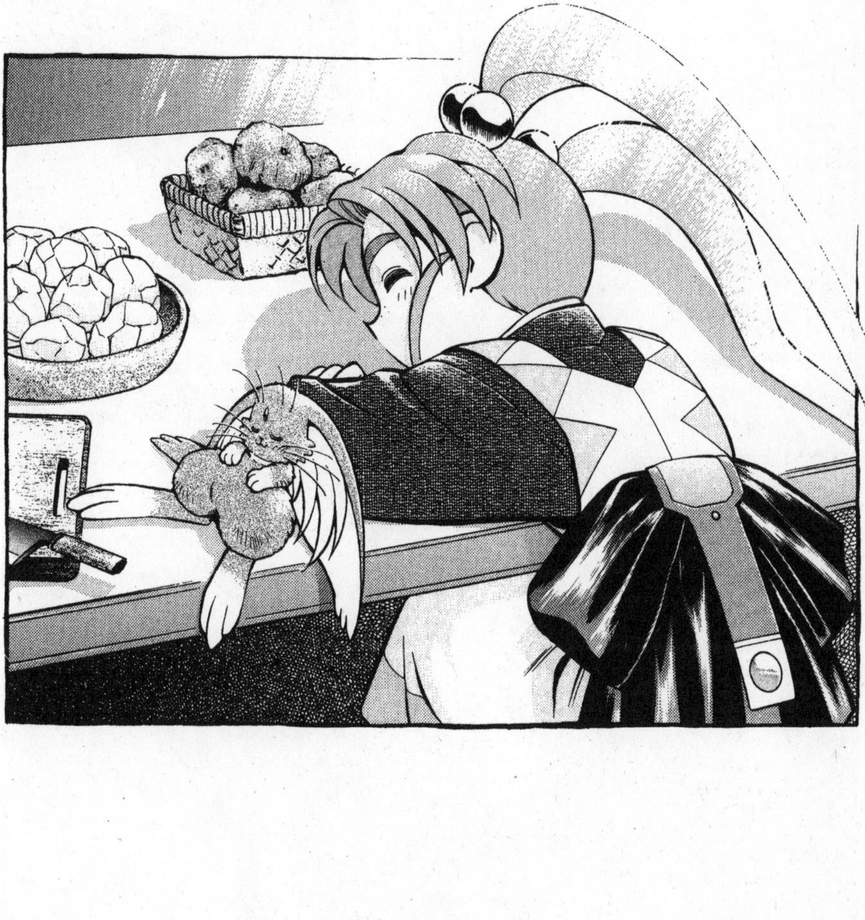

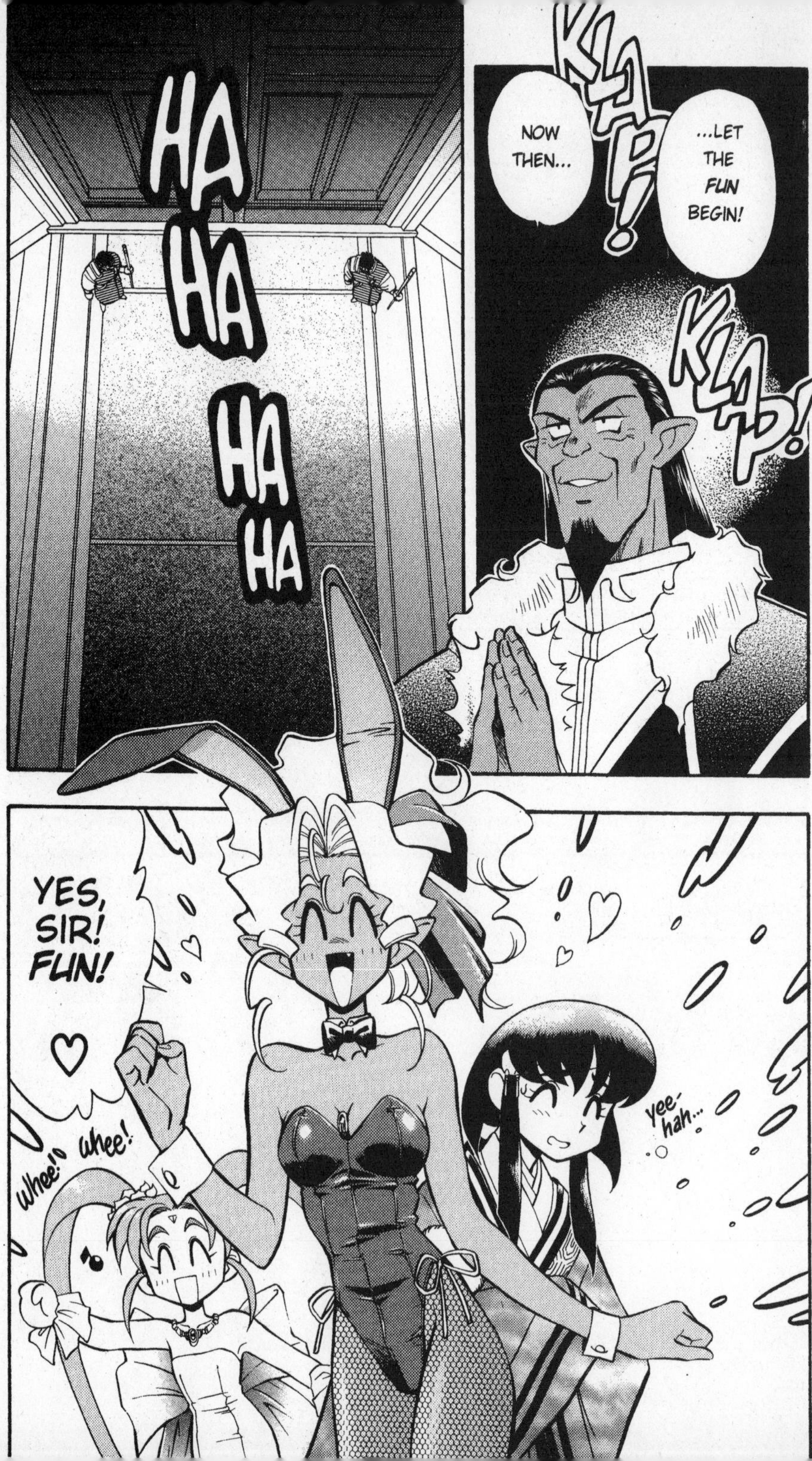
HA
HA
HA
HA
NOW THEN...
KLAP!
...LET THE FUN BEGIN!
KLAP!
YES, SIR! FUN!
whee! whee!
yee-hah...

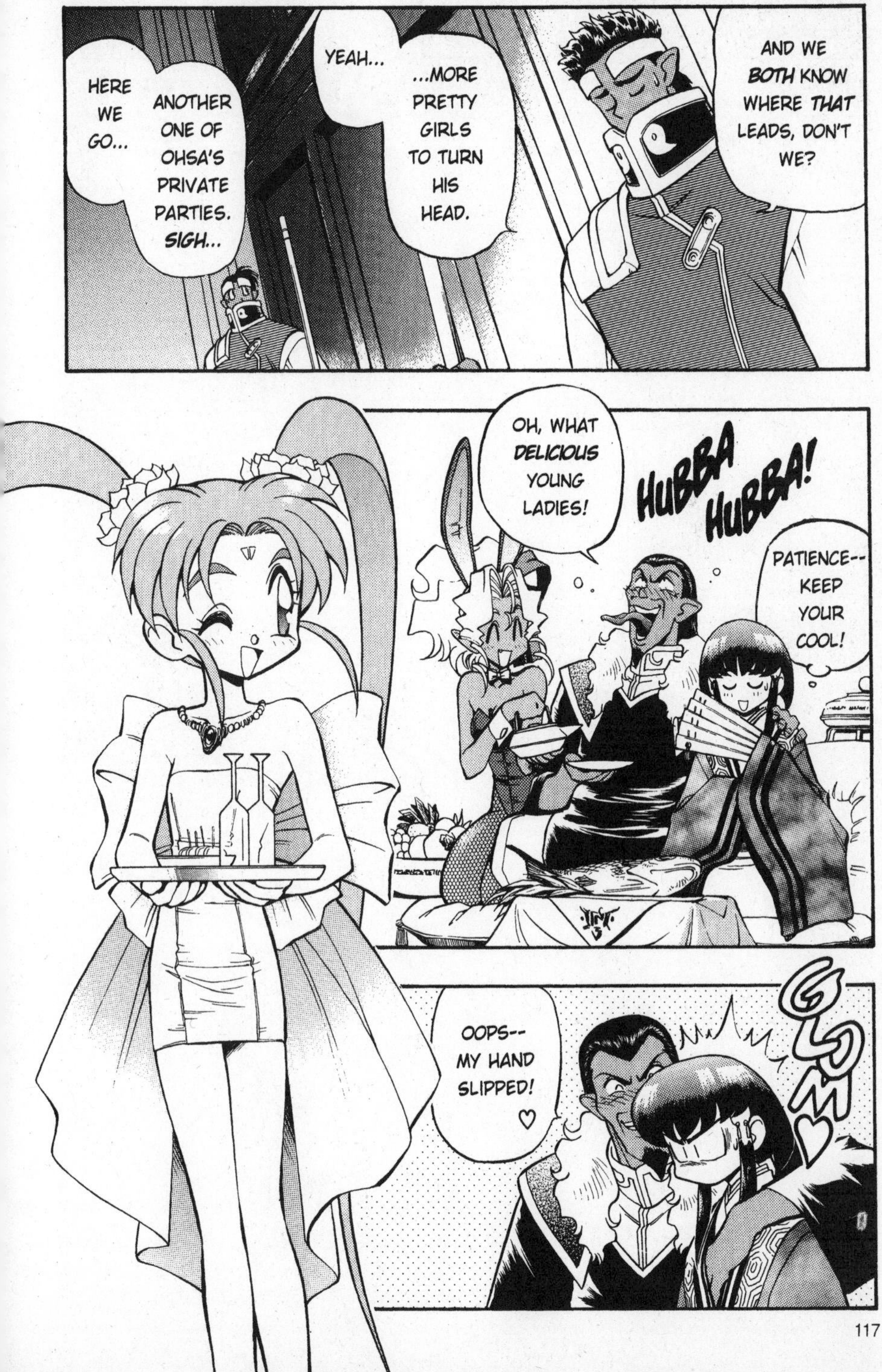
HERE WE GO...
ANOTHER ONE OF OHSA'S PRIVATE PARTIES. SIGH...
YEAH...
...MORE PRETTY GIRLS TO TURN HIS HEAD.
AND WE BOTH KNOW WHERE THAT LEADS, DON'T WE?
OH, WHAT DELICIOUS YOUNG LADIES!
HUBBA HUBBA!
PATIENCE-- KEEP YOUR COOL!
OOPS-- MY HAND SLIPPED! ♡
GLOM ♡

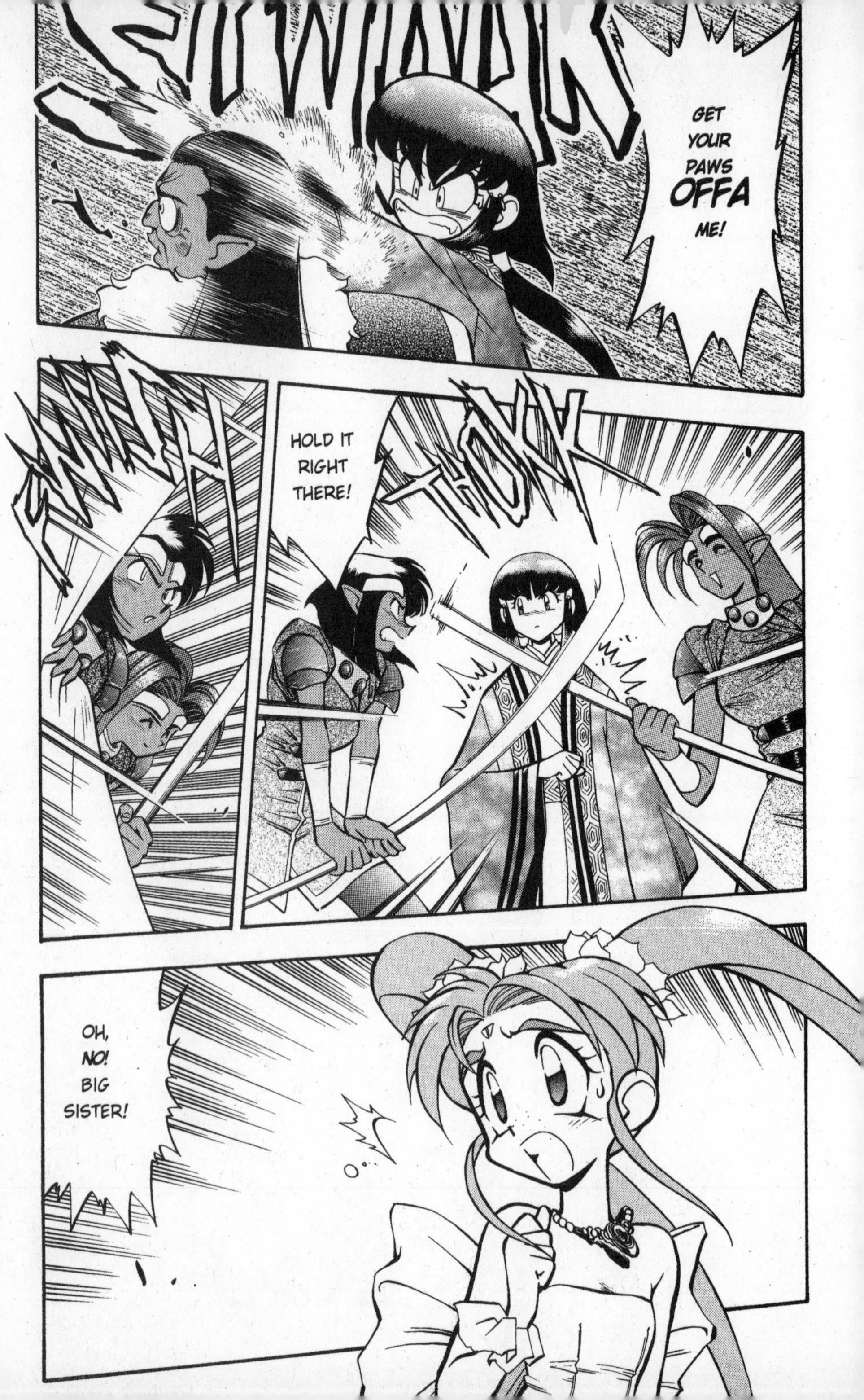
GET YOUR PAWS OFFA ME!
HOLD IT RIGHT THERE!
OH, NO! BIG SISTER!

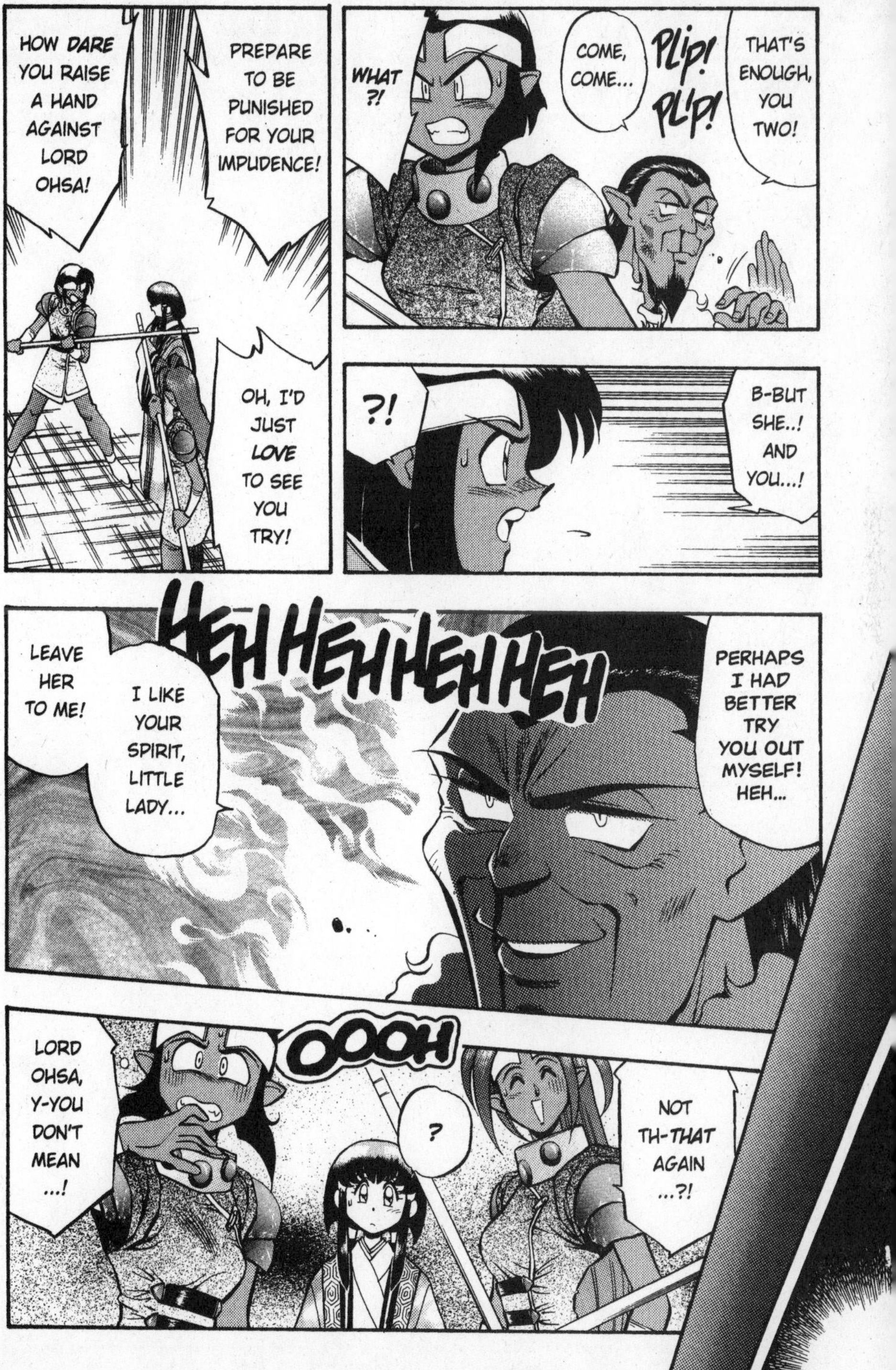
HOW *DARE* YOU RAISE A HAND AGAINST LORD OHSA!
PREPARE TO BE PUNISHED FOR YOUR IMPUDENCE!
OH, I'D JUST *LOVE* TO SEE YOU TRY!
WHAT ?!
COME, COME...
PLIP! PLIP!
THAT'S ENOUGH, YOU TWO!
?!
B-BUT SHE...! AND YOU...!
HEH HEH HEH HEH
LEAVE HER TO ME!
I LIKE YOUR SPIRIT, LITTLE LADY...
PERHAPS I HAD BETTER TRY YOU OUT MYSELF! HEH...
OOOH
LORD OHSA, Y-YOU DON'T MEAN ...!
?
NOT TH-*THAT* AGAIN ...?!

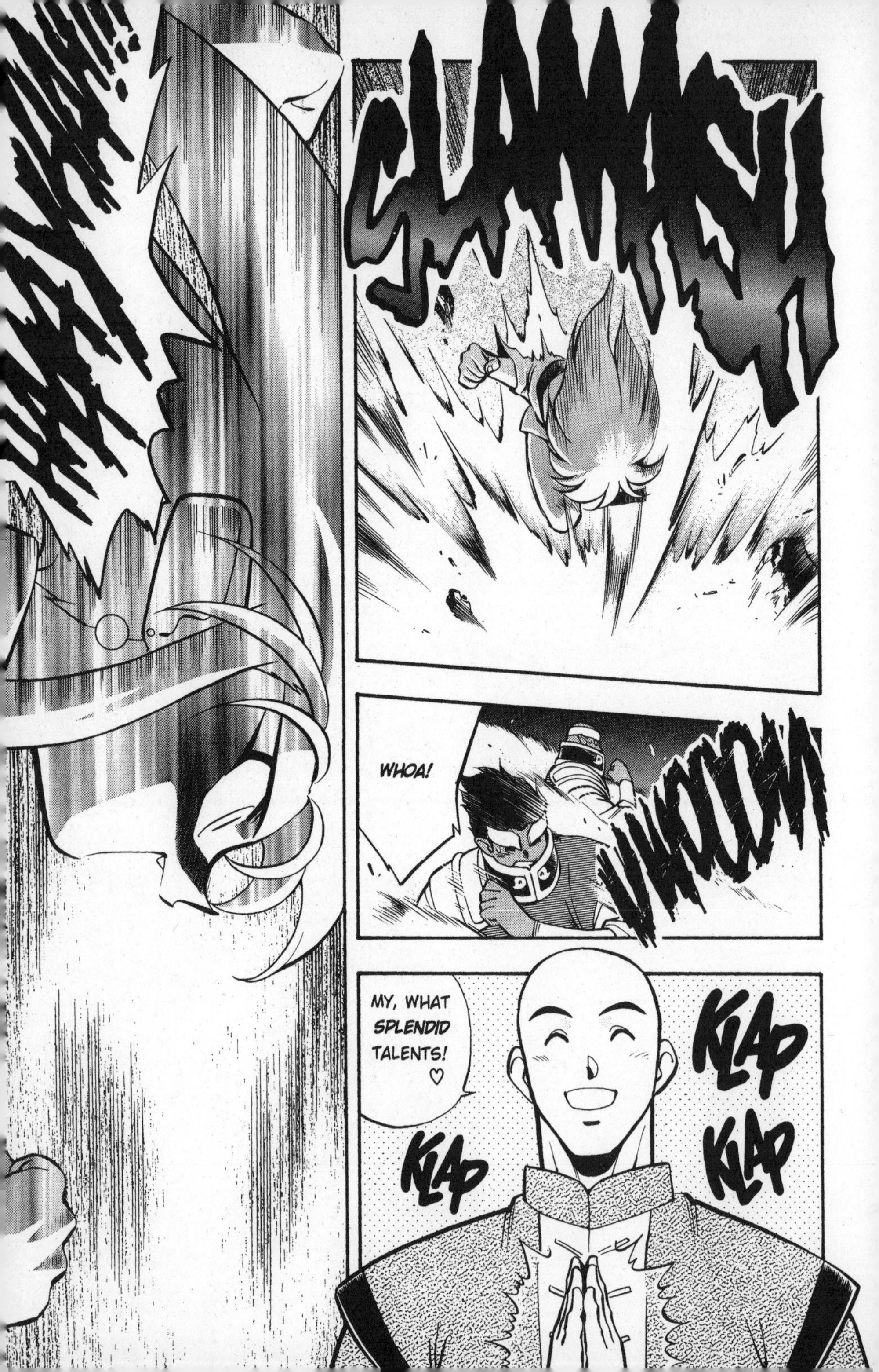
SMAAASH
WHOA!
WHOOOM
MY, WHAT SPLENDID TALENTS! ♡
KLAP
KLAP
KLAP

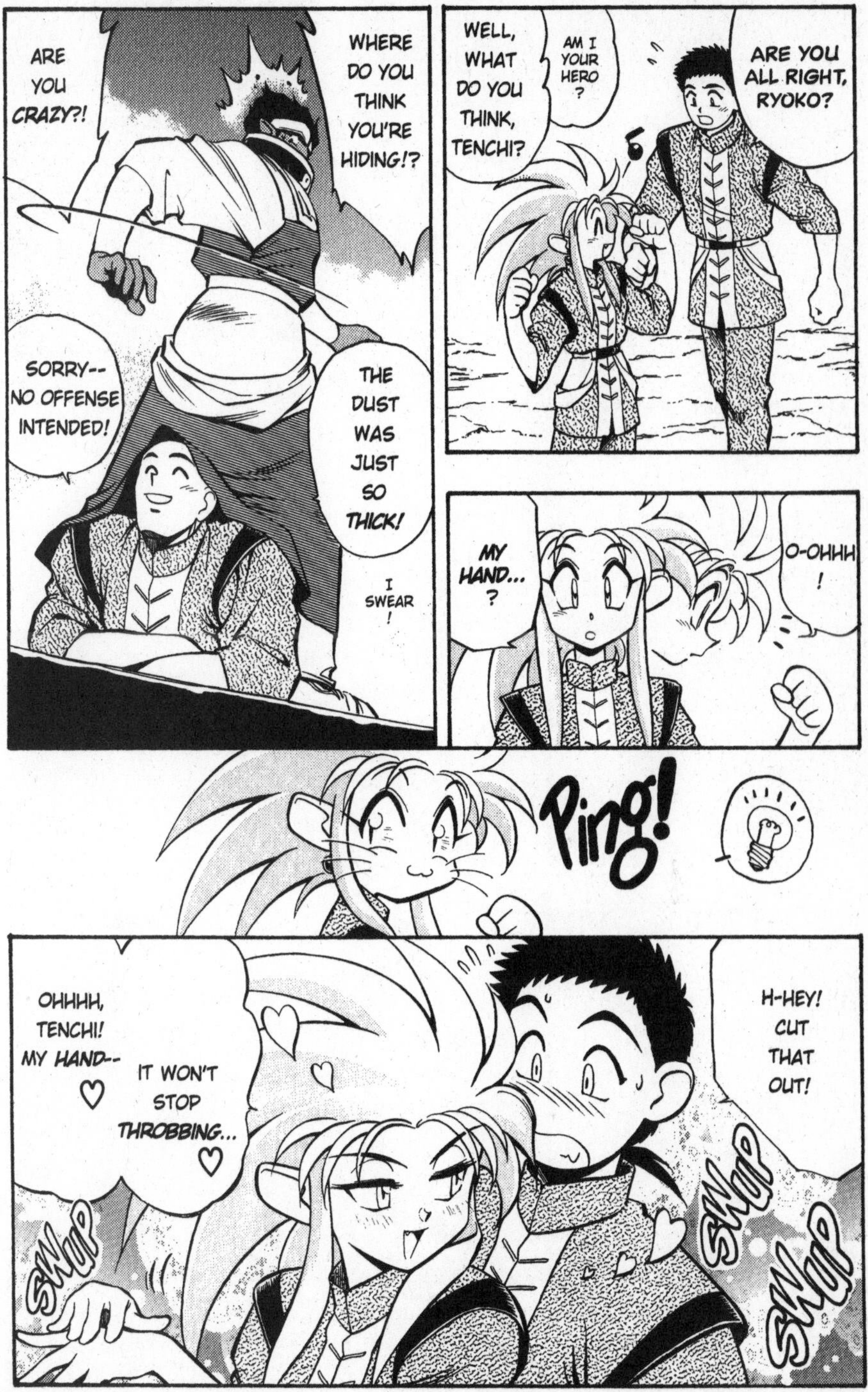
ARE YOU CRAZY?!
WHERE DO YOU THINK YOU'RE HIDING!?
SORRY-- NO OFFENSE INTENDED!
THE DUST WAS JUST SO THICK!
I SWEAR!
WELL, WHAT DO YOU THINK, TENCHI?
AM I YOUR HERO?
ARE YOU ALL RIGHT, RYOKO?
MY HAND...?
O-OHHH!
Ping!
OHHHH, TENCHI! MY HAND-- ♡
IT WON'T STOP THROBBING... ♡
H-HEY! CUT THAT OUT!
SWUP
SWUP
SWUP
SWUP

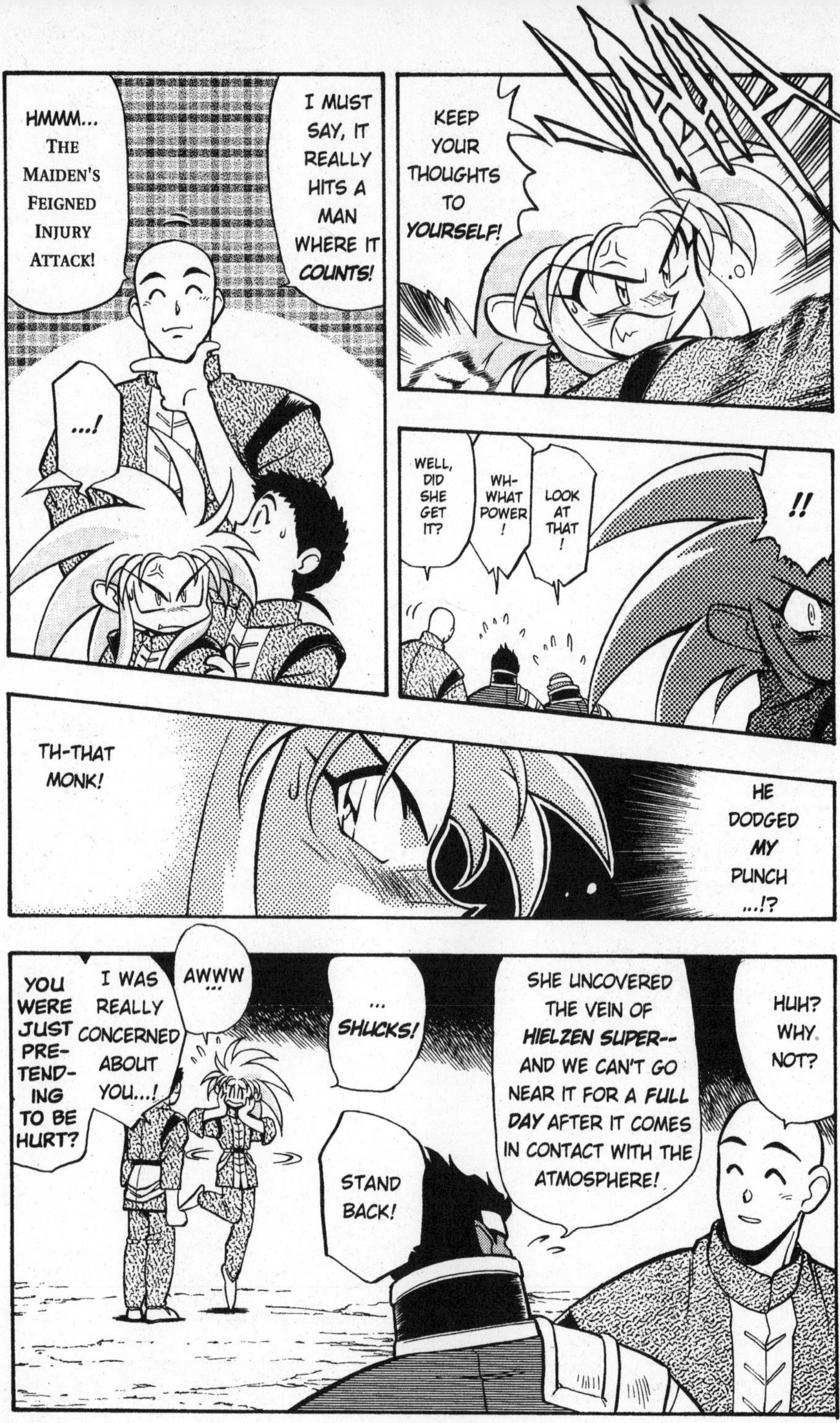
HMMM... THE MAIDEN'S FEIGNED INJURY ATTACK!
I MUST SAY, IT REALLY HITS A MAN WHERE IT COUNTS!
...!
KEEP YOUR THOUGHTS TO YOURSELF!
WELL, DID SHE GET IT?
WH-WHAT POWER!
LOOK AT THAT!
!!
TH-THAT MONK!
HE DODGED MY PUNCH ...!?
YOU WERE JUST PRE-TEND-ING TO BE HURT?
I WAS REALLY CONCERNED ABOUT YOU...!
AWWW...
... SHUCKS!
STAND BACK!
SHE UNCOVERED THE VEIN OF HIELZEN SUPER-- AND WE CAN'T GO NEAR IT FOR A FULL DAY AFTER IT COMES IN CONTACT WITH THE ATMOSPHERE!
HUH? WHY NOT?

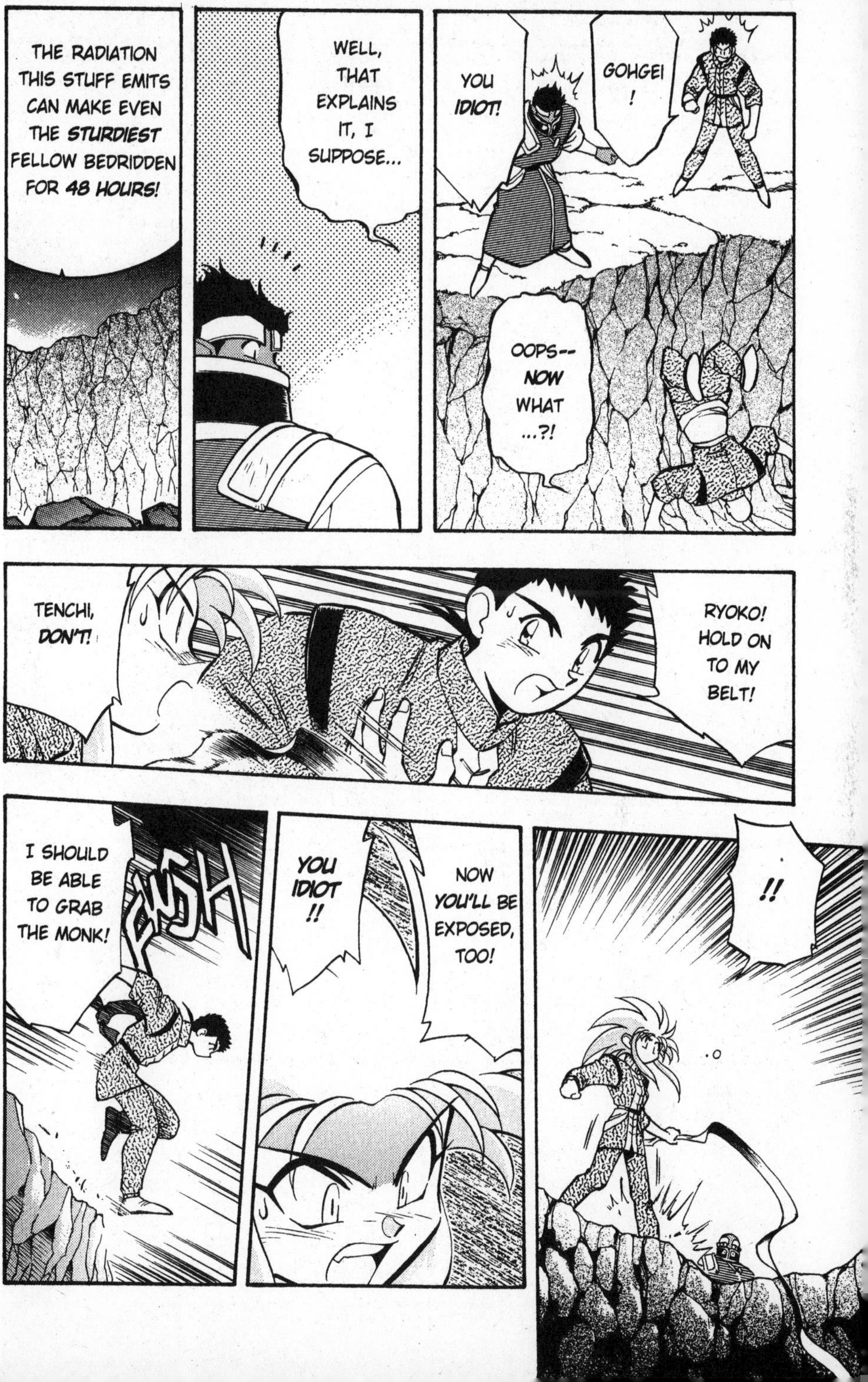
THE RADIATION THIS STUFF EMITS CAN MAKE EVEN THE STURDIEST FELLOW BEDRIDDEN FOR 48 HOURS!
WELL, THAT EXPLAINS IT, I SUPPOSE...
GOHGEI!
YOU IDIOT!
OOPS-- NOW WHAT ...?!
RYOKO! HOLD ON TO MY BELT!
TENCHI, DON'T!
I SHOULD BE ABLE TO GRAB THE MONK!
NOW YOU'LL BE EXPOSED, TOO!
YOU IDIOT!!
!!

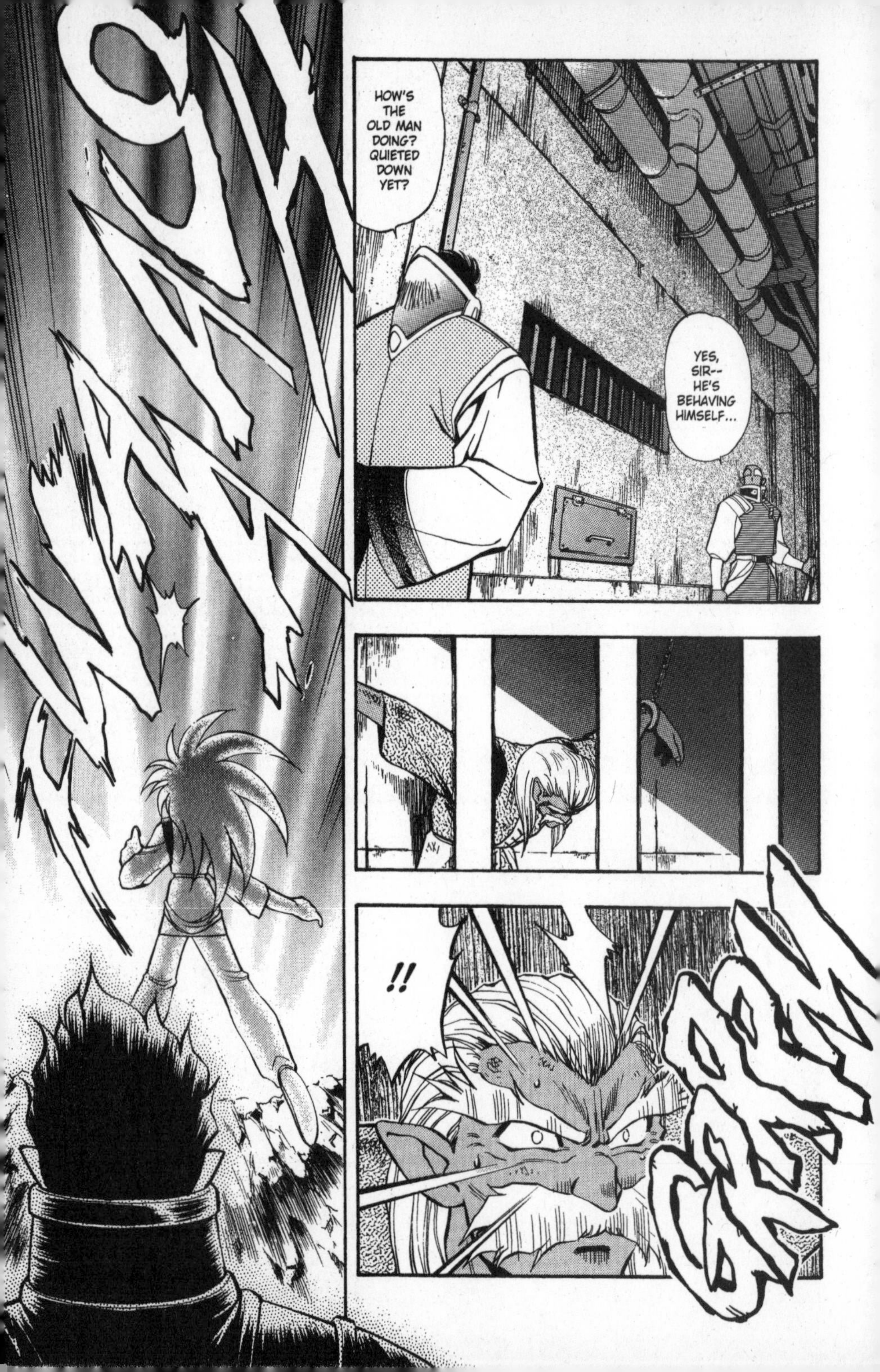
HOW'S THE OLD MAN DOING? QUIETED DOWN YET?
YES, SIR-- HE'S BEHAVING HIMSELF...
!!

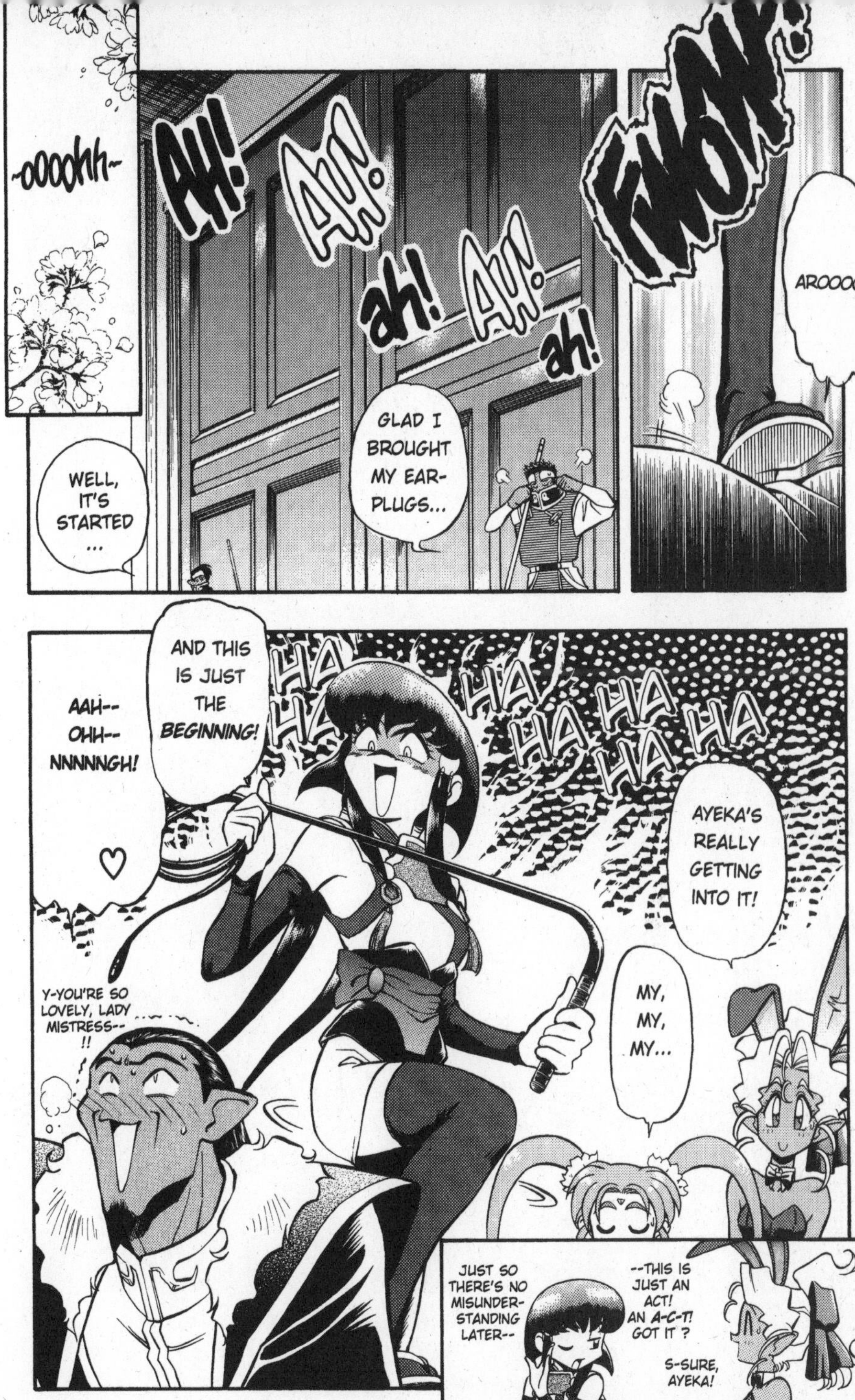
-oooohh-
WELL, IT'S STARTED...
AH! AH! ah! AH! ah!
GLAD I BROUGHT MY EAR-PLUGS...
AROOOOO!
AND THIS IS JUST THE BEGINNING!
AAH-- OHH-- NNNNNGH!
♥
HA HA HA HA HA HA HA HA HA
AYEKA'S REALLY GETTING INTO IT!
Y-YOU'RE SO LOVELY, LADY MISTRESS--!!
MY, MY, MY...
JUST SO THERE'S NO MISUNDER-STANDING LATER--
--THIS IS JUST AN ACT! AN A-C-T! GOT IT ?
S-SURE, AYEKA!

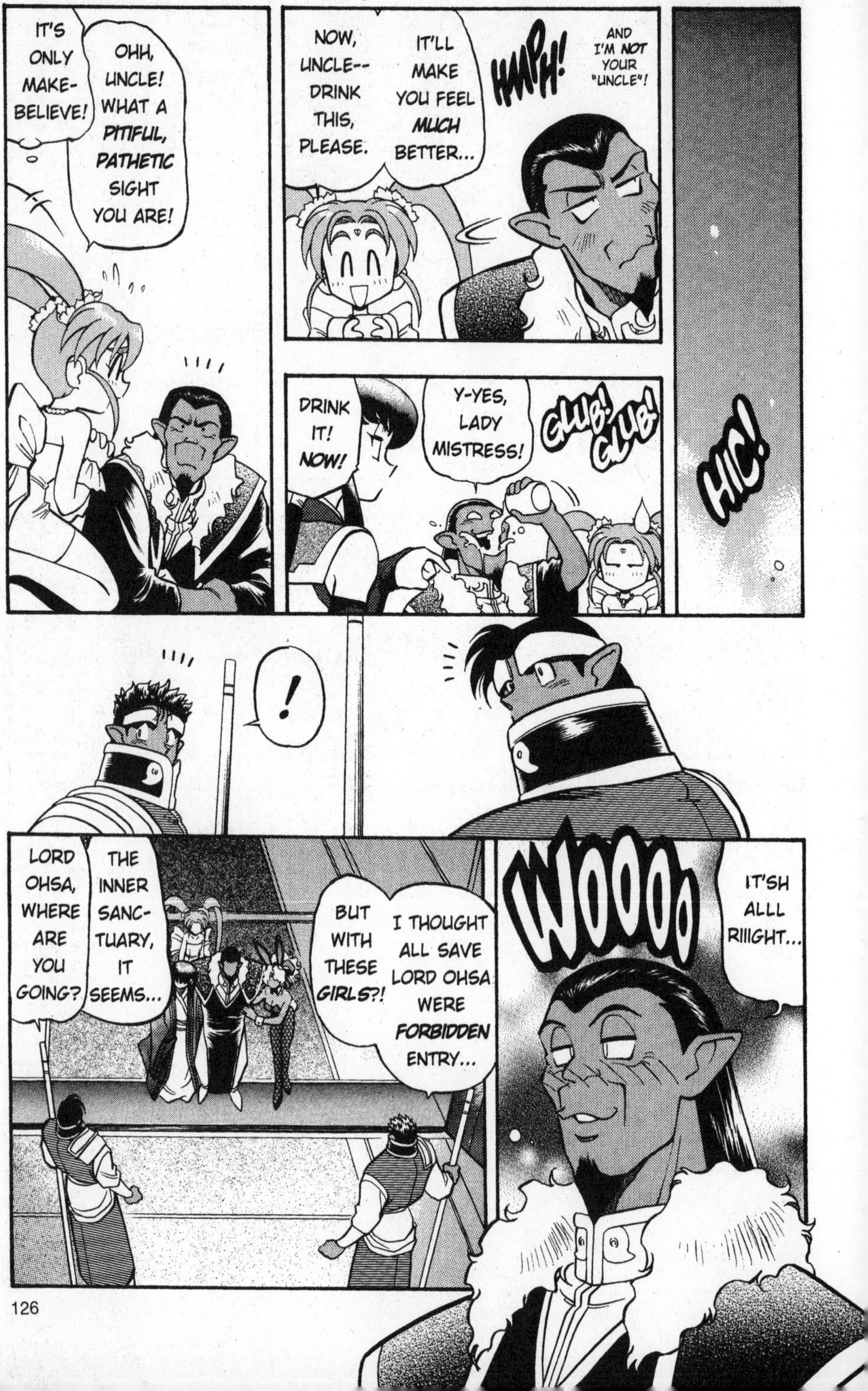

IT'S ONLY MAKE-BELIEVE!
OHH, UNCLE! WHAT A PITIFUL, PATHETIC SIGHT YOU ARE!
NOW, UNCLE-- DRINK THIS, PLEASE.
IT'LL MAKE YOU FEEL MUCH BETTER...
HAAPH!
AND I'M NOT YOUR "UNCLE"!
DRINK IT! NOW!
Y-YES, LADY MISTRESS!
GLUB! GLUB!
HIC!
!
LORD OHSA, WHERE ARE YOU GOING?
THE INNER SANCTUARY, IT SEEMS...
BUT WITH THESE GIRLS?!
I THOUGHT ALL SAVE LORD OHSA WERE FORBIDDEN ENTRY...
WOOOO
IT'SH ALLL RIIIGHT...

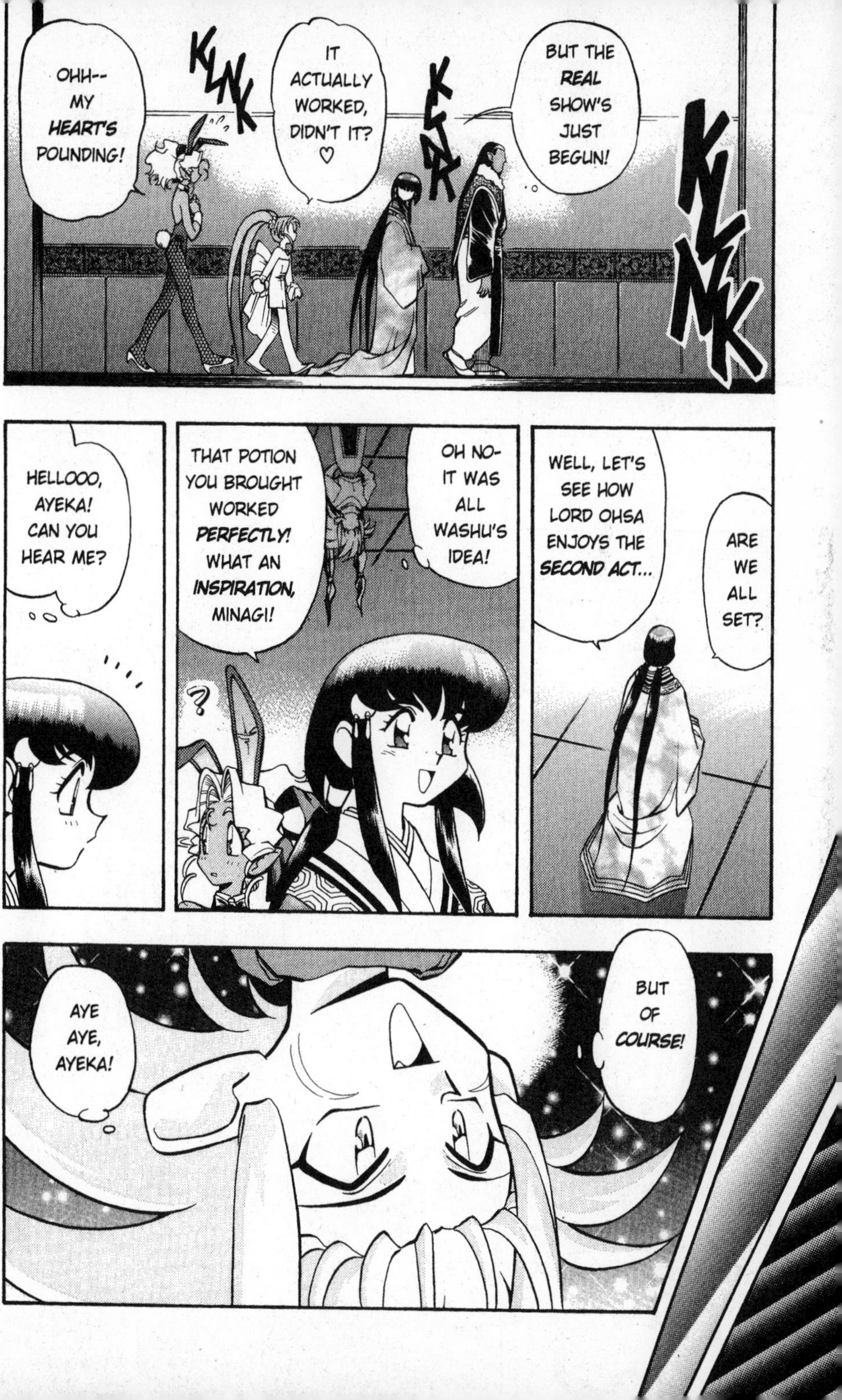
OHH-- MY HEART'S POUNDING!
KLINK
IT ACTUALLY WORKED, DIDN'T IT? ♡
KLINK
BUT THE REAL SHOW'S JUST BEGUN!
KLINK
HELLOOO, AYEKA! CAN YOU HEAR ME?
THAT POTION YOU BROUGHT WORKED PERFECTLY! WHAT AN INSPIRATION, MINAGI!
OH NO- IT WAS ALL WASHU'S IDEA!
?
WELL, LET'S SEE HOW LORD OHSA ENJOYS THE SECOND ACT...
ARE WE ALL SET?
AYE AYE, AYEKA!
BUT OF COURSE!

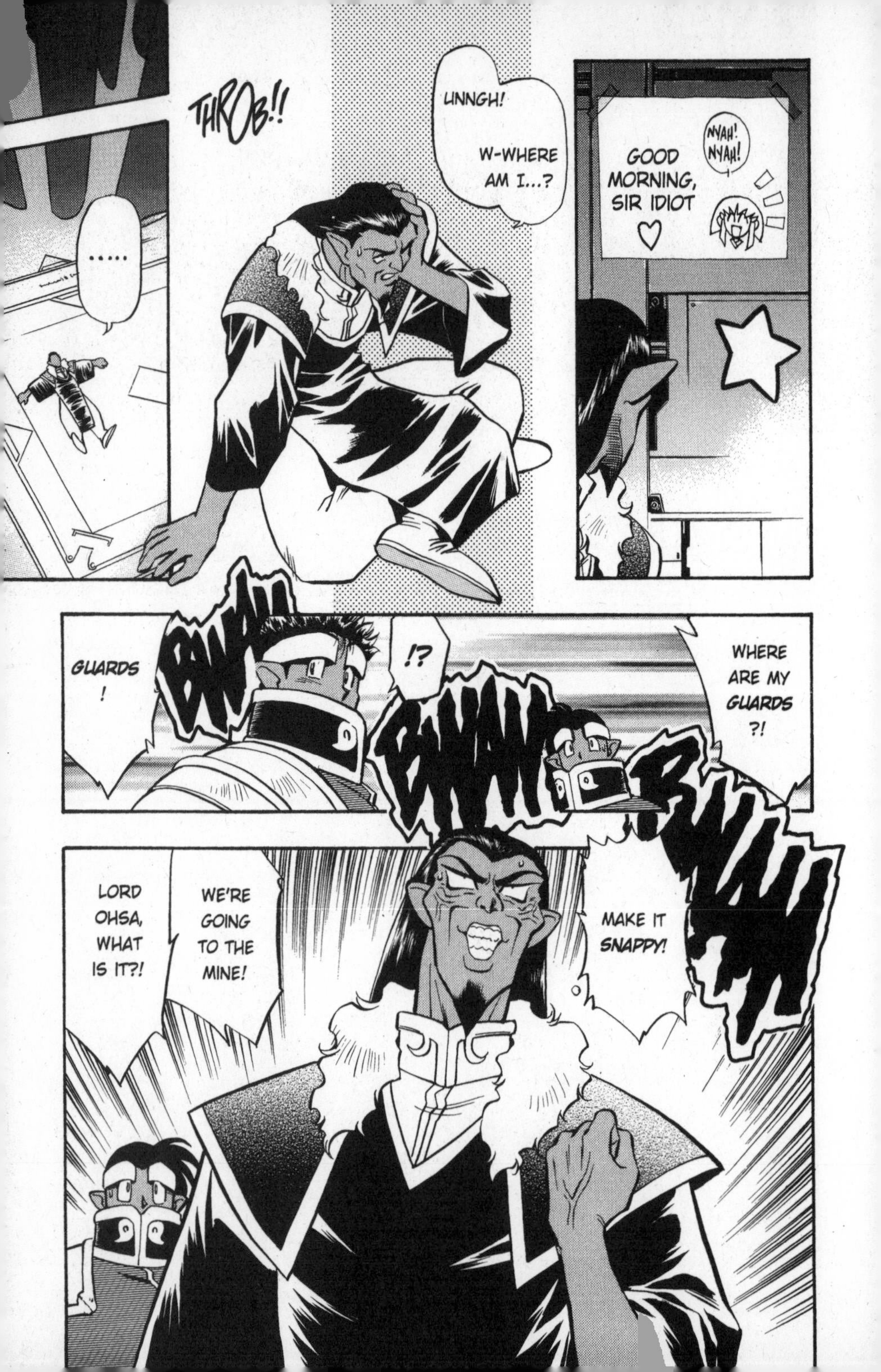
......
THROB!!
UNNGH!
W-WHERE AM I...?
GOOD MORNING, SIR IDIOT ♡
NYAH! NYAH!
BWAM
GUARDS!
!?
BWAM
WHERE ARE MY GUARDS?!
BWAM
LORD OHSA, WHAT IS IT?!
WE'RE GOING TO THE MINE!
MAKE IT SNAPPY!

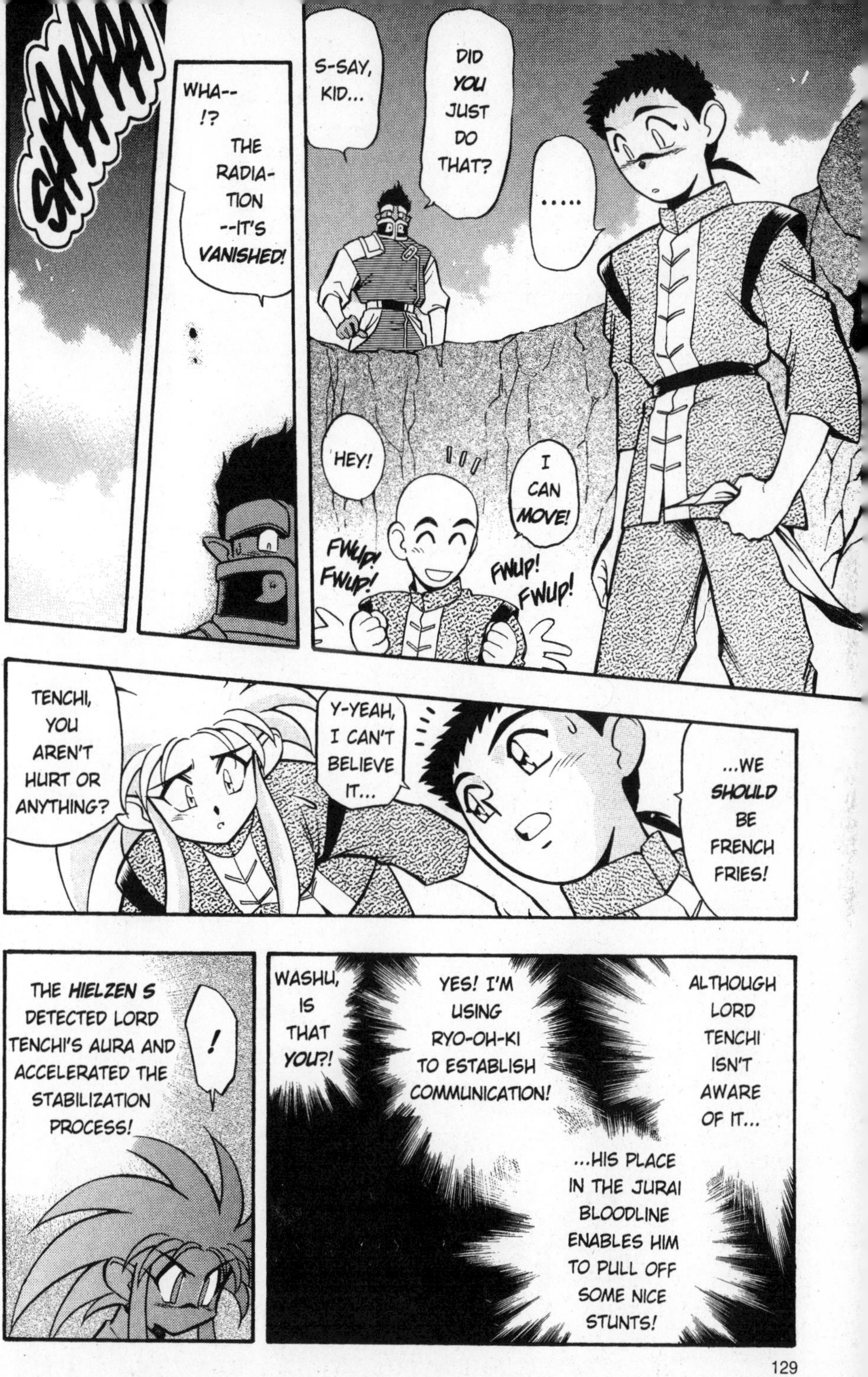
SHAAA!
WHA-- !?
THE RADIA-TION --IT'S VANISHED!
S-SAY, KID...
DID YOU JUST DO THAT?
.....
HEY!
I CAN MOVE!
FWUP! FWUP!
FWUP! FWUP!
TENCHI, YOU AREN'T HURT OR ANYTHING?
Y-YEAH, I CAN'T BELIEVE IT...
...WE SHOULD BE FRENCH FRIES!
THE HIELZEN S DETECTED LORD TENCHI'S AURA AND ACCELERATED THE STABILIZATION PROCESS!
!
WASHU, IS THAT YOU?!
YES! I'M USING RYO-OH-KI TO ESTABLISH COMMUNICATION!
ALTHOUGH LORD TENCHI ISN'T AWARE OF IT...
...HIS PLACE IN THE JURAI BLOODLINE ENABLES HIM TO PULL OFF SOME NICE STUNTS!

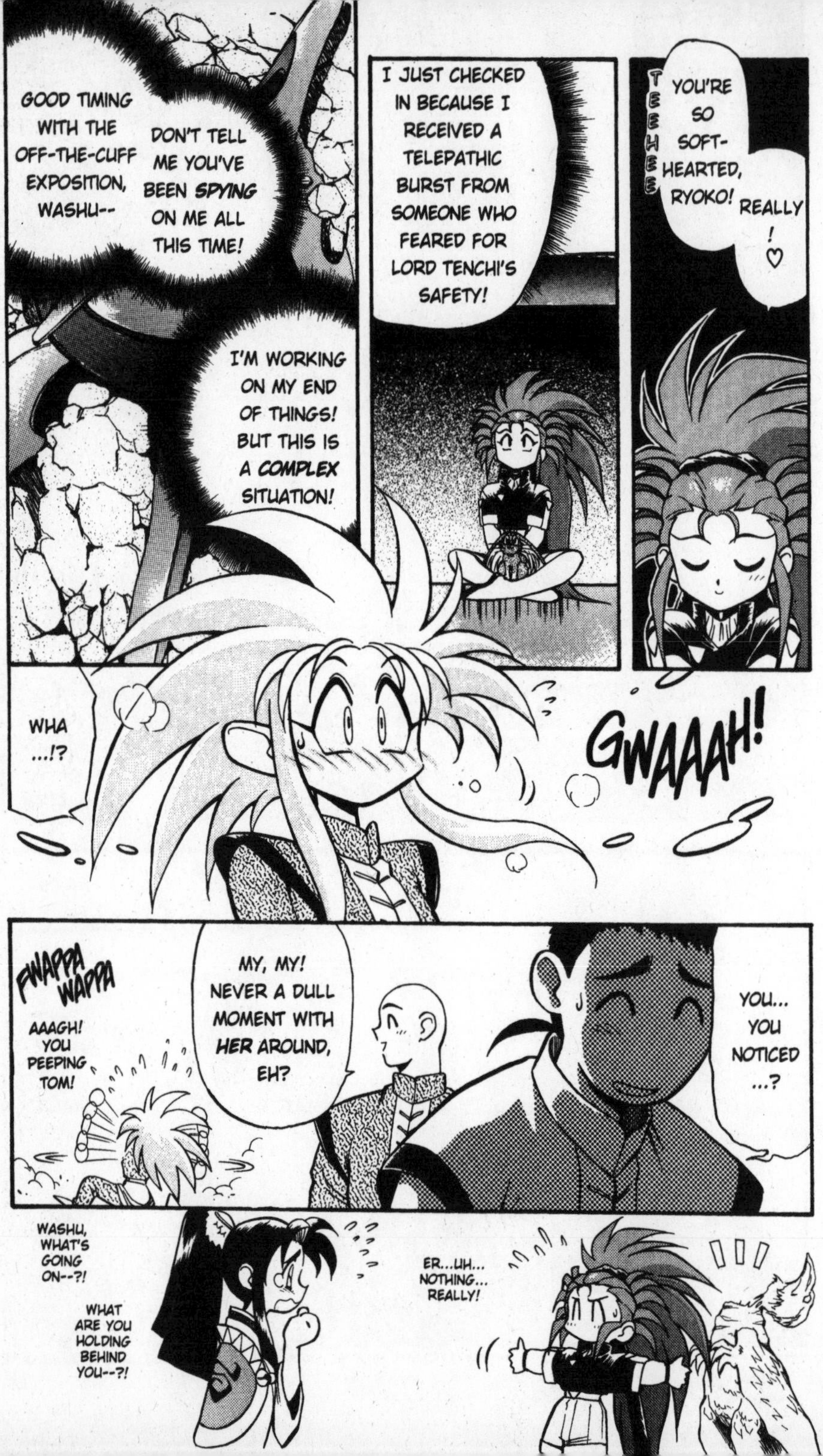
GOOD TIMING WITH THE OFF-THE-CUFF EXPOSITION, WASHU--
DON'T TELL ME YOU'VE BEEN *SPYING* ON ME ALL THIS TIME!
I'M WORKING ON MY END OF THINGS! BUT THIS IS A *COMPLEX* SITUATION!
I JUST CHECKED IN BECAUSE I RECEIVED A TELEPATHIC BURST FROM SOMEONE WHO FEARED FOR LORD TENCHI'S SAFETY!
TEEHEE
YOU'RE SO SOFT-HEARTED, RYOKO!
REALLY! ♡
WHA ...!?
GWAAAH!
FWAPPA WAPPA
AAAGH! YOU PEEPING TOM!
MY, MY! NEVER A DULL MOMENT WITH *HER* AROUND, EH?
YOU... YOU NOTICED ...?
WASHU, WHAT'S GOING ON--?!
WHAT ARE YOU HOLDING BEHIND YOU--?!
ER...UH... NOTHING... REALLY!

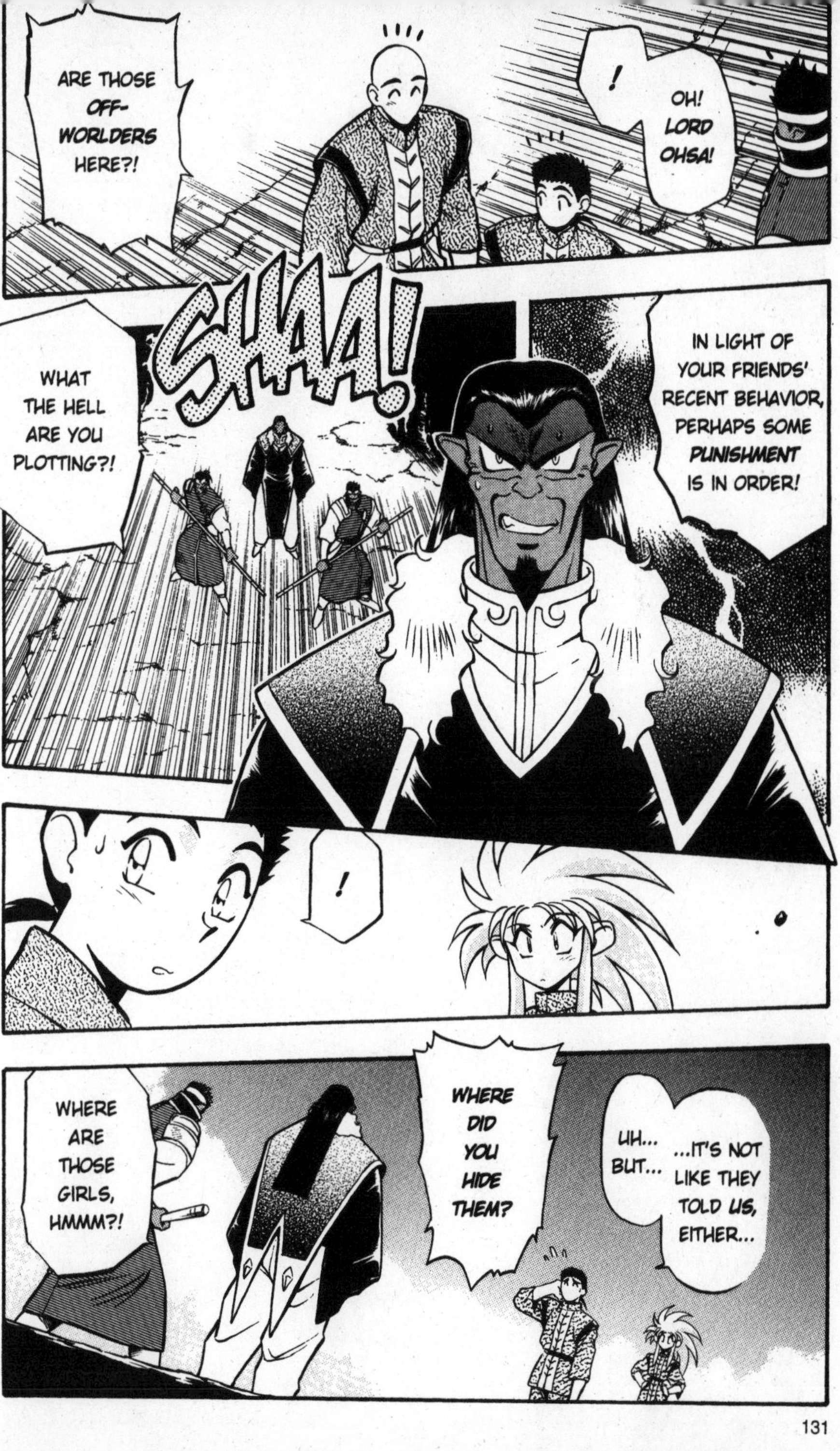
ARE THOSE OFF-WORLDERS HERE?!
!
OH! LORD OHSA!
WHAT THE HELL ARE YOU PLOTTING?!
SHAA!
IN LIGHT OF YOUR FRIENDS' RECENT BEHAVIOR, PERHAPS SOME PUNISHMENT IS IN ORDER!
!
WHERE ARE THOSE GIRLS, HMMM?!
WHERE DID YOU HIDE THEM?
UH... BUT...
...IT'S NOT LIKE THEY TOLD US, EITHER...

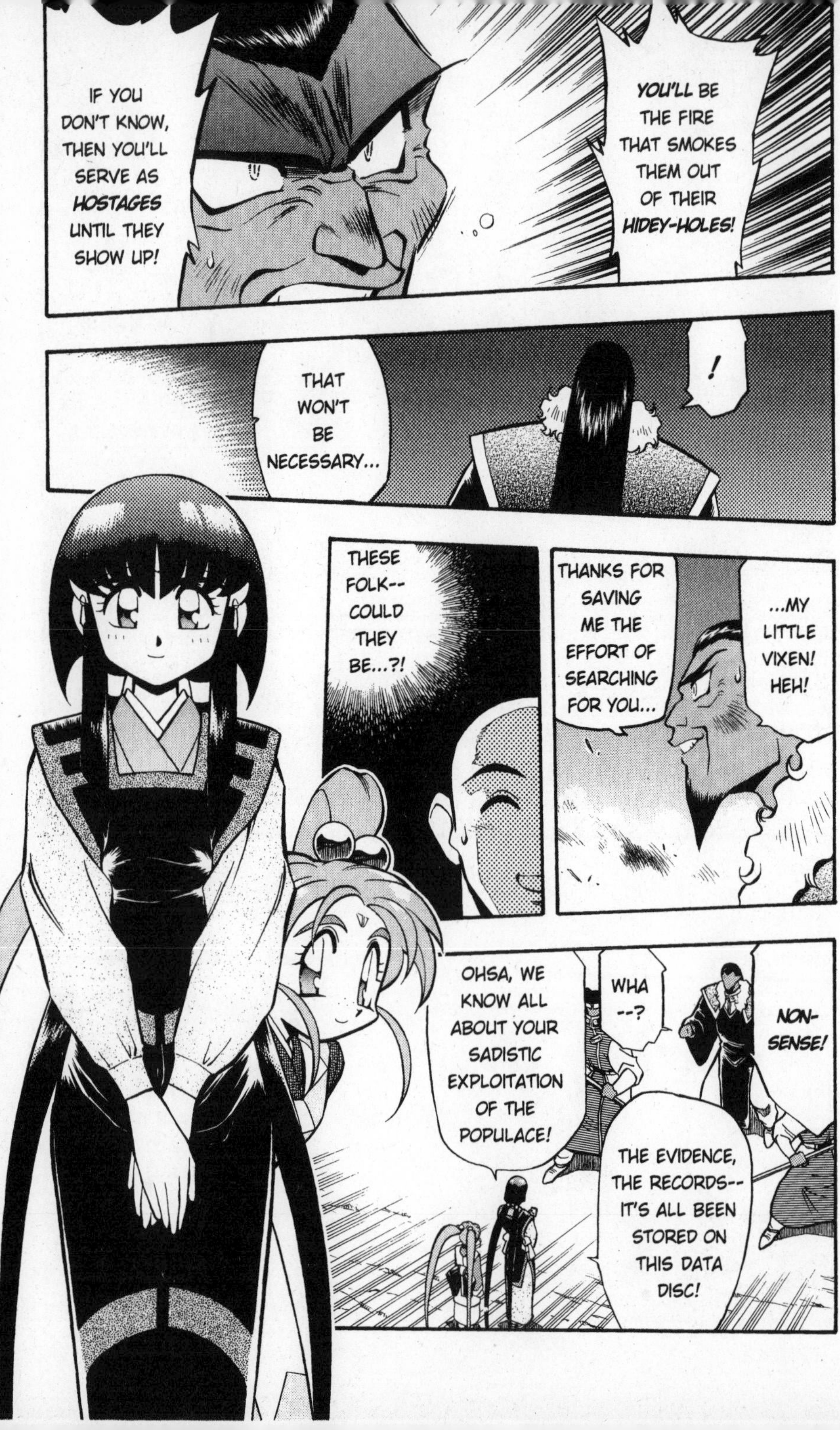
IF YOU DON'T KNOW, THEN YOU'LL SERVE AS HOSTAGES UNTIL THEY SHOW UP!
YOU'LL BE THE FIRE THAT SMOKES THEM OUT OF THEIR HIDEY-HOLES!
THAT WON'T BE NECESSARY...
!
THESE FOLK-- COULD THEY BE...?!
THANKS FOR SAVING ME THE EFFORT OF SEARCHING FOR YOU...
...MY LITTLE VIXEN! HEH!
OHSA, WE KNOW ALL ABOUT YOUR SADISTIC EXPLOITATION OF THE POPULACE!
WHA --?
NON-SENSE!
THE EVIDENCE, THE RECORDS-- IT'S ALL BEEN STORED ON THIS DATA DISC!

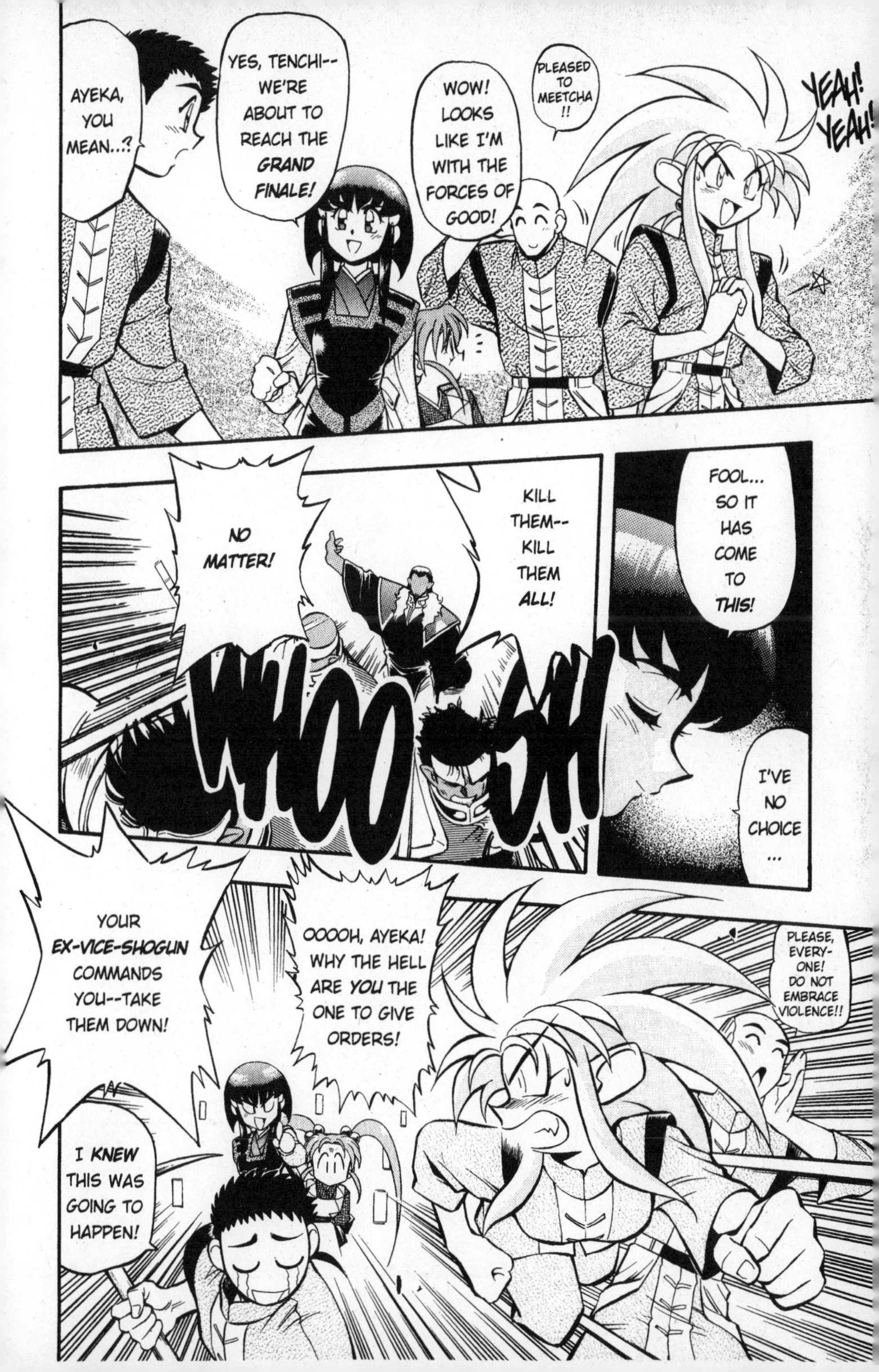
AYEKA, YOU MEAN...?
YES, TENCHI-- WE'RE ABOUT TO REACH THE GRAND FINALE!
WOW! LOOKS LIKE I'M WITH THE FORCES OF GOOD!
PLEASED TO MEETCHA !!
YEAH! YEAH!
FOOL... SO IT HAS COME TO THIS!
I'VE NO CHOICE ...
KILL THEM-- KILL THEM ALL!
NO MATTER!
WHOO-SH
YOUR EX-VICE-SHOGUN COMMANDS YOU--TAKE THEM DOWN!
OOOOH, AYEKA! WHY THE HELL ARE YOU THE ONE TO GIVE ORDERS!
PLEASE, EVERY-ONE! DO NOT EMBRACE VIOLENCE!!
I KNEW THIS WAS GOING TO HAPPEN!

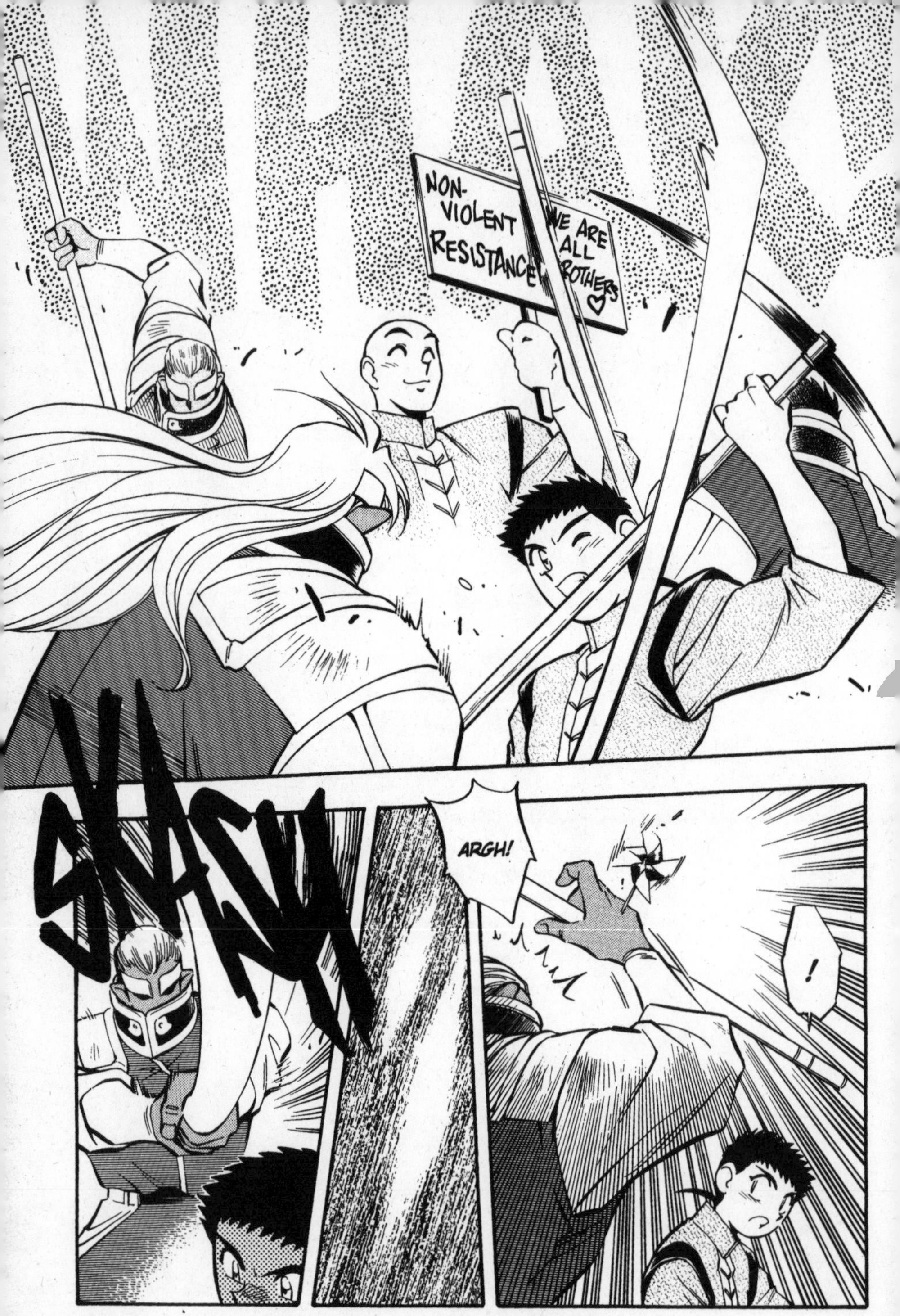
NON-VIOLENT RESISTANCE
WE ARE ALL BROTHERS ♡
ARGH!
!

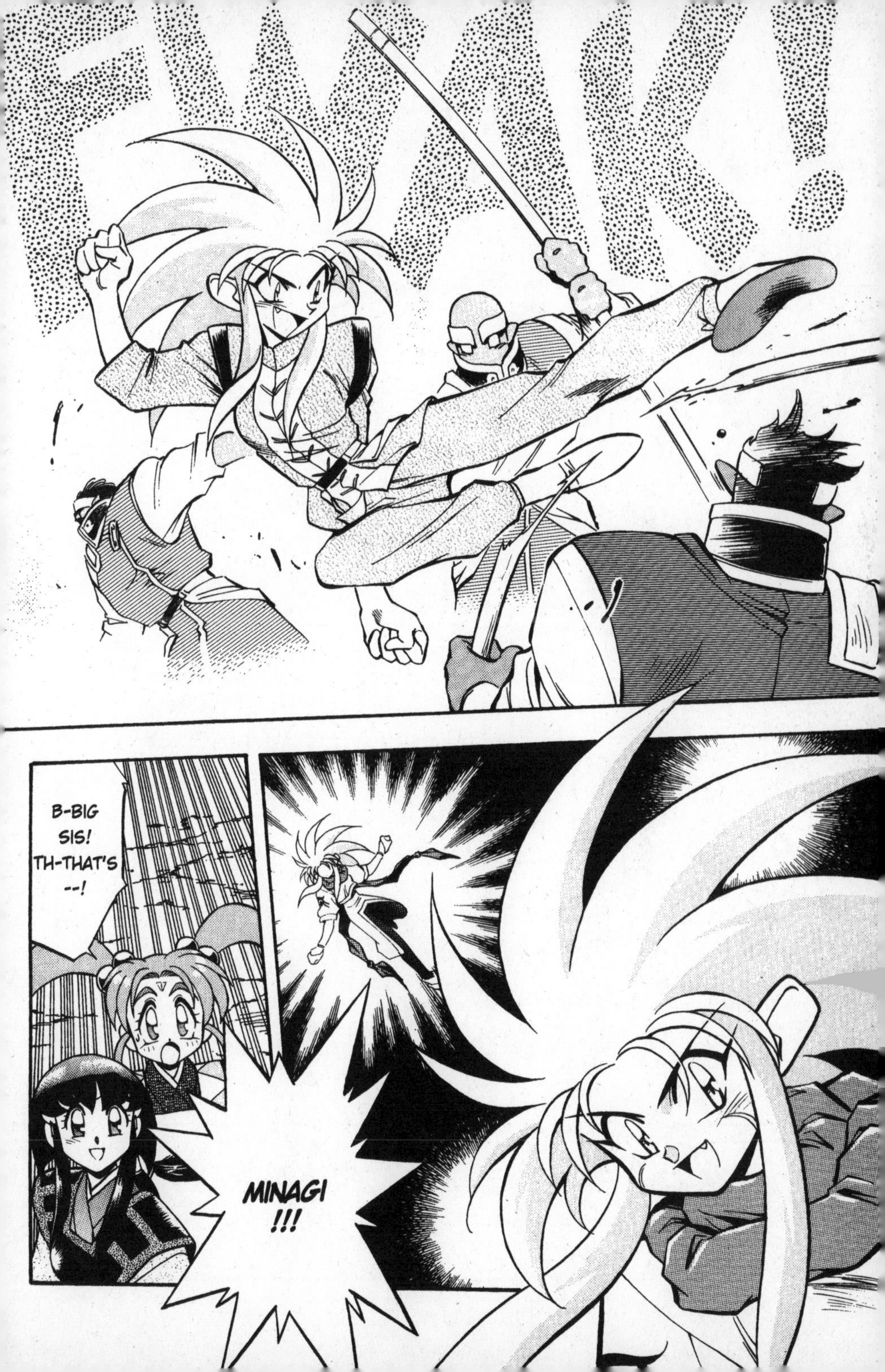
FWAK!
B-BIG SIS! TH-THAT'S --!
MINAGI !!!

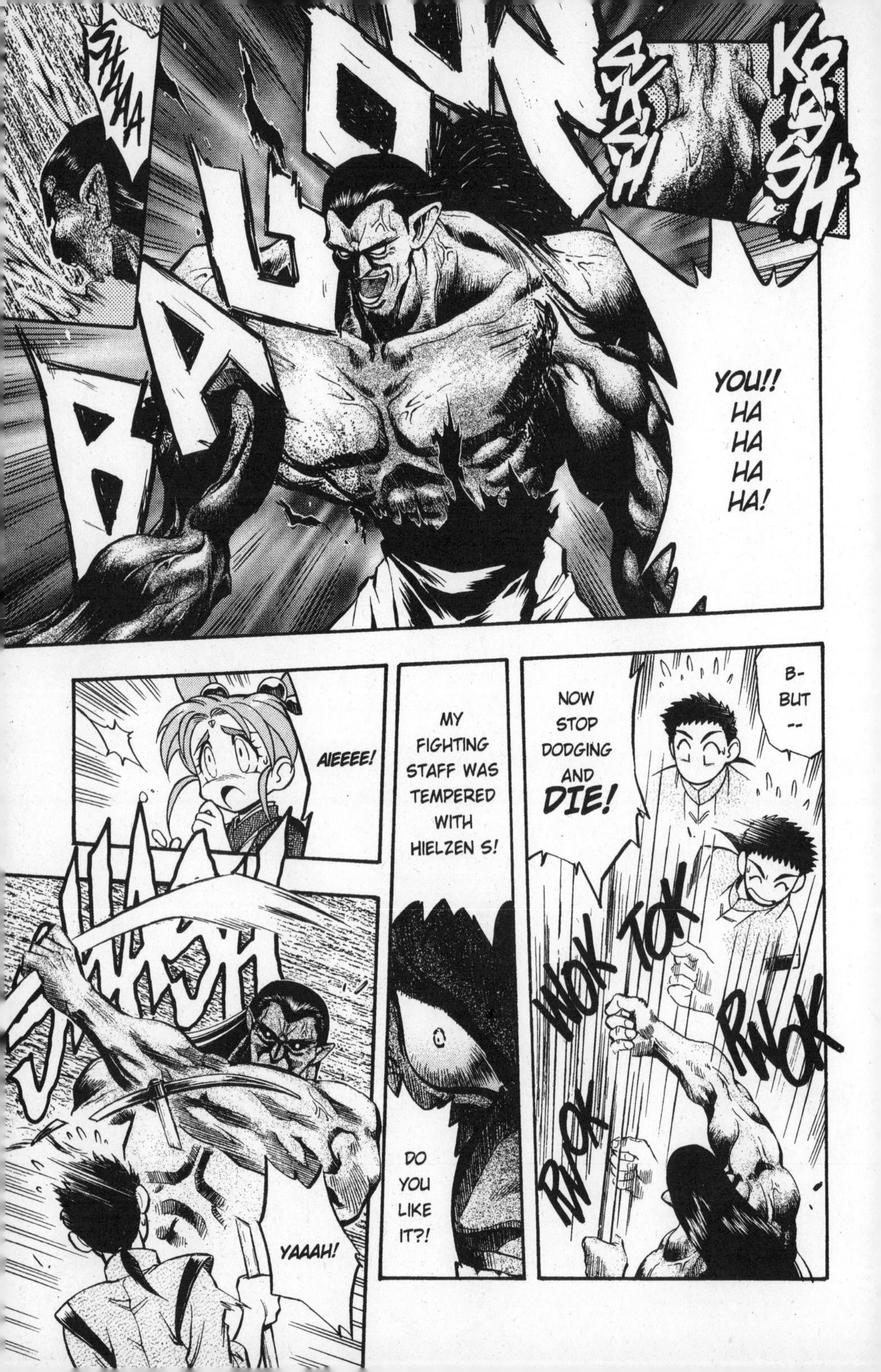
SHWAAA
KRASH
YOU!! HA HA HA HA!
AIEEEE!
YAAAH!
MY FIGHTING STAFF WAS TEMPERED WITH HIELZEN S!
DO YOU LIKE IT?!
NOW STOP DODGING AND DIE!
B-BUT --
WOK TOK
RWOK
RWOK

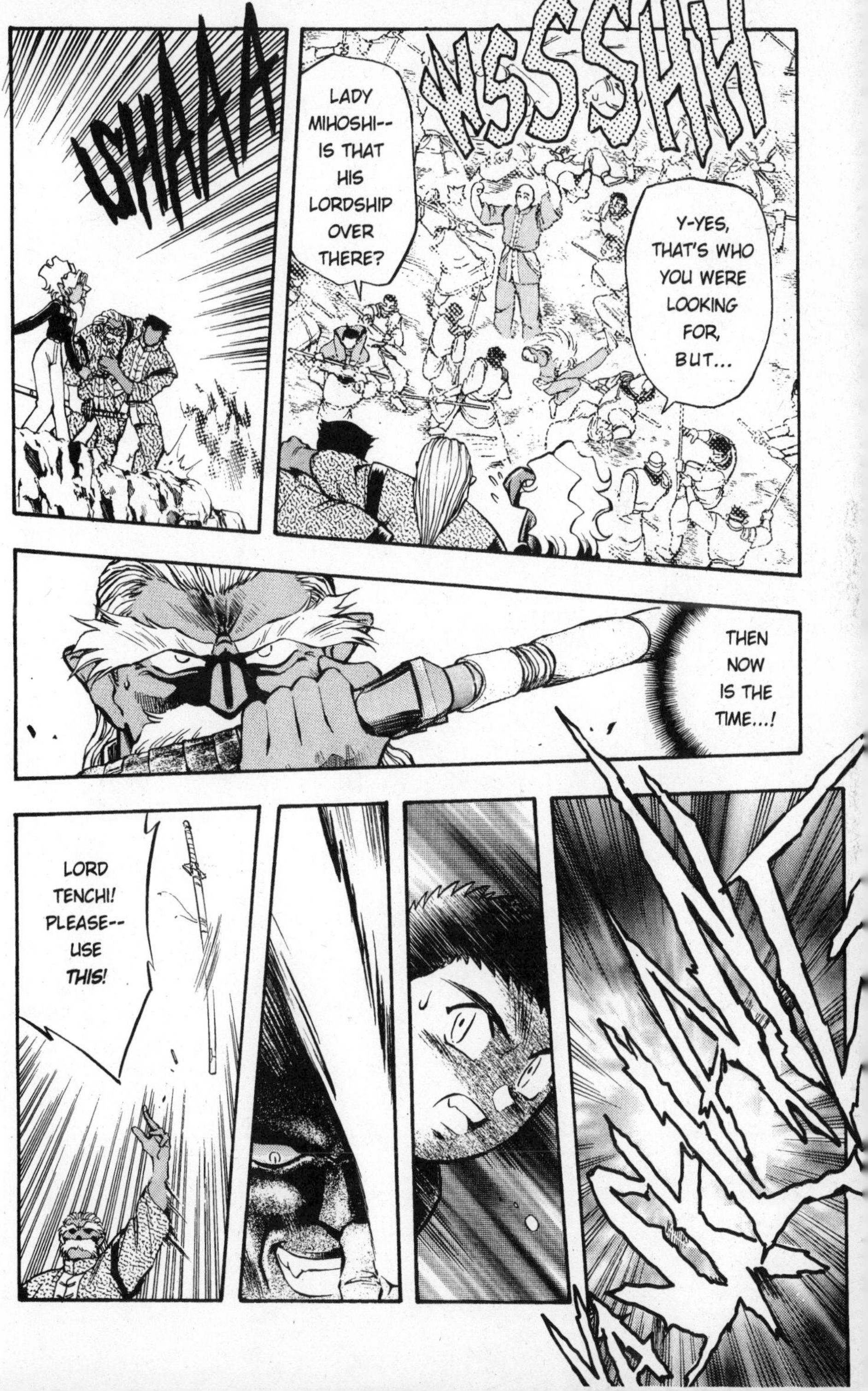
SHAAA
LADY MIHOSHI-- IS THAT HIS LORDSHIP OVER THERE?
WSSSHH
Y-YES, THAT'S WHO YOU WERE LOOKING FOR, BUT...
THEN NOW IS THE TIME...!
LORD TENCHI! PLEASE-- USE *THIS!*

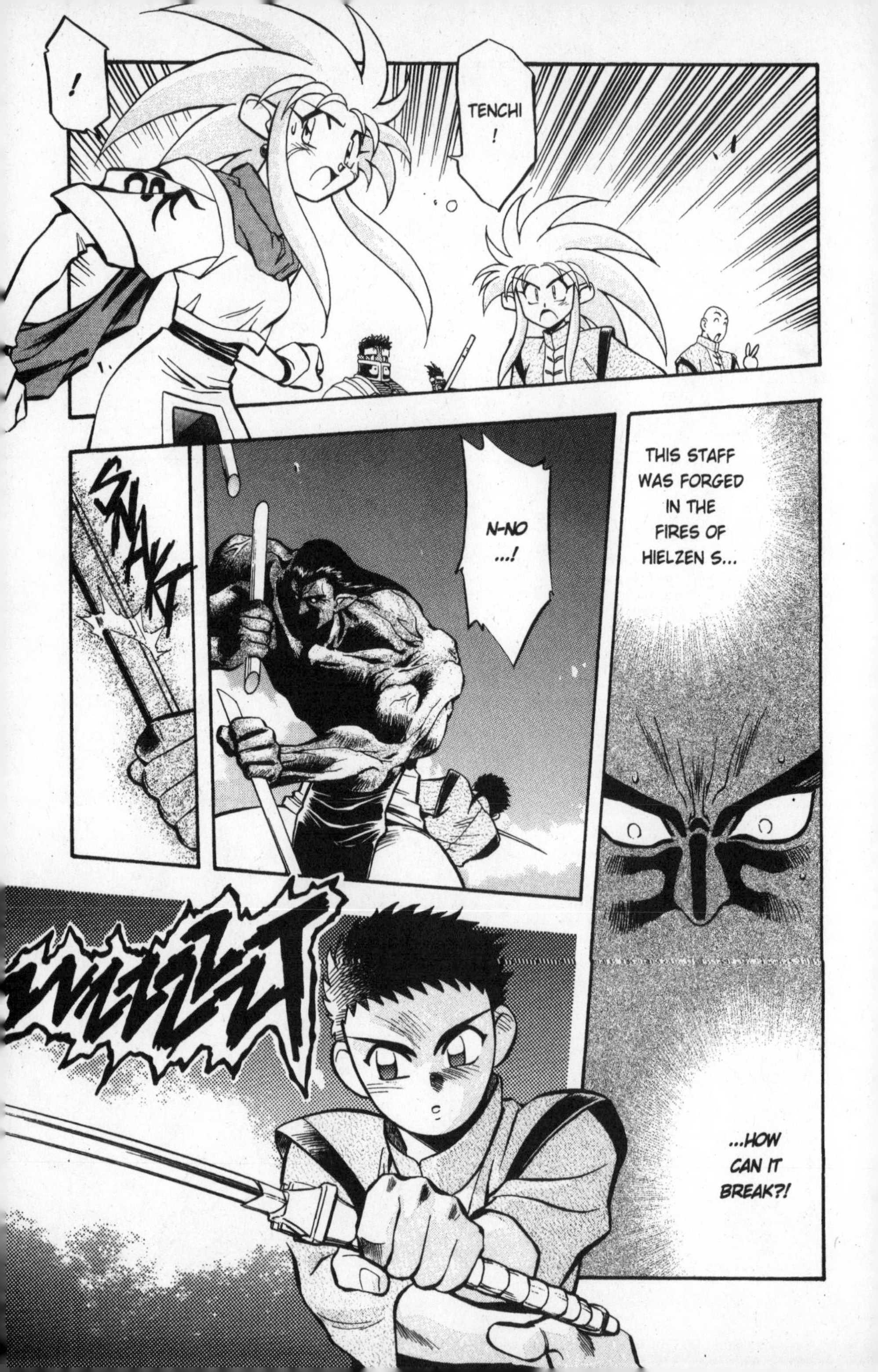
!
TENCHI !
SNAKT
N-NO ...!
THIS STAFF WAS FORGED IN THE FIRES OF HIELZEN S...
WHIZZZT
...HOW CAN IT BREAK?!

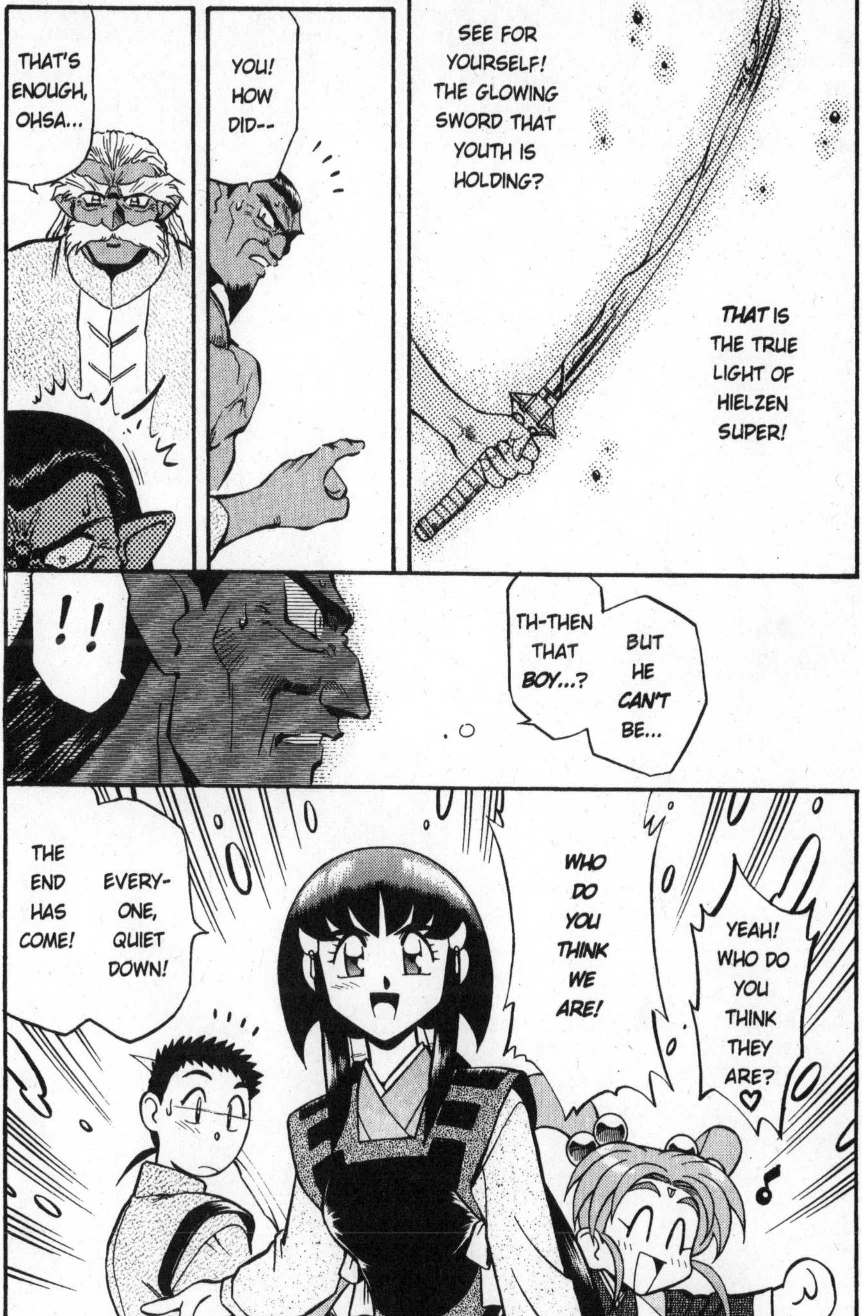
THAT'S ENOUGH, OHSA...
YOU! HOW DID--
SEE FOR YOURSELF! THE GLOWING SWORD THAT YOUTH IS HOLDING?
THAT IS THE TRUE LIGHT OF HIELZEN SUPER!
!!
TH-THEN THAT *BOY*...?
BUT HE *CAN'T* BE...
THE END HAS COME!
EVERY-ONE, QUIET DOWN!
WHO DO YOU THINK WE ARE!
YEAH! WHO DO YOU THINK THEY ARE? ♥

THIS YOUNG MAN IS NONE OTHER THAN HIS ROYAL HIGHNESS, *LORD PRINCE TENCHI* OF THE JURAI ROYAL FAMILY!

AND *I* AM THE FIRST PRINCESS, AYEKA OF JURAI!

HA, HA...

HOW COME SHE GETS ALL THE GOOD LINES?!

WHA-?

YOU ...?!

THE JURAI ROYAL FAMILY?!

H-HMPH! IT -- IT'S A *BLUFF!*

YEAH! THEY'VE GOT NO PROOF!

AH, BUT THERE *IS* PROOF...

...ISN'T THERE, OHSA?

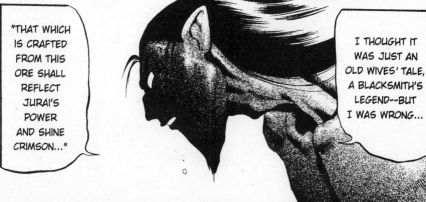

"THAT WHICH IS CRAFTED FROM THIS ORE SHALL REFLECT JURAI'S POWER AND SHINE CRIMSON..."

I THOUGHT IT WAS JUST AN OLD WIVES' TALE, A BLACKSMITH'S LEGEND--BUT I WAS WRONG...

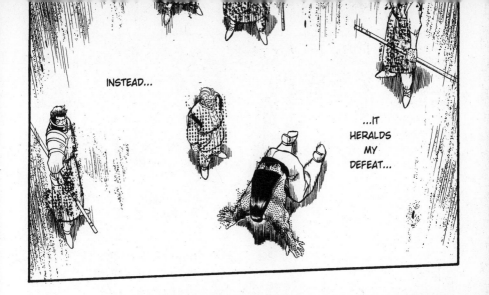

INSTEAD...

...IT HERALDS MY DEFEAT...

WELL, THIS IS FAREWELL, PRINCE...

PLEASE DON'T CALL ME THAT! *PLEASE!*

THANKS TO YOU, I HAVE LIVED TO HOLD MY GRANDCHILD!

YOU HAVE MY DEEPEST GRATITUDE.

GLAD TO BE OF HELP! BUT... ARE YOU SURE IT'S ALL RIGHT? TO KEEP THIS SWORD, I MEAN...

MANY YEARS AGO, A *SWORDSMAN* FROM *ANOTHER WORLD* MET MY PREDECESSOR, A RENOWNED SWORDSMITH...

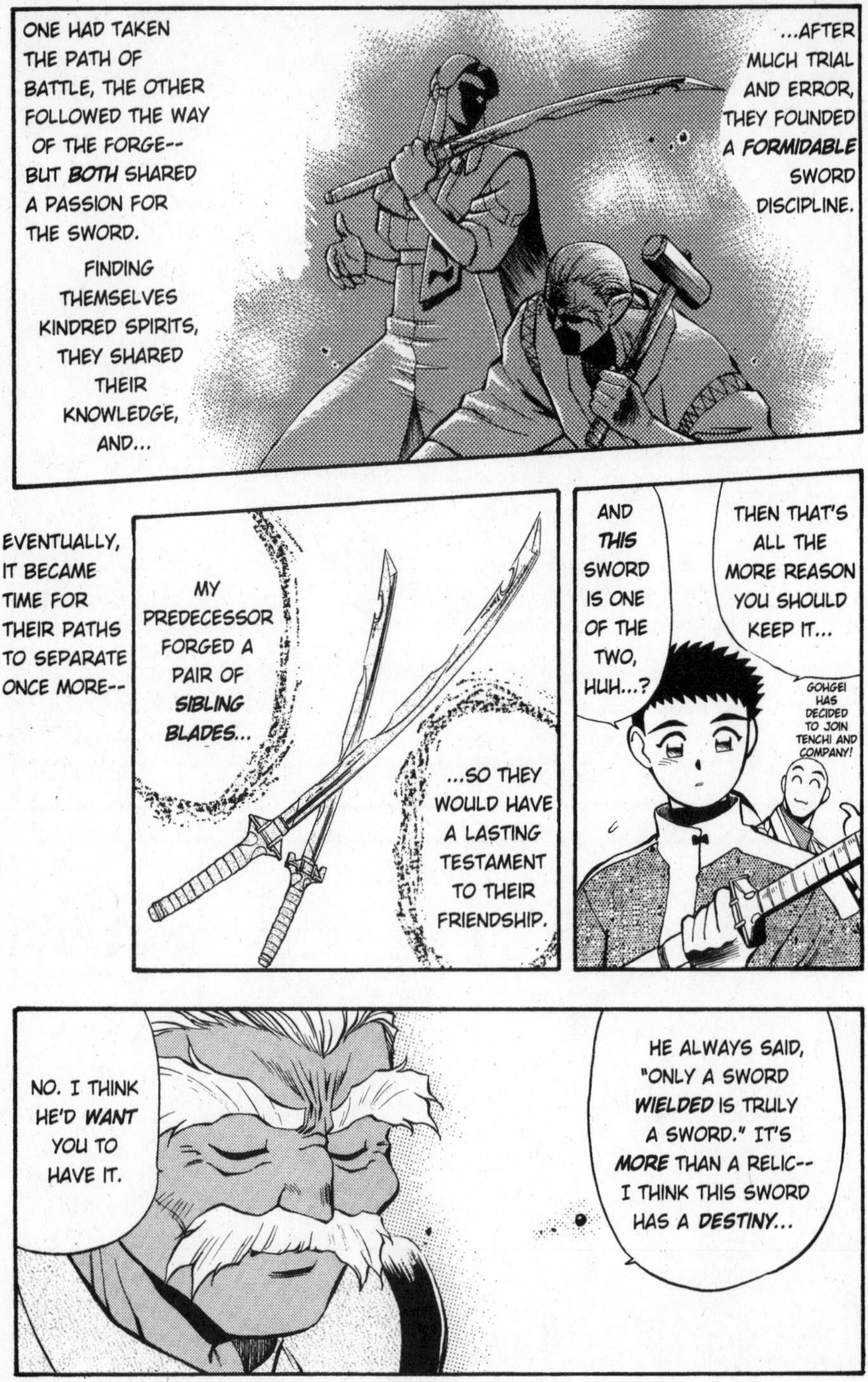
ONE HAD TAKEN THE PATH OF BATTLE, THE OTHER FOLLOWED THE WAY OF THE FORGE-- BUT BOTH SHARED A PASSION FOR THE SWORD.
FINDING THEMSELVES KINDRED SPIRITS, THEY SHARED THEIR KNOWLEDGE, AND...
...AFTER MUCH TRIAL AND ERROR, THEY FOUNDED A FORMIDABLE SWORD DISCIPLINE.
EVENTUALLY, IT BECAME TIME FOR THEIR PATHS TO SEPARATE ONCE MORE--
MY PREDECESSOR FORGED A PAIR OF SIBLING BLADES...
...SO THEY WOULD HAVE A LASTING TESTAMENT TO THEIR FRIENDSHIP.
AND THIS SWORD IS ONE OF THE TWO, HUH...?
THEN THAT'S ALL THE MORE REASON YOU SHOULD KEEP IT...
GOHGEI HAS DECIDED TO JOIN TENCHI AND COMPANY!
NO. I THINK HE'D WANT YOU TO HAVE IT.
HE ALWAYS SAID, "ONLY A SWORD WIELDED IS TRULY A SWORD." IT'S MORE THAN A RELIC-- I THINK THIS SWORD HAS A DESTINY...

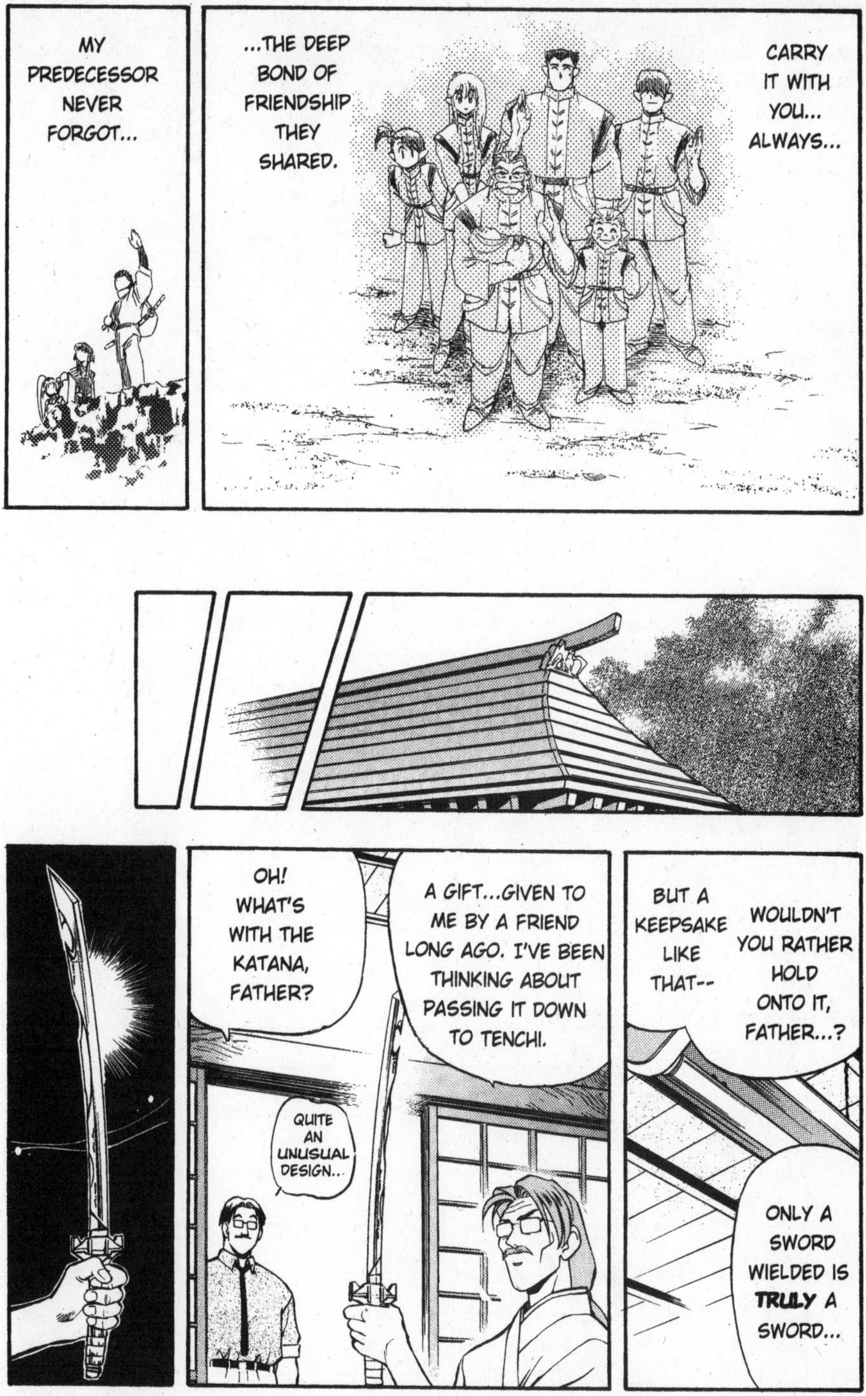
MY PREDECESSOR NEVER FORGOT...
...THE DEEP BOND OF FRIENDSHIP THEY SHARED.
CARRY IT WITH YOU... ALWAYS...
OH! WHAT'S WITH THE KATANA, FATHER?
A GIFT...GIVEN TO ME BY A FRIEND LONG AGO. I'VE BEEN THINKING ABOUT PASSING IT DOWN TO TENCHI.
QUITE AN UNUSUAL DESIGN...
BUT A KEEPSAKE LIKE THAT--
WOULDN'T YOU RATHER HOLD ONTO IT, FATHER...?
ONLY A SWORD WIELDED IS **TRULY** A SWORD...

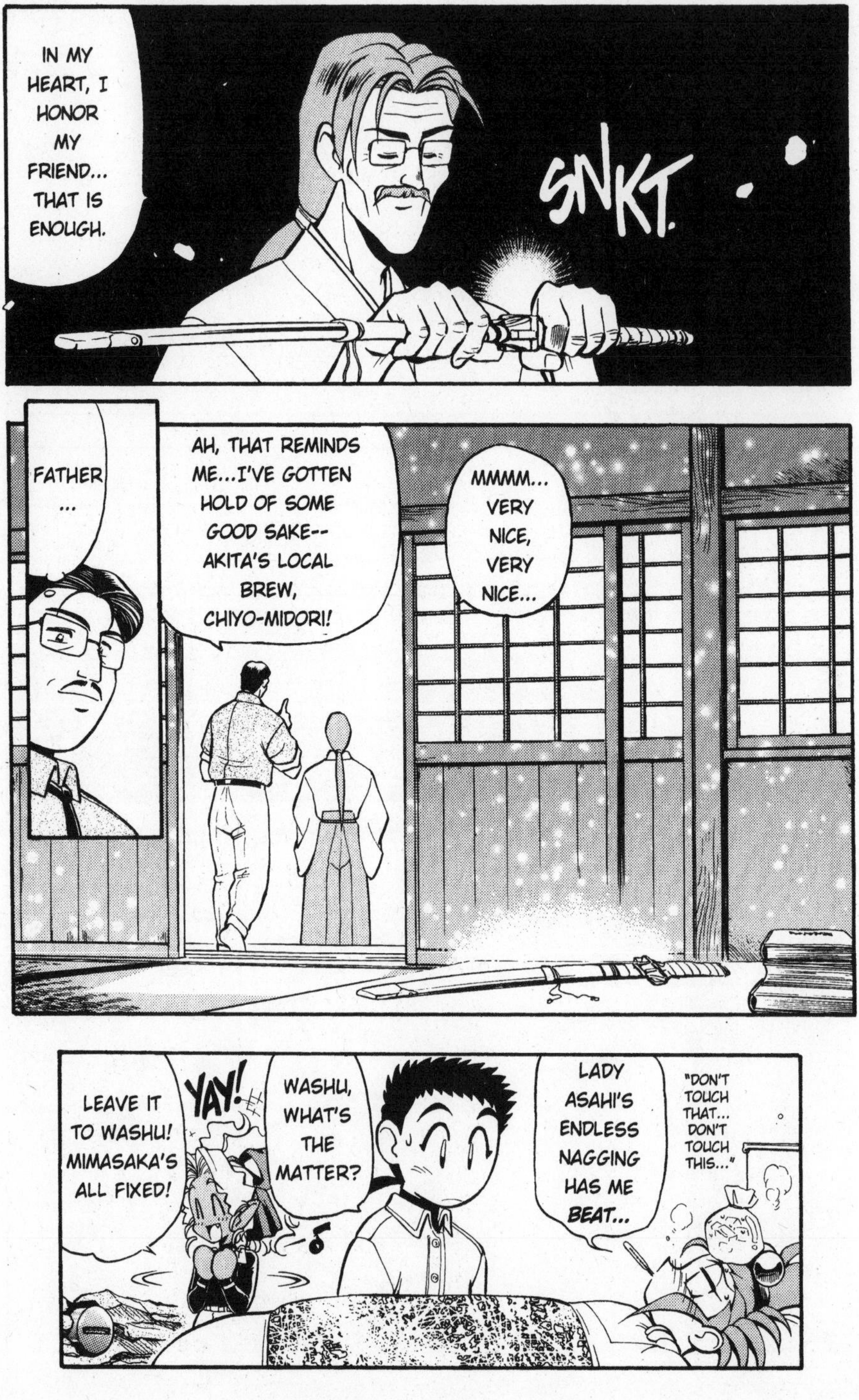
IN MY HEART, I HONOR MY FRIEND... THAT IS ENOUGH.
SNKT.
FATHER ...
AH, THAT REMINDS ME...I'VE GOTTEN HOLD OF SOME GOOD SAKE-- AKITA'S LOCAL BREW, CHIYO-MIDORI!
MMMM... VERY NICE, VERY NICE...
LEAVE IT TO WASHU! MIMASAKA'S ALL FIXED!
YAY!
WASHU, WHAT'S THE MATTER?
LADY ASAHI'S ENDLESS NAGGING HAS ME BEAT...
"DON'T TOUCH THAT... DON'T TOUCH THIS..."

Tales of Tenchi #6
TRANSFORMATIONS

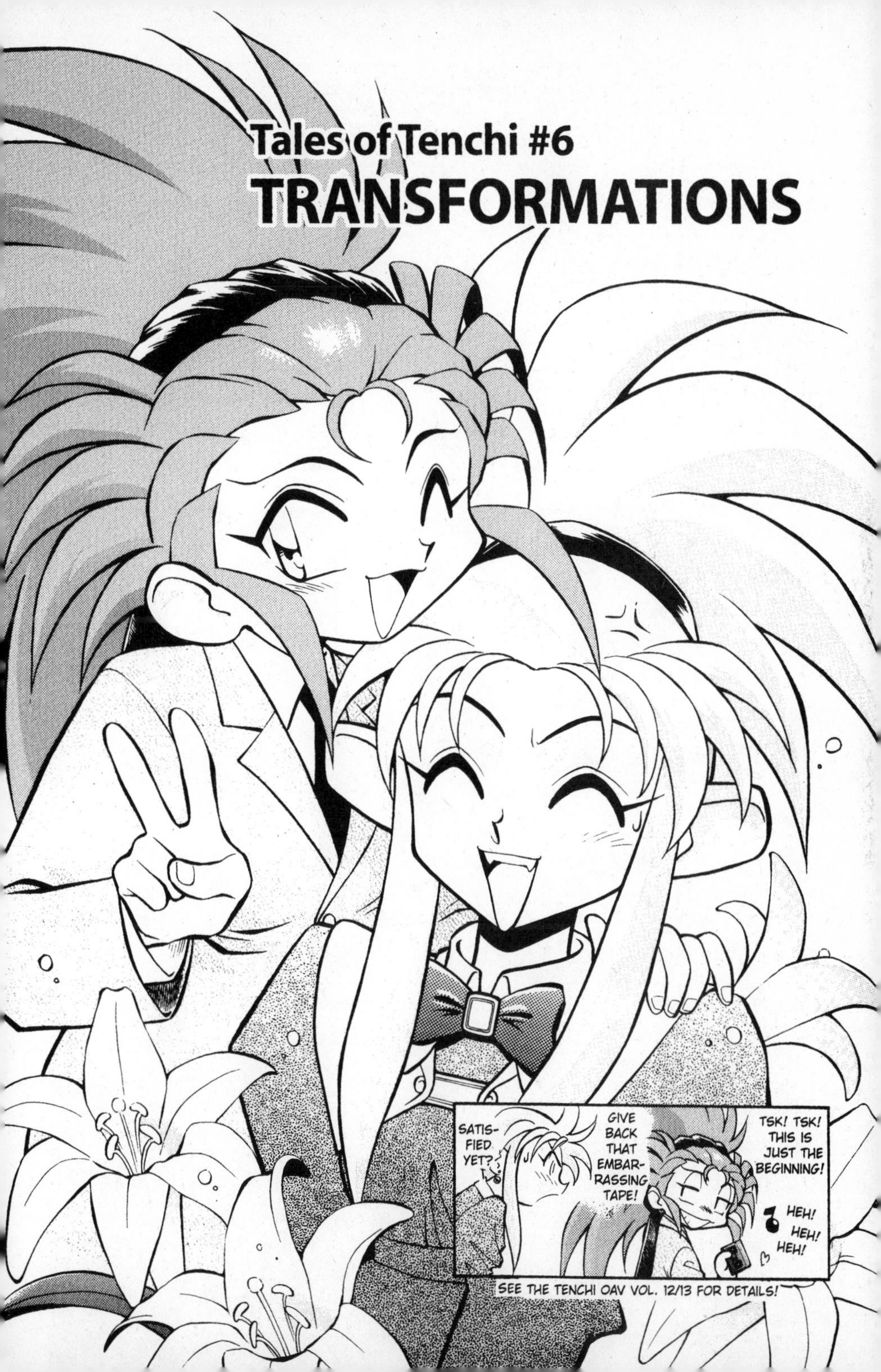
SATIS-FIED YET?
GIVE BACK THAT EMBAR-RASSING TAPE!
TSK! TSK! THIS IS JUST THE BEGINNING!
HEH! HEH! HEH!
SEE THE TENCHI OAV VOL. 12/13 FOR DETAILS!

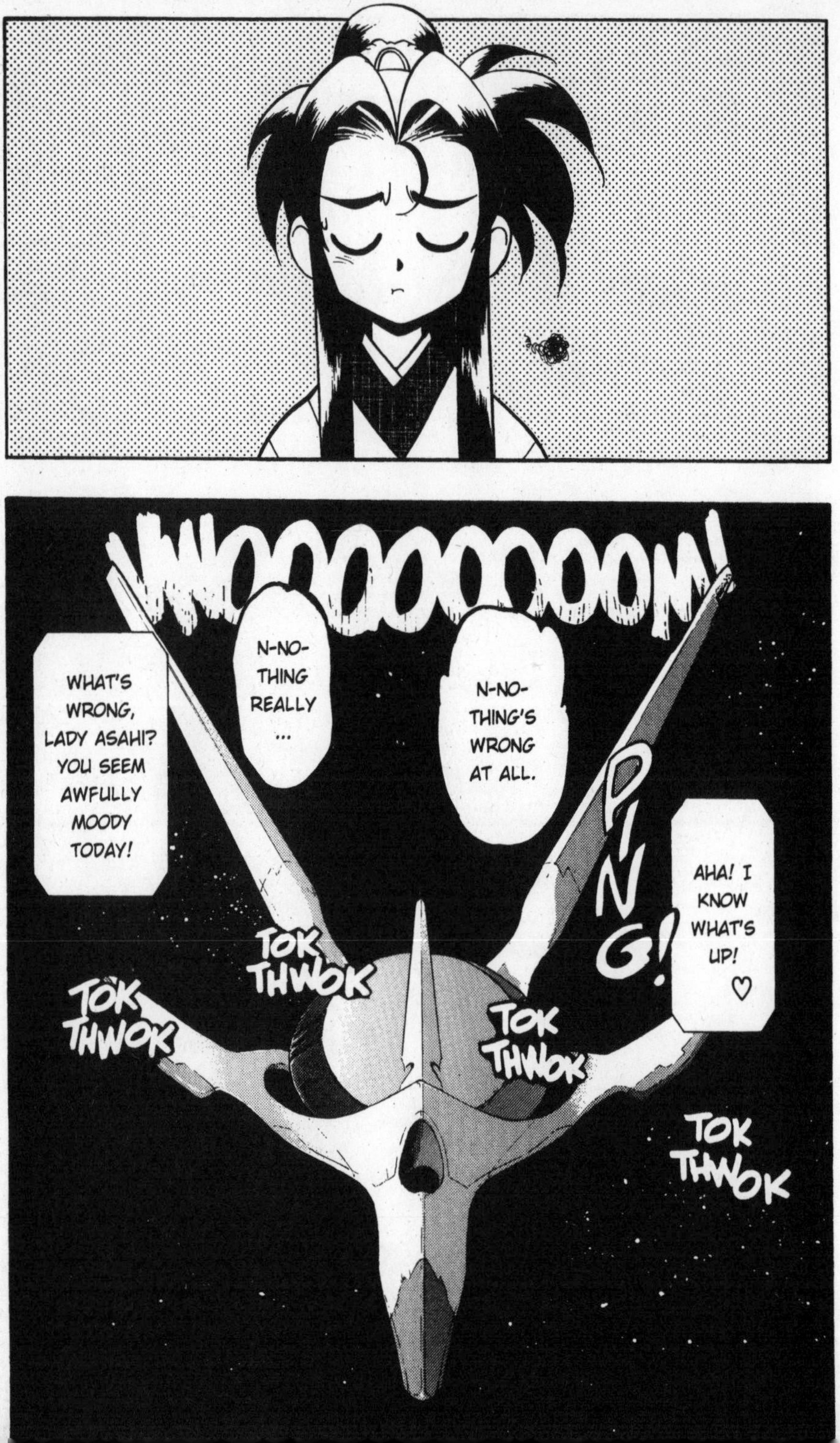
WOOOOOOOOM!
WHAT'S WRONG, LADY ASAHI? YOU SEEM AWFULLY MOODY TODAY!
N-NO-THING REALLY ...
N-NO-THING'S WRONG AT ALL.
PING!
AHA! I KNOW WHAT'S UP! ♡
TOK THWOK
TOK THWOK
TOK THWOK
TOK THWOK

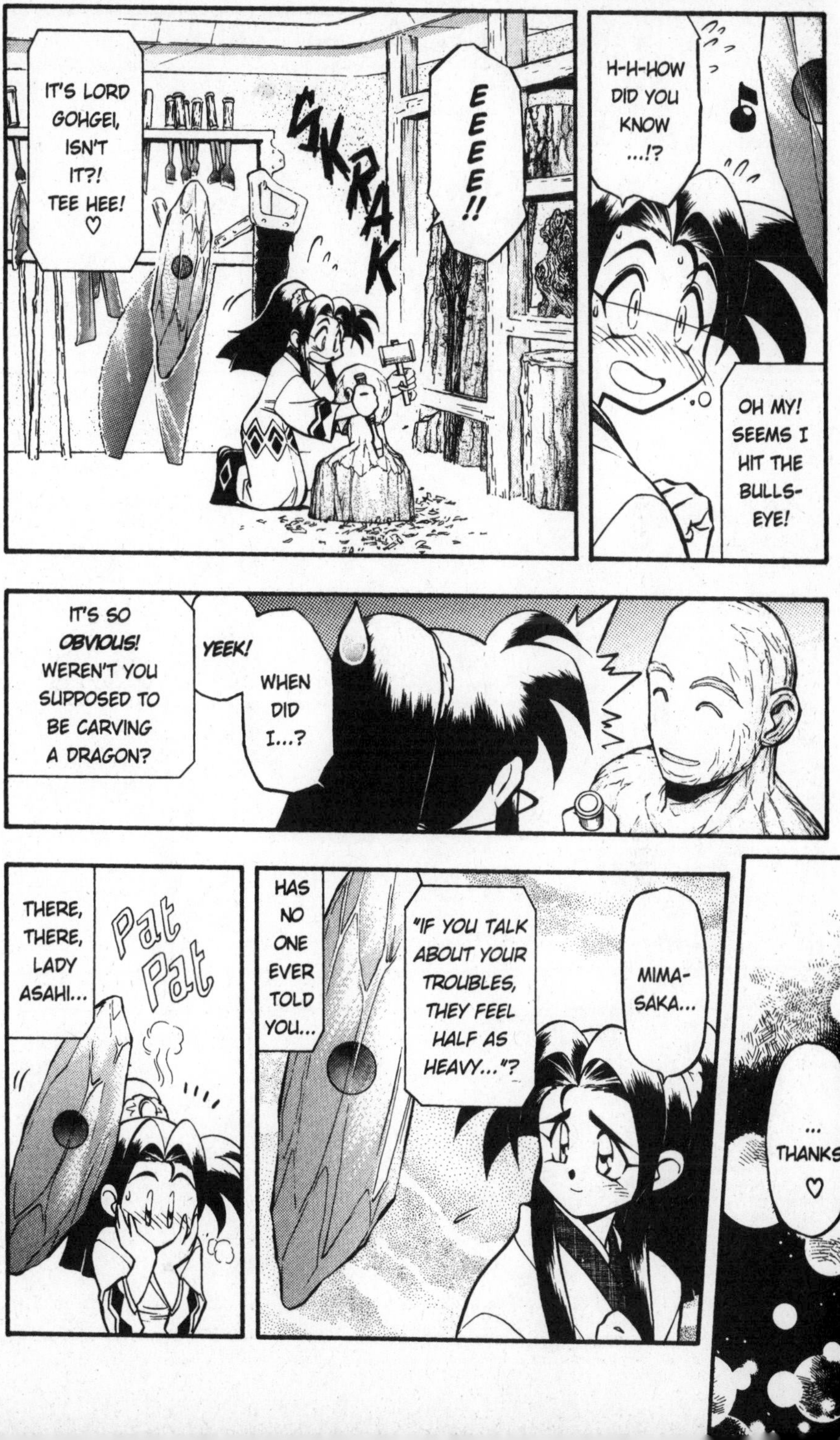
IT'S LORD GOHGEI, ISN'T IT?! TEE HEE! ♡
SKRAK
EEEEE!!
H-H-HOW DID YOU KNOW ...!?
OH MY! SEEMS I HIT THE BULLS-EYE!
IT'S SO OBVIOUS! WEREN'T YOU SUPPOSED TO BE CARVING A DRAGON?
YEEK!
WHEN DID I...?
THERE, THERE, LADY ASAHI...
Pat Pat
HAS NO ONE EVER TOLD YOU...
"IF YOU TALK ABOUT YOUR TROUBLES, THEY FEEL HALF AS HEAVY..."?
MIMA-SAKA...
... THANKS. ♡

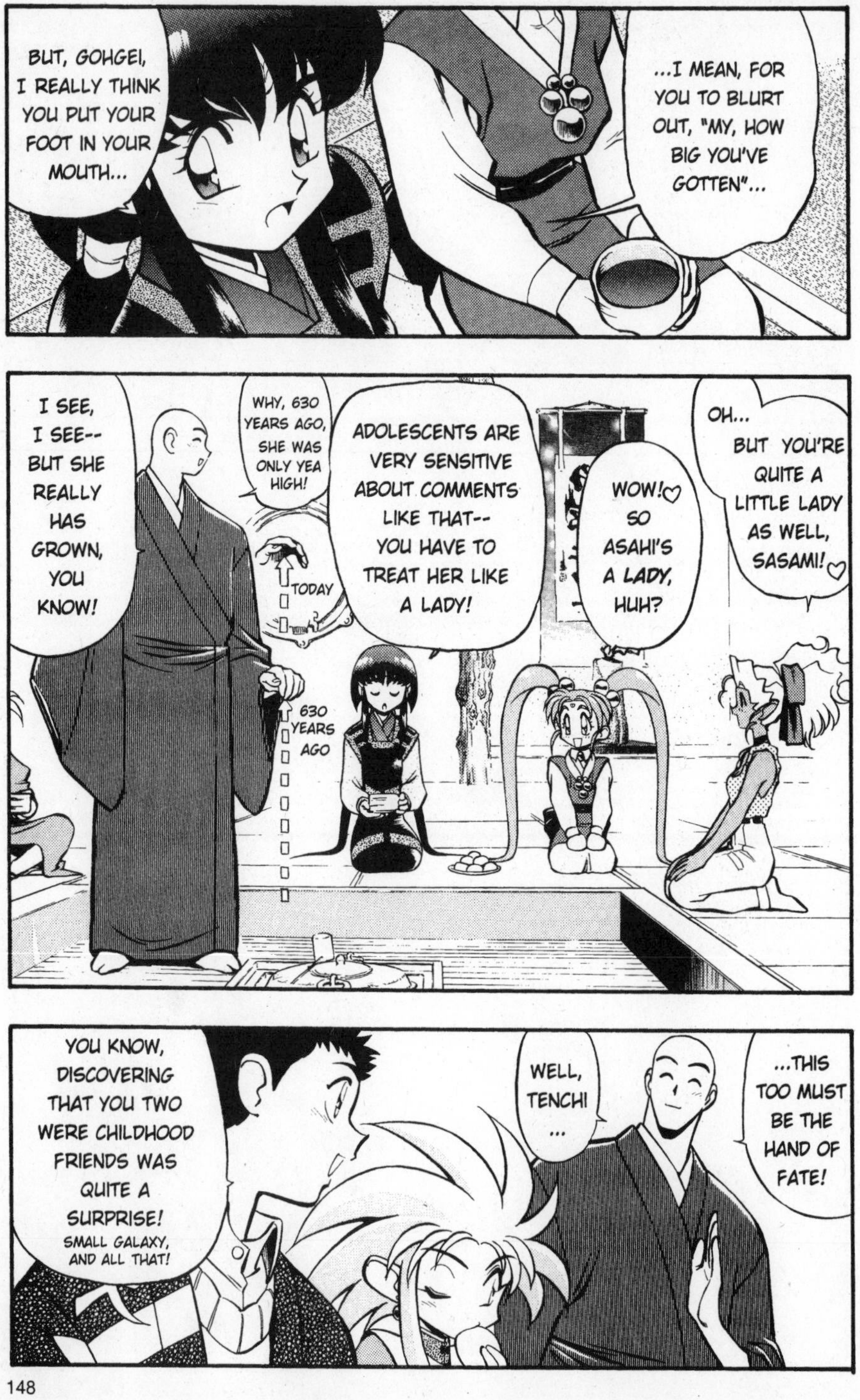
BUT, GOHGEI, I REALLY THINK YOU PUT YOUR FOOT IN YOUR MOUTH...
...I MEAN, FOR YOU TO BLURT OUT, "MY, HOW BIG YOU'VE GOTTEN"...
I SEE, I SEE-- BUT SHE REALLY HAS GROWN, YOU KNOW!
WHY, 630 YEARS AGO, SHE WAS ONLY YEA HIGH!
TODAY
630 YEARS AGO
ADOLESCENTS ARE VERY SENSITIVE ABOUT COMMENTS LIKE THAT-- YOU HAVE TO TREAT HER LIKE A LADY!
WOW!♡ SO ASAHI'S A *LADY*, HUH?
OH... BUT YOU'RE QUITE A LITTLE LADY AS WELL, SASAMI!♡
YOU KNOW, DISCOVERING THAT YOU TWO WERE CHILDHOOD FRIENDS WAS QUITE A SURPRISE!
SMALL GALAXY, AND ALL THAT!
WELL, TENCHI ...
...THIS TOO MUST BE THE HAND OF FATE!

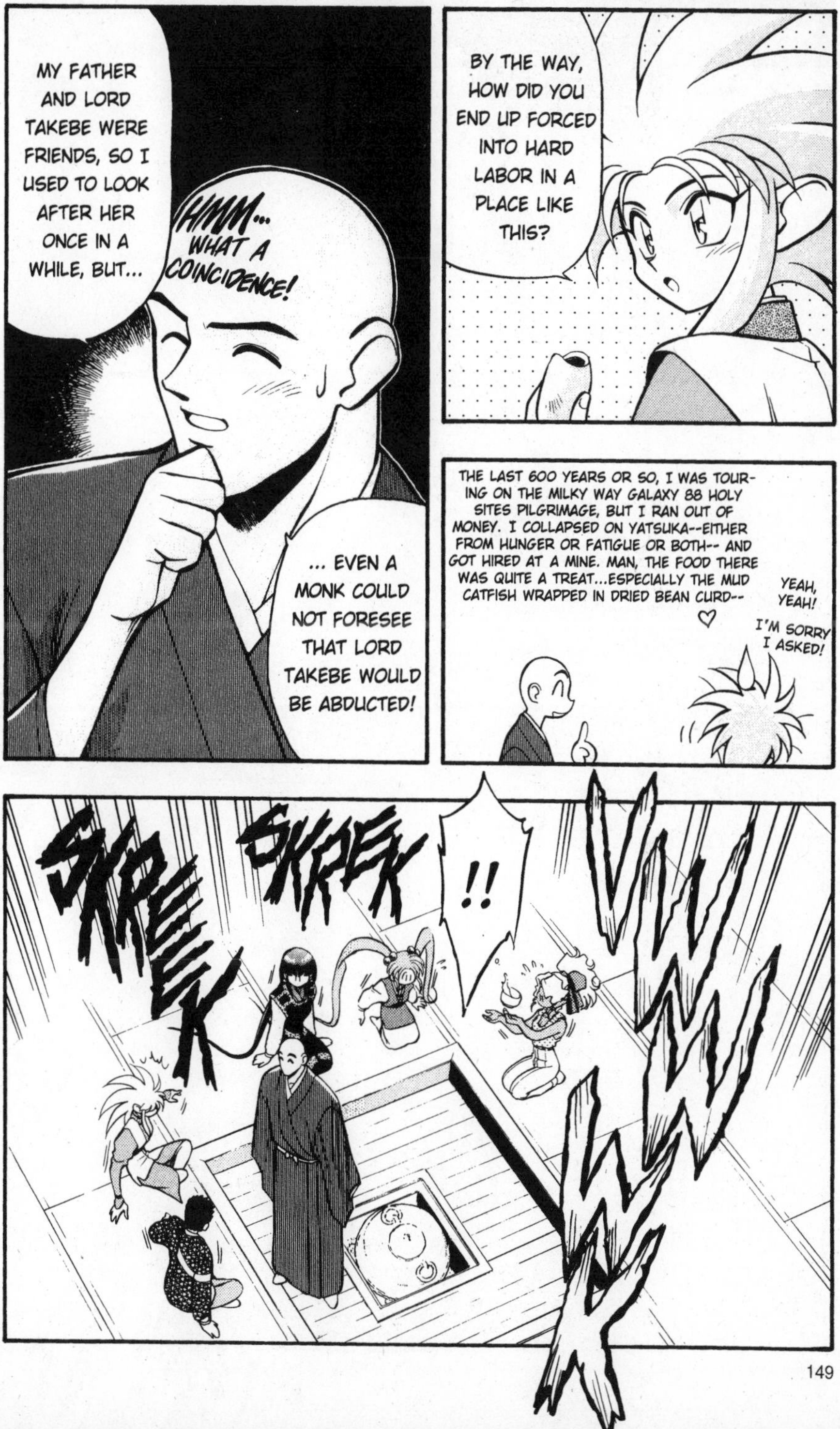
MY FATHER AND LORD TAKEBE WERE FRIENDS, SO I USED TO LOOK AFTER HER ONCE IN A WHILE, BUT...
HMM... WHAT A COINCIDENCE!
... EVEN A MONK COULD NOT FORESEE THAT LORD TAKEBE WOULD BE ABDUCTED!
BY THE WAY, HOW DID YOU END UP FORCED INTO HARD LABOR IN A PLACE LIKE THIS?
THE LAST 600 YEARS OR SO, I WAS TOURING ON THE MILKY WAY GALAXY 88 HOLY SITES PILGRIMAGE, BUT I RAN OUT OF MONEY. I COLLAPSED ON YATSUKA--EITHER FROM HUNGER OR FATIGUE OR BOTH-- AND GOT HIRED AT A MINE. MAN, THE FOOD THERE WAS QUITE A TREAT...ESPECIALLY THE MUD CATFISH WRAPPED IN DRIED BEAN CURD-- ♡
YEAH, YEAH!
I'M SORRY I ASKED!
SKREK
SKREK
!!
VWWWWK

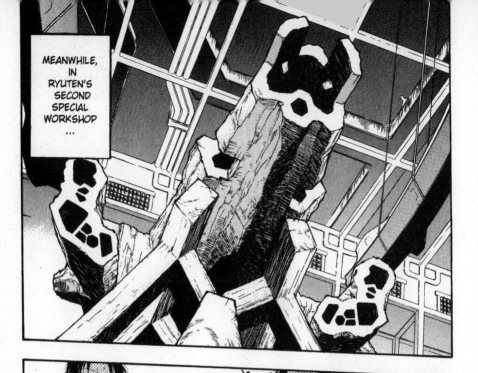

MEANWHILE, IN RYUTEN'S SECOND SPECIAL WORKSHOP ...

GULP!

SHASH

YAH!

FWOOOOOSH

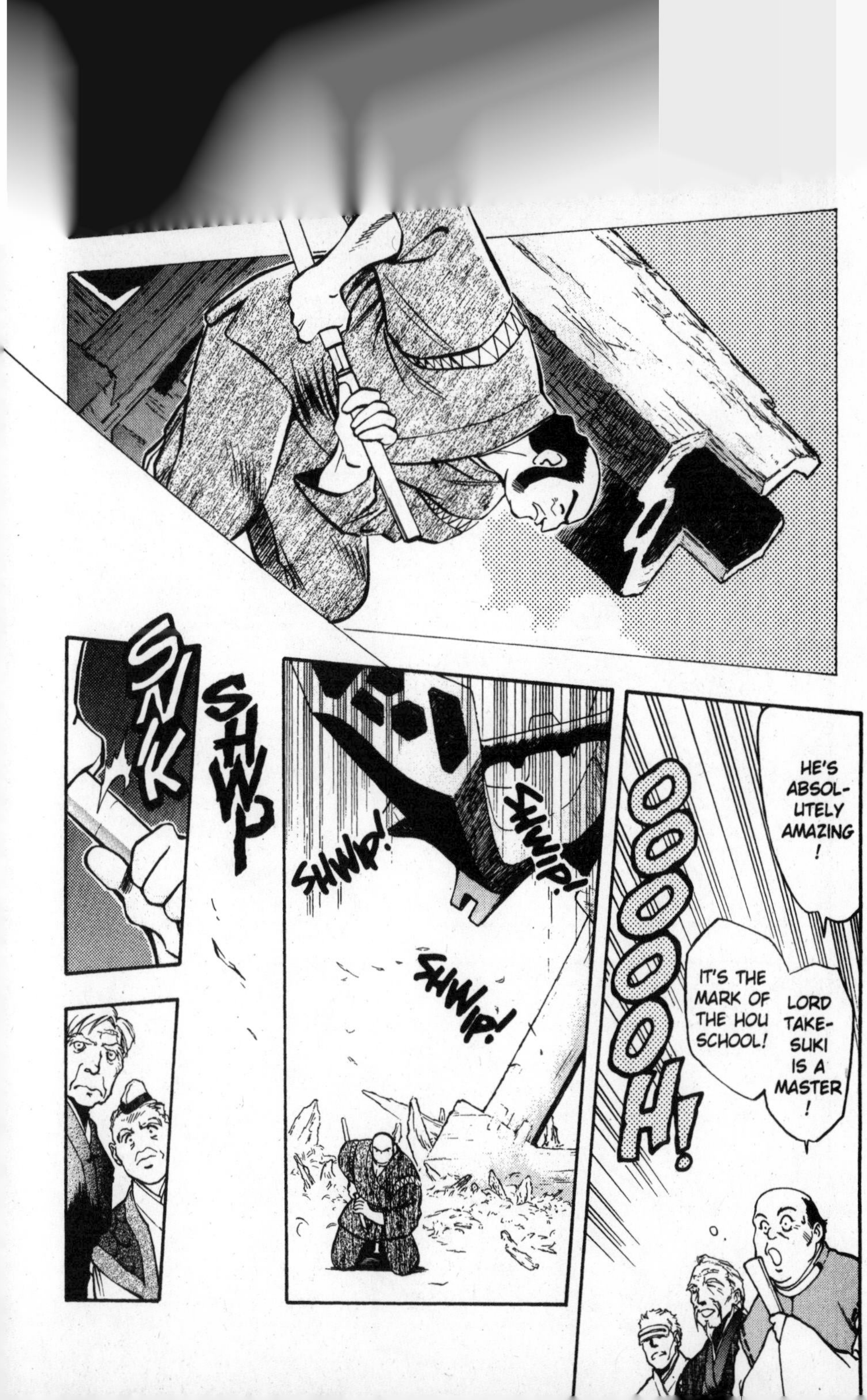
SNIK
SHWIP
SHWIP!
SHWIP!
SHWIP!
OOOOOOH!
HE'S ABSOL-UTELY AMAZING!
IT'S THE MARK OF THE HOU SCHOOL!
LORD TAKE-SUKI IS A MASTER!

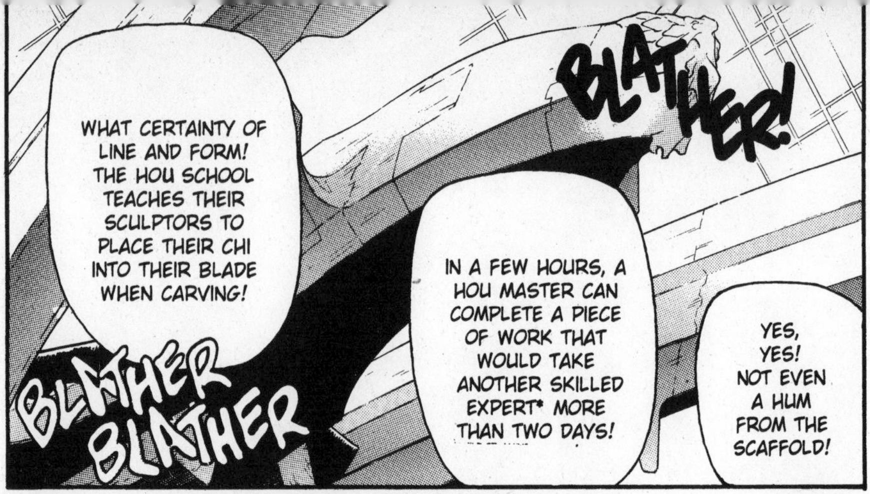
WHAT CERTAINTY OF LINE AND FORM! THE HOU SCHOOL TEACHES THEIR SCULPTORS TO PLACE THEIR CHI INTO THEIR BLADE WHEN CARVING!
BLATHER!
BLATHER BLATHER
IN A FEW HOURS, A HOU MASTER CAN COMPLETE A PIECE OF WORK THAT WOULD TAKE ANOTHER SKILLED EXPERT* MORE THAN TWO DAYS!
YES, YES! NOT EVEN A HUM FROM THE SCAFFOLD!

*MOST OF THESE HUMONGOUS TREE TRUNKS ARE CARVED BY GIANT PILOTED ROBOTS

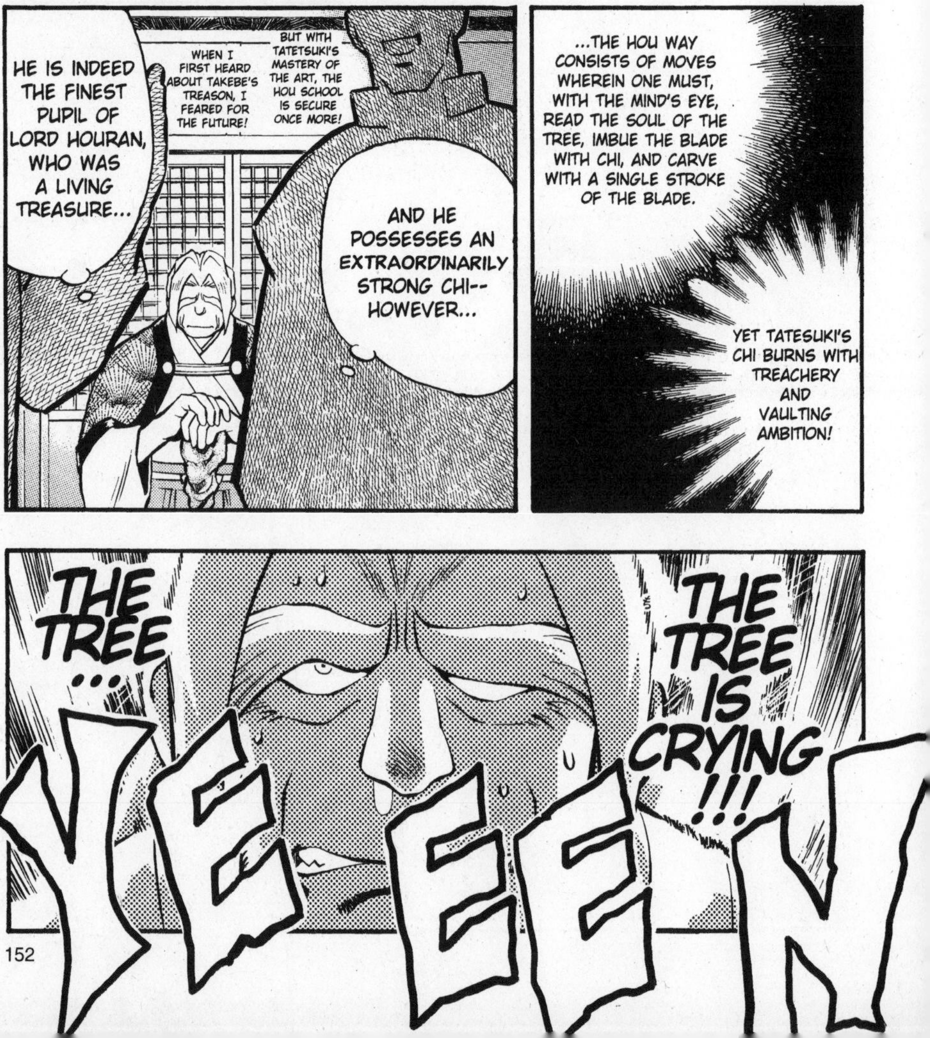
HE IS INDEED THE FINEST PUPIL OF LORD HOURAN, WHO WAS A LIVING TREASURE...
WHEN I FIRST HEARD ABOUT TAKEBE'S TREASON, I FEARED FOR THE FUTURE!
BUT WITH TATETSUKI'S MASTERY OF THE ART, THE HOU SCHOOL IS SECURE ONCE MORE!
AND HE POSSESSES AN EXTRAORDINARILY STRONG CHI-- HOWEVER...
...THE HOU WAY CONSISTS OF MOVES WHEREIN ONE MUST, WITH THE MIND'S EYE, READ THE SOUL OF THE TREE, IMBUE THE BLADE WITH CHI, AND CARVE WITH A SINGLE STROKE OF THE BLADE.
YET TATESUKI'S CHI BURNS WITH TREACHERY AND VAULTING AMBITION!
THE TREE...
YEEEEN
THE TREE IS CRYING!!!

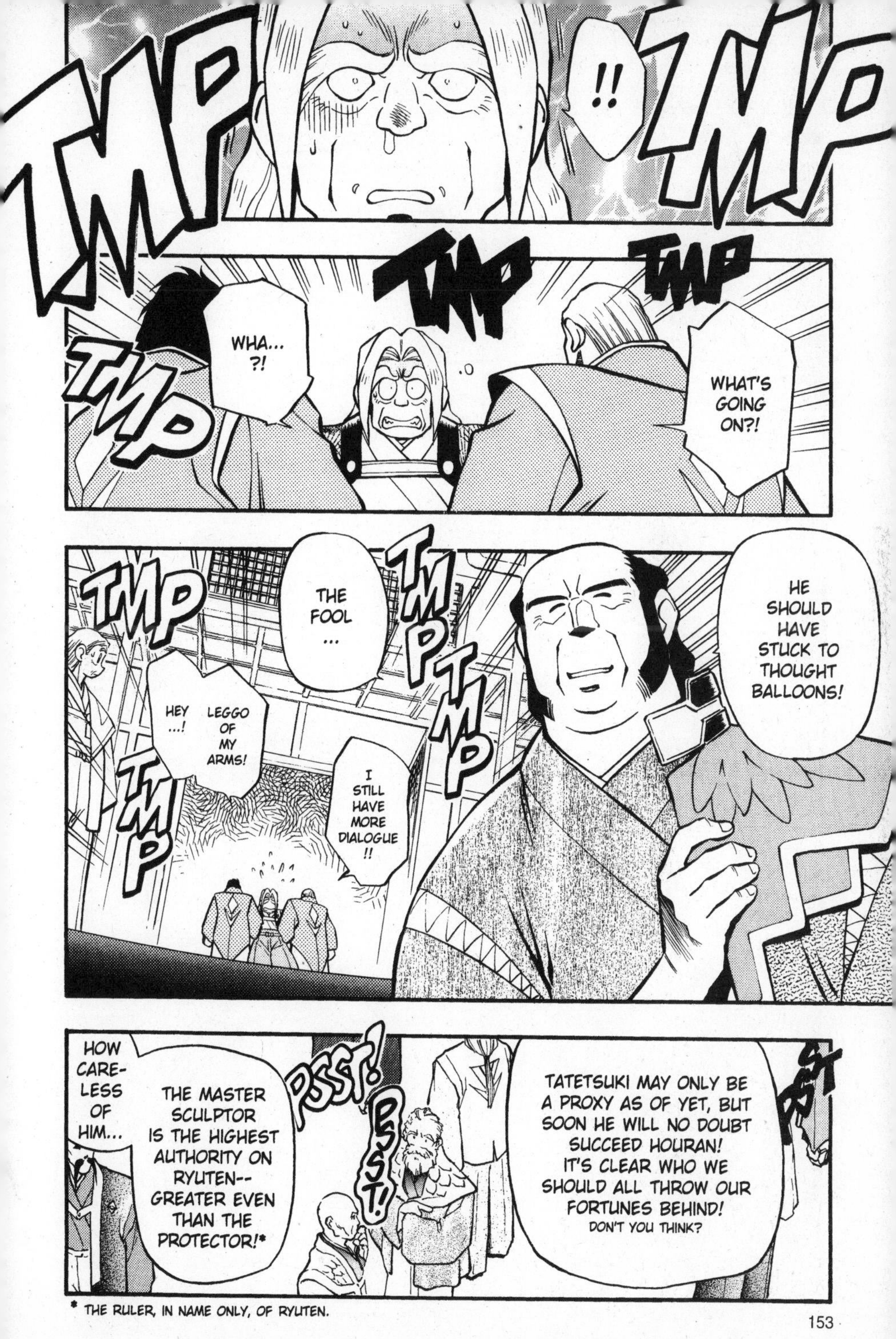
TMP
!!
TMP
TMP
WHA... ?!
TMP
TMP
WHAT'S GOING ON?!
TMP
HEY ...!
LEGGO OF MY ARMS!
TMP
THE FOOL ...
TMP
TMP
I STILL HAVE MORE DIALOGUE !!
HE SHOULD HAVE STUCK TO THOUGHT BALLOONS!
HOW CARE-LESS OF HIM...
THE MASTER SCULPTOR IS THE HIGHEST AUTHORITY ON RYUTEN-- GREATER EVEN THAN THE PROTECTOR!*
PSST!
PSST!
TATETSUKI MAY ONLY BE A PROXY AS OF YET, BUT SOON HE WILL NO DOUBT SUCCEED HOURAN! IT'S CLEAR WHO WE SHOULD ALL THROW OUR FORTUNES BEHIND!
DON'T YOU THINK?
PSST

* THE RULER, IN NAME ONLY, OF RYUTEN.

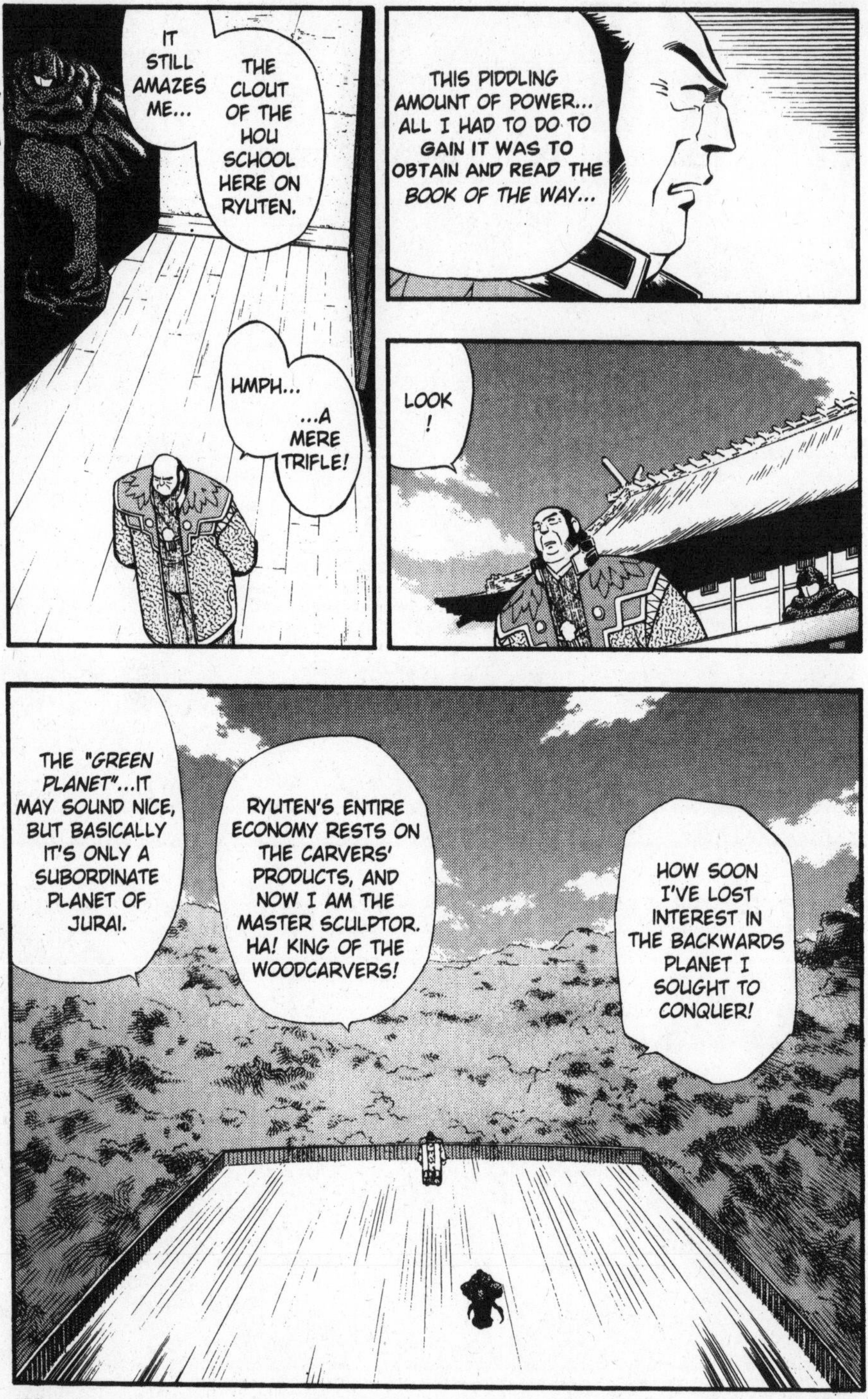
IT STILL AMAZES ME...
THE CLOUT OF THE HOU SCHOOL HERE ON RYUTEN.
HISHIMA
HMPH...
...A MERE TRIFLE!
THIS PIDDLING AMOUNT OF POWER... ALL I HAD TO DO TO GAIN IT WAS TO OBTAIN AND READ THE *BOOK OF THE WAY*...
LOOK!
THE "*GREEN PLANET*"...IT MAY SOUND NICE, BUT BASICALLY IT'S ONLY A SUBORDINATE PLANET OF JURAI.
RYUTEN'S ENTIRE ECONOMY RESTS ON THE CARVERS' PRODUCTS, AND NOW I AM THE MASTER SCULPTOR. HA! KING OF THE WOODCARVERS!
HOW SOON I'VE LOST INTEREST IN THE BACKWARDS PLANET I SOUGHT TO CONQUER!

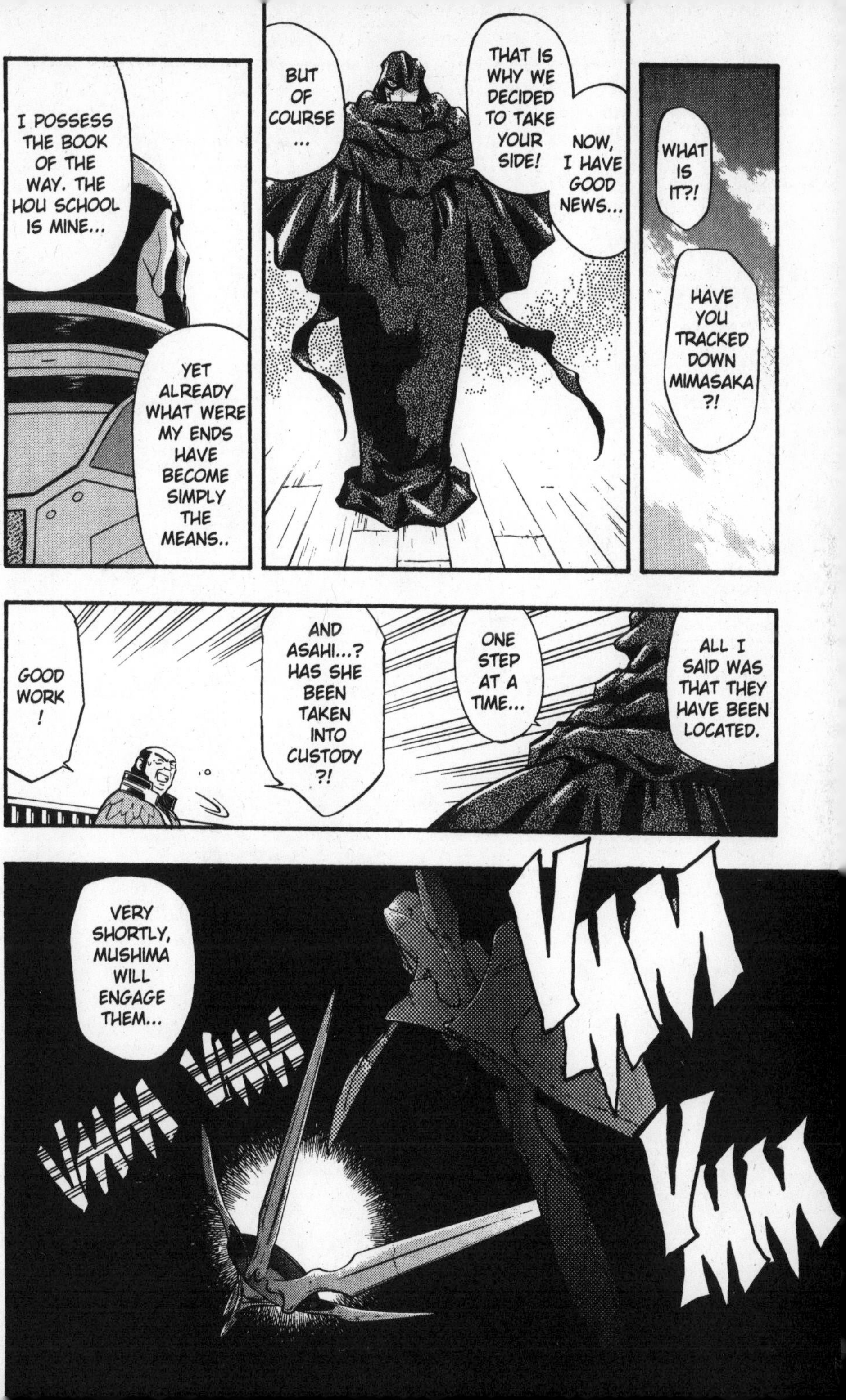
I POSSESS THE BOOK OF THE WAY. THE HOU SCHOOL IS MINE...
YET ALREADY WHAT WERE MY ENDS HAVE BECOME SIMPLY THE MEANS..
BUT OF COURSE ...
THAT IS WHY WE DECIDED TO TAKE YOUR SIDE!
NOW, I HAVE GOOD NEWS...
WHAT IS IT?!
HAVE YOU TRACKED DOWN MIMASAKA ?!
GOOD WORK !
AND ASAHI...? HAS SHE BEEN TAKEN INTO CUSTODY ?!
ONE STEP AT A TIME...
ALL I SAID WAS THAT THEY HAVE BEEN LOCATED.
VERY SHORTLY, MUSHIMA WILL ENGAGE THEM...
VMM VMM
VMM VMM
VMM
VMM

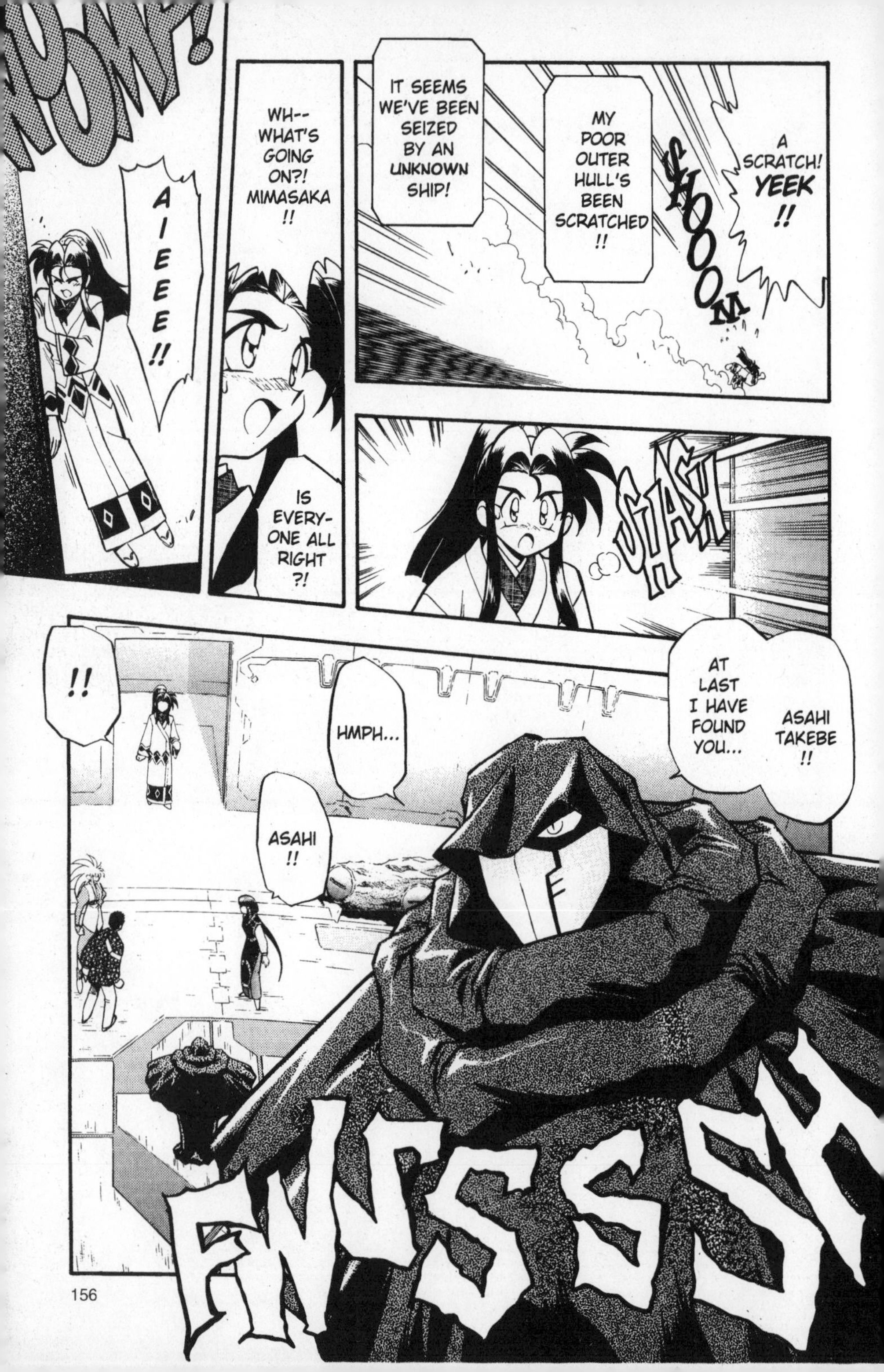
WHOMP!
AIEEE!!
WH-- WHAT'S GOING ON?! MIMASAKA!!
IS EVERY-ONE ALL RIGHT?!
IT SEEMS WE'VE BEEN SEIZED BY AN UNKNOWN SHIP!
MY POOR OUTER HULL'S BEEN SCRATCHED!!
SHOOOM
A SCRATCH! YEEK!!
SHASH
!!
HMPH...
ASAHI!!
AT LAST I HAVE FOUND YOU...
ASAHI TAKEBE!!
FWSSH

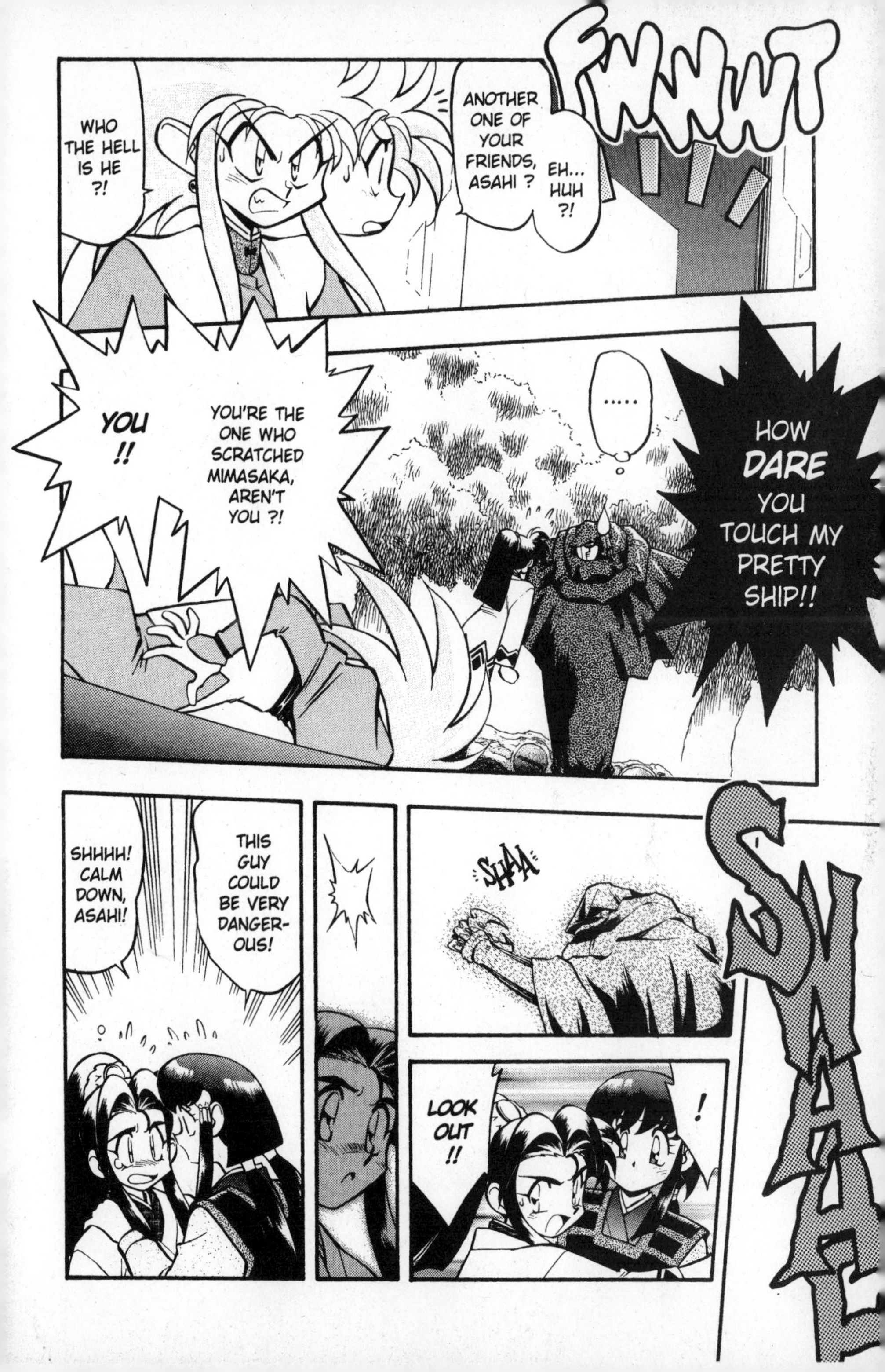
FWNWT
WHO THE HELL IS HE ?!
ANOTHER ONE OF YOUR FRIENDS, ASAHI ?
EH... HUH ?!
YOU !!
YOU'RE THE ONE WHO SCRATCHED MIMASAKA, AREN'T YOU ?!
.....
HOW DARE YOU TOUCH MY PRETTY SHIP!!
SHHHH! CALM DOWN, ASAHI!
THIS GUY COULD BE VERY DANGER-OUS!
SHAA
SWAAA
LOOK OUT !!
!

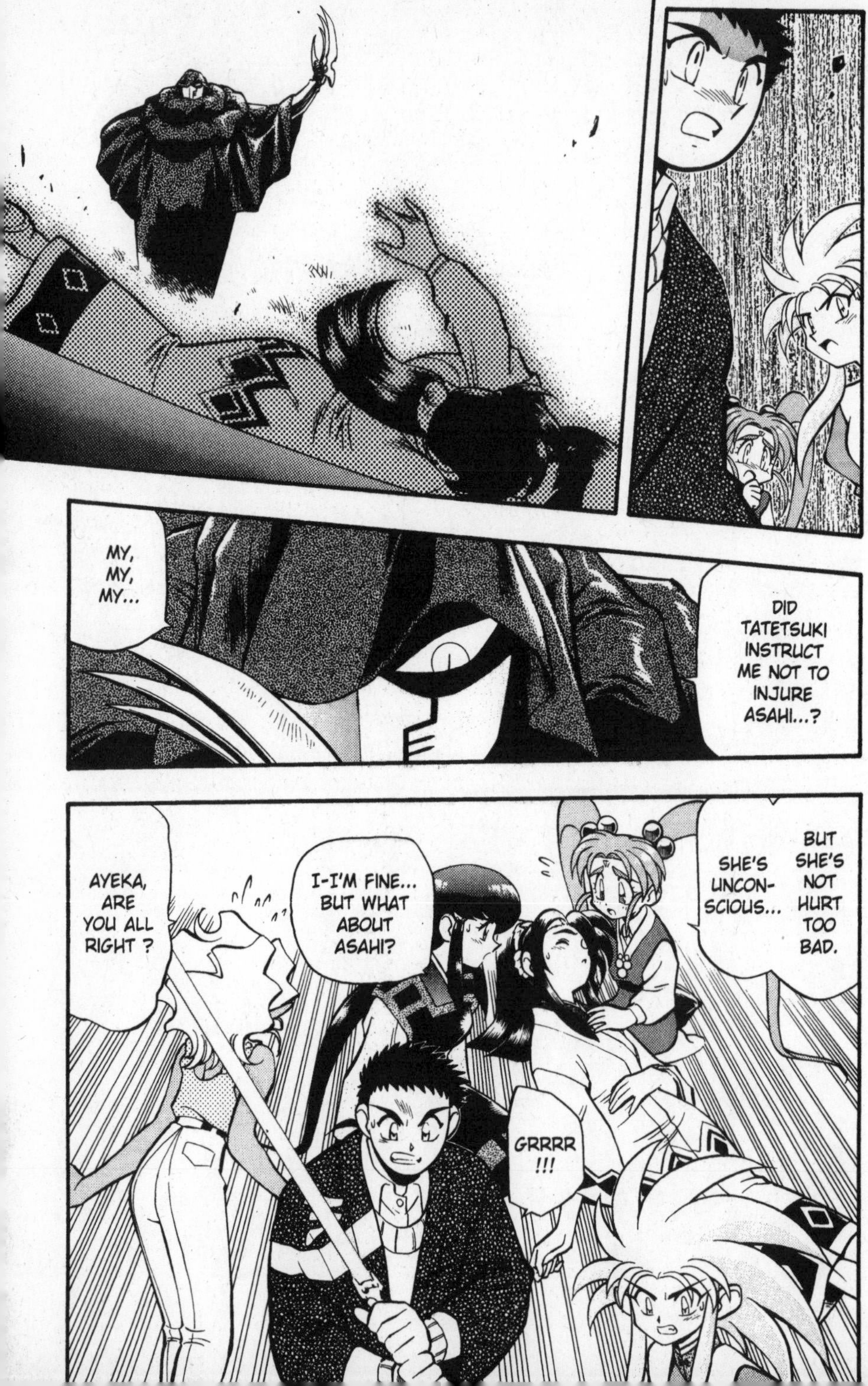
MY, MY, MY...
DID TATETSUKI INSTRUCT ME NOT TO INJURE ASAHI...?
AYEKA, ARE YOU ALL RIGHT ?
I-I'M FINE... BUT WHAT ABOUT ASAHI?
SHE'S UNCON-SCIOUS...
BUT SHE'S NOT HURT TOO BAD.
GRRRR !!!

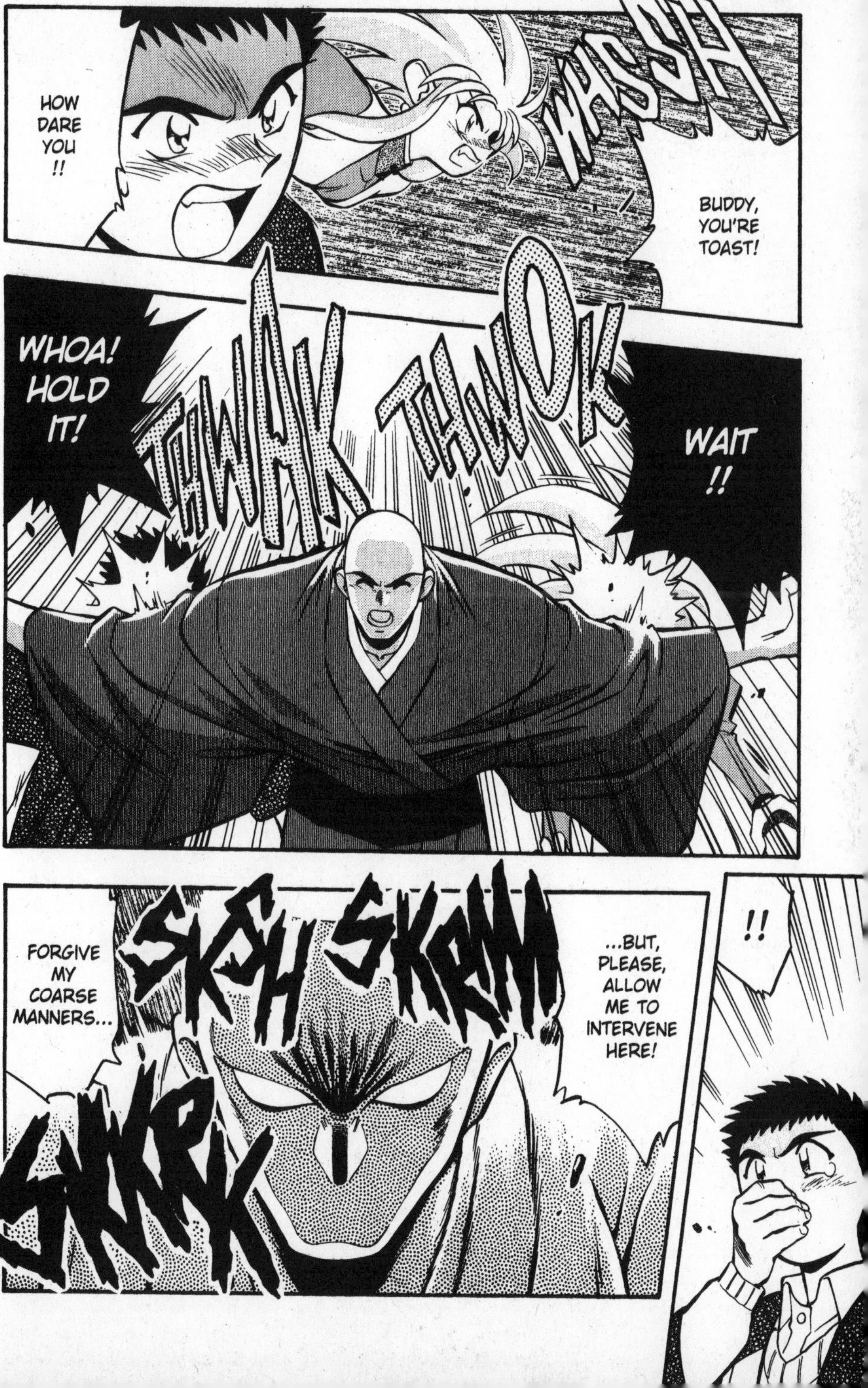
HOW DARE YOU !!
WASSH
BUDDY, YOU'RE TOAST!
WHOA! HOLD IT!
THWAK
THWOK
WAIT !!
FORGIVE MY COARSE MANNERS...
SKSH
SKRM
SHRK
...BUT, PLEASE, ALLOW ME TO INTERVENE HERE!
!!

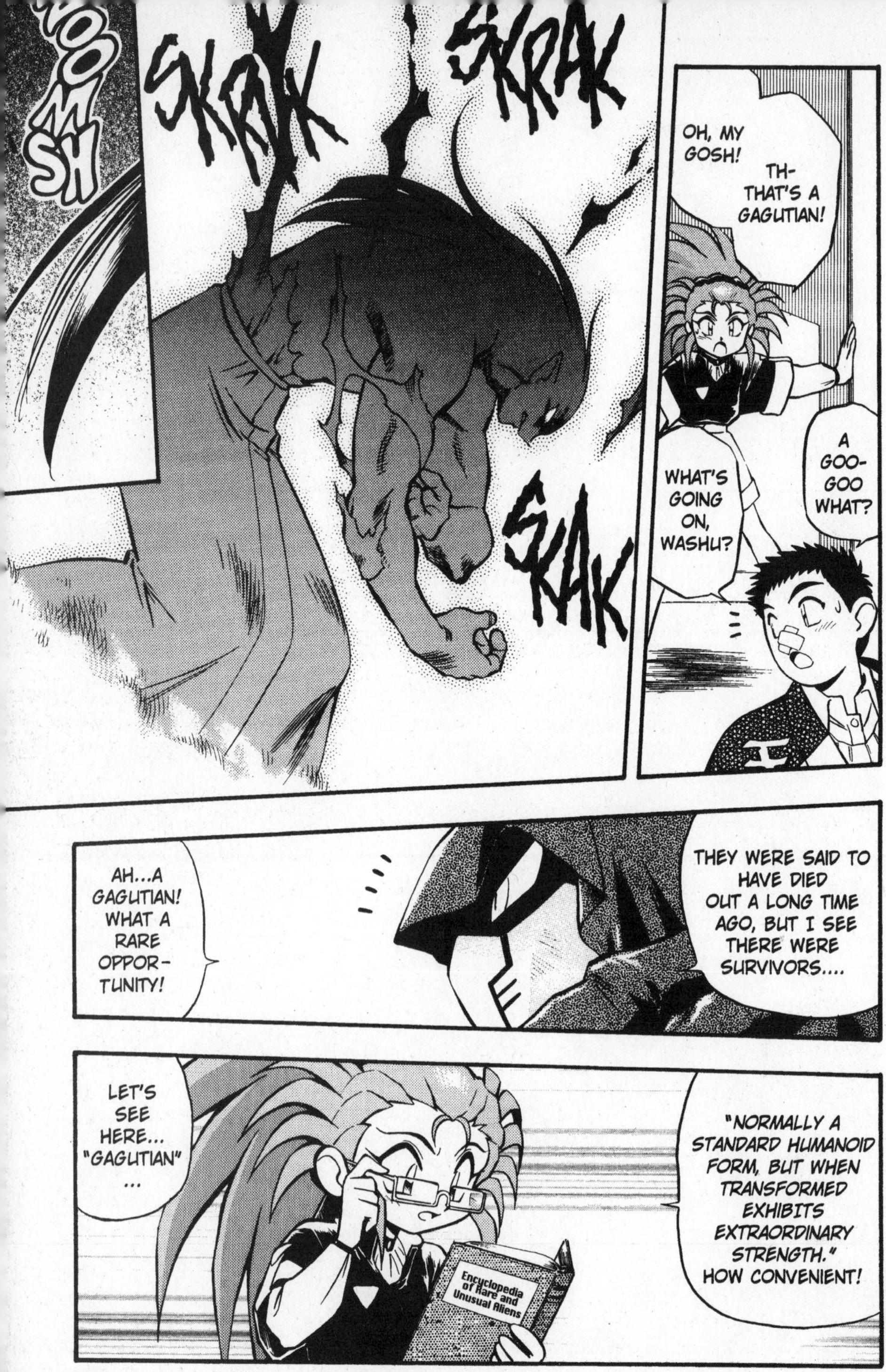
WOOMSH
SKRAK
SKRAK
SKAK
OH, MY GOSH!
TH- THAT'S A GAGUTIAN!
WHAT'S GOING ON, WASHU?
A GOO-GOO WHAT?
AH...A GAGUTIAN! WHAT A RARE OPPOR-TUNITY!
THEY WERE SAID TO HAVE DIED OUT A LONG TIME AGO, BUT I SEE THERE WERE SURVIVORS....
LET'S SEE HERE... "GAGUTIAN" ...
"NORMALLY A STANDARD HUMANOID FORM, BUT WHEN TRANSFORMED EXHIBITS EXTRAORDINARY STRENGTH." HOW CONVENIENT!
Encyclopedia of Rare and Unusual Aliens

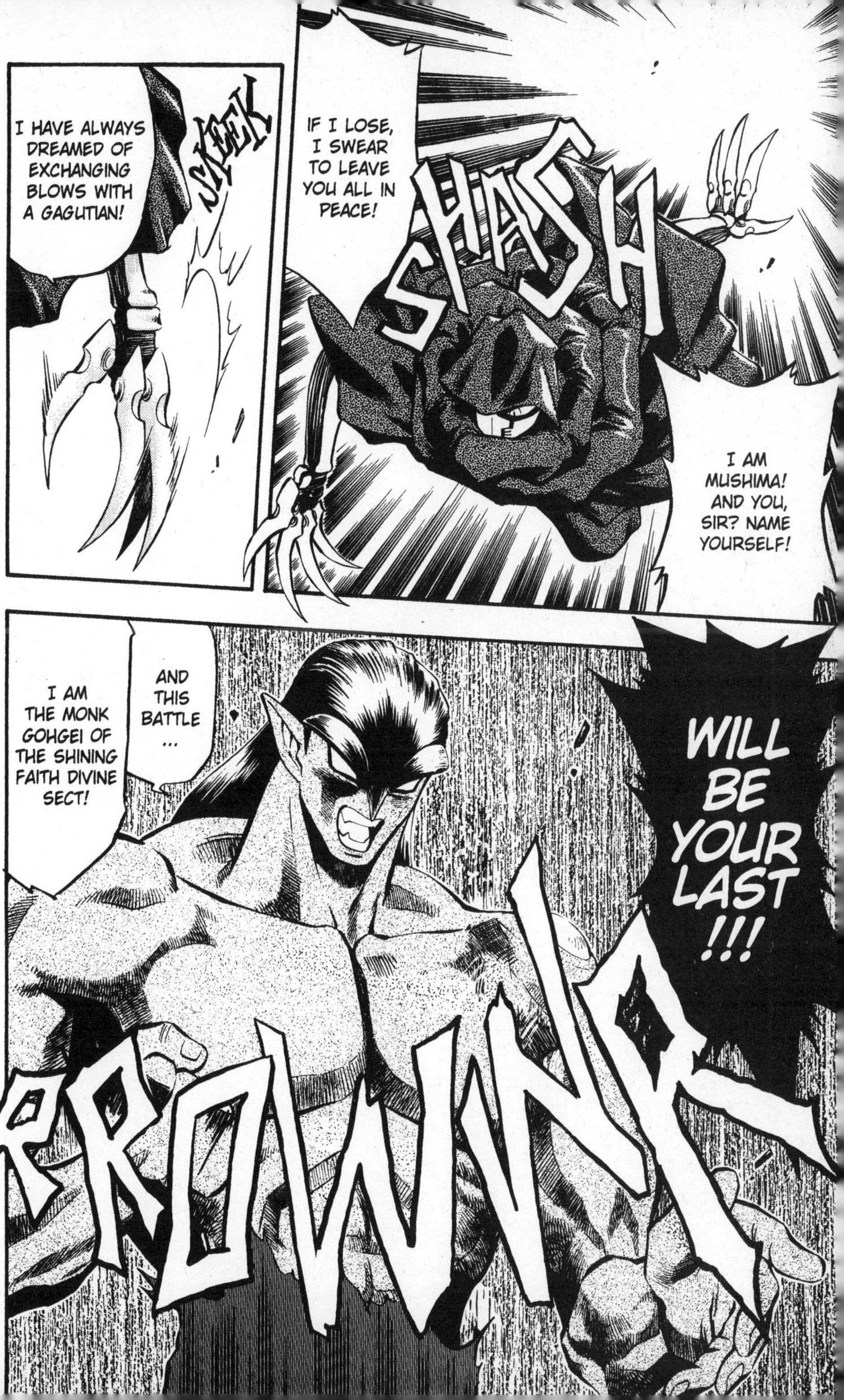
I HAVE ALWAYS DREAMED OF EXCHANGING BLOWS WITH A GAGUTIAN!
SKREEK
IF I LOSE, I SWEAR TO LEAVE YOU ALL IN PEACE!
SHASH
I AM MUSHIMA! AND YOU, SIR? NAME YOURSELF!
I AM THE MONK GOHGEI OF THE SHINING FAITH DIVINE SECT!
AND THIS BATTLE ...
WILL BE YOUR LAST!!!

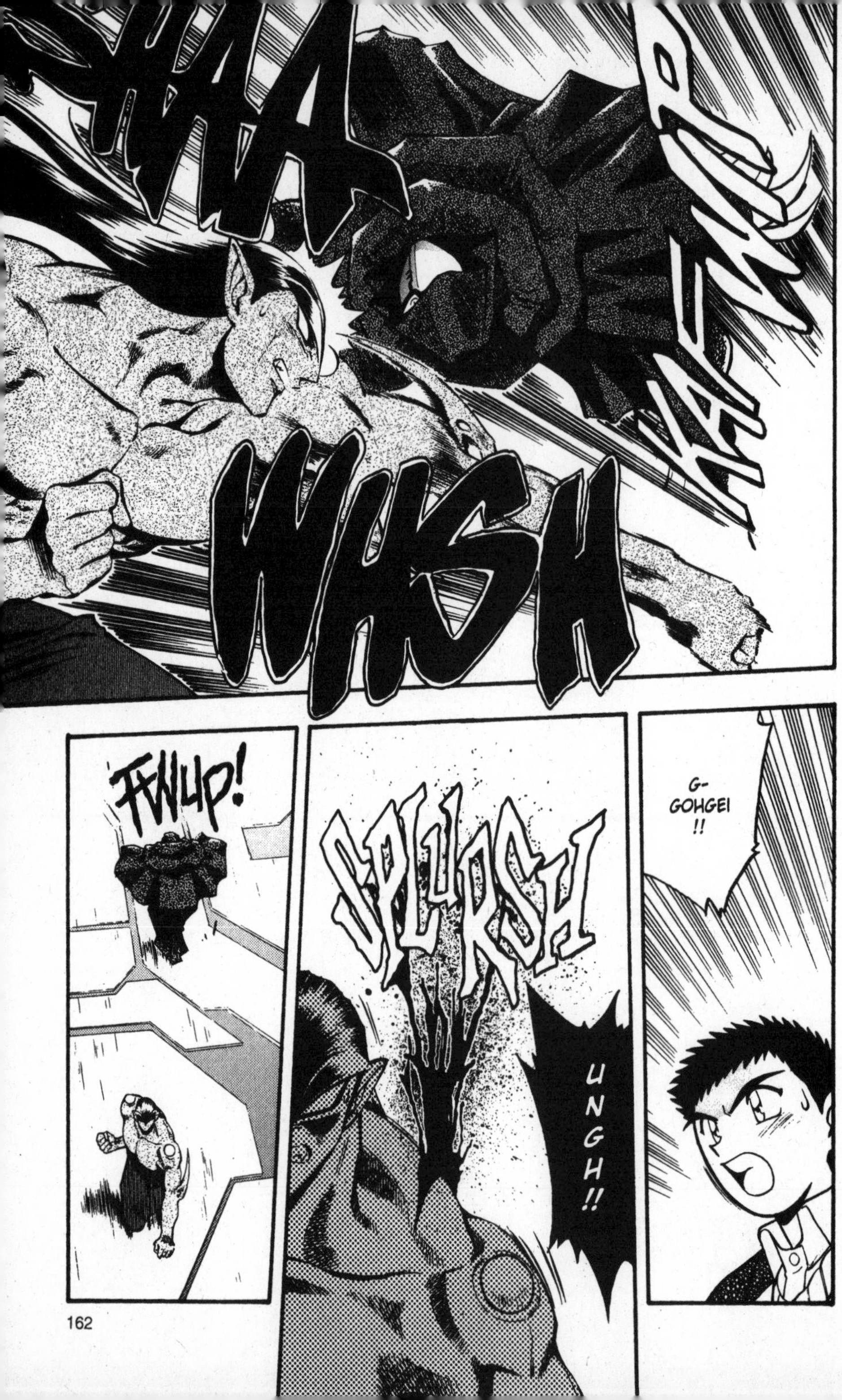

WHSH
FWUP!
SPLURSH
UNGH!!
G-GOHGEI !!

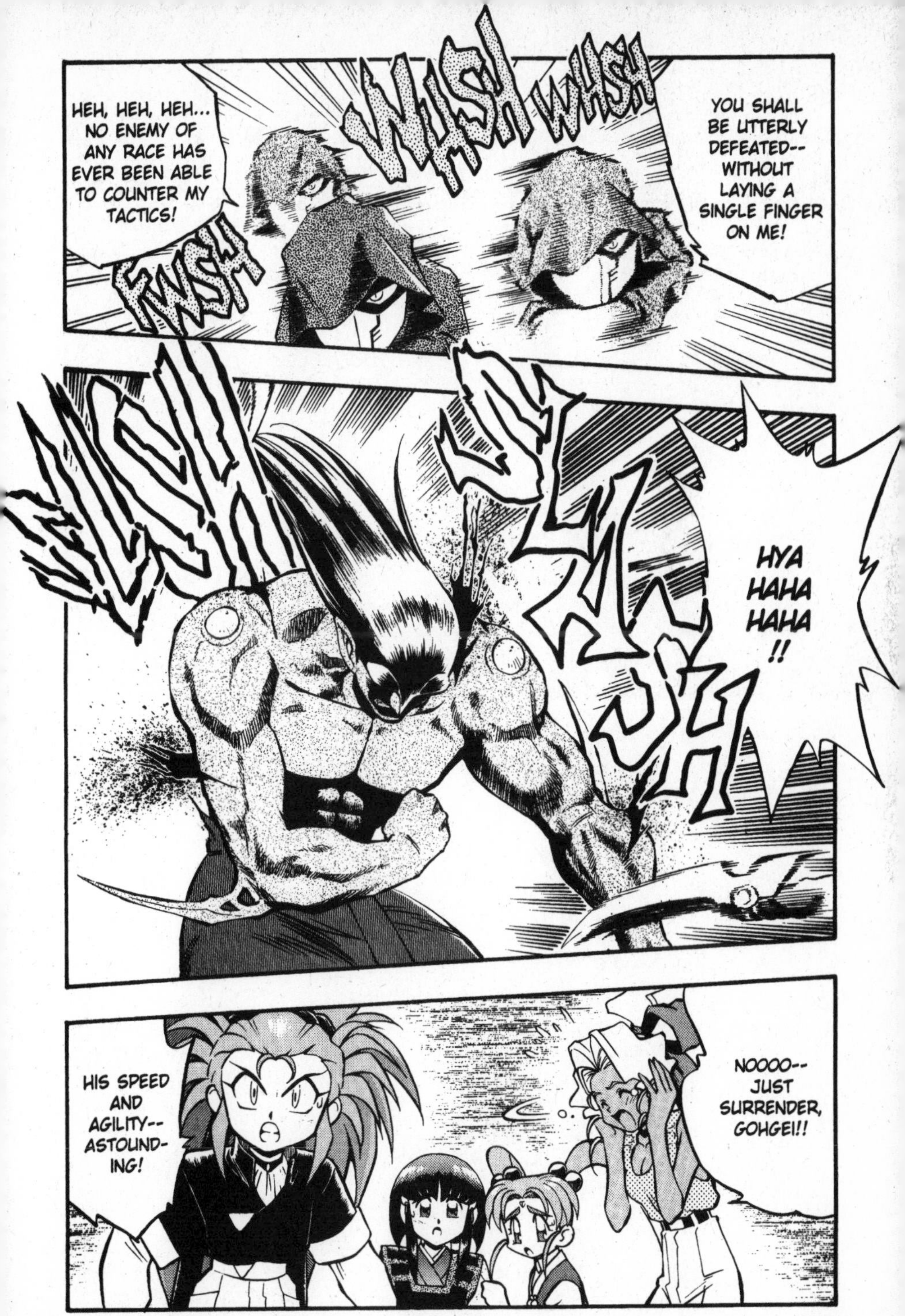
HEH, HEH, HEH... NO ENEMY OF ANY RACE HAS EVER BEEN ABLE TO COUNTER MY TACTICS!
FWSH
WHSH
WHSH
YOU SHALL BE UTTERLY DEFEATED-- WITHOUT LAYING A SINGLE FINGER ON ME!
HYA HAHA HAHA!!
HIS SPEED AND AGILITY-- ASTOUND-ING!
NOOOO-- JUST SURRENDER, GOHGEI!!

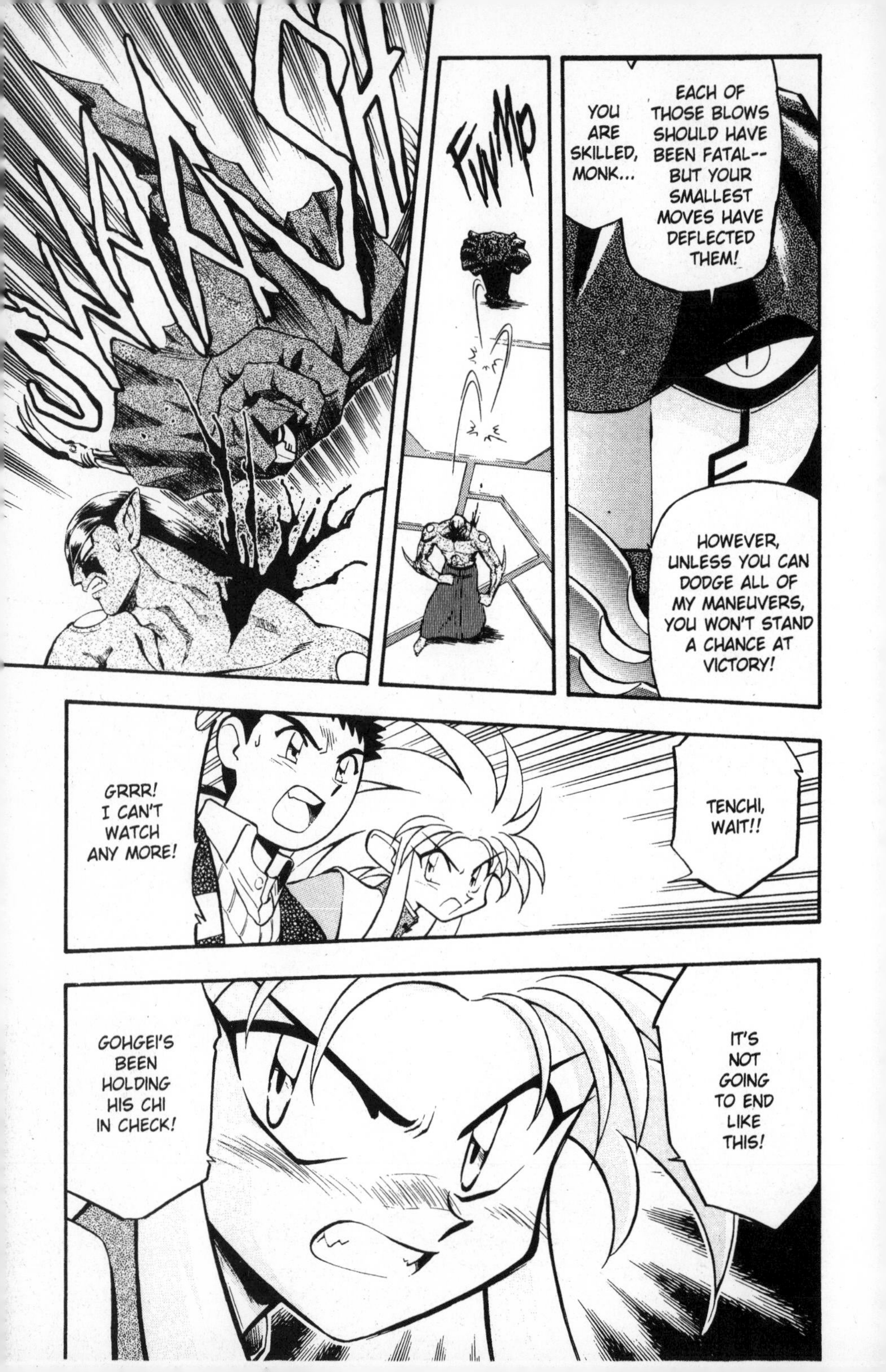
WHASH
FWUMP
YOU ARE SKILLED, MONK...
EACH OF THOSE BLOWS SHOULD HAVE BEEN FATAL-- BUT YOUR SMALLEST MOVES HAVE DEFLECTED THEM!
HOWEVER, UNLESS YOU CAN DODGE ALL OF MY MANEUVERS, YOU WON'T STAND A CHANCE AT VICTORY!
GRRR! I CAN'T WATCH ANY MORE!
TENCHI, WAIT!!
GOHGEI'S BEEN HOLDING HIS CHI IN CHECK!
IT'S NOT GOING TO END LIKE THIS!

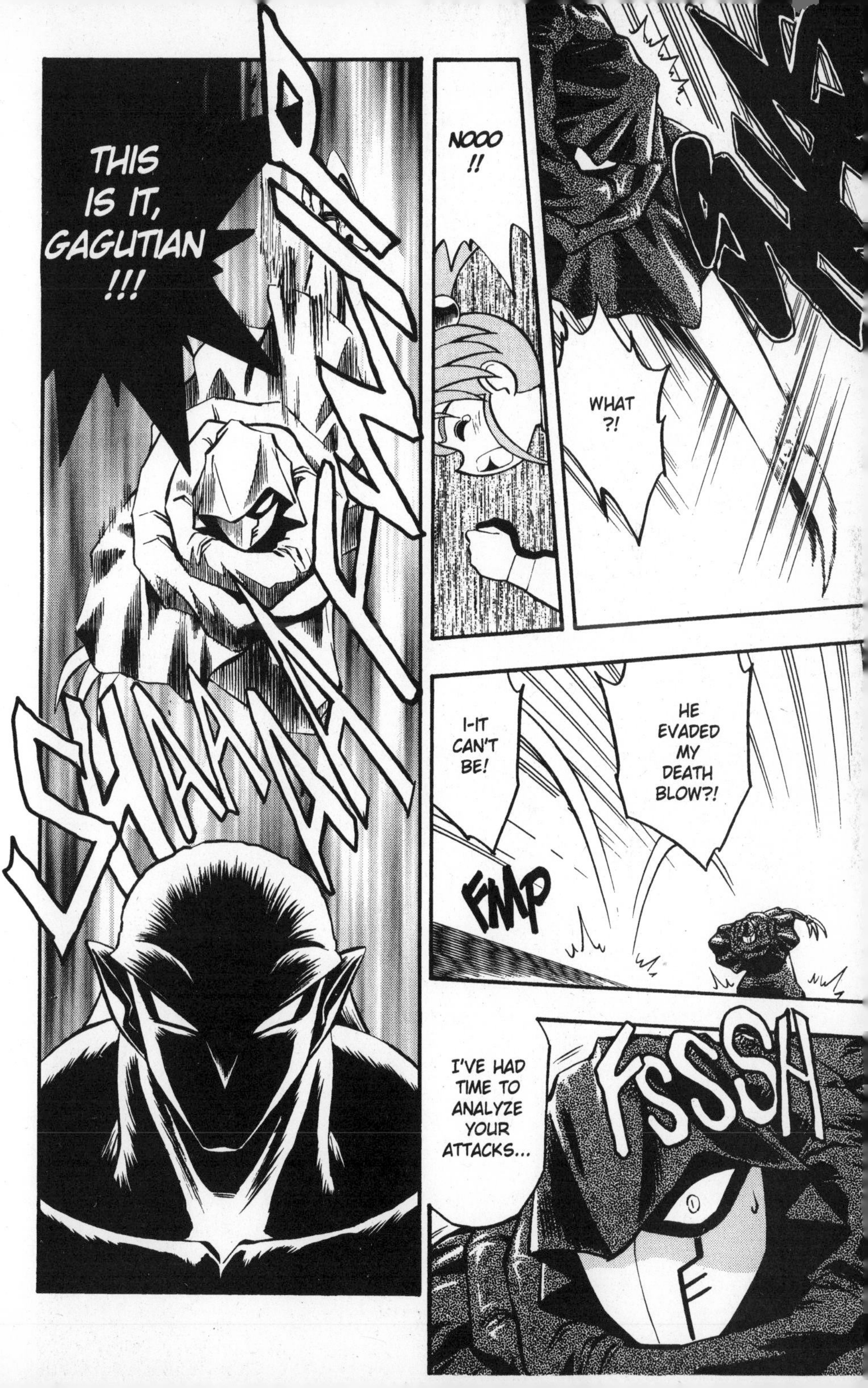
THIS IS IT, GAGUTIAN !!!
NOOO !!
WHAT ?!
I-IT CAN'T BE!
HE EVADED MY DEATH BLOW?!
FMP
I'VE HAD TIME TO ANALYZE YOUR ATTACKS...
FSSSH

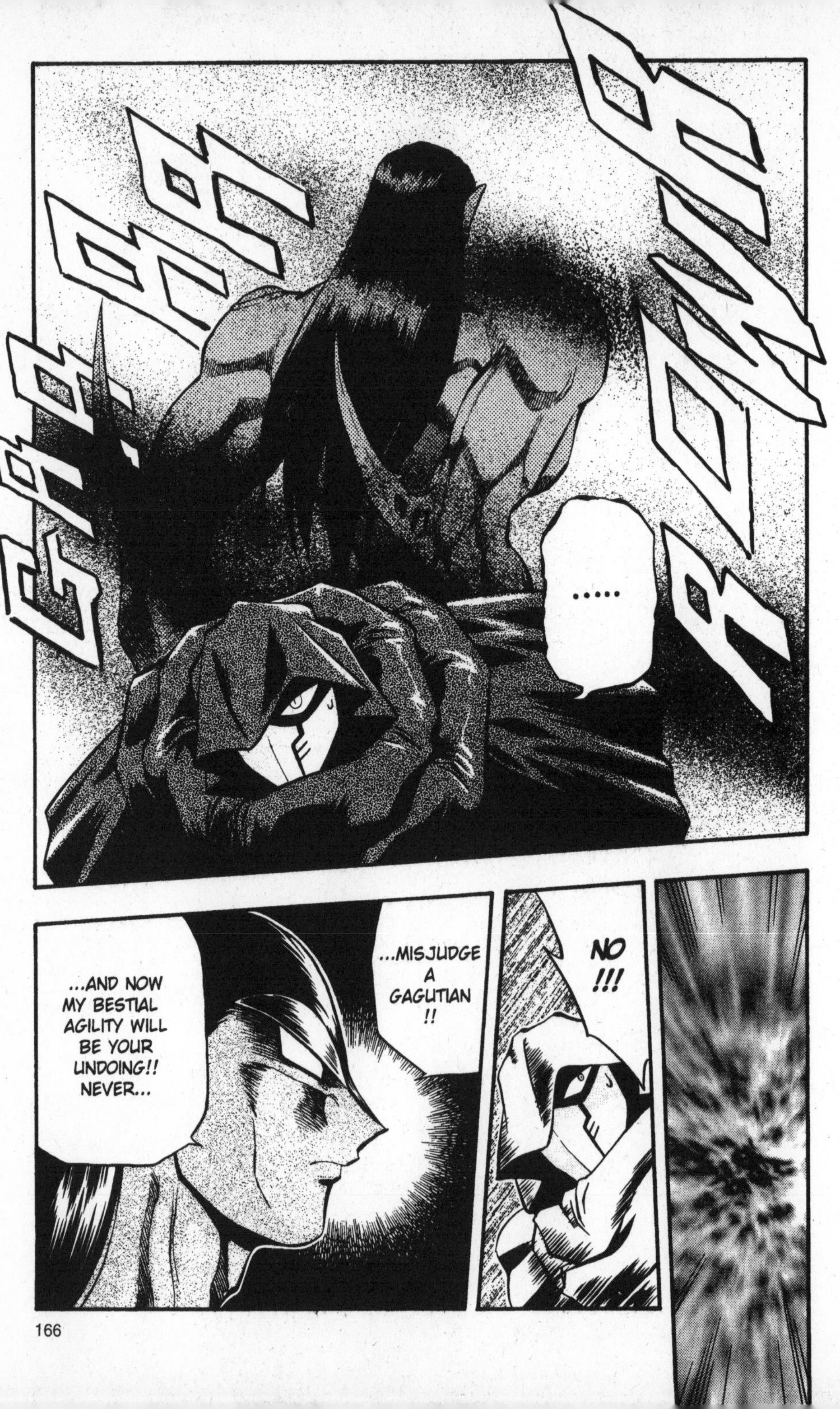
GRABB
.....
...AND NOW MY BESTIAL AGILITY WILL BE YOUR UNDOING!! NEVER...
...MISJUDGE A GAGUTIAN !!
NO !!!

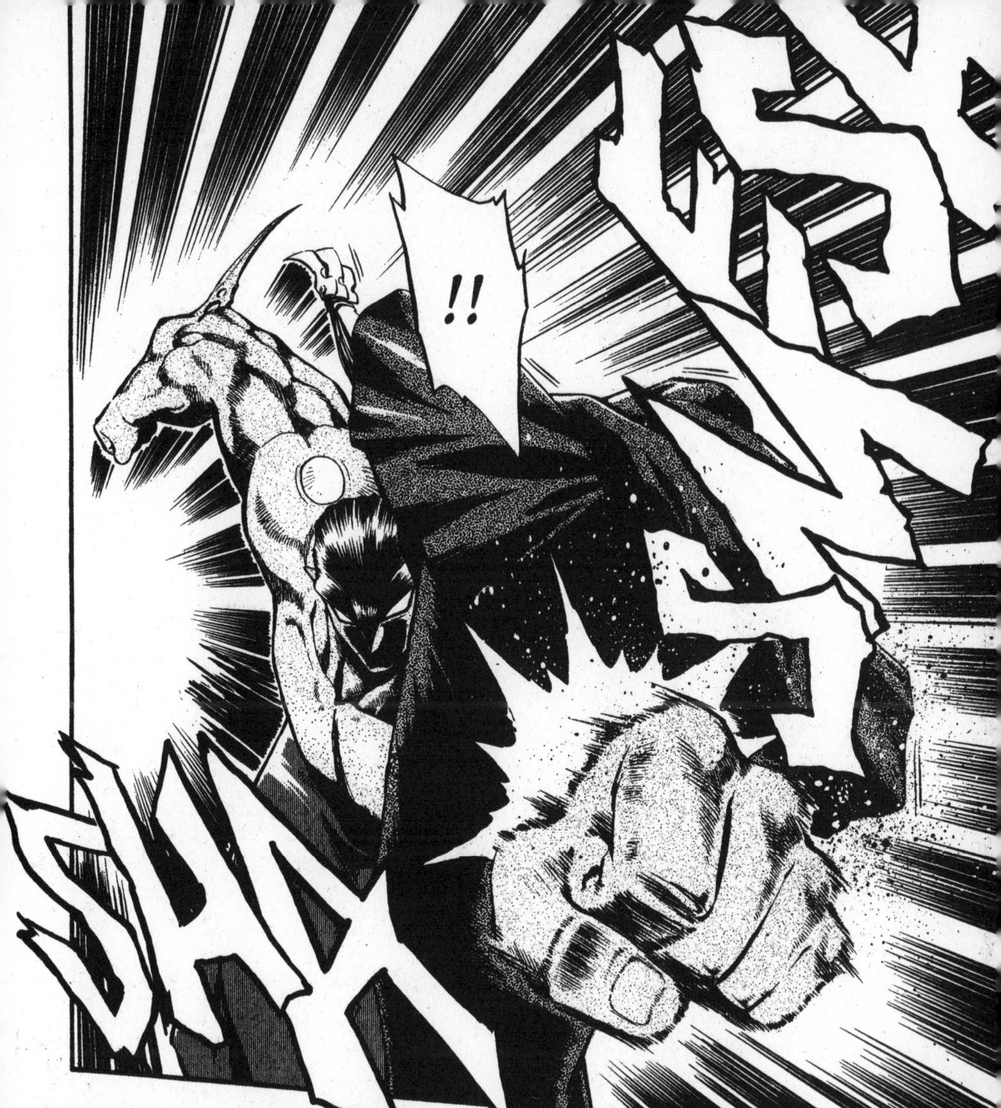
!!

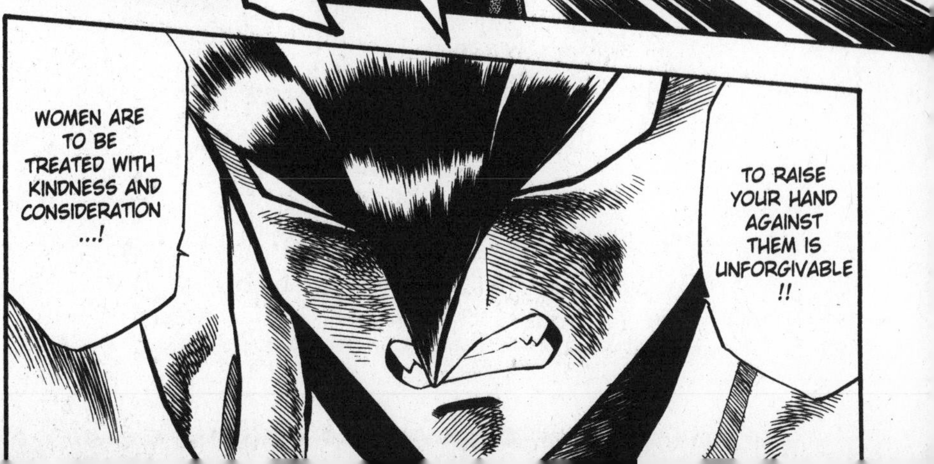
WOMEN ARE TO BE TREATED WITH KINDNESS AND CONSIDERATION ...!
TO RAISE YOUR HAND AGAINST THEM IS UNFORGIVABLE !!

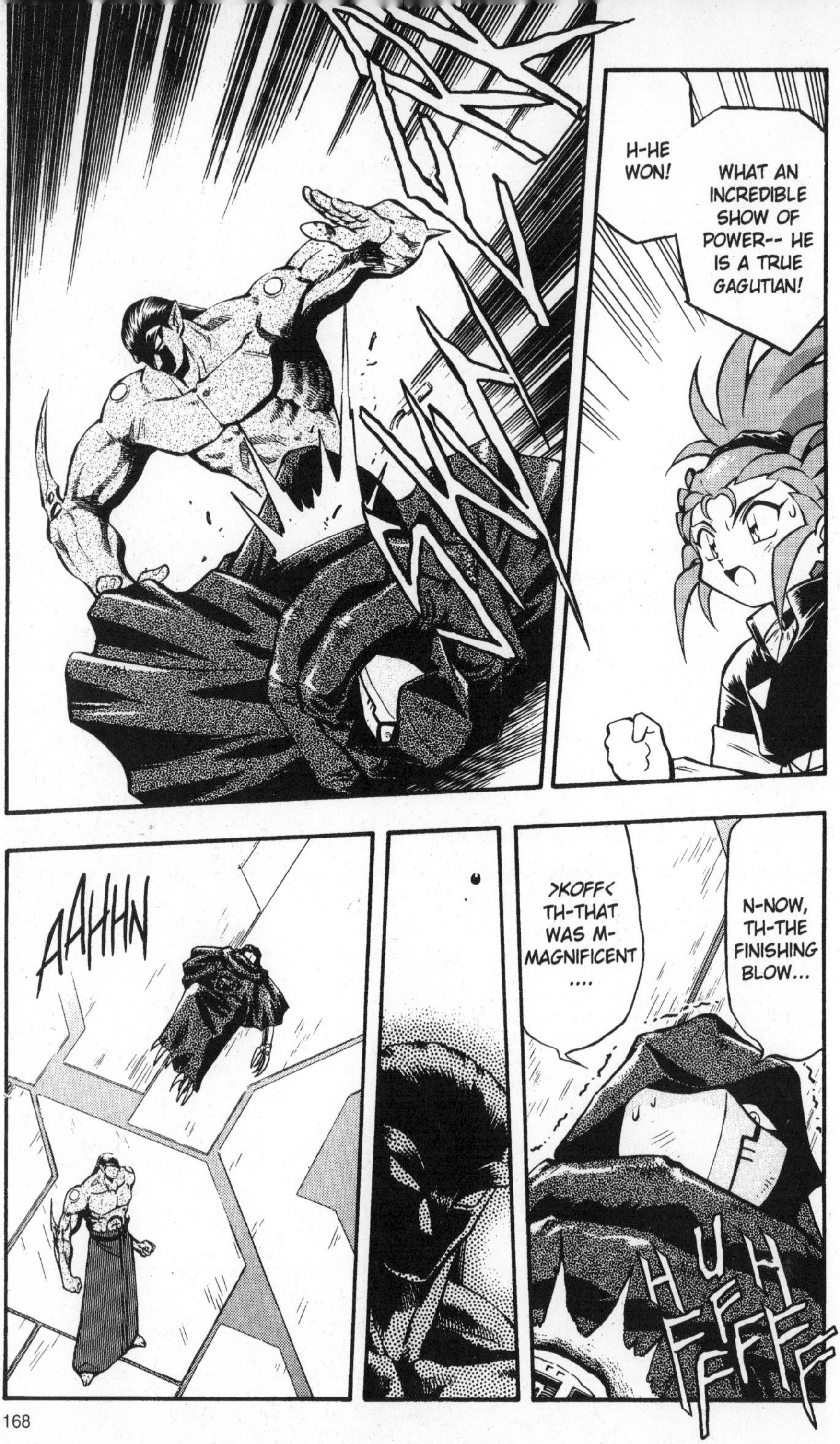
H-HE WON!
WHAT AN INCREDIBLE SHOW OF POWER-- HE IS A TRUE GAGUTIAN!
AAHHN
>KOFF< TH-THAT WAS M-MAGNIFICENT ....
N-NOW, TH-THE FINISHING BLOW...

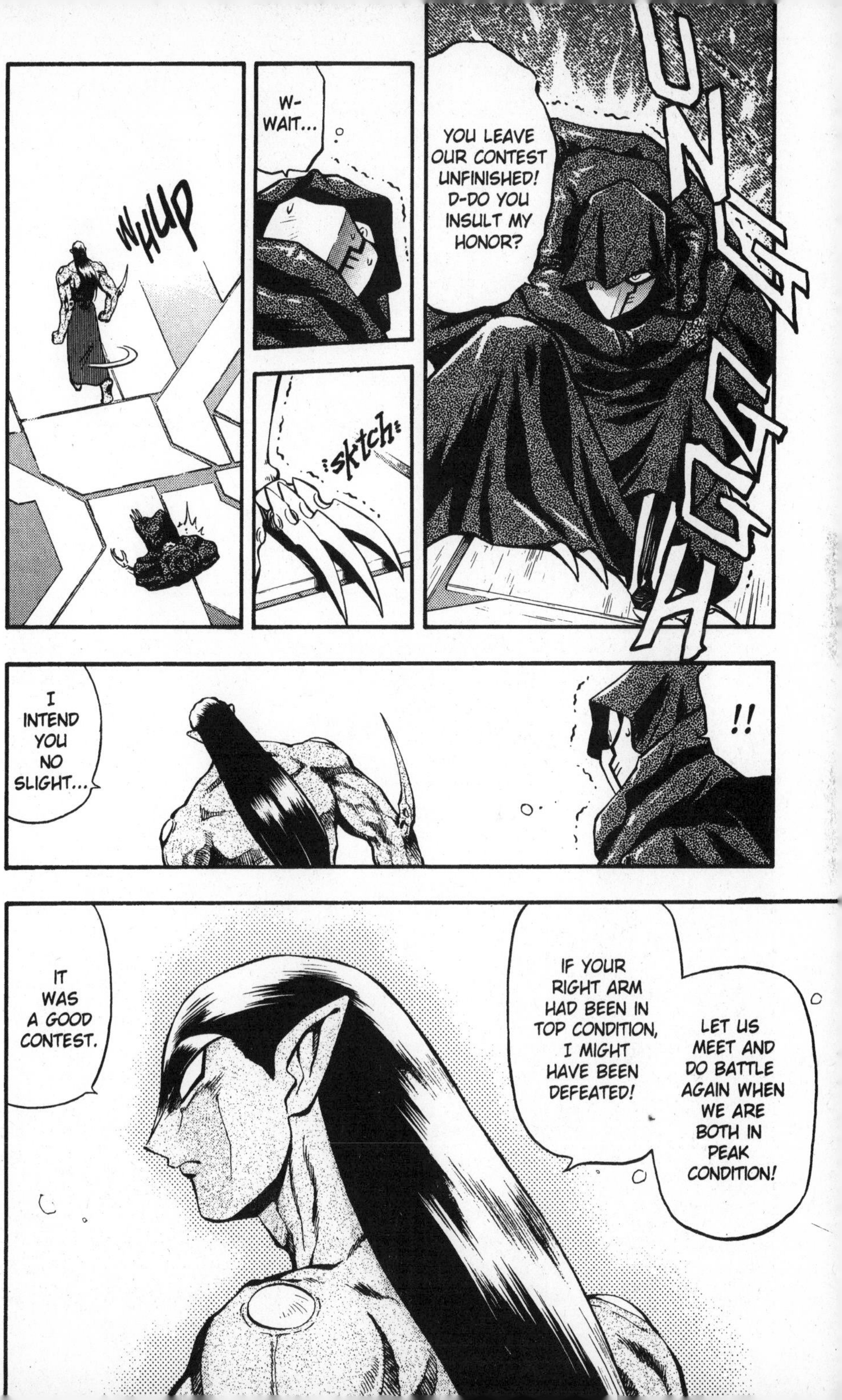
WHUP
W-
WAIT...
sktch
YOU LEAVE OUR CONTEST UNFINISHED! D-DO YOU INSULT MY HONOR?
UNGGGH
I INTEND YOU NO SLIGHT...
!!
IT WAS A GOOD CONTEST.
IF YOUR RIGHT ARM HAD BEEN IN TOP CONDITION, I MIGHT HAVE BEEN DEFEATED!
LET US MEET AND DO BATTLE AGAIN WHEN WE ARE BOTH IN PEAK CONDITION!

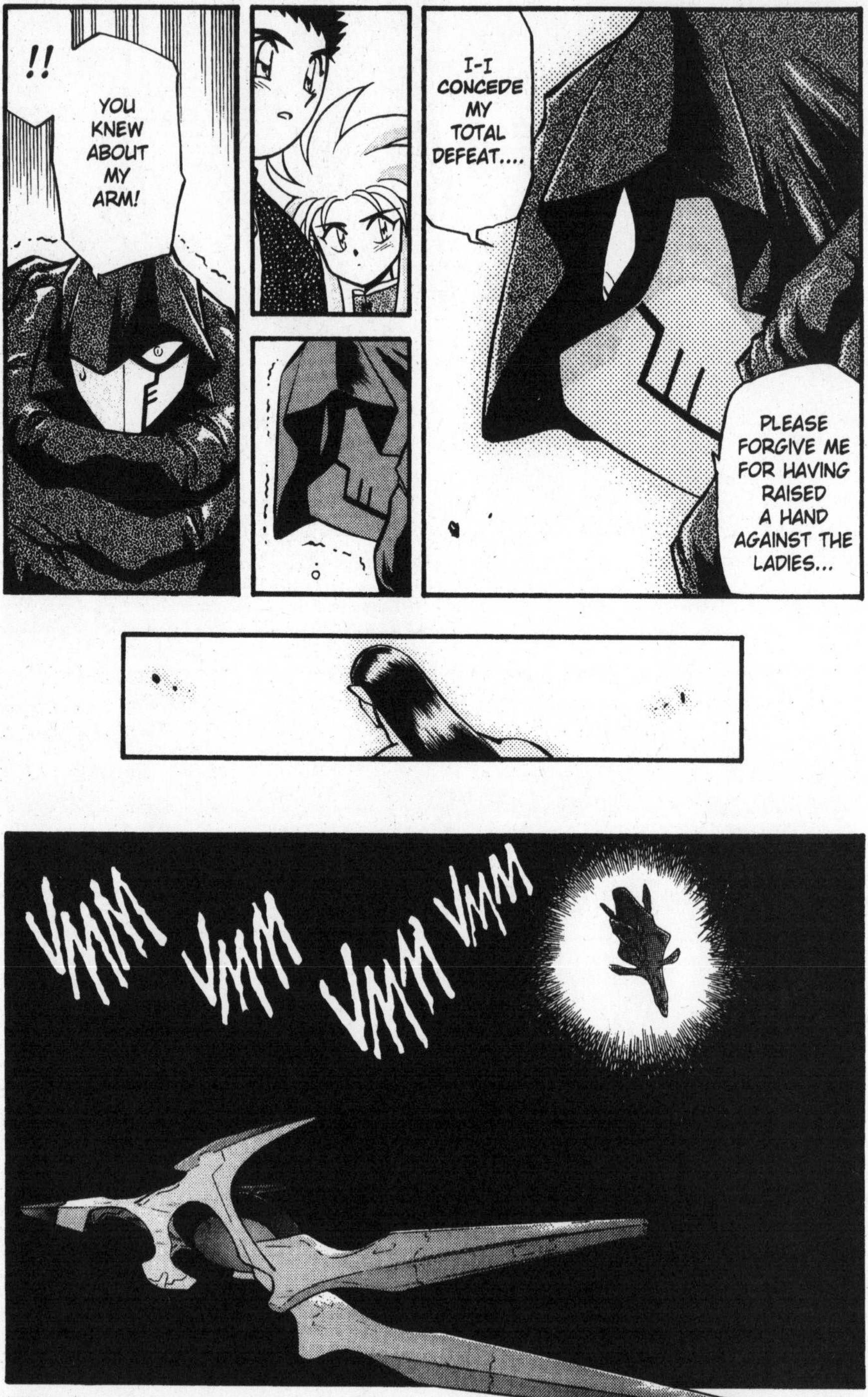
!!
YOU KNEW ABOUT MY ARM!
I-I CONCEDE MY TOTAL DEFEAT....
PLEASE FORGIVE ME FOR HAVING RAISED A HAND AGAINST THE LADIES...
VMM VMM VMM VMM

WHAT ARE THE ODDS...?

F-FIRST, MASAKI KATSUHITO... NOW GOHGEI...

TO EXCHANGE BLOWS WITH SUCH VETERAN WARRIORS HAS BEEN FULFILLING....

I HAVE NO REGRETS !!

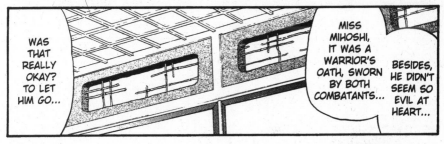

WAS THAT REALLY OKAY? TO LET HIM GO...

MISS MIHOSHI, IT WAS A WARRIOR'S OATH, SWORN BY BOTH COMBATANTS...

BESIDES, HE DIDN'T SEEM SO EVIL AT HEART...

SO MY DEAR GOHGEI RESCUED ME!?

WHY DON'T YOU REST UNTIL WE REACH RYUTEN?

THEY KNOW WE'RE ON OUR WAY, SO THEY SHOULD LEAVE US ALONE UNTIL THEN.

YEAH, YOU'D BETTER GET SOME REST!

TENCHI, A FEW WORDS...

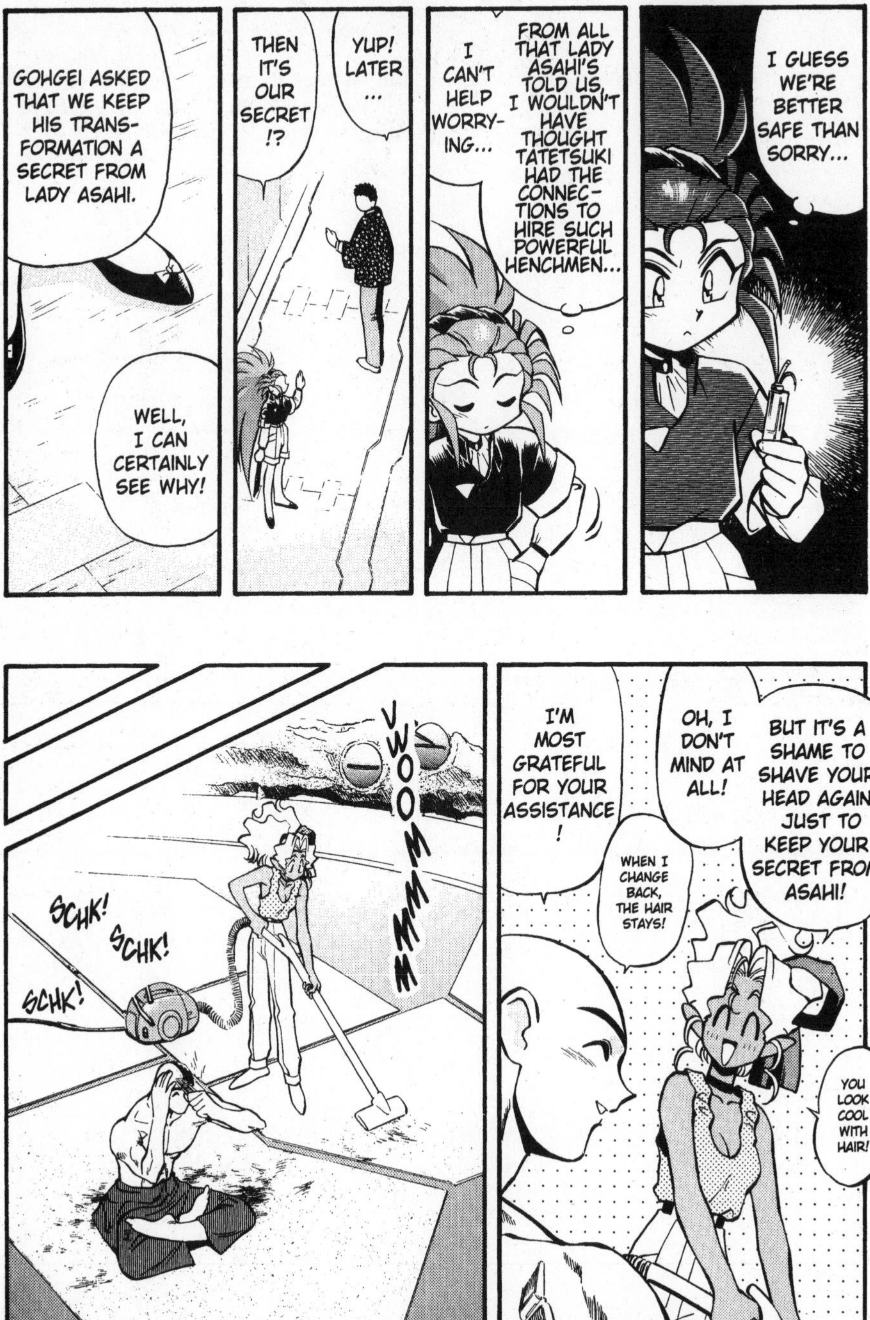
GOHGEI ASKED THAT WE KEEP HIS TRANSFORMATION A SECRET FROM LADY ASAHI.
WELL, I CAN CERTAINLY SEE WHY!
THEN IT'S OUR SECRET!?
YUP! LATER...
I CAN'T HELP WORRYING...
FROM ALL THAT LADY ASAHI'S TOLD US, I WOULDN'T HAVE THOUGHT TATETSUKI HAD THE CONNECTIONS TO HIRE SUCH POWERFUL HENCHMEN...
I GUESS WE'RE BETTER SAFE THAN SORRY...
VWOOOMMMMM
SCHK!
SCHK!
SCHK!
I'M MOST GRATEFUL FOR YOUR ASSISTANCE!
OH, I DON'T MIND AT ALL!
BUT IT'S A SHAME TO SHAVE YOUR HEAD AGAIN JUST TO KEEP YOUR SECRET FROM ASAHI!
WHEN I CHANGE BACK, THE HAIR STAYS!
YOU LOOK COOL WITH HAIR!

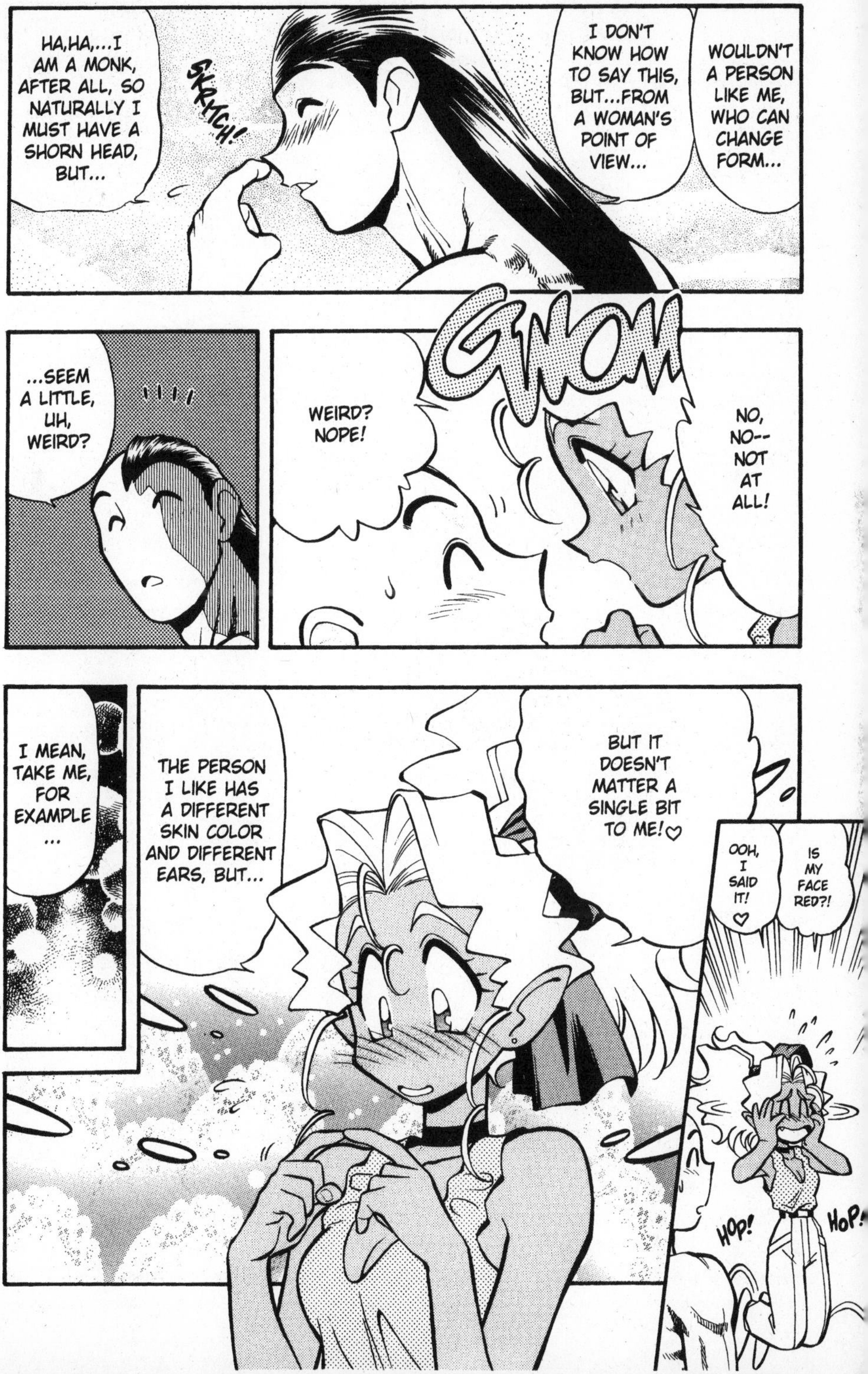
HA,HA,...I AM A MONK, AFTER ALL, SO NATURALLY I MUST HAVE A SHORN HEAD, BUT...
SKRYTCH!
I DON'T KNOW HOW TO SAY THIS, BUT...FROM A WOMAN'S POINT OF VIEW...
WOULDN'T A PERSON LIKE ME, WHO CAN CHANGE FORM...
...SEEM A LITTLE, UH, WEIRD?
GWOM
WEIRD? NOPE!
NO, NO--NOT AT ALL!
I MEAN, TAKE ME, FOR EXAMPLE...
THE PERSON I LIKE HAS A DIFFERENT SKIN COLOR AND DIFFERENT EARS, BUT...
BUT IT DOESN'T MATTER A SINGLE BIT TO ME! ♡
OOH, I SAID IT! ♡
IS MY FACE RED?!
HOP!
HOP!

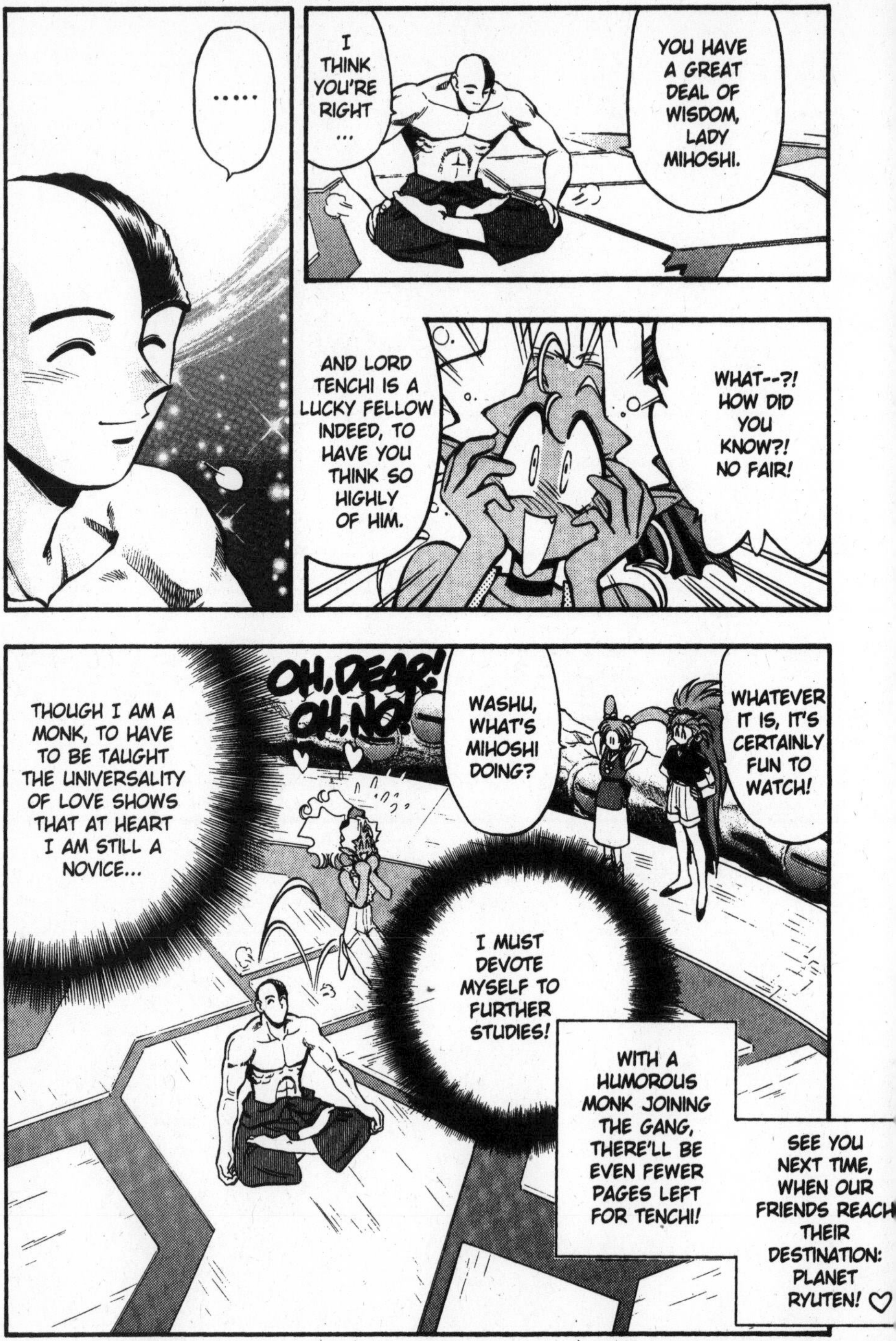
......
I THINK YOU'RE RIGHT ...
YOU HAVE A GREAT DEAL OF WISDOM, LADY MIHOSHI.
AND LORD TENCHI IS A LUCKY FELLOW INDEED, TO HAVE YOU THINK SO HIGHLY OF HIM.
WHAT--?! HOW DID YOU KNOW?! NO FAIR!
THOUGH I AM A MONK, TO HAVE TO BE TAUGHT THE UNIVERSALITY OF LOVE SHOWS THAT AT HEART I AM STILL A NOVICE...
OH, DEAR! OH, NO!
WASHU, WHAT'S MIHOSHI DOING?
WHATEVER IT IS, IT'S CERTAINLY FUN TO WATCH!
I MUST DEVOTE MYSELF TO FURTHER STUDIES!
WITH A HUMOROUS MONK JOINING THE GANG, THERE'LL BE EVEN FEWER PAGES LEFT FOR TENCHI!
SEE YOU NEXT TIME, WHEN OUR FRIENDS REACH THEIR DESTINATION: PLANET RYUTEN! ♡

TO BE CONTINUED...